Buckley

Why Lawsuits Are Good for America:
Disciplined Democracy, Big Business, and the Common Law

The Second Amendment in Law and History:
Historians and Constitutional Scholars on the Right to Bear Arms (editor)

BUCKLEY

William F. Buckley Jr.
and the Rise of
American Conservatism

CARL T. BOGUS

BLOOMSBURY PRESS
NEW YORK · BERLIN · LONDON · SYDNEY

Published by Bloomsbury Press, New York

All papers used by Bloomsbury Press are natural, recyclable products made from wood grown in well-managed forests. The manufacturing processes conform to the environmental regulations of the country of origin.

LIBRARY OF CONGRESS CATALOGING-IN-PUBLICATION DATA

Bogus, Carl T.
William F. Buckley Jr. and the rise of
American conservatism / Carl T. Bogus.—1st U.S. ed.
p. cm.
ISBN 978-1-59691-580-0
1. Buckley, William F. (William Frank), 1925–2008.
2. Journalists—United States—Biography.   I. Title.
PN4874.B796B65 2011
070.92—dc22
[B]
2011012734

First U.S. edition 2011

1 3 5 7 9 10 8 6 4 2

Typeset by Westchester Book Group
Printed in the U.S.A. by Quad/Graphics, Fairfield, Pennsylvania

For Elizabeth, Ian, and Zoe

Contents

Preface

"[It is] no more possible to conduct affairs of state without reference
to political philosophy than it is to do business without money."
—WHITNEY GRISWOLD

William F. Buckley Jr. is one of the most consequential figures in the
latter half of the twentieth century. He refashioned conservatism and
propelled it into becoming a powerful force in American intellectual
and political life. Conservatism as it existed before Buckley was a different philosophy. The rise of modern conservatism as we know it today
would never have happened without Buckley—and the course of history would not have been the same.

Buckley was not a political philosopher with original ideas. He more
or less inherited his ideas from his father and took them for granted. He
took a disparate collection of ideas—some of which were contradictory
or disdained even by leading conservatives of the day—melded them
together, and personally represented this new ideology so appealingly
that many people became Buckley-style conservatives because they passionately admired William F. Buckley Jr. Yet Buckley was no pied piper.
He did not place himself, alone, at the head of a column of followers.
He selected other leaders and promoted them and their ideas. He established not merely a band of followers but a community. He encouraged
wide—but not unlimited—discussion and debate. When he believed
other conservative leaders offered ideas that threatened his core vision,
he deftly marginalized them or decisively excommunicated them. In all
of these ways and more, Buckley created a movement.

This book will focus on the seminal period of the creation of the modern conservative movement, which I believe to be from 1955 to 1968. It was in 1955 that Buckley founded *National Review*, and by 1968—a year of enormous political and social turmoil in America—he had largely completed the process of defining conservatism and fashioning a robust movement to advance it. The introduction includes a section defining what conservatism was before Buckley because that is necessary to understanding how he changed it. And chapter 1 deals with events before 1955, including Buckley's father's experiences in Mexico during the Mexican Revolution, because that is necessary to understanding the environment in which the ideas Buckley inherited were initially formed.

I should tell the reader up front that I am a liberal and thus critical—in some instances, highly critical—of Buckley's ideology. I nevertheless admire William F. Buckley Jr. enormously. He was an imperfect human being as all of us are, but he was a man of marvelous talents. Moreover, as someone who dedicated his career to promoting ideas he believed would be good for America, he was a true patriot. I take solace from knowing that Buckley was not thin-skinned. He could take as well as he could give, and what he could give to liberals and others with whom he disagreed was considerable. He would undoubtedly have disagreed with much in this book, but I hope he would have found my treatment of him and the movement he shaped carefully considered, fair, and provocative in the best sense of the word.

Although I am a committed liberal, I believe liberalism and conservatism are the yin and yang of American political thought. America can achieve no balance and perhaps no wisdom without both of them. Like many, I am disheartened by the present state of partisan animosity. I believe one solution to this state of affairs is to take opposing ideas seriously. That does not mean pulling punches in debate; it means honestly trying to understand the other side. This book is my contribution to that effort.

Introduction

An illustration of a man appeared on the cover of the November 3, 1967, issue of *Time* magazine. The man held a pen in his right hand, its tip casually touching his lower lip, and he peered out at the reader with a droll expression. No identification was necessary. The visage was unmistakable and as instantly recognizable as that of a movie star or high government official. A small caption read WILLIAM BUCKLEY/CONSERVATISM CAN BE FUN.

The story described then forty-two-year-old Buckley's current activities: Buckley wrote a syndicated column, On the Right, which was carried three times per week by 205 newspapers; he edited the conservative journal of opinion *National Review*, which he founded twelve years earlier and that now boasted a circulation of ninety-four thousand; he wrote frequently for other major magazines; he hosted a weekly TV show, *Firing Line*, on which he interviewed—or, perhaps more accurately, debated—many of the nation's most prominent political figures and intellectuals; he even taught a course relating conservative principles to urban problems at the New School for Social Research. Buckley was also the author of seven books, and he had made a big splash two years earlier when he ran for mayor of New York City. Buckley was, moreover, a celebrity. He was a frequent guest on *The Tonight Show* and similar programs. He and his wife, Pat, a handsome and elegant couple—had been recently featured on the cover of *Town & Country*.

Time's article presented three principal themes about Buckley; two were on the mark but the third was terribly mistaken. As the cover suggested, *Time*'s first theme was that Buckley was enormous fun. He had charisma, panache, and a wit that was often breathtakingly surprising. At a press conference during his 1965 New York City mayoral race, for example, Buckley was asked if he really wanted to be mayor. His response: "I have never considered it." When asked how many votes he expected to get, he replied, "Conservatively speaking, one." This prompted a reporter to ask, "What would you do if you *were* elected?" "Demand a recount," Buckley answered.

When, several years later, Buckley was asked why as a conservative complaining about the decadence of American culture he consented to give an interview to *Playboy*, he answered, "To communicate my views to my son." When asked why Robert F. Kennedy consistently refused to appear with him on *Firing Line*, Buckley replied, "Why does the baloney reject the grinder?" It is no wonder that an MIT political scientist told *Time* that Buckley was "an exceedingly witty, attractive and rather insidious spokesman for a point of view for which I have few sympathies." He added, "But if we don't want to die of sheer boredom, the Buckleys should be encouraged."

Time's second theme was that Buckley's brilliance was superficial. The article put it this way: "Buckley is a gifted polemicist; a philosopher he is not." This too was accurate. Buckley was far more clever than thoughtful. Indeed, the article reported that Buckley was then working on a book to be titled *The Revolt Against the Masses*. Though *Time* did not say it, Buckley intended this to be his grand work of political philosophy, in which he would elaborate his breed of conservatism. Buckley ultimately was to produce fifty-seven books, yet he never was able to finish that one. It was not for want of trying. He had devoted his two-month winter vacation in 1964 in Gstaad, Switzerland, to *Revolt Against the Masses*—Gstaad is where he wrote many of his books, writing in the mornings, skiing in the afternoons, and attending dinner parties in the evenings—but his routine failed him this time round. He had produced only ten thousand words, about 10 percent of a book, and what he had gotten down on paper showed that he was floundering. He was simply lost when he sat down and tried to elaborate a coherent political philosophy.

Trying to set forth the basic principles of his philosophy also forced Buckley to confront the fact that many of the ideas he expressed with such verve and wit were inconsistent. Buckley had famously said that he would "sooner be governed by the first two thousand people in the Boston telephone directory, than by the two thousand members of the faculty of Harvard University." This was a clever put-down of what Buckley denounced as the "intellectual elite." The problem was that Buckley was not a populist. A good part of him wanted an elite group to govern America; he just wanted it to be a conservative elite rather than the then-dominant liberal elite.

Time's third theme was that Buckley was too much an individualist to be a leader and not savvy enough about practical politics to make a difference. "Daily, Bill Buckley stands at some conservative Armageddon, but not as the leader of an army or even a division." Buckley was, according to *Time*, "a solitary sniper." "Sometimes," the story said, "even an enemy smiles as Buckley hits the mark; sometimes his own rhetorical smoke obscures the target. Yet he never tires of the battle. Or is it sport?" "Nowhere was Buckley's lack of realism as a politician better demonstrated than in his madcap race for mayor," said *Time*. All Buckley accomplished by running for mayor of New York—and capturing 13.4 percent of the vote in a three-way race—was to drain away votes from the conservative Democrat and thereby elect the candidate Buckley most disliked, liberal Republican John Lindsay. According to *Time*, Barry Goldwater told Buckley, "As a political kingmaker, you're a wrong-way Corrigan."

Time, however, was exceedingly wrong about Buckley's leadership and influence. The magazine's ultimate take on Buckley was that he was entertaining but inconsequential. *Time* argued that Buckley's fatal flaw was his lack of realism, and it offered the following example: "His politics largely formed by the neat formulations of books rather than everyday life, Buckley would like to see a clear-cut ideological division between the two parties: all the conservatives in the Republican Party, all the liberals in the Democratic." Buckley failed to grasp that this was unrealistic, said *Time*, because he "misunderstands the fluid nature of U.S. party politics."

Buckley was certainly entertaining but he was not a mere entertainer. He was a man with a mission—to refashion conservatism and bring it to power—and he pursued that mission prodigiously, relentlessly, and brilliantly. He used every vehicle he could think of to advance his cause.

When, in September 1959, Nikita Khrushchev visited the United States at President Eisenhower's invitation, Buckley had *National Review* rent Carnegie Hall for a protest rally. Remarks by the eleven speakers at that rally—and especially those by the twenty-nine-year-old Buckley—made an impact, not only on the more than two thousand people who attended, but also through media reports on people throughout the country. Buckley would also write a series of spy mysteries, several of which became national bestsellers. These books were fun, but they also promoted Buckley's worldview about the Cold War and foreign affairs.

Because of his wit, playfulness, and élan, Buckley's seriousness of purpose was often underestimated. Buckley ran for mayor of New York City neither for sport nor to win. He ran to use the race as a platform for promoting conservatism. *Time* observed that Buckley's campaign "momentarily fascinated many liberals with some thoughtful proposals," but far more important, Buckley recruited to the movement people with conservative sensibilities.

Buckley founded *National Review* with the goal of reaching "a relatively select group of people, the opinion makers, mostly, and future opinion makers."[1] He hoped this would become a "small, but crucial group" of about 150,000 people. *Time* did not realize just how effectively Buckley was achieving that goal. Nor did *Time* realize how profound an impact Buckley and his cohorts at *National Review* were then having on two generations of future leaders—the generation then on the threshold of power, and the following generation of young men and women who were then in school or college.

When Buckley founded *National Review* in 1955, Barry Goldwater, then forty-six, was the junior senator from Arizona. From time to time, Goldwater's blunt way of speaking got attention, but attention is not the same thing as respect. Few of the nation's kingmakers—key journalists and party leaders—thought of Goldwater as a national figure until June of 1960, when his iconic manifesto, *The Conscience of a Conservative*, was released. The book was an instant bestseller. By the fall, half a million copies were in print, and Goldwater was being discussed as a possible future presidential nominee. Although some of the book was drawn from his speeches, Goldwater himself could not have produced so evocative a statement of conservatism. *Conscience* was ghostwritten by Buckley's brother-in-law and *National Review* associate, L. Brent Bozell. The following fall William A. Rusher, publisher of *National Review*, helped create the National Draft Goldwater Committee, the organization that shoved a reluctant Goldwater—who realized his candidacy was premature and that he was being used to build a conservative constituency for the future—into the 1964 presidential race.[2]

Ronald Reagan was forty-four, a liberal Democrat, and a fan of Franklin D. Roosevelt and the New Deal when Buckley formed *National Review*. Reagan had begun drifting away from acting. He had taken a job the year before as a spokesperson for General Electric. His job was to host *General Electric Theater* Sunday evenings on CBS, and to travel the country speaking at GE facilities in forty states, as well as to civic groups in communities where those facilities were located. By making Reagan's sunny visage the public face of GE, Reagan's boss—Lemuel Boulware, who was in charge of labor relations and public relations—hoped to increase the company's goodwill. Boulware, however, had strong political views: He believed that conservatism would be good for business generally, for GE specifically, and for the country as a whole. He was one of *National Review*'s original financial backers. Boulware gave Reagan (as well as senior GE managers) a reading list, and high on that list were *National Review* and Buckley's syndicated newspaper columns.

Reagan became one of the magazine's earliest subscribers. Because he hated to fly, Reagan's contract with GE stipulated he could travel by train. This gave him plenty of time with Buckley, *National Review*, and other conservative writers assigned by Boulware. Reagan emerged from his seven-year stint with GE as a conservative. *National Review* ideas and rhetoric shaped Reagan's basic message, developed in what friends called The Speech, the talk Reagan gave to countless community groups, constantly refining it until it was pitch-perfect.[3] (Reagan became a national political figure on October 27, 1964, when he delivered a half-hour version of The Speech on NBC in support of Goldwater's presidential campaign.) Reagan gave Buckley and *National Review* much of the credit for his conversion. The year after he assumed the presidency, Reagan awarded the Presidential Medal of Freedom to James Burnham, who was Buckley's de facto number two at *National Review* and author of its foreign policy column titled The Third World War. "I owe [you] a personal debt," Reagan told Burnham when he conferred the medal, "because throughout the years traveling the mashed-potato circuit I have quoted you widely."[4]

The following generation was even more deeply affected by Buckley and his magazine. These were baby boomers, born in the post–World War II era, and raised during a time of both rapidly expanding material wealth and existential anxiety. On the one hand, modern technology was producing an unprecedented cornucopia of benefits for a rapidly expanding middle class—single-family homes, automobiles, televisions, refrigerators, automatic dishwashers, clothes washers and driers, leisure time, vacation travel, and college educations. At the same time, modern technology had produced the equally unprecedented terror of nuclear war. The prospect of a conflagration snuffing out all life on earth was chillingly real. It is no surprise that this generation would become acutely politically aware and seek a worldview that offered both meaning and solutions. The dominant culture was liberal, and those who turned left for answers readily found thinkers who spoke to them. But young people of conservative sensibilities felt lost until they discovered Buckley and his magazine.

Karl Rove was about fifteen when he discovered *National Review* at the Sparks, Nevada, library. "I eagerly awaited its arrival each week, devouring articles using words I didn't know (such as denouement) but whose meaning I could often guess," Rove said in his autobiography. "I couldn't get my hands on Buckley's books quickly enough. At age fifteen I laughed out loud all the way through *The Unmaking of a Mayor,*" he continued. Rush Limbaugh has written: "I grew up on *National Review* and Mr. Buckley. Aside from my father, he's the most influential man in my life." When, as a young lawyer, future Supreme Court Justice Samuel Alito applied for a job in the Department of Justice, he wrote in his application: "When I first became interested in government and politics during the 1960s, the greatest influences on my views were the writings of William F. Buckley, Jr., the *National Review*, and Barry Goldwater's 1964 campaign." That is how Alito signaled to Reaganites then in charge of the department that he was one of them.

Conservative historian George H. Nash writes:

> As the only significantly avowedly conservative journal of opinion for a long time after 1955, *National Review* was far more in-

dispensable to the Right than any single liberal journal was to the Left . . . If *National Review* (or something like it) had not been founded, there would probably have been no cohesive intellectual force on the Right in the 1960s and 1970s. To a very substantial degree, the history of reflective conservatism in America after 1955 is the history of the individuals who collaborated in—or were discovered by—the magazine William F. Buckley, Jr. founded.[5]

When we consider *Time*'s article from our present vantage point, we cannot help being struck by its statement that Buckley was unrealistic—evidenced, according to *Time*, by Buckley's wish that the Republican Party become exclusively conservative and the Democratic Party exclusively liberal. Yet *Time* magazine was not wrong; Buckley's view was, in fact, unrealistic based on the realities of 1967. What happened, quite simply, is that Buckley and his colleagues changed America's political realities. It was a feat so great that it is almost impossible to overstate.

Conservatism was moribund when Buckley founded *National Review* in 1955. The Republican Party had consistently rejected conservatism's champion, Senator Robert A. Taft of Ohio, in favor of a series of progressives: Wendell Willkie in 1940, Thomas E. Dewey in 1944 and 1948, and Dwight D. Eisenhower, who when elected president in 1952 identified himself as a "modern Republican" and a "liberal Republican." Conservatism was on its deathbed not only in the realm of active politics but in the intellectual world as well. In his 1950 book, *The Liberal Imagination*, the acute observer of the American scene Lionel Trilling had written: "In the United States at this time liberalism is not only the dominant but even the sole intellectual tradition. For it is the plain fact that nowadays there are no conservative or reactionary ideas in general circulation."[6]

Conservatism was not merely out of favor; it was disrespected. The leading public intellectuals of the day—people such as Lionel Trilling, Arthur Schlesinger Jr., and John Kenneth Galbraith—looked down on both conservatism as a philosophy and those who were foolish enough to subscribe to it. This was not new; a century earlier, John Stuart Mill had called conservatives the "stupid party." Social scientists were now saying research showed that Mill was right. Political scientist Herbert McClosky conducted a series of sophisticated studies involving thousands of subjects. First, he tested and refined questionnaires that determined how liberal or conservative someone was; then he correlated those results with other instruments that revealed characteristics about the individual subjects. "By every measure available to us," McClosky wrote in the *American Political Science Review* in 1952, "conservative beliefs are found most frequently among the uninformed, the poorly educated, and so far as we can determine, the less intelligent."[7] Only 12 percent of the most conservative group had some college education compared to 47 percent of the most liberal group. It is perhaps telling that McClosky labeled the most conservative group "Extreme Conservatives" and the most liberal group "Liberals," as if only people with very conservative views were extreme.

On an "Awareness Scale" that McClosky said reflected "not only actual knowledge but also the clarity of one's grasp of the social process, past and present" and also served "as a crude intelligence test," 66 percent of Extreme Conservatives scored low while only 9 percent scored high. The Liberal group was just the opposite: Only 9 percent scored low and 54 percent scored high. A separate measure of "Intellectuality" produced nearly identical results. "The data show clearly . . . that the most articulate and informed classes in our society are preponderantly liberal in their outlook," he wrote. McClosky also gave his subjects psychological tests and found that conservatives were more submissive, alienated, bewildered, suspicious, hostile, rigid, and pessimistic, and had far lower self-confidence and higher levels of guilt than liberals—differences that remained after controlling for education and social status.

Of course, not all conservatives were dull witted or dysfunctional, but conservative causes attracted far more than their fair share of kooks and bigots. Even Buckley privately lamented, "Why is it our side is afflicted with all the loonies?"[8] One of Buckley's first lessons in just how prevalent undesirables were in the conservative ranks occurred in 1959 when he decreed that no one on the masthead of the *National Review* could write for *American Mercury*, the journal once edited by the great H. L. Mencken that had since become virulently anti-Semitic. When his edict became public, Buckley found himself pelted with angry letters from

National Review subscribers who were also faithful readers of *American Mercury*. To one such letter writer who demanded that Buckley cancel his *National Review* subscription, an exasperated Buckley replied:

> I have this day instructed the circulation department to cancel your subscription to *National Review* and to make you an appropriate refund. I have also instructed the department that it is not to enter a subscription from you in the future, unless it comes accompanied by a sworn affidavit to the effect that you will no longer pester us with any of your ignorant letters.[9]

By becoming its most prominent adherent, Buckley gave conservatism a new image. Buckley was well educated, accomplished, wealthy, handsome, self-assured, cosmopolitan, witty, and apparently erudite. Not only had he been educated at Yale but even as a student he had made Yale sit up and take notice. As chairman of the *Yale Daily News* (the paper's equivalent of editor in chief), Buckley seized the comfortably liberal campus by its lapels and shook it with biting conservative editorials. Just two years out of college, he wrote a nationally bestselling book, and four years later founded what would become the most influential journal of political opinion of its time.

Buckley seemed to have six careers—magazine editor, newspaper columnist, writer of nonfiction books and articles, novelist, host of a weekly television show, and public speaker—any one of which would have been a full-time occupation for most mortals. He is surely one of the most prolific writers in American history, leaving behind fifty-seven books, four thousand newspaper columns, and four hundred articles and book reviews, not only in *National Review* but other magazines such as the *New Yorker* and *Esquire*. Moreover, Buckley did not merely do many things; he did many things superlatively well. He won not only the Best Columnist of the Year Award (1967), but also an Emmy for Outstanding Achievement (1969), an American Book Award for Best Mystery in paperback (1980), and a Lowell Thomas Travel Journalism Award (1989). He also received the Presidential Medal of Freedom from President George H. W. Bush in 1991.

It was not merely Buckley's talents that caused young men and women to so admire—and secretly desire to emulate—him, it was his style and elegance as well. Buckley's baritone voice and unique speech pattern made him sound learned, aristocratic, and perhaps slightly British. His language was sprinkled with the most wonderful, arcane words—words such as gallimaufry, rodomontade, belletristic—that sent even professors scurrying for dictionaries. He was not showboating (at least, not entirely). He used these words precisely and naturally, just as much in private letters as in published writings.* Veteran publishers thought using such words ill advised. William Loeb, publisher of the archconservative *Manchester Union Leader*, sought to go over the young editor's head by warning Bill's father, Will Buckley, about the foolishness of using such words. "The word 'usufructs' has no place in any popular magazine, and is one of the reasons the circulation of *National Review* doesn't go up any faster," Loeb wrote to Will in a private letter.[10] The reply Loeb received came directly from Bill. It read:

> I am sorry you don't like words like "usufruct." I think one of the most precious possessions of the English speaking world is a large and very subtle vocabulary. I believe everyone should make a modest effort to pass on to the next generation as beautiful and flexible a language as he inherited. That responsibility the editors of *National Review* undertake, in a moderate way, to assume.[11]

When Bill began writing a syndicated newspaper column, James J. Kilpatrick, editor of the *Richmond News Leader*, warned him against forcing upon editors "a vocabulary they simply cannot bring to the day's page."[12] Buckley did seem thereafter to try to rein in his vocabulary for his newspaper column, although not for magazine articles, books, or public appearances. Bill turned out to be right: *National Review* readers liked being talked up to. It made them feel part of a highbrow community.

If Buckley was fun to read, he was positively galvanizing to listen to or watch, all the more so because he sliced up debating partners and constantly delighted audiences with his wit. And enthralled high school

---

*In a profile for the *Atlantic* (July/August 2009), Garry Wills wrote that Buckley sometimes was unsure of the meanings of his big words and misstepped. If so, this is an etymological debate at the highest level.

and college students also knew that Buckley lived an enviable life: He was married to a beautiful woman, skied in Switzerland, sailed (twice across the Atlantic Ocean), enjoyed music and high culture, and counted among his friends famous writers, movie stars, and at least one president.

Buckley's first contribution to conservatism, therefore, was to become its most visible representative. When people thought of conservatives, they no longer thought of simpletons and screwballs, or even the admirable but gray Senator Robert A. Taft, but of Buckley. Committed conservatives felt safe coming out of the closet to friends and co-workers; young men and women of conservative sensibilities had someone to emulate. Having Buckley as a leader made it possible to assemble a conservative army—the very army, in fact, that in 1967 *Time* magazine did not think existed. Subscribers to *National Review* were not merely readers of a magazine; they were part of a movement.

Buckley was not just the public face of conservatism; he was also its commander in chief who made many of the strategic and tactical decisions that determined the fate of the conservative movement. His first task was to decide who should write for and edit *National Review*, and then to recruit them. Many of the people Buckley wanted were prima donnas. They had to be wooed, and once on board, required attentive care and feeding. There was intramural strife. Some members of the *National Review* inner circle disliked other members; some believed that views advocated by others were apostasy. In recruiting—and then keeping happy and productive—a cadre of conservative thinkers with large egos, eccentricities, and interpersonal animosities, Buckley exercised the same kinds of skills that General Dwight David Eisenhower deployed in leading fellow generals Sir Bernard Montgomery, George Patton, and Charles de Gaulle. Making his role especially challenging was Buckley's relative youth. It would have been easy for a callow young man to be steamrolled by more established and experienced luminaries of the conservative firmament.

Buckley, however, was up to the challenge. He was young but not callow. His interpersonal skills—which he consciously developed during a tour in the army—were considerable. He knew how to flatter without kowtowing. He was charming. He was generous. He genuinely liked people, and respected them for their particular skills (while recognizing their deficits). But Buckley also possessed the will to lay down the law when necessary, and because he held all of the *National Review* common stock with voting rights, he had the ability to do so.

Buckley became so respected that he was also able to read individuals and groups out of the conservative movement. In 1955, it was difficult to draw distinctions between reputable and disreputable conservatives, to demark the boundaries of responsible conservatism, to discern when debate was healthy and when it was dangerously divisive. Repudiating fellow conservatives would be viewed by some as treasonous. Buckley would be told time and again that conservatives must hang together or they would all hang separately. But Buckley understood that if conservatives were to shed the image of being wacky, dysfunctional, and anti-intellectual, they had to separate themselves from the kooks. In addition, while a healthy movement benefits from a considerable breadth of views and robust discussion, it also needs to remain coherent. Buckley's determinations to amputate gangrenous limbs comprise some of the most intriguing portions of the story to come. It was sometimes uncertain whether the surgery itself would prove fatal.

For Buckley, *National Review* was a vehicle for fashioning a new political philosophy and bringing it to political power. He never saw the magazine merely as a pulpit for preaching to the converted; he was particularly interested in readers who could be brought into the fold. "I want the students, the professors, the tentatively interested readers, who are looking in, many of them, wondering whether conservatives have the right idea," he explained.[13] Among other things, Buckley persuaded financial backers to provide free *National Review* subscriptions to students and school libraries.

Buckley was also the principal financial engine for the magazine. No national journal of opinion—whether *National Review* or magazines on the left such as the *Nation* and *New Republic*—has ever been able to sustain itself on subscriptions and advertising alone. When he launched the magazine, Bill's father helped by plunking down $100,000 (the equivalent of more than $750,000 today), and Bill raised more than $300,000 by selling debentures and nonvoting stock to a few other wealthy conservatives. The need to raise money never ended however. Buckley did not enjoy fund-raising, but he devoted considerable portions of his time to it nonetheless. Moreover, he never personally drew a salary from *National Review*.[14] In 1959, he got an agent to book him on the lecture circuit for a couple of weeks in both the fall and the spring. His typical speaker's fee in the early years was $300 to $400 per lecture plus expenses, about $2,100 to $2,800 in today's dollars.

Buckley's greatest contribution was redefining conservatism. Almost from its founding, *National Review* became the quasi-official organ of the movement. Conservative views were those that *National Review* published. In his role as editor in chief, from the time the magazine was founded in 1955 until 1990 when he retired from that position, Buckley not only commissioned articles and hired and fired the magazine's regular columnists but—with the exception only of when he was vacationing or on the lecture circuit—was the principal editor of the editorial section and decided whether or not to run every signed article published by the magazine.[15] Buckley determined not only *National Review*'s editorial positions but, far more importantly, who would write for the magazine, what they would write about, which arguments would be presented and which would not, and how much space and prominence would be given to particular topics and writers. When editors or writers drifted too far from what he deemed permissible, Buckley, as he himself put it, banished them.[16] These cumulative decisions fashioned conservatism. Thus, what Buckley was unable to do reflectively—sitting down to write a great treatise of conservatism—he did intuitively in response to the flow of current events.

Journals of opinion have exerted a special influence on American politics and policy. The *Nation* was an important voice during the progressive era, and both the *Nation* and the *New Republic* were vital promoters of the New Deal. It was the examples set by these magazines that persuaded Buckley that the conservative movement needed a journal of opinion. But *National Review* became much more than the right's counterpart to those journals. Its circulation grew to exceed that of any other opinion journal, but that is not what most differentiated it. Buckley, and thus *National Review*, personified American conservatism in a way unparalleled by other journals. Readers of other magazines read an article and thought, *That's interesting!* Subscribers of *National Review* read an article and thought, *That's what conservatives think! That's how conservatives think!*

* * *

Buckley did not act alone. Despite all of his individual achievements, he was more the conductor of an orchestra than a one-man band. The orchestra was, of course, the writers and editors of *National Review*, and the expanding conservative intellectual community it spawned. Buckley not only recruited established figures for his magazines but he also discovered some of the greatest new talents of his time, among them Garry Wills, Joan Didion, John Leonard, George F. Will, David Brooks, and Richard Brookhiser, all of whom began their careers (or in Will's case, began writing for a general audience rather than for scholarly journals) at *National Review*. Today, of course, Wills, Didion, and the late John Leonard are considered liberals. They are some of the writers who strayed too far from conservative doctrine and either departed voluntarily or were banished by Buckley.

The principal battles and intrigue at *National Review* that led to redefining conservatism, however, were not between conservatives and liberals. They were among conservatives. Besides Buckley, three figures are of special importance to this story.

The first is Russell Kirk. Like Buckley, Kirk was propelled to fame as a young man. Kirk was an obscure, thirty-five-year-old assistant professor of history at what is now Michigan State University when, in 1953, he wrote *The Conservative Mind: From Burke to Eliot*, a book that has been described as the "landmark study" that provided conservatives "with a sense that their movement had inherited a serious intellectual legacy."[17] *Time* magazine greeted its publication with an especially long and laudatory review, and the first printing sold out by the end of the month. Kirk's book was so successful that he resigned his appointment at Michigan State to earn his livelihood as an independent writer and lecturer in the conservative establishment. More than half a century later, *The Conservative Mind* is still widely read, and it is considered one of the iconic conservative texts.

Kirk rooted conservatism in the philosophy of eighteenth-century British statesman Edmund Burke. "Burke's is the true school of conservative thought," Kirk declared. Burke believed that societies had become constructed in particular ways for particular reasons, even though the reasons were not always apparent. For Burke, this did not mean that change should be resisted. On the contrary, Burke was a reformer, and Kirk acknowledged that Burke was both a liberal and a conservative.

Burke believed that changes should be made carefully and with a healthy respect for the risks of unintended consequences. Cultures were different, and their differences gave rise to different governments, societal structures, and religions. No form of government was universally best; no great religion possessed greater truth than others. Burke was a pragmatist who eschewed overarching philosophies. Public policy had to take into account a host of factors including sociology, economics (Adam Smith considered Burke one of the few people who truly understood his theories), and most especially history.

When William F. Buckley founded *National Review*, Kirk, quite understandably, was one of the people he most wanted to recruit. Kirk was happy to come on board. But when Kirk saw the magazine's masthead, he was much less happy. Kirk stunned Buckley by vehemently objecting to having his name "cheek by jowl" on the masthead with two libertarians. Buckley tried to assuage Kirk, explaining that *National Review* was dedicated to reexamining the nature of conservatism by presenting a variety of viewpoints. Kirk would have none of it. He considered libertarianism a threat to the republic. If libertarians were to be on the masthead, Kirk's name would have to be removed. He agreed to write a regular column titled From the Academy for *National Review*, but he would not lend his name as an editor to any periodical that welcomed libertarians.

A second individual of importance is one of the libertarians whose name on the masthead so upset Kirk, namely, Frank S. Meyer. Meyer, who was forty-six when Buckley founded *National Review*, had studied at Princeton, Oxford, and the London School of Economics, where he had become a committed communist. He served the party as educational director in Illinois and Indiana before making a dramatic switch to the political right. Buckley appointed Meyer book review editor, and also assigned him a regular column called Principles and Heresies.

One thing that Kirk and Meyer had in common was their iconoclasm: Kirk lived a nearly Luddite existence without radio and phonograph in remote Mecosta, Michigan; Meyer lived a nocturnal existence—his workday generally began around five P.M. in rural Woodstock, New York. Another thing they had in common was that they both converted to Catholicism. Kirk, who had been brought up by non-church-going parents, converted to Catholicism when he was forty-six. Meyer, who had been raised Jewish, made the final submission on his deathbed. (Jeffrey Hart was a third member of the *National Review* circle who converted to Catholicism.) In fact, Catholicism—or more precisely, a right-wing Catholic tradition—was integral to Buckley and *National Review*'s philosophy, particularly in the early years when the magazine routinely published articles about Catholic theology.

Despite these personal similarities, Meyer and Kirk both saw themselves as ideological adversaries. It is often said that Frank Meyer was the architect of "fusionism," sometimes described as fusing libertarianism and traditional conservatism. That is not entirely correct. The confusion originates from an article by Brent Bozell that made such a claim, but in fact Meyer wrote a subsequent article "to plead innocent" to Bozell's "indictment."[18] Meyer explained he advocated fusing libertarianism with virtue, not with traditional conservatism. While traditional conservatives also place great importance on virtue, the disagreements between the two schools of thought are profound and irreconcilable. Libertarians believe in the transcendent importance of the individual while traditional conservatives stress the importance of the community. Libertarians want the free market to be as unregulated as possible while traditional conservatives believe that big business, if unconstrained, can impoverish national life and threaten freedom. Libertarians believe a strong state threatens freedom while traditional conservatives believe that a strong state—properly constructed to ensure that too much power does not accumulate in any one branch—is necessary to ensure freedom.

Libertarians and traditional conservatives even disagree about such fundamental issues as what words such as *freedom* and *liberty* mean. Libertarianism is elaborated from a set of abstract principles. Its first principle is that there is an overarching natural right that no government may legitimately curtail: "the right to live your life as you choose so long as you don't infringe on the equal right of others."[19] By contrast, traditional conservatives prefer specifics to abstractions. "Abstract liberty, like other abstractions, is not to be found," Edmund Burke famously declared.[20] To Burke, Kirk, and other traditional conservatives, rights come not from God, nature, or a priori reasoning; they are products of experience. They are, in the best sense of the term, socially constructed.

Frank Meyer argued that the state has only two natural functions:

"to protect the rights of citizens against violent or fraudulent assault and to judge in conflicts of right with right."[21] He believed that government should maintain police, courts of law, and a military to protect citizens against foreign assault, but little else. "To give to it in addition any further power is fraught with danger," he wrote.[22] The idea that government should provide institutions and public services that citizens cannot profitably furnish fits comfortably with Burkean philosophy but not with libertarianism.

To traditional conservatives such as Russell Kirk, libertarianism would lead to decadence, deterioration, and decay. Kirk believed that by glorifying the individual, the free market, and the dog-eat-dog struggle for material success, libertarianism weakened community, promoted materialism, and undermined appreciation of the things that truly matter, namely, "the permanent things" of true community: tradition, love, learning, and aesthetics. Kirk lambasted libertarians for holding up capitalism as an absolute good. True conservatives, he maintained, valued not the individual acquisition of property but what can be created by and for "true community, the union of men, through love and common interest, for the common welfare."[23] He argued that "economic self-interest is ridiculously inadequate to hold an economic system together, and even less adequate to preserve order."

Kirk and Meyer both understood that Burkeanism and libertarianism were incompatible. They saw their philosophies engaged in a death struggle for the soul of conservatism. Their animosities became personal. It was evident to all that Meyer actively hated Kirk.[24] Though Buckley admired Kirk, Kirk surely understood that he could never prevail within the councils of *National Review* for the simple reason that Buckley was a libertarian. If Kirk were to help traditional conservatism prevail over libertarianism, his best chance was to remain outside of *National Review*, make common cause with other Burkeans, and try to rally conservatives to their flag. Yet Kirk rejected that approach.[25] An important part of the story is why that came to be.

The third member of the *National Review* family who warrants special attention is James Burnham. Compared to Buckley and Russell Kirk, James Burnham, fifty years of age in 1955, was a grown-up. He looked and acted the part: He wore impeccably tailored suits and was exceptionally well mannered. Like his coeditors, Burnham possessed a stellar academic pedigree: He graduated first in his class at Princeton, earned a master's degree from Oxford, and had been a tenured professor at New York University. He authored six books about the future of the world, international affairs, and the struggle between the West and communism. Moreover, Burnham was, or at least had been, famous—far better known than Kirk or Buckley. His first nonacademic book, *The Managerial Revolution*, published fifteen years earlier, had been not merely a bestseller but a sensation: It sold more than two hundred thousand copies in the United States alone and was translated into fourteen languages. Burnham's book inspired many of the ideas in George Orwell's *1984* and appears in the novel under a different name.

Buckley and Burnham had met briefly and under improbable circumstances in 1950. Buckley, having just graduated from Yale and looking for a way of avoiding being called back for service in the Korean War, decided to apply for covert work with the CIA. Burnham was then secretly working in Washington, D.C., for the CIA's Office of Policy Coordination, and when Buckley presented himself to be interviewed at a CIA safe house in Georgetown, it was James Burnham who interviewed him.[26] This brief meeting presumably had nothing to do with Buckley's hiring Burnham for *National Review* five years later however. Buckley wanted Burnham to be the magazine's foreign policy editor and to write a regular column titled The Third World War. Considering Burnham's marquee appeal, it is easy to understand why Buckley considered him a catch. Yet for several reasons, Burnham was a strange choice. For one thing, Burnham had no formal training in foreign affairs. His academic training was in English literature. For another thing, Burnham did not fit easily into the conservative mold. His favorite Republican was liberal Nelson Rockefeller, who—to the consternation of his fellow editors—Burnham repeatedly wanted *National Review* to endorse for president.

Burnham had also been a former communist, a Trotskyite to be exact. He had been a regular correspondent of Trotsky and one of Trotsky's most trusted American supporters. Burnham served Trotsky and the Communist Party for seven years as a writer and editor of socialist journals but became disillusioned with communism when the Soviet Union invaded Poland. Burnham was one of no less than seven former communists among the small circle of editors and contributors for *National*

Review. (The others were Meyer, William S. Schlamm, Will Herberg, Whittaker Chambers, Max Eastman, and John Dos Passos.) The magazine liked to suggest these three men had become vigorous anticommunists because they had seen communism firsthand. The alternative explanation is that these were people who desperately needed ideology and doctrine, and when an ideological system to which they had clung became unacceptable, they had to find another.

The second explanation, however, fits Burnham only up to a point. Burnham was a theorist when it came to the Cold War. Believing "containment" was an inadequate policy for dealing with international communism—a "guarantor of ultimate defeat," as he put it[27]—Burnham developed the competing strategy of "rollback." Thus, Burnham did not merely want to contain communism within the areas already under its sphere of influence, including Eastern Europe; rather, he advocated an aggressive approach of rolling back communism and liberating areas under communist control. This would be accomplished principally through political warfare, or "polwar," which would consist of propaganda, psychological warfare, sabotage, subversion, and guerilla warfare. But on other topics, Burnham was far less doctrinaire, and often viewed as a pragmatist. Burnham became Buckley's closest confidante outside his own family and the de facto number two at *National Review*, the person who made decisions when Buckley was unavailable.

Jeffrey Hart, a longtime senior editor at *National Review*, says that Burnham was invaluable because he moderated Buckley's tendencies; he stopped Buckley and the magazine from becoming too libertarian, too religious, too doctrinaire.[28] Buckley's sister Priscilla, who served as managing editor of *National Review*, says that Burnham insisted that practical considerations, experience, and facts be taken into account and thereby kept Buckley and the magazine anchored in reality and stopped them from drifting too far into ideological abstractions. Burnham was also a force for maintaining a sense of dignity. He was not opposed to spirited attacks on political opponents but he was offended by attacks that were sophomoric or mean-spirited, and therefore provided a force for restraint.

Burnham was the first neoconservative. Irving Kristol famously said, "A neoconservative is a liberal who has been mugged by reality."[29] What Kristol meant was that the world was a hard place. Some people were bad, some people were lazy, and it was a mistake to coddle them. Crime had to be deterred with swift and certain punishment, undiminished by pathos for criminals' unfortunate childhoods or indigent circumstances. Government handouts to the poor only made them dependent. It was better to make people stand on their own feet and hold them account-able for their actions. The "neoconservative" label was first used by Kris-tol and a group of former liberals—including, notably, Kristol and Norman Podhoretz—in the 1970s and 1980s. At first, neoconservatives were primarily focused on domestic policies, but over time they became more interested in foreign affairs—and applied the same thinking to the international stage. The world, they argued, was a dangerous place. Some nations were our enemies. The communist bloc was bent on world domination, and it was not going to be dissuaded from its ambitions through negotiations and mutual understanding. America had to rely on military might. It had to be tough. In November 1979, Jeane Kirk-patrick wrote an article titled "Dictatorships and Double Standards" that became a neoconservative classic. She argued that America should not be squeamish about using double standards for dictatorial regimes. Where it was in our self-interest to befriend anticommunist dictators, we should do so. "Liberal idealism need not be identical with masochism, and need not be incompatible with the defense of freedom and the na-tional interest," she wrote. James Burnham advocated such views long before these other thinkers, which is why historians H. W. Brands and Richard Brookhiser have called him the original neoconservative.[30]

Burnham believed that American military might should be used not only for defense—not just to deter or repulse attacks on America and its allies—but offensively as well. Communism should not only be con-tained but pushed back. America should project its way of life (capitalism even more than democracy) across the globe through force, sometimes applied covertly and, when necessary, overtly. The world is a dangerous place; evil exists; adversaries cannot be reasoned out of pursuing their goals. In the end, the only effective weapon is force. As Burnham saw it, America did not need to be afraid. Its military was the most powerful on earth. Yet its leaders—the liberals especially—were timid, gullible, and naïve.

It is a paradox that Burnham was generally a force for moderation and yet an extreme hard-liner within foreign affairs, where his influence was greatest. Buckley considered Burnham the preeminent expert in that sphere. Burnham's views about the Cold War became conservative orthodoxy. If Buckley had selected someone else as *National Review*'s foreign affairs expert, conservatism may have developed differently. It was not preordained, for example, that conservatives would wind up supporting the war in Vietnam. The traditional conservative position was to be suspicious of foreign military adventures. Garry Wills, for example, privately argued that the war was not sensible on either anti-communist or conservative grounds.[31] A Burkean who believed that studying the history and culture of Vietnam was essential to under-standing what was feasible would have concluded that the war was un-winnable, no matter how many troops were sent or how many bombs were dropped. Had Buckley, in 1955, selected a Burkean instead of Burnham as the magazine's expert on foreign affairs, it is possible the conservative movement would have wound up criticizing Lyndon Johnson for pursuing a futile war instead of criticizing him for not pursuing the war aggressively enough. Had that occurred, Johnson, who harbored deep misgivings about the war even as he escalated it, might have reversed course in the early stages of the conflict. But it was not mere chance that Buckley selected Burnham; he did so be-cause Burnham's neoconservative approach was consistent with his own predilections.

Conservatism today is a three-legged stool. It is based upon liber-tarianism, religious conservatism, and neoconservatism. We think of these as three distinct schools of thought that developed separately and have different constituencies. There are, moreover, fundamental disagree-ments among the three schools. Social conservatives consider abortion a critical issue. Libertarians believe that government should not regulate morality and outlaw private conduct such as abortion or drug use. Neo-conservatives tend to consider drug use socially corrosive and therefore warranting governmental regulation, and abortion a private matter that the government should not regulate. Yet, despite these and other differ-ences, all three schools were able to make common cause in the conser-vative movement because William F. Buckley Jr. was himself a libertarian, a religious conservative, and a neoconservative. As a result, he and *National Review* defined conservatism in a way that accommodated all three schools of thought.

But the coalition among those groups is now breaking down. We are entering a new period of ideological searching and transformation for both conservatism and liberalism. This is partly due to the "March of Dimes effect," the phenomenon that occurs when a cause has achieved its goals. In 1938, President Franklin D. Roosevelt founded the March of Dimes organization to defeat polio. Twenty years later, the Salk and Sabin vaccines had wiped out polio, and the March of Dimes had to decide whether to go out of business or take on another cause. (It took the latter course.) Similarly, modern liberalism and conservatism have both realized many of their defining goals. Two of liberalism's greatest causes—the civil rights movement and the women's movement—have largely succeeded. Liberalism has also had considerable successes with the consumer and the environmental movements, though the latter may now face its greatest challenge in climate change. Although another important cause of liberalism, the war on poverty, has largely been a failure, liberalism is uncertain about whether, or how, to attempt to wage that war again. Meanwhile, modern conservatism's most important cause was realized when the Soviet Union ended and Russia and China began converting to market economies. Some conservatives have tried replacing anticommunism with the war on terror as a defining cause, but that may not succeed.

Of course, liberals and conservatives have not joined hands, poured each other glasses of champagne, and celebrated unity. Just the opposite has happened: We are experiencing hyperpartisanship. Paradoxically, it is confusion within each camp—not certainty—that fuels the vehemence. It is because each side can't see its own compass clearly that makes it so distrustful and defiant whenever the other side suggests a direction.

The tea party movement is one manifestation of our entering a time of ideological reconsideration. The tea parties were ignited by a fear that government bailouts of banks, financial institutions, and automobile manufacturers meant the end of capitalism, even though those decisions were made by both the George W. Bush and Barack Obama administrations. Tea party members are considered generally conservative—but they did not rush to defend conservative battlements. They instead created new organizations and often supported unorthodox politicians over established conservatives. The tea parties too are searching, and even they do not yet know exactly for what.

This book is about the rise of modern American conservatism—about the last time conservatism was refashioned. I hope that by examining that period, conservatives may gain a better understanding of the direction they now wish to take. Although this book is about the rise of modern conservatism, I believe it can be just as helpful to liberals looking to the future. We often get a better grasp of our own perspective by reflecting on opposing perspectives; sometimes, in fact, that is the best method of self-understanding. It is for these reasons that I believe the story of William F. Buckley Jr. and the rise of American conservatism is not only interesting, but also relevant to our present moment.

To appreciate how Buckley changed conservatism, we must first understand what conservatism was before Buckley and *National Review*. For that we need an appropriate benchmark—a gold standard of conservatism before 1955, if we can find one. It is natural to look first to the conservative journals of opinion, but that will not do. When *National Review* began publishing in 1955, it filled a void. Although two conservative journals then existed, both were troubled. The *Freeman* had begun publishing in 1950 under the slogan "a fortnightly for individualists."[32] Taking its name from a journal coedited by Albert Jay Nock in the 1920s, the new venture included John Chamberlain and a number of other veteran editors and writers. However, circulation was low, the magazine was in financial distress, and the editors became embroiled in angry fights over whether to defend Joseph McCarthy or to endorse Taft or Eisenhower for the 1952 Republican nomination. It is unclear whether the split was precipitated by financial or editorial reasons, but either way Chamberlain and the magazine's other top talents walked out in 1953. The following year, the *Freeman* was converted into a monthly and devoted itself largely to publishing essays on libertarian economics and otherwise ignoring the political and policy issues of the day. It quickly receded in importance.

With a circulation of ninety thousand, *American Mercury* had a far larger readership as well as a distinguished heritage. *American Mercury* was cofounded in 1924 by the journalist and cultural and literary critic H. L. Mencken, and become famous publishing works by the likes of F. Scott Fitzgerald, William Faulkner, Carl Sandburg, and Sherwood

Anderson. When in 1926 a prosecutor declared an article about a prostitute obscene, H. L. Mencken rushed to Cambridge, Massachusetts, to personally sell the offending issue to a prominent clergyman who had raised the hue and cry over the scandalous article. Thus, Mencken got himself dramatically arrested, and proceeded to challenge censorship in the courts. (He won.) *American Mercury*, however, was badly buffeted by the Great Depression. Under new editorial leadership in 1950, it changed its format from a primarily literary journal to a journal of conservative opinion. Only two years later, however, J. Russell Maguire purchased the magazine. Maguire was a miscreant. He had been convicted of both violating the securities laws by deliberately manipulating stock prices and making excess profits selling guns to the armed forces during World War II. He had other problems too. Under his ownership, *American Mercury* became a crude tract of loony conspiracy theories and vile anti-Semitism.

Nor can we benchmark conservatism before Buckley by looking to the philosophy of a consensus among conservative writers or to that of a preeminent conservative intellectual. No group or individual is adequate to the purpose.

Happily, however, there is someone who can serve as the quintessential exemplar of conservatism before Buckley: Robert A. Taft, the United States senator from Ohio from 1939 until his premature death, at age sixty-three, in 1953.[33] Taft was known as Mr. Republican because he was generally considered the real leader of his party in Congress even while others held the formal leadership positions. "Taft is the man you want to see," Republican senate majority leader Wallace White famously told reporters in 1946, acknowledging that it was Taft who really spoke for the Republicans. Taft was the conservative favorite for the Republican presidential nomination in 1940, 1948, and 1952. There were conservatives both to the right and left of Taft, but they all admired—and followed— him. Taft was also considered "the dominant conservative of his time," and "the very model of the American conservative."[34] To understand what conservatism was before Buckley changed it, we need to spend a little time understanding Taft's political philosophy and the background that shaped it.

* * *

Bob Taft came from formidable stock. His grandfather Alphonso was born in Vermont, graduated third in his class at Yale University (where he cofounded the secret society Skull and Bones), went on to Yale Law School, and then moved to New York City to practice law. Reflecting a temperament that would epitomize three generations, Alphonso was repulsed by what he considered to be the materialism and self-centeredness of New York. "Money is the all in all," and the "great mass of men" are characterized by "notorious selfishness and dishonesty," he said. He moved to Cincinnati, where he became involved in the Whig Party and subsequently in the Republican Party, at a time when it was still very much the party of Lincoln. He was a city councilman and then a judge on the Superior Court of Cincinnati, during which time he courageously handed down a decision prohibiting compulsory Bible reading in the public schools. In 1876, seeking rectitude for an administration blemished by scandals, President Ulysses S. Grant appointed Alphonso Taft to his cabinet, where Taft served briefly as secretary of war and then attorney general. After Grant left office, Alphonso moved back to Cincinnati and lost two races for governor of Ohio, one against Rutherford B. Hayes. Taft believed, in part, that he lost those elections because of his decision against Bible reading in the schools.

Alphonso and his wife, Louise, had five sons and a daughter. All of the boys followed their dad into Yale, the study of law, and the Republican Party. One of those boys was William Howard Taft. William outperformed his father by ranking second in his class at Yale College.* It was an omen of things to come. William became a Superior Court judge at age thirty-two, and handed down a decision—in this instance a decision against a secondary boycott by bricklayers—that created a national hubbub. He (and his son Robert) would be forever after distrusted by labor unions. Soon thereafter President Benjamin Harrison appointed William solicitor general of the United States, a post in which he served for two years before returning to Ohio to take a seat on the U.S. Court of Appeals for the Sixth Circuit. For several years he served simultaneously as judge and dean of his law school alma mater, the Cincinnati Law School.

---

*Three generations of one family probably never compiled a more stellar academic record at Yale. Another of Alphonso's sons, Peter, was valedictorian of his class.

Howard Taft's ambition was to live a life in the law culminating in a seat on the United States Supreme Court, but to please his wife, who wanted him to pursue a career in politics, he accepted the position of governor-general of the Philippines. He received high marks in that post for building schools and roads and improving the economy, and four years later President Theodore Roosevelt brought Taft back to Washington as his secretary of war. The two men became mutual admirers and fast friends, and Roosevelt designated Taft as his successor. With Roosevelt's blessing, Taft received the Republican nomination and was easily elected president in 1908.

Roosevelt and progressive Republicans enthusiastically supported Taft in the election, but in office Taft disappointed them by being bullied by the right-wing Republican leadership in Congress into supporting high tariffs and also by failing to aggressively pursue conservation.[35] Taft was a progressive in many other ways. He supported a constitutional amendment authorizing the income tax, directed the Interstate Commerce Committee to regulate railroad rates, and aggressively fought big business by filing more than eighty antitrust suits. The Rough Rider was not mollified however. He returned from his African safaris to challenge Taft for the Republican nomination in 1912, and failing in that effort, ran for president on the Progressive Party ticket. The hapless Taft, who was so personally pained over Roosevelt's rejection that he literally wept, ran third in a four-candidate race, behind Woodrow Wilson and Teddy Roosevelt and ahead of Eugene V. Debs. Taft spent the next eight years on the faculty of the Yale Law School. His lifelong dream came true in 1930 when President Warren G. Harding nominated him as chief justice of the United States Supreme Court. He served nine happy years in that position, once stating, "I don't remember that I was ever president."

Robert A. Taft, Will's oldest child, was born in Cincinnati in 1889, when his father was a superior court judge. At thirteen, his parents sent him to board at the Taft School in Connecticut, the elite prep school founded and then personally run by his uncle Horace Taft. Bob followed the family path to Yale College, and like his father was tapped for Skull and Bones. He was a junior at Yale when his father became president. Bob capped a three-generation trajectory by graduating first in his class. As there was no family tradition about where to study law, Bob was free to go where he wanted for law school, and he chose Harvard. Bob was in his last year of law school when he watched his father try to rally the Republican faithful in the 1912 presidential campaign by claiming that Teddy Roosevelt was advocating theories "as Socialistic as anything that has been proposed in the countries of Europe."[36] That statement, as Bob surely understood, fell somewhere between hyperbole and hokum; it was also ironic considering that one of the candidates in the race, Eugene Debs, was a real socialist.

When Bob graduated from law school, William Howard Taft was so eager that Bob return to Cincinnati to pursue a career in law and politics that without even discussing it with Bob he made arrangements for Bob to join a law firm headed by a former colleague at the Cincinnati Law School, negotiating for his son, who was not only valedictorian of his class but also an editor of the *Harvard Law Review*, the breathtaking starting salary of nothing. ("I don't want you to be anxious about the compensation you are getting," Will told his son. "You can count on me to give you enough to live on but not to splurge on.") Bob would have to learn to develop his own clientele, but as the son of a former president this may not have been difficult.

Bob was practicing law in Cincinnati when World War I broke out. He originally opposed American involvement, but when Germany instituted unrestricted submarine warfare, Taft, along with many Americans, favored America's joining the Allies. After being rejected for military service because of poor eyesight, Taft looked for another way to serve. He admired the relief work Herbert Hoover had done for Belgium before America entered the war. Hoover now headed the American Food Administration, and Taft signed on as an assistant counsel. Taft found that the agency suffered from "red tape and delay and confusion," and his experience left him skeptical about bureaucracies. He caught Hoover's eye however. When the war ended, Hoover took the twenty-nine-year-old Taft to Europe as legal adviser to the American Relief Administration.

"Famine is the mother of anarchy," Hoover declared. In Europe, however, Taft witnessed how shortsighted nations can be. The Allies refused to permit food shipments to former neutrals or enemies. Under pressure from Hoover, the Allies relented with respect to neutrals but long maintained a ban on food shipments to former enemies. Taft's biographer,

James T. Patterson, says that this experience did not transform Taft into an isolationist. Taft later would support the League of Nations, the World Court, and the United Nations, but he would have a narrow, and as Patterson puts it, "legalistic" view of international organizations, believing their role should be limited to promulgating international law and adjudicating disputes but not as actively guaranteeing peace.

After returning to Cincinnati, Taft supported Herbert Hoover for the 1920 Republican presidential nomination. Taft—the man who would become the standard-bearer for conservatism—said he supported Hoover because it was "necessary to nominate a moderate progressive who will defend the existing system . . . avoiding Socialism and Radicalism on one hand and reaction on the other."

Hoover lost the nomination to Warren G. Harding, but Taft had a success of his own: He was elected that fall to the Ohio House of Representatives. Bob Taft spent six years in the state assembly, his final year as speaker, followed by one term as a member of the state senate. He was particularly interested in tax policy. He was not a fan of the sales tax, which he considered regressive—a tax "reaching the taxpayers in proportion to their expenditures rather than in proportion to their income and property." Taft preferred an income tax. Moreover, he preferred taxing investment income to taxing income on labor. Major newspapers praised Taft for devising a plan to replace the state tax on an investor's total holdings with a 5 percent tax on investment income only, and for successfully maneuvering his proposal through the legislature. Taft argued that by making the investment tax less burdensome and bringing it line with that of other states, Ohio's revenues would actually increase because fewer investors would avoid the tax by failing to report or moving out of state.

Bob Taft's most courageous episode in the state legislature may have been his decision to fight the Ku Klux Klan on bills outlawing Sunday dancing and requiring public schoolteachers to read ten Bible verses to their classes every day. The Klan was then powerful in Ohio, and these measures were popular in the wider population. When the bill banning dancing on Sundays passed the assembly 82 to 11, Taft knew the Bible reading measure would pass regardless of what he did. He also knew that when his grandfather had run for governor, he had paid a heavy political price for his judicial opinion against compulsory Bible reading.

Nevertheless, Bob not only voted against the measure but also made a passionate speech against it on the floor of the assembly. Scripture may be considered great literature, yet "in it religion overshadows all else," and religion should be taught only in churches, he said. The newspapers gave his speech prominent coverage. The bill passed, as expected, but the governor vetoed it.

Like other conservatives, Bob Taft was hostile to Franklin D. Roosevelt and the New Deal. Sometimes, especially when speaking to Republican groups, he equated the New Deal with socialism. The New Deal, he said, "would practically abandon the whole theory of American government, and inaugurate what is in fact socialism." When he seconded Alfred M. Landon's nomination at the Republican National Convention in 1936, Taft praised Landon as someone who would "tell the people that they cannot enjoy fancy government improvements and socialistic experiments without paying for them." When he ran for the United States Senate in 1938, Taft called FDR's farm program "socialism with a vengeance," and when he was preparing to contest Eisenhower for the his party's presidential nomination, he told a Republican national committeewoman that "if we get Eisenhower we will practically have a Republican New Deal Administration with just as much spending and socialism as under Mr. Truman."

Yet, notwithstanding the polemics, Taft's views were not ideologically hard-edged. He rejected some New Deal programs but accepted others. His instinct was to oppose business regulation. He was skeptical about government bureaucracies and devoted his maiden Senate speech to opposing increased funding for the Tennessee Valley Authority. He opposed deficit spending, but if the budget was not going to be balanced by restricting spending, he favored increasing the income tax. In the early days of the New Deal, he favored price controls for oil and coal, some forms of debtor relief, and spending $3 billion (but no more) for public works programs. He supported old-age pensions, increasing payments for the health of mothers and children, and some unemployment insurance under Social Security, but he did not want to extend coverage too far.

Patterson says that "Taft did not believe in laissez faire," although perhaps it is more accurate to say that Taft was not a laissez-faire absolutist.[37] The free enterprise system "has certain definite faults," Taft observed. He believed that government should combat poverty both for moral and practical reasons. "If the free enterprise system does not do its best to prevent hardship and poverty, it will find itself superseded by a less progressive system which does," he declared. The federal government should "put a floor under essential things to give all a minimum standard of living, and all children an opportunity to get a start in life." Taft cosponsored legislation to provide federal assistance for both FHA loans to home buyers and for building public housing for the needy.

Although Taft's default position was against governmental action, once he became interested in an issue he immersed himself in data and reached a pragmatic conclusion. Following a 1943 visit to Puerto Rico where he saw desperate poverty, Taft studied the causes of poverty, concluded that poverty and poor educational systems were intertwined, and became a staunch advocate of federal aid to education. When fellow conservatives gave Taft a dose of his own medicine by denouncing federal support for education as socialistic, Taft shrugged off the ideological objection, remarking that "education is socialistic anyhow, and has been for 150 years."

Some conservatives who held elitist—and in some instances racist—views believed that government wasted money by spending it on poor, or black, students. Taft was an elitist. But he was a meritocratic elitist, not an aristocratic elitist, and he was not a racist. He believed that positions of responsibility in government should be held only by the very best people, but he defined that in terms of ability, not lineage or social standing. He spoke plainly about racial concerns. "I see no reason to think that inequality of intellect or ability is based on racial origin," he said. He spoke out against poll taxes, and argued that blacks were entitled to greater representation in city councils and legislatures. In 1942, when even liberals such as Franklin Roosevelt and Earl Warren, then governor of California—panicked by fears of a possible Japanese invasion on the West Coast, as well as outright racism—advocated interning Japanese Americans, Taft was the only member of Congress to question the proposal.[38]

Taft stood up for the rule of law even when it was risky for a politician to do so. In October 1946, Taft denounced the Nuremberg Trials, in which eleven high officials of the Third Reich had just been found guilty of war crimes and sentenced to death. Taft argued that these

Nazis, as despicable as they were, had been tried for crimes created after the fact, something the United States Constitution characterizes as ex post facto laws and prohibits. "The trial of the vanquished by the victors cannot be impartial no matter how it is hedged about with forms of justice," he declared. This was an enormously unpopular position to take in the wake of World War II and may have cost him the 1948 Republican presidential nomination. Taft earned, however, the admiration of a young man then running for Congress in Massachusetts—John F. Kennedy—who later made Taft's stand on the Nuremberg Trials the subject of one of the chapters in his Pulitzer Prize–winning book, *Profiles in Courage*.

Taft may be most remembered for the 1947 Taft-Hartley labor law. Labor has always considered the Taft-Hartley Act to be tilted heavily in favor of management. That was not Taft's intent however. He strongly believed in the rights to bargain collectively and to strike. When a year earlier President Truman asked Congress for legislation empowering him to draft strikers who jeopardized the national welfare, Taft stopped the bill in the Senate.[39] "Strikes cannot be prohibited without interfering with the basic freedom essential to our form of government," he declared. In drafting Taft-Hartley, Taft wanted to strike a fair balance between labor and management. Because the National Labor Relations Act declared certain management practices to be unfair, Taft believed that certain labor practices—including secondary boycotts, that is, boycotts by unions not directly involved in a dispute but in solidarity with a striking union—be classified as unfair as well. Labor denounced the bill in passionate terms, and Truman vetoed it, but the House overrode the president's veto 331 to 83 and the Senate did so by 68 to 25.

When Taft saw how his law was working, he himself came to believe it too heavily favored management. In 1949, he proposed revisions, including moderating the ban on secondary boycotts. To win wider support, Taft also included a few changes that unions did not like, including giving the president authority to seek injunctions against strikes threatening the national welfare. Labor, however, refused to support Taft's effort. It insisted on a complete repeal of the act. The Senate passed Taft's proposal, but both Taft's and the unions' bills died in the House. Both presidents Eisenhower and Kennedy made similar efforts to amend Taft-Hartley, but those efforts failed as well. As time marched on, labor became progressively weaker, and the opportunity to better balance Taft-Hartley was lost. The law remains virtually unchanged to this day.

Before Pearl Harbor, Taft—and most conservatives—opposed American involvement in World War II. Their slogan was America First. "We should be prepared to defend our own shores, but we should not undertake to defend the ideals of democracy in foreign countries," Taft said in April 1939. When Hitler invaded Poland five months later, however, Taft voted to allow munitions shipments to Britain and France, although he demanded that munitions only be sold on a cash-and-carry basis. When, during the following year, Roosevelt was looking for additional ways to help the beleaguered British, Taft privately confessed to "great uncertainty" about the course America should take. "The prospect of seeing England and France overwhelmed by Germany is one which I look forward to with the greatest misgivings," he wrote to a friend. However, shortly before the Republican National Convention in June 1940, Taft found himself at a party attended by many influential people, including the journalist Dorothy Thompson. Wendell Willkie told his fellow guests that he would rather vote for Roosevelt than support a Republican who opposed aiding the Allies, and Taft angrily disagreed. The discussion became heated, and was widely reported by the press.

Pearl Harbor, of course, ended the debate about American involvement in World War II and started discussions about America's role in the world after the war was over. Taft became the leading spokesperson against idealism. He attacked both Roosevelt's goal of ending "freedom from want" and Willkie's "one world" vision as naïve. His solution for postwar peace was once again legalistic. He supported the United Nations, but—true to form—he put his faith more in the International Court of Justice than in the Security Council, which he recognized would be hamstrung by the veto. Taft hoped the court would eventually achieve the same moral authority internationally that the Supreme Court enjoys domestically. "If we can establish an international law and a Court to apply it," he said on the floor of the Senate, "the moral force of those decisions may well dominate in time public opinion of the world, so that no nation dare defy it."

Born of American experience of the First World War, Taft's isolationism was originally a desire to stop America from becoming embroiled in old—and from America's point of view—pointless European conflicts. But during the Second World War, his isolationism underwent a subtle metamorphosis. Its new core was resistance to the Cold War idea of promoting democracy and Western values abroad through force of arms. "I do not believe," he once said, "that any war can be justified as a crusade." To hold otherwise, one "must admit that the Soviets have a right to crusade to impose Communism on the rest of the world." Moreover, Taft also opposed trying to buy loyalty from other nations through foreign aid. He saw that as a form of economic imperialism. While he was willing to furnish modest levels of foreign aid to nations that needed help, he cautioned, "If we throw our dollars around and try to run the show, we are going to give the Communists further arguments against us for trying to be imperialistic."

Even before the Second World War ended, Taft foreshadowed Eisenhower's famous warning about the military-industrial complex. He was concerned that America was becoming "a garrison state" and what that meant for the character of the nation, and he believed that an effort to bring Pax Americana to the world would be imperialistic. Taft sometimes became downright angry opposing steep increases in the defense budget, notwithstanding claims by the president and joint chiefs that the expenditures were necessary to protect America from the communist threat. Taft argued that the Soviets did not want war. In part, that was because they knew they would lose, but Taft also pointed out that the Soviet Union did not invade Western Europe at the end of the war when Europe was helpless.

Taft worried that treating the Soviet Union as an adversary might become a self-fulfilling prophecy. He opposed the formation of NATO in 1949 because it would "give the Russians the impression, justified at least to themselves, that we are ringing them about with armies for the purpose of taking aggressive action when the time comes." He believed stationing large numbers of troops in Europe was unnecessarily provocative. And he cautioned against demonizing the Russians. "I see no reason for the President and the Secretary of State and everybody else calling the Russians names on every occasion," he said in 1951.

Taft was not always consistent, and at times he sounded like a rabid cold warrior. He accused the Truman administration of being "soft toward communism." Curiously, he seemed more willing to defend allies in Asia than in Europe. (Some attributed this to Taft's spending four formative years in the Philippines.) He wanted to publicly commit to defend Formosa, arguing that this would stop a communist advance without any appreciable risk because there was "not the slightest evidence that Russia will go to war with us because we interfere with a crossing to Formosa." At times, Taft could sound positively McCarthyesque. He accused the State Department and "its procommunist allies" of wanting "to get rid of Chiang [Kai-shek and the Chinese Nationalists] and were willing at least to turn China over to the Communists for that purpose." As for Joseph McCarthy himself, Taft privately called him reckless yet publicly urged him on.

Although Taft had generally supported the Truman administration on the Korean War, when Truman fired Douglas MacArthur, Taft suddenly changed his tune, calling for an escalation of the war. Truman argued that bombing targets in Manchuria or blockading Chinese ports might provoke Russia to enter the war. Taft pooh-poohed those concerns, declaring that "we have repeatedly assumed the risk of war in Europe, and there is no reason why the same policy should not be followed in Asia." He was widely criticized for contradicting everything he said about Europe. Why would the Soviets consider American troops in Europe provocative and not be provoked by an expanding theater of war on their doorstep? Why should America be more willing to defend Asian rather than European allies?

It was, in fact, Taft's position on Europe that caused Dwight David Eisenhower to run for president, and probably to do so as a Republican. Friends were telling Eisenhower that he should seek the presidency because he was the only man who could lead America.[40] Eisenhower was not eager to do so, but was considering whether duty to country compelled him to run. He agreed with his friends' assessment about Truman, then floundering in the Korean War, whom he considered a man of integrity but over his head in the presidency. Taft, however, was a man of ability, and Eisenhower considered himself roughly in accord with Taft's views on domestic policy. The problem was NATO and the defense of Europe. Eisenhower had the capacity to think strategically. He recognized that the advent of nuclear weapons changed everything. Conventional war between powers armed with nuclear weapons was obsolete, and nuclear war between such powers was unthinkable. Eisenhower, the man who orchestrated military cooperation among the Allies during World War II, believed that America's commitment to NATO was imperative. It created a standoff that required both sides to resolve disputes without resorting to force, and it provided time for East and West to seek a more enduring peace.

In January 1951, shortly before Eisenhower left for Europe to assume the position of supreme commander of NATO, he invited Taft to a secret meeting at the Pentagon. Before the meeting, Eisenhower had two aides draft a statement that read, "Having been called back to military duty, I want to announce that my name may not be used by anyone as a candidate for President—and if they do I will repudiate such efforts." The two men had a long meeting alone. Eisenhower asked Taft whether he and his associates in Congress would "agree that collective security is necessary for us in Western Europe—and will you support this idea as bipartisan policy?" Eisenhower then offered Taft a deal: If Taft answered yes, Eisenhower would spend his next years in Europe; if Taft's answer were no, then Eisenhower would "probably be back in the United States." The import of that statement could not possibly have been lost on Taft; these two men were considered the principal rivals for the 1952 Republican presidential nomination. Taft hemmed and hawed. Eisenhower said that what mattered were not the details but an agreement in principle to support NATO. Taft said that he could not in good conscience make such a deal. After Taft departed, Eisenhower called back his two aides and tore up his statement. For his part, Taft told companions as he left the Pentagon, "By God, that's a man."

When Eisenhower won the 1952 Republican presidential nomination, the two men made a different deal.* In return for delivering the enthusiastic support of the conservative wing of the party, Taft got Eisenhower to issue a joint statement. Its principal rhetorical feature was Eisenhower's agreement that the fundamental issue in the campaign was "liberty against the creeping socialism in every domestic field." More substantively, Eisenhower agreed to a budget target of $600 billion, to cut taxes to that level, and to defend major provisions of the Taft-Hartley Act. Eisenhower also agreed that he would not "discriminate" against Taft supporters when he formed his administration.

---

*Before switching votes to be with the winner, delegates cast 595 votes for Eisenhower, 500 for Taft, 81 for Earl Warren, 20 for Harold Stassen, and 10 for Douglas MacArthur.

Quite surprisingly, the statement described and acknowledged the differences on foreign policy between the two men, papering them over as "differences in degree." Liberals in the party called the statement the "Surrender at Morningside Heights" (the two men met at Eisenhower's residence in the Morningside Heights section of New York City).

After he became president, Eisenhower was pleasantly surprised by how well he got along with Taft, who was then Senate majority leader. "Senator Taft has been the model of cheerful and effective cooperation," Eisenhower wrote in his diary on February 7, 1952. Taft freely and frankly gave Eisenhower his advice and the benefit of his experience, which Eisenhower valued. Eisenhower discovered that Taft was more liberal than he had realized on a number of domestic issues such as federal aid to education, old-age pensions, and public housing—indeed, Taft was more liberal on these issues than Eisenhower.[41] "In some things," Eisenhower wrote in his diary shortly after Taft died, "I found him extraordinarily 'leftish.'"

Eisenhower especially appreciated Taft's efforts to keep both wings of the party together. When Eisenhower nominated Charles E. "Chip" Bohlen as ambassador to the Soviet Union, Senator Joseph McCarthy launched a bombastic campaign against his confirmation. Bohlen had been at Yalta, and even though he had principally served as an interpreter, his mere presence at the infamous conference was enough for McCarthy to accuse him of being one of "the architects of disaster" and in "one hundred percent cooperation with the Acheson-Hiss-Truman regime." McCarthy suggested that Bohlen's FBI contained evidence of disloyalty, and battles raged over whether the FBI files would be made public. Taft maneuvered the nomination to confirmation through the turbulent waters. He worked out an arrangement in which he and Senator John Sparkman, the 1952 Democratic vice presidential candidate, examined the FBI files, and then jointly certified that Bohlen's record was unblemished. Bohlen was confirmed 74 to 13. Eisenhower wrote in his diary that "the mass of Republican senators . . . in general will follow Taft's lead," and that "Taft held the mass of Republicans squarely in line."[42]

Among the baker's dozen of votes against Bohlen was that of a newly elected senator from Arizona named Barry M. Goldwater. Goldwater's vote surprised Eisenhower. Eisenhower wrote in his diary that most of the senators who voted against Bohlen were "the most stubborn and essentially small-minded examples of the extreme isolationist group in the party," but Goldwater, along with Senator John Bricker of Ohio, "seemed to me a little bit more intelligent than the others." This was a precursor of things to come. A new conservatism was on the horizon: one not steeped in isolationism that characterized conservatives such as Taft who had come of age during World War I.

Taft's work with Eisenhower was short-lived. Only about a quarter into the first year of the Eisenhower administration, Taft discovered he had cancer. Before the end of July, he was dead.

How should we sum up the conservatism of Robert A. Taft? First, Taft believed in the free market, but he was not a free market absolutist. He believed the free market worked well and generally should be left alone, but he also believed it had deficiencies and that government should provide the necessary adjustments. Second, he was not an idealist. He was not enamored with grand schemes, foreign or domestic, and he was especially skeptical about the abilities of government bureaucracies. Third, Taft believed in balanced budgets. His first instinct was to achieve balance by holding spending in check, but when that was not possible he preferred raising taxes to running deficits. Fourth, he was a pragmatist. Facts and reasoning trumped ideology. Once he studied an issue, he went where the data and analysis led him. His pragmatism allowed him to work with people across ideological boundaries because he could talk about issues in terms of facts.[43] Fifth, Taft believed in equality of opportunity. He believed government had to assure reasonable opportunities for all by providing minimum standards of living and high-quality schools. Sixth, he opposed imperialism in any form. He believed that America should lead by example and not project its values across the globe through military or economic means. Finally, Taft placed his greatest faith in the rule of law, and wanted to nurture that ethos at the international level.

What kind of conservative, then, was Robert Taft? Despite his general faith in the free market, he was certainly not a libertarian. Libertarianism is based on the negative view of liberty; that is, libertarians define liberty as being free from coercion, whether by the government or others. That is why they oppose governmental regulation in almost all its forms. Because he placed such a high premium on equality of opportunity, Taft clearly believed in the positive vision of liberty. Under that view, real liberty is having the capacity for self-determination—a reasonable opportunity to do with one's life what one wishes.

A reporter once asked Robert Taft whether he had read *The Conservative Mind* by Russell Kirk. He had not. "There are some questions that I have not thought very much about, but I'm a politician, not a philosopher," he remarked. Presumably, the reporter asked Taft if he had read Kirk's book because he thought the two men held similar views. And indeed they did; both generally followed the Burkean-style conservatism that we also call traditional conservatism. Taft did not need to study Burke, Kirk, or political philosophy to generally follow this school of thought. He followed it because he was raised in it, because it was the conservative zeitgeist of his time, because his own instincts and sensibilities took him in the same direction.

Putting aside for the moment who Taft agreed with or how to characterize his conservatism, the main point to be made is that Taft best defines the conservatism of his day. That does not mean that all conservatives agreed with Taft in all things. But conservatives agreed more with Taft than with any other individual; he was their acknowledged leader and consensus choice for president over the course of four presidential elections. Taft, therefore, fairly represents mainstream American conservatism during the 1940s and up until his death in 1953. By locating Taft, we have a basis of comparison and a means of gauging how conservatism changes.

We shall see the first tremors begin two years before Taft's death when Buckley publishes *God and Man at Yale*. We shall see the tectonic plates begin to shift dramatically when, two years after Taft's death, Buckley founds *National Review*. But first we must learn how William F. Buckley Jr. became the person who changed American conservatism.

CHAPTER 1

The Making of the Man Who Remade Conservatism

William F. Buckley Jr.'s ideology was not the product of study and reflection. It was practically inherited. Bill and nine siblings were brought up by powerful and opinionated parents. Their father had made a small fortune in the oil business, and until high school they lived in a velvet cocoon.[1] Except for one year in an English boarding school, Bill, and his siblings, were homeschooled by professional tutors and coaches at the family estate, Great Elm, in the bucolic town of Sharon, Connecticut. When the children reached adulthood, they discovered, somewhat to their own surprise, that they all held a common and distinct political philosophy. There wasn't an ideological black sheep among them.

Much has been written about the family dinner table, at which the children supposedly were expected to present their views about current events and defend them under rigorous questioning from their father. The children, we are led to believe, underwent an almost deliberate program of political indoctrination.[2] In private interviews, however, two of the children—Priscilla and James, the third and fourth oldest of the ten siblings—assure me that the portrayals of political science seminars at the family dinner table are grossly exaggerated if not downright fallacious.[3] There was, in fact, not especially much discussion about politics within the Buckley household, at least not overtly. That does not mean there was no conversation about politics. The children knew, for example, that their parents subscribed to the America First doctrine, which held that America should not become embroiled in the Second World War, and that they considered Franklin D. Roosevelt's New Deal socialistic. But that was about as far as the expressly political talk went in the Buckley household.

How then did Bill and his siblings acquire their distinctive political philosophy? Something more powerful than dinner table political science seminars was going on in the Buckley household: A father was telling his children evocative stories about his experiences in Mexico. William Frank Buckley Sr.—Will—as he was called—lived in Mexico during his own politically formative years. Will was in Mexico from ages twenty-seven to forty, when the president of Mexico expelled him for conspiring to overthrow the government. These were also the years that shaped modern Mexico, the period of the Mexican Revolution. The stories Will told his children were focused more on his own adventures than on the philosophical differences among the factions fighting for control of Mexico. When the children became older, they wondered whether their father's stories had been exaggerated—for their father was a dramatic storyteller, and he knew how to make a tale more colorful for children. But whether Will's stories were entirely true is beside the point. Bill and his siblings believed them, at least while they were children.

Will's stories may not have been overtly political, but they reflected a particular way of looking at the world that was forged during his experiences in Mexico. He assimilated his children into that worldview just as other parents assimilate their children into their particular realities: by describing the world and explaining events against a backdrop of particular assumptions. Will's children themselves recognize that their father's years in Mexico molded both his perception of the world and their own. Reid Buckley, the third youngest of the ten siblings, writes that his father's "experiences in Mexico stamped our father's character and beliefs ever after, in turn indelibly stamping the assumptions, attitudes, perspectives, and political inclinations of his children."[4]

To understand Bill's political philosophy, therefore, we have to understand his father's worldview, and to do that, we must understand Will's time in Mexico. As ironic as it may seem, the seminal influences of the new conservatism flow from Will Buckley's experiences during the Mexican Revolution.

*   *   *

Will Buckley was born in 1881 into a family of Irish immigrants living in San Diego, Texas. Most of the residents in this town of two thousand in southern Texas were of Hispanic origin. While English was used in the public schools, Spanish was spoken more often in town generally, and Will was bilingual from an early age. Will's father was, in turns, an insurance salesman, the elected sheriff of Duval County, and a sheep rancher. Will's mother was a devout Catholic, and the children were tutored in Latin and Catholicism by Father John Peter Bard, a parish priest from the Basque region in Spain who is described in a book published privately for the Buckley family as "a scholar and linguist" and a man of "rugged individualism."[5] Father Bard had a strong influence on Will. The relationship was so strong, in fact, that Will continued as an altar boy for Father Bard for more than fifteen years, returning to San Diego to assist his mentor during college vacations even after the Buckley family had moved away. One of the undercurrent themes in the Buckley family book is that even as a young boy in Texas, Will learned to distrust both the people and the government. The book states, for example, that during his childhood in San Diego, Will "knew firsthand of armed rising and rebellions, and of the ruthlessness of the Texas rangers."

In the fall of 1900, Will entered the University of Texas at Austin, which was then, as it is now, the premier state university in Texas. By majoring in Spanish, in which he was already fluent, Will was able to earn eight course credits by simply taking the final examinations and quickly leaped ahead to advanced courses in Spanish literature. His proficiency in Spanish also allowed him to earn money by coaching other students in Spanish and working as a translator in the university's land office. He joined a fraternity and was elected editor in chief of *Cactus*, the university yearbook. While Will was in college, his father died, and the family moved to Austin. Will's sister Priscilla took a position as a schoolteacher, helping to put Will, brothers Claude and Edmund, and sister Eleanor through the University of Texas.

A story about Will's undergraduate days is revealing. At a basketball game between the University of Texas and St. Edwards College (now St. Edwards University), a Catholic school in Austin, played on the latter's home court, tempers were running high when a priest serving as referee made a call in favor of St. Edwards. A Texas student in the audience yelled, "That damn priest is lying." Will immediately flattened him with a powerful punch.

After earning their bachelor's degrees, Will and his brothers continued on to law school at the University of Texas. In 1908, Will, a newly minted lawyer, decided to seek his fortune in Tampico, Mexico. Tampico, a seaport on the Gulf of Mexico, is in the heart of Mexico's oil-producing region. For two years, Will worked for another lawyer whom he described in a letter to a friend as "a crook." He quit working for this man, and for a period of about a year—without resources or friends to fall back on—had no source of income. Will did not give up however. He opened his own law office, in which he was joined by his brother Claude and later brother Edmund as well. The Buckley boys gambled all they had—and more—on developing a practice that would represent the large oil companies. They took a large loan and sunk it into fitting out a handsome office and hiring top-notch staff. They persuaded a local judge to leave the bench and join the firm. To cultivate their image as lawyers for big companies, they took the bold step of turning down small business clients, though they surely could have used the revenue. Their gamble paid off: The Buckley brothers won over the big companies—they represented the likes of Standard Oil, British Petroleum, and Companie Française—and their practice became extremely profitable.

Will, however, was soon bored by legal practice, and he increasingly turned to business. He invested profits from his law practice in real estate. He leased or purchased land from peasants and in turn leased those lands to oil companies. By 1914, he owned land valued at more than $100,000 (the equivalent of more than $2 million today). In that same year, he founded the Pantepec Corporation of Mexico, the first of a series of oil exploration companies that eventually would make him rich.

When Will arrived in Mexico, Porfirio Díaz was the nation's president.[6] Díaz had come to power thirty-two years earlier through an armed revolution against a former dictator under the slogan "effective suffrage and no reelection." Once in power, however, Díaz himself became a permanent, absolute ruler. He justified his rule in two ways. First, he maintained cosmetic constitutionality: When the constitution became an impediment to remaining in office, he amended it to permit him to run for reelection or extend his term, maintaining the fiction that his dictatorship was lawful and sanctioned by the people. Second, Díaz and a powerful group of supporters and advisers known as the *científicos* maintained that because the population was largely illiterate, Mexico was not ready for true democracy. What the nation needed first, they argued, was a sustained period of stability, a *Porfiriato*, to bring to Mexico capitalism, industrialization, education of the masses, and development of a middle class.

On several fronts, Díaz and the científicos made progress. They built infrastructure: roads, ports, factories, electric plants, and especially railroads. When Díaz came to power, Mexico had four hundred miles of railroad track; by the time Will arrived in Mexico, there were twelve thousand miles of track. Díaz and the científicos built new schools to train teachers, and they tripled primary school enrollment. Literacy increased. By the time Will arrived in Mexico, a majority of people in the Federal District of Mexico City could read and write, and national literacy rates had increased from less than 15 percent in the pre-Díaz era to nearly 20 percent. During the first two decades of Díaz's rule, Mexico's gross national product increased by 8 percent per year.

Progress, however, came at a price. The científicos believed that people of pure Spanish or other European descent were racially superior to Mexico's indigenous peoples or to the mestizos, that is, the people of mixed European and native Indian ancestry. The white population, which constituted less than 20 percent of the country, was largely concentrated in the central plateau, especially in Mexico City and Guadalajara. Within these areas, a professional class developed that was loyal to Díaz, but it was small and racially restricted. Throughout the rest of Mexico, the Díaz government allowed the rich white elite to become superrich by acquiring enormous tracts of land. Seventeen families came to own 20 percent of the entire country; half of Mexico's land was held by three thousand families. They took these lands by hook and by crook—sometimes through outright force, sometimes by concocting fraudulent deeds that corrupt government courts said were valid. Community landholding fell from 25 percent to just 2 percent of the nation's land.[7] Moreover, little of the growth in GNP trickled down to the lower and middle classes. According to historians Robert M. Buffington and William E. French, the economic growth "only exacerbated the traditional incongruities in Mexico's economic and social structures. Not surprisingly, the rich got richer and spent much of their new wealth on imported luxuries."[8]

The Díaz government encouraged U.S. and European entrepreneurs to develop businesses in Mexico. The científicos argued that this was the most efficient means for bringing the ethos of capitalism and economic development to Mexico. But a sort of conspiracy of thieves took hold. The government protected foreign entrepreneurs with favorable tariffs and with courts that—when presented with disputes between native Mexicans and foreign enterprises—routinely ruled in favor of the foreigners. In return, the foreign entrepreneurs enriched the government officials and Mexican elites through both legitimate business arrangements and outright graft.

What the científicos portrayed as foreign investment that was valuable to Mexico, others saw as rank exploitation. Foreign firms built and operated textile mills and other factories. Foreigners owned 90 percent of the incorporated value of these industries, with Americans owning 70 percent.[9] Foreign enterprises engaged in extensive mining operations in the north, extracting silver, gold, lead, copper, and zinc. United States companies controlled 75 percent of the mines. Along the Gulf of Mexico, foreign firms—with local headquarters in Tampico—drilled for oil. During Will Buckley's time there, Mexico was the world's second-largest oil-producing nation. U.S. firms controlled 38 percent of that business; British and other European firms were also heavily represented.

What about the Catholic Church? Mexico was a devoutly Catholic nation. Did the church not stand up for her people? Díaz's predecessor had sought to weaken the church through anticlerical Laws of Reform, aimed in part at reducing the church's large landowning. Díaz, however, devised a more nuanced approach. In a secret pact with the archbishop of Mexico, Díaz agreed not to enforce the Laws of Reform, although he slyly kept them on the books as sort of a hanging sword of Damocles. In return, the archbishop agreed to give Díaz veto power over all ecclesiastical appointments, and to encourage parish priests to preach fidelity to the government.

For the most part, Díaz was able to maintain his rule through collaborations with elites, foreign entrepreneurs, and the church, as well as through savvy manipulation of the press. He paid handsome subsidies to newspaper publishers and editors as long as he liked what they printed, and he permitted "opposition" newspapers as long as their criticisms were carefully circumscribed. When faced with protests, Díaz quashed them with dramatic cruelty. When native Indians in the Mexican state of Hidalgo rebelled at having their ancestral lands stolen, Díaz's rurales—a quasi-military state police force—buried the protestors up to their necks and then trampled them to death on galloping horseback. As aspirations slowly rose, disenchantment rose. Workers in the textile and mining operations began to unionize, and violence flared between strikers and an American employer in the mining region in the north.

The series of events leading to the Mexican Revolution began in 1910, two years after Will Buckley arrived in Mexico. An unlikely man— Francisco Madero, the thirty-seven-year-old scion of Mexico's fifth-richest family—wrote a book condemning the dictatorship in blistering terms. He accused Díaz of "patriarchal politics" that was causing a "corruption of the spirit, the disinterest in public life, a disdain for law and the tendency towards deception, towards cynicism, towards fear." "We are sleeping under the cool but harmful shade of a poisonous tree," Madero warned. He demanded a return to the Constitution of 1857, with a president selected through a genuine democratic vote and barred from reelection. Madero sold much of his property, used the money to form a new political party, and set out on a nationwide speaking tour during which he was drawing crowds in the tens of thousands. Díaz had Madero arrested on trumped-up charges of plotting armed insurrection. This persuaded Madero that armed revolution was in fact the only route to reform. Madero escaped from jail and called for an armed national uprising, which (probably because he believed in the occult and for mystical reasons considered the time propitious) he declared would begin about seven weeks hence, at precisely six P.M. on Sunday, November 20, 1910.

Madero's call for revolution released dammed-up frustration with the Díaz regime. Two men with large followings answered Madero's call. The first, in hardscrabble northern Mexico, was Pancho Villa. To some, Villa was nothing more than a bandit who looted for his own benefit. To others, he was a Mexican Robin Hood. One thing is indisputable: The charismatic but semiliterate Villa revered Madero, in part because Madero was an intellectual. Villa raised forces composed of cowboys, miners, sharecroppers, and lumberjacks, and acquired arms, horses, and money by raiding rich haciendas. The second man, in the rich sugar-producing state of Morelos immediately south of the Federal District, was a mestizo named Emiliano Zapata. Zapata was principally interested in land reform. Peasants, living in small villages, had once farmed their own small plots. The científicos considered this backward, and the Díaz regime had supported policies that enabled the haciendas to swallow up land, impress the peasants into a form of peonage, and eliminate the villages. Just as Madero was beginning to call for revolution, Zapata was getting his start as a revolutionary by exposing hacienda deeds as fraudulent. His goal was to restore land to the peasants. His movement was the most genuinely revolutionary in Mexico. He adopted as the slogan of his movement Land and Liberty! and declared, "It is better to die on your feet than live on your knees." In keeping with the true revolutionary spirit of his movement, Zapata's forces included soldaderas, that is, women soldiers.

In May 1911, Díaz realized he could not defeat the revolutionaries. He resigned and went into exile in France. Five months later, in what was probably Mexico's first truly free and fair election, Francisco Madero was overwhelmingly elected president. Madero, however, was a babe in a viper pit. Because he was a moderate reformer who was fearful of revolutionary fever getting out of hand, Madero foolishly instructed both Villa and Zapata to disband their forces.[10] Meanwhile, he refused to purge the right-wing *porfiristas* from their governmental positions, oblivious that they were sharpening their knives behind his back. Only a few months after Madero's election, Porfirio Díaz's nephew—with secret assistance from the United States ambassador to Mexico, Henry Lane Wilson, who was acting without the knowledge of the State Department or President Taft—launched a counterrevolutionary attack on Mexico City. On February 18, 1912, the man Madero entrusted with the defense of the government, General Victoriano Huerta, betrayed him. Huerta had Madero arrested. Three days later, Madero was killed by a supposedly unknown assassin while being transferred between prisons. Huerta then declared himself ruler of Mexico.

Three separate revolutionary forces then moved against Huerta: reconstituted forces led by Pancho Villa, which were soon dubbed the

Division of the North; Zapata's army of peasants and sugar production workers in Morelos; and Constitutionalists led politically by Venustiano Carranza and commanded militarily by Álvaro Obregón.[11]

Carranza, who came from an aristocratic, landowning background, had been Madero's minister of war. When Madero had tried to tamp down the revolutionary fervor to make his government more acceptable to right-wing elements, Carranza warned him: "A revolution that makes concessions commits suicide." Carranza had also warned Madero about the danger of leaving porfiristas in the government. When Madero failed to heed his warnings, Carranza resigned the cabinet position and ran for governor of his home state of Coahuila on a platform of local democracy and municipal autonomy. After his election, Carranza improved the state's schools. He also tried to improve workers' conditions in the mines, but here he ran headlong into the entrenched power of the foreign mining companies and was less successful. Obregón's father had been a wealthy landowner, but for political reasons his property had been confiscated long before Obregón was born. As a result, Obregón had been brought up by well-educated parents thrust into modest circumstances. Most of their children became schoolteachers. Obregón, however, turned out to have natural military talent, and became a military commander for Madero. After Madero's murder, Obregón raised an army of six thousand men in the northern Mexican state of Sonora.

The Constitutionalists were the least revolutionary of revolutionaries. While they demanded free presidential elections and advocated for workers' rights, the Constitutionalists were principally a movement of the middle class and local elites. Unlike Zapata and Villa, they had little interest in land reform.

In January 1913, Woodrow Wilson became president in the United States. Wilson was interested in Mexican affairs, and quickly took matters into his own hands. Wilson valued democracy above all else, and he was not about to recognize an autocrat like Huerta who overthrew an elected president in a military coup. Wilson dispatched John Lind, a former congressman and governor of Minnesota, as his personal envoy to Huerta. Lind informed Huerta that the United States would recognize the Huerta government only on the condition that Huerta hold free elections for president and agree not to stand for election himself.

Huerta rejected the proposal in a deliberately insulting way, implying that Wilson was grossly ignorant of Mexican affairs. More consequential matters followed. In September 1913, Senator Belisario Domínguez denounced Huerta's rule in a speech to the Mexican Congress. Huerta had Domínguez arrested, and a few days later Domínguez's bullet-riddled corpse turned up in a ditch. When the Mexican Congress passed a resolution calling for an investigation into Domínguez's murder, Huerta's troops marched into the Assembly and demanded that the resolution be retracted. When legislators refused, seventy-four of them were imprisoned. Huerta then held a sham election for the presidency. Although he was constitutionally precluded from standing for reelection, Huerta claimed to be reelected as a write-in candidate and declared he had to honor the wishes of the people. This stiffened Wilson's resolve to help drive Huerta from power.

By the early spring of 1914, Constitutionalist armies were on the outskirts of Tampico, where Will Buckley and the oil companies were located. On April 9, federal troops in Tampico arrested a small landing party of sailors from an American warship. Why exactly this occurred is unclear. Some speculate the federal soldiers had been jumpy as a result of the advancing Constitutionalist forces. In any event, the federal troops soon set the American sailors free. The admiral of the U.S. fleet was not easily placated, however. He demanded a formal apology. The local commander referred this diplomatic request to Mexico City. On hearing of the demand, a reportedly inebriated Huerta ordered that no apology would be made.

Woodrow Wilson seized upon this incident as an excuse to intervene in the struggle between Huerta and the rebels, with the object of precipitating Huerta's downfall. Wilson ordered American naval forces to intercept a German vessel bound for Veracruz with arms for Huerta, and to seize the customhouse in Veracruz to prevent any further delivery of arms to the combatants. U.S. Marines landed in Veracruz expecting no opposition. When the citizens of Veracruz saw foreign invaders on their beaches, however, they, together with one thousand cadets from the Veracruz Naval Academy, rushed to defend their shores, and a genuine battle erupted. U.S. warships opened fire on the civilians and the cadets with their heavy guns, resulting in hundreds of civilian casualties (nineteen American marines were killed in the battle). Within a few days, six thousand U.S. Marines were on the ground, fifteen American warships were off the coast, and the United States firmly held the seaport of Veracruz, where it was in position to control the importing of arms to the warring factions. The United States military commander, General Funston, asked Will Buckley to serve as civil governor of Veracruz, but Buckley—furious with Wilson for not supporting the Huerta regime—refused.[12] For Buckley, Huerta represented stability, government by an educated class, and protection of private property, including that belonging to the church and to foreign nationals like himself. The revolutionaries offered mob rule, sacrilegious attacks on the church, and legalized—but morally unjustified—theft of private property to reward their followers. Buckley considered Wilson a naïve idealist. Not only was Wilson supporting democratic ideals in a country unprepared for them, he was working to remove the only government that could be counted on to protect American business.

Wilson, however, was wrestling with the very pragmatic decision of which rebel force to support. It was not an easy choice. Carranza had never been a friend of the United States, and in the wake of nation-wide anger over the slaughter of Mexican civilians on the beach of Veracruz, the Constitutionalists denounced Wilson's incursion. Villa, meanwhile, declared that he supported the American occupation at Veracruz. He told the American consular that no drunkard (Villa was referring to Huerta) was going to drag him into a war with a friend. These statements were probably genuine. Villa's biographer, Frank McLynn, writes, "At this stage of his career, Villa was notably pro-American. He took Woodrow Wilson's moral posturing seriously and for a time looked on him as a kind of American Madero."[13] American businesses with interests in Mexico, however, started to lean on Wilson to support the more moderate Constitutionalists over the more radical alliance of Villa and Zapata.

On July 15, 1914, following two decisive battles at which Villa routed federal armies, Huerta resigned and departed for exile in Barcelona. Huerta's military commanders made arrangements to surrender the Federal District to the Constitutionalists, which they considered preferable to allowing Zapata's forces to take the District. (This turned out to be a mistake: Constitutionalist soldiers plundered Mexico City.) Meanwhile, Zapata began to implement his Plan of Ayala, a program of radical land reform, in Morelos. When on October 10, 1914, representatives of all of the revolutionary groups met at the Convention of Aguascalientes, the alliance between Villa and Zapata became stronger, and tensions between them and the Constitutionalists became more pronounced. Henceforward, Villa and Zapata would be known as the Convention Alliance because they recognized the Convention of Aguascalientes as the supreme authority of Mexico.[14]

The Convention adopted in principle Zapata's Plan of Ayala for all of Mexico, agreeing to incorporate it into a new national constitution. Americans held one quarter of the land subject to redistribution. Zapata and Villa also advocated nationalization of Mexico's petroleum reserves. When the Constitutionalists took the position that property rights should be respected, Wilson finally decided whom to support. Although he was worried about Carranza's history of anti-Americanism, Wilson considered Obregón reliable. And American businessmen were telling him their interests would be more secure under the Constitutionalists than under a government satisfactory to the Convention alliance.[15]

In November 1914, the American forces in Veracruz furnished the Constitutionalists with twelve thousand rifles, millions of rounds of ammunition, artillery, machine guns, trucks—and 1,250 boxes of sodium cyanide, which is used for creating poison gas. Americans turned over Veracruz and its strategically important port as well. And on October 19, 1915, President Wilson recognized Carranza as president of Mexico. Through this series of actions, Wilson strengthened what previously had been the weaker revolutionary group.*

Full-scale civil war broke out as the Constitutionalist and Convention forces turned on each other. Constitutionalist forces controlled the Federal District, and declared themselves the rightful government of Mexico. It was a bleak time for Mexico City. Obregón pillaged every-

---

*Wilson's intervention in the Mexican Revolution paralleled his involvement four years later in the Russian civil war, when he sent eight thousand U.S. troops to Vladivostok, Russia, to protect retreating Czechoslovakian forces and ensure that American arms and material intended for the White Army did not fall into Bolshevik hands. The main differences were that the Polar Bear Expedition, as the American force was called, was working in collaboration with British forces, and wound up in direct combat with Bolshevik forces.

thing of value to fund the war effort. He also desecrated churches and humiliated priests partly for political reasons and partly out of pure hatred. Constitutionalist armies commanded by Obregón won a series of decisive battles over Villa's forces in the north, while Zapata's forces of true believers held off superior Constitutionalist forces thrusting south into Morelos. In a strategy born of frustration, Villa attacked Columbus, New Mexico. Wilson responded by ordering General John J. Pershing to lead twelve thousand American troops into Mexico on a mission—called the Punitive Expedition—to kill or capture Villa and take retribution on his troops. But Villa evaded the American invaders, and his image as a national hero grew. Carranza—now president—was forced to demand that Pershing leave Mexico. For his part, Villa declared that henceforth Americans would be prohibited from owning any property or engaging in any economic activity in Mexico. (He later gave up this vow, and allowed U.S. companies to return to areas under his control as long as they paid taxes to him.)

In early 1917, the Constitutionalists won widespread support by writing a new constitution that guaranteed minimum wages, union rights, government-sponsored health care, and land reforms. Their constitution declared, "Ownership of the lands and waters within the boundaries of the national territory is vested originally in the Nation," which had "the right to impose on private property such limitations as the public interest may demand." This principle extended to all natural resources beneath the land and waters, including minerals, ores, precious stones, petroleum, and natural gas. To the dismay of the hacendados, the constitution provided that large estates would be divided to "develop small landed holdings." To the dismay of American and other foreign companies, the constitution also provided that either the federal or state governments could declare that private property constituted a public utility and expropriate it on payment of compensation equal to its assessed value for tax purposes. Only Mexicans had a right to acquire ownership in real property. The state could grant a similar right to foreigners provided that they agreed to "consider themselves as nationals in respect to such property, and bind themselves not to invoke the protection of their governments in matters relating thereto." However, foreigners were absolutely prohibited from owning land within a hundred kilometers of the nation's borders or shores. Moreover, the constitution provided that "foreigners may not in any way participate in the political affairs of the country."

The 1917 Constitution of Mexico also included provisions aimed at curtailing the power of the Catholic Church and creating a separation of church and state. It guaranteed to all of the people of Mexico a free public—and secular—education. It declared that "the standard which shall guide such education shall be maintained entirely apart from any religious doctrine and, based on the results of scientific progress, shall strive against ignorance and its effects, servitudes, fanaticism, and prejudices." The constitution also stated that because the state would not condone agreements resulting in the "restriction, loss or irrevocable sacrifice of the liberty of man, whether for work, education, or religious vows," monastic orders were prohibited. The constitution provided that while "everyone is free to embrace the religion of his choice and to practice all ceremonies, devotions, or observances of his respective faith, either in places of public worship or at home," public religious ceremonies outside of homes or places of worship were prohibited. The constitution provided that religious institutions could not hold real property. "Places of public worship are the property of the Nation, as represented by the Federal Government, which shall determine which of them may continue to be devoted to their present purpose," it declared.

Historians suggest that the reforms may have been more strategic than ideological, that is, the Constitutionalists constructed the reforms to win public support rather than out of genuine revolutionary commitment.[16] The reforms were successful nonetheless; they satisfied many people and helped the Constitutionalists consolidate power. Support for Villa and Zapata waned, and the regions under their control shrank.

On April 10, 1918, a Constitutionalist scheme to assassinate Zapata succeeded. It was a precursor of what was to come: Eventually every revolutionary leader would suffer a similar fate. On November 26, 1919, Constitutionalist forces captured General Felipe Ángeles, a man greatly admired for erudition and integrity. Ángeles himself had been a Constitutionalist before switching allegiances to Villa. Wanting a quick execution but with a pretense of following the law, Carranza had Ángeles publicly tried by a military tribunal. The scheme backfired. Ángeles was duly found guilty and executed, but not before making a powerful impact. As had Socrates, Ángeles refused an opportunity to escape and used his trial as a final opportunity to educate the people. He turned a speech in his own defense into a ringing oration about the benefits of representative democracy, social welfare, and the nobility of free individuals. He exalted Villa and Zapata, and blamed Carranza for Mexico's continuing civil strife. Five thousand people—many weeping or quoting memorable passages from his speech—attended Ángeles's funeral. The episode left Carranza politically enfeebled.

Now Carranza and Obregón turned on each other. Obregón declared that he would run for president. Unable to stop him through the democratic process, Carranza accused Obregón of plotting to overthrow the government and ordered his arrest. This precipitated actual armed rebellion by Obregón. Carranza fled Mexico City (taking with him all of the gold bars in the national treasury). Before he found a safe haven, he was betrayed by a Constitutionalist leader whom he trusted and was killed by snipers.

Pancho Villa had no political ambitions of his own. It was Carranza he found unacceptable; with Carranza dead he was willing to bring civil war to an end. Villa cut a deal with the provisional president of Mexico, Adolfo de la Huerta: Villa would retire peacefully to a 163,000-acre hacienda, where he would be protected by a large contingent of bodyguards; he would demobilize his forces; and the government would provide eight hundred Villistas with money and land. Obregón was reportedly furious with the deal but agreed to honor it nonetheless. To do otherwise would have been perceived as standing in the way of bringing peace to Mexico, which by now had suffered ten years of revolution and civil war. In December 1920, Obregón became president of Mexico. He placated remaining Zapatistas by accepting limited land reform in Morelos, and Mexico appeared at peace.

We know what Will Buckley thought about these events because on December 6, 1919, he testified at length about them before a subcommittee of the United States Senate Foreign Relations Committee investigating American foreign policy toward Mexico.[17] Buckley was more interested in communicating his views to members of the Senate than the senators were interested in hearing them. Buckley testified on a Saturday before a counsel for the subcommittee. There is no evidence that any senator attended the session. Nevertheless, his testimony fills seventy-six pages of the Congressional Record. It was an impressive performance: Buckley displayed his deep knowledge of Mexican affairs and a facility for communicating his ideas simply and forcefully. He also revealed attitudes that would greatly influence his son's ideology.

Buckley was in sympathy with Díaz and the científicos—and with their rationale for nondemocratic rule. "To understand the Mexican situation it must be understood in the beginning that the present is more or less the normal condition of Mexico; the era of peace during the Díaz regime from 1876 to 1910 was an abnormal period in the history of the country," he told the subcommittee. Díaz's regime provided stability for a country incapable of democratic government. Moreover, it provided a period of time for the development of a middle class. "There was no such thing as a middle class in Mexico before the Díaz regime, and the people of the middle class were the strongest advocates of the Díaz regime, for without peace and order it could not subsist." As Will Buckley saw it, the Díaz regime was "the only decent government [Mexico] ever had."

Buckley conceded, however, that the Díaz government had little interest in the great mass of people—the "submerged eighty percent," as Buckley put it, borrowing the phrase from President Woodrow Wilson. "This class has never received any consideration or protection in Mexico during the regime of Porfirio Díaz," said Buckley. Nevertheless, he believed it pointless to give democratic power to an illiterate people living hand to mouth. He also believed these people did not much care how their nation was governed. All this group "wants is to be let alone and be allowed to live in peace and receive those material necessities that are indispensible for the maintenance of life," Buckley told the subcommittee. He continued: "I do not contend that this is all the 80 per cent of the population are entitled to, but I do contend, and history shows, that material benefits must come first and that a people does not concern itself with the niceties of government or universal suffrage until after it is provided with bread and clothes."

Buckley did not explain how the circumstances of the downtrodden mass would improve under a regime that gave it, in his own words, "no consideration or protection." Either he believed that somehow these people were properly in the care of their betters or he believed that the welfare of the great mass of people was of less importance to the nation than that of the upper classes. Either way, Buckley believed that Mexico should be governed by an aristocracy of the well bred and well educated. "The American Government has disregarded the history of the last 100 years, which shows that up to the present time Latin American countries may only be ruled successfully by their educated classes, and that the mass of the people are not yet prepared to exercise the attributes of democracy," Buckley said. Even though Buckley favored the Díaz government, he respected Madero's supporters, whom he described as "Mexicans of the old Liberal type and included in its ranks some of the finest men in Mexico." By contrast, he called post-Madero "radicals of an inferior social type."

Buckley had nothing but disdain for President Wilson, whom he blamed for Mexico's problems. "There is no doubt that the American government is largely responsible" for the "plight" and "suffering" of the Mexican people, he told the subcommittee. President Wilson blundered by failing to support Huerta—the man who led a counterrevolution against Madero and sought to reestablish autocratic rule. The American government "placed the bandits in power by destroying Huerta." While Buckley admitted that the "cultivated Mexican . . . would never have chosen Huerta for president of his own free will," he argued that Huerta was nonetheless "the lesser of several evils."

Why did Buckley prefer Huerta to Carranza? He gave two answers to that question, and we can infer a third answer as well. The first answer is that the Constitutionalists were anticlerical. Huerta also attacked the church and its priests, but the Constitutionalists did so far more viciously, especially Obregón.[18] Second, the Constitutionalists were anti-American. Carranza had always been opposed to American economic imperialism. He believed that American companies were exploiting Mexico's people and resources, and when he became president he made it known that he intended to nationalize the Tampico oil fields.[19] This hit Buckley where he lived.

Buckley related a conversation he had with an official of the Carranza government named Luis Cabrera. "Mr. Cabrera very frankly told me that the menace of the American in Mexico must be removed and that the only way to do this was to drive him out of the country and take his property," Buckley told the subcommittee. Buckley told Cabrera that the American government would never permit that to occur. Cabrera, said Buckley, "smiled" and "explained to me that Mr. Wilson was an advanced liberal, a great Democrat, whose concern was for the people of the world and was not limited to the narrow bounds of the United States." Buckley then described an incident that convinced him Cabrera had been right. In 1916, Mexican employees of an American oil company in Tampico went on strike and seized the refinery. The American superintendent of the refinery demanded that Mexican authorities restore possession to his company, to no avail. The superintendent then confronted the commander of American warships in the harbor and "demanded of him that he and the property of his company be given protection," claiming that was permitted under international law. The American naval commander declined to intervene because doing so would have contravened the policy of the American government.

Buckley explained to the subcommittee the changes that the 1917 Constitution of Mexico made with respect to private property. "This 'modern concept of property' as a 'social function' has found expression in Carranza's Mexico and Trotsky's Russia," Buckley declared. "Thus has Carranza accomplished three of the great bolshevist objects of the revolution—the abolition of private property, the crippling of the church, and the expulsion of the foreigner."

Near the end of his testimony, Buckley read a petition that eighty-four American businessmen in Tampico sent to President Wilson shortly after the U.S. Navy commander refused to protect a refinery from striking workers. These businessmen wanted the American government to protect them and their business interests in Mexico, apparently with military force if required. What justified such an intervention in the internal affairs of another sovereign nation? The petition explained, "We submit to our Government that we believe that we are in this country not by the grace or favor of the Mexican authorities but because we have the right to be here." That statement not only reflects the arrogance of Americans who believed they were in another sovereign nation not as its guests but by right, it also reflects a belief that the ownership of property is sacrosanct—so sacrosanct as to transcend national interest.

This highlights a fundamental difference between Porfirio Díaz,

Victoriano Huerta, and the revolutionaries. Díaz and Huerta protected private property—whether in the hands of hacendados, the church, or foreign companies—pretty much regardless of how that property was acquired or the consequences for the nation. Buckley characterized the principle that a nation owns all land and natural resources as "bolshevism," but that principle was not as extreme as Buckley assumed. Even Theodore Roosevelt had declared, "Every man holds his property subject to the general right of the community to regulate its use to whatever degree the public welfare may require."[20]

In Buckley's eyes, Madero's folly was his desire to bring democracy—but not radical reforms—to a nation with a submerged 80 percent. Such a thing was not possible. When people mired in poverty were given power, including the power of the ballot box, they would use it to appropriate property that belonged to others. This is why Buckley told the subcommittee that Mexico was "not fitted" for democracy. Yet one might argue that Mexico's upper class demonstrated, over a period of more than three decades during the Díaz government, that it was no better at setting aside self-interest.

What was it Buckley wanted the United States to do? His main message was that the United States should support the aristocracy in overthrowing the Constitutionalist government. Buckley himself was secretly engaged in such efforts. Earlier that year, he had supported an unsuccessful coup against the Carranza government led by General Manual Peláez. Buckley told the subcommittee that the United States should take unilateral action and strongly criticized the Wilson administration for participating in two pan-American conferences about Mexico. "I think we should settle this matter with Mexico without reference to Latin America or what Latin Americans or anyone else thinks," he told the subcommittee.

Reid Buckley writes that his father was "so appalled by the bungling of Washington [with respect to the Mexican Revolution], he would be an isolationist thereafter, until Pearl Harbor." It is a curious reaction as Will Buckley had been as much an interventionist with respect to Mexico as had Wilson. Their only difference was that Wilson intervened to put the Constitutionalists in power while Buckley wanted him to intervene to keep Huerta in power.

Two years after Buckley's appearance before the Senate subcommittee, Obregón would expel Buckley from Mexico, and confiscate his Mexican holdings, for participating in another counterrevolutionary coup.

In the Buckley household mythology, this period during Will's life was portrayed as romantic and heroic. Writing about the Mexican Revolution, William F. Buckley Jr. says, with black-and-white clarity, that "the counterrevolutionaries were decent men, and those in power barbarians." For him, as for his father, a neat division could be made between good guys and bad guys. No accounting was made for the fact that counterrevolutionaries Félix Díaz and Victoriano Huerta were duplicitous and brutal; that revolutionaries such as Zapata, Villa, and Ángeles genuinely desired to help the people; or that one might say that during the thirty-five years of Porfirio Díaz's regime, the upper class and foreign corporations had been engaged in a kind of banditry, carried out not with guns and knives against particular individuals but with political influence against the people as a whole.

Will's worldview was communicated in wonderful stories about his exploits.[21] There were several stories about Will's facing down Pancho Villa. In a story about Will's first encounter with Villa, Will was taking a train to deliver the payroll of a large U.S. company. Afraid that the train might be held up by Villa, Will hid the payroll—in the form of rolls of gold coins—in the bottom of phlegm-filled spittoons. As Will feared, Villa had learned about the gold shipment, and he and his caballeros held up the train. Villa's men found the gold coins when one of them accidently knocked over one of the spittoons. Villa placed his pistol to the skull of a conductor who a few minutes earlier had sworn that there was no gold on the train. According to his own story, Will stepped forward and declared, "Don't hurt that man. I hid the gold. He knew nothing about it." When Villa threatened to shoot the conductor anyway because he was whimpering so pathetically, Buckley saved the man's life by telling Villa that he was "too great a man to shoot a wretch like this conductor."

A story about the purported last encounter between Buckley and Villa is set in a famous historical scene: the dinner between Villa and Zapata at Xochimilco on December 4, 1914. The dinner is famous because it was a public celebration—complete with bands and children's choirs—of the first, and as it turned out, only meeting between Villa and Zapata.[22] According to the story, Will, who had been having trouble on his land in Tampico from marauding Villistas, arrived at the dinner uninvited, strode to the head table where Villa and Zapata were seated, and declared to Villa, "The next time one of your men puts his foot on my property he will be shot." The stunned assemblage fell silent. Hands drifted to pistols. After a few hair-raising moments, Villa chuckled and promised Will Buckley that he would not be bothered again.

These and other stories about Will's adventures in Mexico are about how a man without a dime in his pocket makes his fortune through raw intelligence, grit, determination, and courage—accomplishing this in a society not far from anarchy.[23] Will Buckley's tales were akin to Wild West stories, outdoing the standard genre because the hero is not a simple cowboy but a professional man—a lawyer—who became an entrepreneur. He is surrounded by charlatans and bandits. Government is of no help: Local officials are ineffectual or corrupt; national governments are downright dangerous. With the sole exception of the Díaz regime, all of the competing forces in Mexico are more interested in power than in governing for the sake of the nation, and are capable of cruelty and venality. What sets Will Buckley apart from iconic figures who symbolize the transcendent power of the individual—such as Ayn Rand's fictional protagonists John Galt and Howard Roark, or celluloid heroes such as Indiana Jones—is his religiosity. Will Buckley is not merely a self-aggrandizer. He is virtuous, and for him his virtue comes from the only source from which true virtue can come, namely, from his devotion to God and the one true church.

People are profoundly influenced by their parents. Typically they either accept their parents' perceptions of the world or actively struggle to see the world differently. Robert A. Taft and William F. Buckley Jr. fall in the first group; they both contentedly inherited their worldviews. It is illuminating, therefore, to compare the progenitors—to compare Will Buckley with both Alphonso and William Howard Taft. At first, we are struck by important similarities: All three men were extraordinarily intelligent and successful; all became lawyers; all were imbued with a deep sense of patriotism. But there are profound differences. The Tafts eschewed materialism and a career devoted to the pursuit of wealth.

Alphonso migrated to Cincinnati because he found New York City too materialistic. Will Buckley pursued wealth, even gambling his life to make his fortune. The Tafts devoted themselves to the law; Will Buckley quickly became bored by the law and threw it over for business. The Tafts were by sentiment Midwesterners; Will Buckley was by sentiment a Texan, which is to say a blend of South and West. The Tafts were communitarians; Will Buckley was an individualist. The Tafts valued prudence; Will Buckley valued boldness. The Tafts were motivated by a sense of noblesse oblige to serve in government; Will Buckley disdained government. The Tafts thought religion belonged in the private sphere. Will Buckley spent his formative years in a nation that did not have a tradition of separation of church and state, and did not expect religion and government to be confined to separate spheres. Moreover, for Will Buckley the church and anticommunism were more important than democracy. It is no surprise that later he was warmly inclined to the regime of Francisco Franco in Spain.[24]

On a trip to New Orleans five years before he was expelled from Mexico, Will Buckley met a twenty-two-year-old woman named Aloïse Steiner. Her father was a banker. Aloïse had spent two years at the H. Sophie Newcomb Memorial College, the coordinate women's college at Tulane University. She was beautiful, wrote short stories and poems, and was a deeply pious Catholic. According to some reports, she also liked to describe herself as a "daughter of the Confederacy."

Will was immediately smitten and proposed after only a few days. They were soon married, and Aloïse moved to Mexico with her new husband. Their marriage was an exceedingly happy one and lasted until Will's death, forty years later. They had ten children together—six girls and four boys. Bill, born on November 24, 1925, was number six.

In 1929, Will took the family for two years to France, where he was trying to raise money for an oil exploration investment business, and then for another year to England. In 1933, the family returned to the States and settled in a forty-seven-acre estate named Great Elm in Sharon, Connecticut. Will headquartered his business in New York City, but he wanted to raise his family in a more pastoral setting. Sharon, a small town in the bucolic Northwest Highlands region of Connecticut, is adjacent to Dutchess County, New York, home of the Roosevelt estate at Hyde Park. Sharon today remains largely unchanged from the time the Buckleys settled there. The town center is small, green, and nearly unblemished by stores or sidewalks. The private Hotchkiss Library, designed in 1893 by the architect who also designed the gated community of Tuxedo Park, New York, faces the town hall from across the town green. Radiating out from the town center are large estates, many with horse stables and grounds for riding and steeplechasing. Will routinely spent the workweek in New York City, returning home on weekends. Aloïse ran a household with an expanding number of children and a staff of about ten, consisting of nannies, governesses, tutors, horse grooms, and other servants and assistants.

Although most Americans would have perceived the Buckleys as residing in the highest stratosphere of the upper class, genuine aristocrats considered the Buckleys pretenders. The American aristocracy of the time was Protestant, indeed overwhelmingly Episcopalian or Presbyterian. Their sons went to the Ivy League or to elite liberal arts colleges such as Amherst and Williams, and their daughters to the Seven Sisters. Even more importantly they attended one of the socially proper prep schools—a group of schools that sociologists number at no more than sixteen.[25] The Buckleys were nouveau riche Catholics, and Will was the product of a public school and a state university. Making matters even worse were persistent rumors that Will was only a step from financial disaster. There was, in fact, some truth to that rumor—until 1939, when Buckley's Pantepec Oil Company (named after a Mexican river where Buckley purportedly eluded revolutionaries who were chasing him) struck oil in Venezuela.[26] After 1939, the Buckleys were genuinely wealthy by anyone's standards. While no one outside the family knows what Will was worth, some estimates place Will's personal wealth at roughly $20 million in the mid-1950s, the equivalent of roughly $140 million today.

Although Aloïse had come from a family that her son Reid classifies as "petite bourgeoisie," the aristocracy of New Orleans was more pluralistic and permeable than that of the Northeast, and the Steiners did not feel excluded from elite society.[27] Now, however, Aloïse felt cold disdain from her blue-blooded neighbors. She was bitterly stung. She took pleasure not only in associating with the right people, but letting others know she did so. She kept a silver tray near the front door, in which she placed visiting cards of the European dukes and barons and the business cards of American governors and generals, captains of industry, and other personages who called on Great Elm. Every day she shuffled the cards so that another one was placed on top. The tray was there to impress— to flaunt the family's connections. Not everyone in the family was enamored with the tray. When he was a teenager, second-eldest John had a fake card printed. One side read, "Lady Chatterly"; the reverse side said, "And Lover." John placed the fake card on top of the pile in the silver tray. When the prank was discovered, Will was amused. Aloïse was not.[28]

Being rebuffed by society may have made other nouveau riche parents obsessed with winning acceptance by the upper class, beginning with efforts to have their children admitted to one of the proper prep schools. That was not the Buckley way. Although Aloïse felt the sting of exclusion during her early years in Connecticut, Will and Aloïse did not feel inferior because the aristocracy rejected them. They knew that a bold, self-made entrepreneur like Will was not the inferior of scions of social register families with inherited fortunes and jobs on Wall Street or in the headquarters of large corporations. By excluding his family, the aristocrats confirmed Will's perception of them as an effete and self-satisfied group that honored the possession—rather than the acquisition—of wealth.

Will and Aloïse's reaction to their rejection by the Establishment took on a political dimension. Aristocrats were influential in both political parties. The Republican Party included the likes of Henry Stimson, Henry Cabot Lodge, and Leverett Saltonstall. The Democratic Party was home to patricians such as Franklin Delano Roosevelt, Francis Biddle, W. Averell Harriman, and Dean Acheson—to pick four men who were alumni of just one of those proper schools—namely, Groton.[29] With few variations, the aristocracy in both parties held similar ideological views that their prep schools deliberately reinforced. This has been described as a social gospel philosophy that believes in continuous social progress and assumes that capitalism, though good overall, suffers from certain unchristian practices.[30] As it would turn out, many of the politicians and public intellectuals whom Bill later came to especially dislike happened to come from aristocratic families, including (with their prep schools): Nelson A. Rockefeller (Deerfield), John V. Lindsay (St. Paul's), William Scranton (Hotchkiss), Henry Cabot Lodge Jr. (Middlesex), Arthur M. Schlesinger Jr. (Exeter), and Gore Vidal (Exeter). By contrast, Bill Buckley became warm friends with liberals such as John Kenneth Galbraith and Norman Mailer, who were products of public schools and the middle class. Bill also had special antipathy for the three Kennedy brothers, whose father, like Will Buckley, was nouveau riche Catholic but instead worked at having his children accepted by the upper class, sending John to Choate and Robert and Edward to Milton Academy. The Kennedys, moreover, were ultimately accepted by the aristocracy because they accepted the Establishment's ideology—liberalism—as the one true faith. Conservatives have long disliked what they refer to as the Eastern Establishment.[31] For William F. Buckley Jr., the animosity was not just political; it was also personal.

The subtle snubs from their aristocratic neighbors helped produce an extremely close-knit family. The Buckley children squabbled at times, as all siblings do, but generally only at home. They fiercely stuck up for one another outside the household. And they tended to stick together, unusually so. Reid Buckley, the eighth child, writes that "at a party, we would always be found gathered together and chatting animatedly, paying little attention to the friend whose birthday we had been invited to celebrate or the other girls and boys. There was simply no one else in the world as interesting to us as we were to ourselves."[32] In ages, they spanned two decades: The oldest—Aloïse, generally called Allie—was twenty and a student at Smith College when Carol, the youngest, was born. Allie was born before Will was expelled from Mexico, as were the next two children, John and Priscilla. The next four—James, Jane, Bill, and Patricia (Trish)—were born in the States before the Buckleys left for Europe. Reid and Maureen were born in Paris, and Carol arrived after the family returned to the States. For schooling, meals, and other purposes, Will and Aloïse generally divided their children into three groups: the four oldest, the middle four, and the two youngest. Bill was therefore most often thrown together with Jane, Trish, and Reid, an arrangement about which he often complained. If he were closest to one of his siblings during childhood, it was probably Trish, and because she—a year and half his junior—adored Bill.[33] In adulthood, James and

Priscilla would become closest to Bill: Jim because he managed Bill's 1965 campaign for mayor of New York City, and three years later became a major conservative figure in his own right when he was elected United States senator from New York on the Conservative Party ticket, and Priscilla because she worked closely with Bill as managing editor of *National Review*.

Childhood for Bill and his siblings was close to idyllic. "Summers were seasons of unmitigated pleasures for us," Bill wrote. The children frolicked in the pastures and woods at Great Elm. The estate also had swimming pools, tennis courts, and riding stables—complete with a groom and an assistant. Several times a week the children went sailing on nearby Lake Wononscopomuc. They went pheasant hunting in the fall and skiing in Switzerland in the winter. And as was the case with their neighbors, the Buckleys devoted particular attention to equestrian pursuits. Bill Buckley's memoirs include a picture of him at about fifteen years of age jumping a hurdle on horseback while Will—dressed in a sport coat, tie, and straw hat—is timing him with a stopwatch. Bill relates an incident when his younger sister Trish won a blue ribbon at the annual Dutchess County horse show, at which the Buckley family maintained a box adjacent to that of Franklin Delano Roosevelt. The winner traditionally rode around the ring waving and nodding to applauding spectators. "When she rode by the president's box," Bill writes, "FDR applauded lustily, whereupon Trish abruptly turned her pigtail head to one side," thereby slighting the president.

Trish could hardly be blamed. At about the same time, her parents were writing letters to the editor in the local newspaper excoriating FDR for the lend-lease program, under which America was providing England with warships and other material to defend itself against Nazi Germany. And after Sharon residents expressed outrage over the circulation of an anonymous leaflet that not only denounced lend-lease but condemned England and accused FDR of dishonestly attempting to embroil America in the war, Will admitted that he was the leaflet's author.

An often-told story is that Will believed in taking advantage of young children's natural ability to learn languages, and that to make them fluent in three languages he employed a Spanish-speaking nurse to care for the children until age five, at which time they were transferred to a French-speaking governess. English was, according to this story, Bill's third language. This is what accounts for the unique Buckley speech pattern that sounded patrician to most ears.[34] Like many other stories of the Buckley household, however, this is exaggerated. During the time the family lived in France—when Bill was four to seven years of age—the four older children were under the care of a French governess. They were also old enough to attend a French-speaking school, and thus became fluent in French. They were less well versed in Spanish however. Meanwhile, the younger group of children had Mexican nurses and became fluent in Spanish, but they did not become as well versed in French.[35] English was always the primary language of the household, and none of the children spoke a foreign language before English.

The idiosyncratic Buckley speech pattern was the product of complex influences. One parent had a Texas accent modified by years in Mexico, the other had a Southern accent, and there was a fair amount of French and Spanish being spoken around the house. Moreover, in 1938 Will sent Bill and two of his sisters to English boarding schools for a year. While the real reason he did this was that Aloïse was in the midst of a dangerous pregnancy and doctors worried she might not survive childbirth, Will told the children he was sending them to England to improve their elocution. Bill, then twelve, attended the St. John's Beaumont School, a boarding school near London operated by Jesuit priests, while his sisters attended a girls' boarding school. It shows just how hard Bill was willing to work for his father's approval that Bill returned to America with a distinct British overlay to his accent.

With the exceptions of the several years in Paris for the older children and the year in England for Bill and two of his sisters, the Buckley clan was homeschooled through eighth grade. Will set up a homeschool in a small building immediately behind the main house at Great Elm, and he sent around a circular to three hundred families in the Sharon area inviting them to consider sending their children to his homeschool in order to avoid the "blight of Liberalism and Communism they will encounter in almost all elementary schools." His school, he assured parents, would not be in any fashion "progressive." Three children from the area eventually attended Will's school along with the Buckley children. One of them was the daughter of the local Episcopal minister; her name was then Audrey Cotter, but she later became famous under the stage name Audrey Meadows. Will engaged two full-time teachers—one American, the other British—and supplemented them with additional tutors and coaches for music and extracurricular activities.

Will purchased curricula from the Calvert School, a venerable home-schooling organization in Baltimore. The children used Calvert materials for academic subjects, which they studied in the mornings. In the afternoons, they received additional instruction in a wide assortment of sports and hobbies, ranging from golf and ballroom dancing to bird-watching and carpentry. The most important extracurricular was music. Great Elm had an organ and five pianos, and the Buckley children were required to practice piano forty-five minutes per day.

The children regularly visited the private Hotchkiss Library on the Sharon Green, less than a mile away from Great Elm. The library had a well-stocked children's room and a wonderful librarian named Mary Mackay, who got to know each of the children's individual tastes and alerted them to new arrivals that she thought they would enjoy. Bill Buckley's last public appearance, in the fall of 2008, was at a fund-raising event for Hotchkiss Library, at which he, four of his siblings, and his son Christopher read from their books.

In the mid-1930s, the family began to spend increasing amounts of time during the summer in Camden, South Carolina. At first they rented houses, but in 1940—the year after Will struck oil in Venezuela—they purchased an estate in Camden named Kamschatka, which included an expansive three-story home complete with colonnades and balconies, and well-manicured grounds that included formal terraces. In many ways, Will and Aloïse found Southern culture more congenial, including in attitudes toward race. Reid Buckley writes of his parents that "they were born into their times and stamped indelibly, lifelong, by the attitudes of their times. The Negro race was on the whole inferior. The average Negro was, they thought, incapable of competing with white people in a modern industrial economy."[36]

Reid recounts how, after the second Vatican Council decreed that black men could be ordained as priests, his mother prayed about whether she would be able to receive communion from a black priest, should the unlikely necessity ever arise.[37] Will was also plagued with anti-Semitism. Bill Buckley once remarked that if, when he were an adult, someone in his presence made the kind of remark about Jews that he routinely had heard at his family dinner table during his youth, he would have been required to leave the room.[38] As we shall see, Bill successfully shed his parents' anti-Semitism at a relatively early age, but his attitudes toward race were far more complicated.

When it was time for high school, Bill was sent to the Millbrook School, where his two older brothers, John and Jim, were already enrolled. Millbrook was then new—it had been established by its headmaster, Edward Pulling, nine years earlier—and had only sixty students and a few buildings on a beautiful campus in Dutchess County, New York, about ten miles from Great Elm. The choice reflected Will's rejection of the aristocracy. In selecting Millbrook, Will shunned elite prep schools such as Hotchkiss, which is only six miles from Great Elm; Kent or Taft, which were also relatively nearby; or even Portsmouth Abbey, a Catholic boarding school in Rhode Island that, because it is Catholic may not be quite as acceptable as the proper sixteen, is nevertheless considered "prestigious" and "within the elite tradition"—and is the school that Bill would ultimately select for his son Christopher.[39]

Bill excelled academically at Millbrook, especially in English, and was permitted to skip a year. He was also particularly strong in music and debate, and he founded the school yearbook. But Bill was not as successful socially. In fact, he was rather disliked by students and teachers, who considered him to be haughty and arrogant. He also rubbed some the wrong way for being, as Buckley himself put it, "obnoxiously Catholic" in a school that was expressly Protestant. Bill was also politically pedantic; he lectured not only classmates but also even faculty members about politics. Moreover, Bill was championing isolationist America First views, which were distinctly unpopular at Millbrook. Of course, the America First position was bombed to smithereens on December 7, 1941, and Bill—as well as his parents and brother Jim, who had been engaging in America First activities at Yale—immediately stopped opposing American involvement in World War II.

During Buckley's senior year at Millbrook, Albert Jay Nock published *Memoirs of a Superfluous Man*, which became Bill's favorite book.[40] Nock, born in 1870, was a public intellectual. He was the author of a number of books, including an acclaimed biography of Thomas Jefferson, but he was best known as an essayist. Nock began as a liberal writing for the *Nation*. Over time, however, he became a libertarian. In 1920, Nock helped establish the *Freeman*, and he served as co-editor of the magazine. Managerial skills were not his forte, however. He also preferred spending most of his time in Europe. So after four years, he gave up his editorial position and rededicated himself to writing exclusively. His work had flair and elegance, and his essays were published by leading literary magazines such as *Atlantic Monthly* and *Harper's*. Nock was seventy-three when he published *Memoirs of a Superfluous Man*. It was the capstone of his career—his most widely read book, and his last. He died two years later. There was good reason that Nock's book came immediately to Bill's attention: Nock was a friend of Will Buckley's and a periodic luncheon guest at Great Elm.

Memoirs of a Superfluous Man was a libertarian manifesto. In it, Nock railed against statism and collectivism in all forms. He drew no distinctions among different forms of government. "Communism, the New Deal, Fascism, Nazism, are merely so-many trade-names for collectivist Statism, like the trade-names for tooth-pastes which are all exactly alike except for the flavoring," Nock wrote.[41] The problem, as he saw it, was that governmental power will inevitably be turned against the individual. "In proportion as you give the State power to do things *for* you, you give it power to do things *to* you; and the State invariably makes as little as it can of the one power, and as much as it can of the other," he explained.[42] Somewhat incongruously, Nock argued that "if a régime of complete economic freedom be established, social and political freedom will follow automatically."[43] But Nock was not clear about what kinds of government, if any, foster complete economic freedom. They were not republican or democratic governments; Nock said that they had been no more successful at promoting freedom than autocracies and monarchies.[44] Though Nock did not expressly say so, he appeared to lean toward anarchism. *Memoirs* was a particular kind of libertarian manifesto, however, for Nock did not admire capitalists. He denounced "economism"—a term he coined for the belief that life should be devoted to "the production, acquisition, and distribution of wealth"—just as zealously as he denounced statism.[45] Economism was the American philosophy, said Nock, and that was one of the reasons (along with American imperialism) that he preferred Europe.[46] Nock believed that people should live for higher purposes, such as appreciation of knowledge and beauty. Or at least he believed that the small number of people who had the capacity to appreciate knowledge and beauty should do so; Nock was so great an elitist that he opposed universal literacy.[47] Most people, he argued, lacked the capacity to comprehend anything of value, and the main function of universal literacy was to extend the reach of advertising.

Undoubtedly, neither Will nor Bill accepted all of Nock's views. They must have felt that Nock's preference for spending most of his time in Europe evidenced a lack of patriotism. And they could not have much liked Nock's views about religion: Nock was an ordained Episcopal priest who became disenchanted with organized Christianity and left the clergy. Nock believed that Jesus had preached about a universal loving God and the brotherhood of man, and nothing more. Jesus's teachings, thought Nock, were exclusively about human conduct, and said nothing about the kingdom of God, or about building a church. But Nock's radical libertarianism, combined with his rejection of materialism, resonated. For Bill, Nock's appeal was probably heighted by his erudition and literary skill, as well as an elitism that was based on intelligence and right thinking rather than lineage or wealth. Bill admired Nock greatly—both then and later. As an adult, Bill Buckley acquired the handwritten manuscript of Nock's Jefferson biography, and clearly treasured it as one of his prize possessions.[48]

When Bill graduated from Millbrook in June 1943, World War II was raging across Europe and the Pacific. Although the Allies were gaining the upper hand, the final result of the great conflict was still in doubt. Allied forces had recently defeated the German Panzer Army under Rommel in North Africa and were preparing to invade Sicily, but the invasion of Normandy was a year away. German forces were launching a counteroffensive in the Ukraine and had retaken Kharkov. German U-boats were extracting a terrible toll on Allied shipping, sinking twenty-seven merchant marine ships during March 1943 alone. The world was beginning to learn that the Nazis were committing unspeakable acts against humanity, but the Allies were still unprepared to do anything about it. Six months earlier, British foreign secretary Anthony Eden told the House of Commons that the Nazis were committing mass murders of Jews in Europe but could only vow to avenge those crimes someday in the future. In the Pacific, the U.S. Navy won the decisive victory at Midway a year earlier, but a great deal of American blood would have to be spilled before the final victory. American marines were conducting amphibian invasions in the Solomon Islands; their assaults on the Marshall Islands and the Marianas, at Iwo Jima, Okinawa, Corregidor, and in Manila were all to come.

Having skipped a grade, Bill Buckley was seventeen when he graduated from Millbrook, and he would not be drafted until he turned eighteen. While many young American men wanted to fight, Bill was not among them. He told his father he wanted to "land a desk job of some sort." Will also hoped to keep Bill out of combat. With the plan of getting Bill into either the army or navy advanced language school and then assigned to intelligence work, Will took the family to Mexico during the summer of 1943 so that Bill could brush up on his Spanish.

Bill was inducted in June 1944 and sent to basic training at Camp Wheeler in Georgia. The advanced language school plan did not work out. Bill's backup plan was Officer Candidate School. He was accepted and sent to OCS at Fort Benning, also in Georgia. Bill found the physical training grueling. But even more difficult were Bill's relationships with fellow trainees, drill sergeants, and officers. He was offended by their manners. Bill wrote to his father that he found many of the men "crude, coarse, vulgar and highly objectionable in some respects." He was disturbed by eating shoulder to shoulder and sleeping in the same quarters with black soldiers. Bill was used to being around black people at Kamschatka in South Carolina, but he was accustomed to being served by them. Bill was also put off by what he viewed as the lack of intelligence and education in his fellow soldiers—enlisted men and commissioned officers alike. Bill wrote to his mother how resentful he felt "when I am bossed around by a person with no education." This, Bill wrote, brought out his "recalcitrance," which in turn interfered with his forming friendships.

Bill's blaming recalcitrance for his lack of friends makes it sound as if he became quiet and withdrawn, but that was not so. The problem was much the reverse: As had been the case at Millbrook, Bill was an insufferable know-it-all. One person with whom Bill did make friends, Charles Ault, reported that Bill was outspoken, particularly about politics. According to Ault, Buckley "was very vocal about the Democrats in general and Roosevelt in particular," and that he expressed himself "vociferously" on these topics.

Bill was in officers' training while World War II was at its blood-soaked zenith. He entered OCS just as Allied troops were landing in Normandy and U.S. Marines were invading Saipan. America was being led during the war by an immensely popular president. Yet Buckley was lecturing his fellow soldiers—most of whom were older than he—on how FDR had maneuvered America into a war that was not in the national interest. He also let them know he considered himself morally superior. Before men left Fort Benning on a leave, a platoon leader suggested they take condoms with them. Bill loudly sneered that *he* did not need to do so.

One might think that someone as smart as Buckley would have the good sense to shut up, but good sense is not something Bill Buckley had in great supply when he entered the army. He was immature and inexperienced. He had been homeschooled and attended a small, homogeneous private high school. The lieutenant who commanded Buckley's unit in OCS later said that he thought Bill failed "to come to grips with" the reality of war. He and his fellow officers were watching men graduate and then learning only a few weeks later that they had been killed in action. Some OCS trainees had already served in combat as enlisted men. For these men, training was serious business. But during one competitive exercise, Bill made a group of men he was leading stop so that he could pick a flower, and another group won. No wonder Charles Ault considered Bill a "smart-ass" and "effete"—and this was the one man who befriended Buckley.

One can only imagine what life was like for Buckley under these circumstances. Few soldiers can be expected to be tolerant of those who tell them that they are about to risk their lives for an unworthy cause. It is unlikely that drill sergeants and fellow trainees treated Buckley with mere indifference. And Bill no longer had the luxury of retreating to his family's bosom on the weekends. Soon after his arrival at Fort Benning, his stress manifested itself in such an acute case of acne that he almost failed a medical examination.

Bill knew he had to learn to adjust. He worked hard to understand his problems and present a different face to the world. He wrote Trish a letter asking for advice about how to conceal his attitude of superiority. He also took to heart advice that a priest in Camden, South Carolina, had given him years earlier: Be quiet, generous, interested in others, and inconspicuous. In a letter to his mother, Bill wrote that his "greatest achievement" in the army was his "success in social relations." And to his father, Bill wrote the following:

> I don't know whether you were aware of this while I was at Millbrook, but I was not very popular with the boys. After a good deal of self-analysis, I determined that the principal reason for this revolved around my extreme dogmatism—particularly in matters concerning politics and the Catholic Church. I could not understand another point of view; it seemed to me that someone who was not an isolationist or a Catholic was simply stupid.[49]

But in the army, Bill wrote, he "learned the importance of tolerance and the importance of a sense of proportion about all matters." He learned to make friends of all kinds of people, including those who "were atheistic, and even immoral." He had found he could be friends with people as long as they had a "good sense of humor, a pleasant personality and a certain number of common interests."

Buckley graduated from Officer Candidate School by the skin of his teeth. His superior officers decided to commission him only after a long and contentious debate. And much to his relief, the army did not send Bill to a combat theater. He spent five months as an infantry training officer at Fort Gordon, Georgia. Then his fluency in Spanish finally paid off: He was sent to Fort Sam Houston in San Antonio, Texas, to do counterintelligence work. Buckley arrived at Fort Sam Houston, however, on August 15, 1945—the day that the Japanese surrender was announced—and in a delicious irony he was reassigned to teach sexual hygiene to Mexican recruits. Less than a year later, he was honorably discharged.

In September 1946, a much-matured William F. Buckley Jr.—just shy of his twenty-first birthday—entered Yale University as an undergraduate.

As had been the case with Millbrook, Will decided where Bill would go to college, and it is said he made that decision ten years earlier. Why Yale rather than Harvard or, for someone for whom Catholicism was so important, Georgetown or Notre Dame? Was Will suspicious of Harvard, which had educated not only archvillain Franklin Delano Roosevelt but also the notoriously liberal members of FDR's famous Brain Trust—Adolf Berle, Benjamin Cohen, Thomas Corcoran—not to mention Jewish Supreme Court justices Louis Brandeis and Felix Frankfurter? Were the Catholic universities not good enough? No one knows Will's thinking. For whatever reason, he decided that his boys should go to Yale, and, in turn, James, Bill, and Reid all did.

At Yale, the Buckleys found that neither their religion nor their politics stopped them from being warmly welcomed by the most exclusive groups. All three were tapped by Skull and Bones, Yale's most prestigious secret society. Moreover, Bill at least was a member of the Fence Club, which C. Wright Mills identified as one of Yale's most socially selective fraternities and a 1956 Yale student pamphlet described as "the most pretentiously snobbish organization at Yale." In fact, Fence so wanted to recruit Bill that—at Bill's demand—it reversed itself and accepted for membership Tom Guinzburg, a friend of Bill's whom Fence had previously rejected because he was Jewish.

Bill's academic record at Yale was solid but not stellar. He graduated with an average of 85, boosted by extremely high grades in Spanish courses, a language in which he was already fluent.[50] He scraped by with a 70 in a two-semester physics course, and he earned a 92 in a music course. Otherwise, his grades ranged between 80 and 90, even in English, notwithstanding his extraordinary talent. Two Buckley biographers report that he majored in economics—perhaps based on Bill's book *God and Man at Yale*, which focuses on Yale's economics department—but that is not so.[51] Bill took only four economics courses. It is not clear whether Yale then had a system of formal majors (no major is listed on Bill's Yale transcript), but Bill took nine political science courses, more than in any other discipline. Moreover, his adviser was political science professor Willmoore Kendall. Bill also took a smattering of courses in history, philosophy, and sociology.

Bill's extracurricular activities, however, made him a star at Yale. In his freshmen year, he tried out for both *Yale Daily News* and the debate team, and his extraordinary gifts for both journalism and debate were immediately recognized. He was one of three selected for the freshman debate team. One of the others was L. Brent Bozell Jr., the son of a nationally prominent advertising executive from Omaha, Nebraska, who would become an important figure in both Buckley's personal life and the history of the conservative movement.

Bozell and Buckley became a powerful debate team. Bozell was the more eloquent orator; he would twice win Yale's public speaking prize. Buckley shone at rebuttal. The debate team coach described Bill as a "terrific infighter" with a "flair for the dramatic." He was not equally effective on both sides of an argument; he was far more effective advocating a conservative rather than a liberal position. The Bozell-Buckley team specialized in acid wit and sarcasm. Their style did not appeal to everyone. One judge commented, "You'll never persuade me by your sarcasm and your denigrating references to your opponent." But on the whole, their style worked. Buckley even used pantomime to ridicule opponents. When an opponent argued that a proposal Bozell and Buckley were supporting would lead to disaster, or asked the audience to feel sympathy for victims, Buckley would pretend to play a violin or histrionically dab his eyes with a handkerchief. Buckley deployed this technique against an Oxford University debate team that visited the United States during the fall of 1949 and had trounced all of the other Ivy League colleges before reaching Yale. A large crowd turned out to watch the contest. Just as an Oxford debater was reaching the crescendo of his argument, Buckley drew a handkerchief from his pocket and waved it in a manner that at Yale signaled everyone was to rise and sing the college fight song. The audience tittered with amusement, leaving the Oxford speaker confused and discombobulated. Bozell and Buckley won by unanimous vote.

Buckley also debated politics and affairs of the day in other venues, such as the Political Union, where students debated about political candidates and issues. His style was much the same. Thomas Emerson, then a young law professor at Yale, debated Buckley several times on a radio show. Emerson said that Buckley was "really vicious" but effective nonetheless. "I was no match for him at all," Emerson conceded.

It was at Yale that Buckley developed his inimitable style. He learned to walk a fine line between cutting attack and good-natured teasing. He was savage but playful. He could be nastily sarcastic but have a twinkle in his eye and a smile on his lips. William Sloane Coffin, who would later become famous as a Yale chaplain and liberal political activist but was then a Yale undergraduate one class ahead of Buckley, liked Bill. Coffin thought that while Buckley was arrogant, it was a cocky arrogance, not a smug arrogance. "He was a prima donna, and he knew it, but he could be kidded about it," said Coffin.[52] Buckley almost certainly would not have been able to pull this off had it not been for his two years in the army. Buckley's style, however, was not all a persona he put on. It reflected the man within. Buckley zealously believed in his cause and disdained the opposing view; nevertheless, he had a genuine reservoir of goodwill.

Buckley was even more successful at the *Yale Daily News.* He was a naturally fluid writer—in his later days, he could write a thousand words in half an hour—and he produced more stories than any other freshman. As early as his freshman year, he set his sights on becoming chairman (what other papers call editor in chief) of the newspaper. This required being elected chairman by fellow editors in the fall of his junior year. Buckley did not doubt that he was the best person for the job: "I will definitely stand out, by virtue of ability, industry, experience, conscientiousness, and self-confidence as the next logical chairman," he wrote to his father. Judging by the extraordinary journalistic talent he displayed throughout his career, Bill was almost certainly right. But Bill worried that personality shortcomings might cost him the position. "I am so terribly afraid," his letter to his dad continued, "that because of the remnants of the difficulties I have in arousing spontaneously friendly relations, I will not be elected." As Bill saw it, democracy was the problem. "Were it an appointive position, I would most certainly get the office," he told his dad. Buckley assumed that a person in charge, a boss, would be fairer than the group. The group would recognize Bill's superior talent, but therein lay a problem. "As you probably well know," he told Will, "there is a tendency in human beings to resent obviously superior ability . . . a tendency to be reluctant to vote for the man who so obviously should have the job."

Yet despite his fears, Bill's interpersonal skills were now up to the challenge. His principal competition was his friend Thomas H. Guinzburg, the Jewish boy Buckley had insisted that Fence admit. Guinzburg was an alumnus of the elite Hotchkiss School and the U.S. Marines. He was both good-looking and extremely talented: Later in life he would marry starlet Rita Gam and become publisher of Viking Press. Over a drink, Bill asked Tom what his ambitions were with regard to the *Yale Daily News*. Tom said he wanted to be managing editor because he was more interested in managing the news department than in writing editorials. "That's good because I want to be chairman, and we'll make a terrific team," Bill replied. In his sophomore year, Buckley was unanimously elected chairman of the *Yale Daily News* by secret ballot. Guinzberg was elected managing editor. They were to take the helm the following year, serving from February 1, 1949, in their junior year, to February 1, 1950, a few months before they were to graduate. It would be one of the most scintillating and provocative years in the history of the nation's oldest college newspaper.

The *Yale Daily News* had typically focused on campus matters—student government, sports, fraternity charity drives, and the like. Buckley and Guinzburg started covering national stories, even sending reporters to New York or Washington on occasion. But the greatest change was on the editorial page. Buckley wrote blistering right-wing critiques of current events at a time when conservatism was not entirely respectable in intellectual circles. Hoover and the Depression had discredited conservatism. The New Deal had worked. Lord John Maynard Keynes had revolutionized economics, showing why government regulation of the economy was essential. Benjamin Cardozo and Louis Brandeis had infused the law with a similar dynamism, buttressing the case for government regulation of business by administrative agencies and courts. Intellectuals were reading John Dewey, Reinhold Niebuhr, Bertrand Russell, and Walter Lippmann. During Buckley's tenure as chairman of the *Yale Daily News*, Arthur Schlesinger Jr. published his liberal manifesto, *The Vital Center*. Liberalism was the accepted wisdom. People were accustomed to Robert Taft's brand of conservatism, which stressed prudence, caution, and humility in substance and in style, but Buckley threw Molotov cocktails. He wrote editorials excoriating liberals as hypocrites and calling for religion to "rally against godless materialism whose headway in the last 30 years threatens civilization." His writing was elegant, his style more than brash. Philosophy professor Paul Weiss said Buckley "was the most extraordinary editor of a college newspaper that Yale had ever seen or I had ever heard of. The faculty and the students waited every day to have the issue appear. It was electric, dynamic, horrendous; to read it was to be shocked."

Buckley provoked a firestorm of controversy with a series of scathing attacks on Raymond Kennedy, a sociologist and one of Yale's most popular teachers. Buckley accused Kennedy of disparaging religion in his classroom. "Mr. Kennedy never makes the positive assertion that God does not exist. Instead his beliefs form an inarticulated hypothesis for this thesis," argued Buckley.[53] Buckley's evidence was a few quotes that Buckley had transcribed from Kennedy's classroom, such as "chaplains accompanying modern armies are comparable to witch doctors accompanying tribes," and "religion is a matter of ghosts, spirits and emotion." Buckley was not complaining that Kennedy was trying to indoctrinate his students. As Buckley saw it, a college should indoctrinate its students—but in correct and moral positions. Buckley complained that Kennedy was advocating erroneous and immoral views. Letters to the editor defending Kennedy and attacking Buckley poured in—from students and faculty alike. The chair of the sociology department demanded to know whether Buckley's editorial—which had been unsigned—represented the views of the editorial board. William J. C. Carlin, vice-chairman of the *Yale Daily News*, who wrote his own editorials for the paper two days per week, challenged Buckley's implication that Yale students needed to be protected from Kennedy's views. "If any student is willing to accept uncritically every opinion and interpretation with which he is confronted, he doesn't deserve to be at Yale," Carlin wrote. Professor Kennedy was given two full columns to defend himself.

Criticism did not suppress Buckley; he thrived on it. Several months later, he accused the Yale faculty of being filled with so-called Reds. He denounced efforts to form a civil rights group at Yale, arguing that most civil liberty groups were riddled with communists. Fashioned by other hands, such arguments might sound slack witted. But by clothing his arguments with formal syntax and elegant writing, Buckley could make the outlandish seem dignified. He employed subtle and clever techniques of argument. He implied civil rights groups included communists by praising the ACLU for banning communists from membership, which, he said, made the ACLU "the only decorous civil rights committee of which we have knowledge."[54]

At the end of his tenure at the paper, Buckley received a letter from William DeVane, dean of Yale College, which read:

> As you come to the end of your editorial duties, you deserve the congratulations of the entire community for making the *News* the most lively college newspaper in the country, past or present. Of course, neither I nor a lot of other people agreed with your editorial position on a lot of points—but the paper was alive and could not be ignored. As a matter of fact, it was read eagerly because significant things were said, important issues debated. That, I believe, is the *summum bonum* of journalism. Heartiest congratulations.

Buckley was the most prominent, respected, and controversial member of his class. The Yale administration invited him to be the student speaker at Alumni Day in his senior year—an event designed to make alumni glow with enough good feeling about Yale to reach for their wallets—and then realized the gamble they were taking. The secretary of Yale invited Buckley to come to his office to rehearse his speech. Buckley realized this was a ploy to find out what he intended to say and refused. Instead, Buckley gave a copy of his speech to the Yale News Bureau, where it was read with horror and passed up the chain until it reached the president of the university. Administrators should not have been surprised: Buckley's speech was a screed against the decadent liberalism of Yale. He accused Yale of not adequately fostering Christianity and free enterprise, and called for disciplining professors such as Raymond Kennedy. Yale, he said, was failing as an "educational leader" and leading its students "only to confusion." The administration asked Buckley to revise the speech. Buckley made some small modifications and sent a revised draft back with an ultimatum: He would be willing to give the speech without discussing further revisions, or he would not speak at all. Buckley believed the administration would be forced to let him speak: The event was the next day, and there was no time to recruit another student speaker. He was surprised and hurt when the administration accepted his invitation to withdraw.

Yale administrators must have had heart palpitations when, shortly thereafter, the graduating class selected Buckley to give the Class Day

Oration. This time they were helpless. But this speech was before a different audience—one largely composed of students rather than alumni, for whom Buckley's Alumni Day speech had been tailored—and as a result Buckley decided to give a different speech. Buckley delivered a ringing right-wing jeremiad about defeating communism, but he did not make Yale the center of his bull's-eye. University administrators undoubtedly breathed a deep sigh of relief. Yet, though they did not then know it, they had not dodged the bullet. Their decision not to allow Buckley to deliver the Alumni Day speech would come back and haunt them in ways they did not then imagine. Buckley had decided on a different means of telling alumni that Yale was betraying its mission.

Shortly after graduation, Bill married Patricia Taylor. He had met his wife the summer before in Vancouver, Canada. Bill's sister Trish had become friends with Taylor at Vassar College. Trish, who had herself become engaged to Bill's debating partner, Brent Bozell, decided that Pat was marriage material for Bill. "Pat looks like a queen, she acts like a queen, and is just the match for Bill," Trish told her family. Pat was nearly six feet tall, elegant, beautiful, and witty. At Trish's suggestion, the Taylors extended an invitation to Brent and Bill to visit Vancouver during the summer before their senior year, and the boys had accepted. As the story is told, Brent and Bill arrived in Vancouver on a Sunday, and on Thursday evening—the evening before he was to return home—Bill insisted that Pat excuse herself from a card game because he had speak to her immediately. "Bill, what do you want?" Pat demanded when she entered the library. Thereupon, Bill proposed. "Bill," Pat regally replied, "I've been asked that question many times. To the others I've said no. To you I say yes. Now may I please get back to my hand?"

Pat's family, however, took persuading. Pat's father, Austin Taylor, a baron of gold, timber, and oil, was one of the wealthiest men in Canada—far wealthier than Will Buckley. Moreover, the Taylors were members of the High Anglican Church of Northern Island, and taken aback at the thought of their daughter marrying a Catholic. However, after some interfamily negotiations about the wedding—the ceremony would be performed by the archbishop at the Roman Catholic cathedral in Vancouver, following which an Anglican bishop would bless the couple at a reception at the Taylor's estate—both families agreed to the match. Bill and Pat were married on July 6, 1950. The couple settled in New Haven, and Bill went to work turning his Alumni Day speech into a book.

Bill Buckley burst onto the national stage the following year as author of *God and Man at Yale*. This remarkable book reflects both the paradox of William F. Buckley Jr. and how he ultimately shaped American conservatism. It is brilliantly written; it takes one's breath away to realize it was written by a twenty-four-year-old. Buckley's distinctive literary style was already fully mature. His writing is like a sharp sword in a velvet scabbard. He attacks opposing ideas and—even more so their advocates—ad hominem. His specialty is ridicule. But the cutting force is sheathed in a tone of discursive formality, and his argument appears to proceed carefully step-by-step. Buckley always sounds thoughtful and learned.

In *God and Man at Yale*, Buckley condemned Yale for failing to effectively indoctrinate its students in two ideals: Christianity and a brand of pure laissez-faire economics that Buckley calls "individualism." Buckley considered these ideals the bedrock of the nation, and he argued that Yale's duty was to inculcate its students in these ideals. Faculty who did not subscribe to these orthodoxies should be fired, he argued. Buckley's research showed him that the university's trustees were all professed Christians, and most were lawyers, politicians, and businessmen who, Buckley assumed, must have been "overwhelmingly favorable to free enterprise." They must, he wrote, "certainly be anxious that students . . . also be persuaded, in so far as possible, to espouse similar views." But Yale was not doing that. Although the religion department was academically "everything one could wish" and most faculty were Christians, teachers nonetheless were failing to "proselytize the Christian faith."

The economics department was even worse, for "the net influence of Yale economics [is] thoroughly collectivist." Only four of nine full professors in the economics department were "forthright defenders of individualism." The rest were Keynesians who embraced some governmental regulation. Buckley so effectively ridiculed the textbooks used in Yale's introductory economics courses that it can be difficult to resist concluding that the authors must have been fools—until one considers that these texts were used by hundreds of colleges and universities, including not only elite institutions such as five other Ivy League colleges, Chicago, MIT, and Stanford, but also by flagship state universities in every region of the country, Catholic colleges including Holy Cross and Xavier, and the U.S. service academies. How likely was it that all of these colleges had selected patently absurd textbooks and needed a twenty-four-year-old to point out their folly?

Why was it that Yale was failing to do what its trustees and administrators so obviously desired? "What I call a failure to Christianize Yale was not due to any lack of sympathy or understanding of religion" on the part of the Yale administration but rather "to the shibboleths of 'academic freedom' that have so decisively hamstrung so many educators in the past fifty years," Buckley wrote. Yale would not tolerate a racist or anti-Semite on its faculty, he argued, and its immediate past president stated that Yale would not "knowingly hire a Communist." Thus, Buckley argued, academic freedom was a myth, and it should not have stood in the way of proper indoctrination of students. For Buckley, there were no shades of gray. If academic freedom could not be absolute and free of contradictions, it should have been discarded entirely.

While Buckley purports to raise and demolish opposing arguments, he never considers that a university's mission is not to indoctrinate students but to teach them how to think for themselves. Buckley writes that he himself came to Yale believing that "a rigid adherence to Christian principles" was good for the individual, and that free enterprise and limited government were good for the nation. While he concedes the latter view was based on "only a scanty knowledge of economics," Buckley considered increased knowledge worthwhile only if it supported his existing beliefs. As Buckley himself put it, he had "looked eagerly to Yale University for allies against secularism and collectivism."

Buckley later would be strongly criticized for confusing education with indoctrination, but he would only claim that he was not confused at all. Eight years later Buckley wrote that "education is largely a matter of indoctrination any way you look at it." Did he consider this a regrettable though unavoidable state of affairs? No. "I firmly believe," he would declare, "that most professors are to some extent indoctrinators, and that those who are not to any extent indoctrinators, should be."

God and Man at Yale was published by the Henry Regnery Company. Regnery Publishing today describes itself as "the nation's leading conservative publisher" and boasts that it has "published most of the great thinkers and writers of the conservative movement" over its sixty-year history. In 1951, however, the Henry Regnery Company was three years old. All of the few books it had published lost money, and the company was hanging by a thread. As soon as Henry Regnery read the manuscript, he was genuinely enthusiastic about publishing *God and Man at Yale*. But his enthusiasm grew when Will Buckley committed $19,000 (the equivalent of more than $155,000 today) for his son's book—$3,000 for printing costs and getting the book out faster, $10,000 for promotion, and $6,000 that went directly to Bill Buckley to fund a personal publicity tour.

With a four-page foreword by well-known, conservative journalist John Chamberlain, Regnery released the book in October 1951. It had been Will Buckley's idea to publish the book that month to coincide with Yale's 250th anniversary celebration. On the day of release, the manager of the Yale Co-op bookstore called Regnery with an urgent order for more copies; customers wanting the book had lined up on the sidewalk before the store opened. But it wasn't only Yale students and alumni who were interested in *God and Man at Yale*. By the end of November, the book was number sixteen on the *New York Times* bestseller list. Fortified by Will Buckley's promotional support, Regnery had optimistically printed a first run of five thousand copies. Within six months, it sold thirty-five thousand copies of *God and Man at Yale*. The book was such a phenomenon that in addition to book reviews in many periodicals, *Time* and *Newsweek* ran news articles and *Life* magazine published an editorial about it.

Some of the credit for the book's enormous success—or perhaps some of the blame—belongs to Yale University. As Dwight MacDonald put it at the time, Yale "reacted with all of the grace and agility of an elephant cornered by a mouse." Buckley had called the president of Yale, A. Whitney Griswold, during the previous summer to let him know the book was coming out. It must have been a call Bill delighted in making; Griswold was responsible for withdrawing Bill's invitation to deliver the Alumni Day speech a year earlier. Buckley was, in effect, telling Griswold: I've turned the speech that you did not let me give into a book. Buckley says that Griswold was "reserved" but polite, and that he told Buckley that of course he had the right to express his views. But Griswold was rattled. Word of the book had already reached him, and according to the rumor mill Will Buckley was going to send a copy to every Yale alumnus. (In fact, Will Buckley purchased just seventy-five copies of his son's book.) After a ham-handed attempt through an intermediary to try to persuade Bill not to publish, Griswold launched a campaign to disparage Buckley and the book. Griswold's assistant sent a letter to one prominent trustee stating that "we intend to take the offensive in this matter and not sit by waiting for complaints to roll in when the book is published."

In November 1951, the *Atlantic* published a three-page review of *God and Man at Yale* by McGeorge Bundy. Bundy is best known to history as national security adviser to presidents Kennedy and Johnson, and as an early supporter and later opponent of America's involvement in Vietnam. In 1951, Bundy was an associate professor of government at Harvard who had achieved recognition for coauthoring a book with Henry L. Stimson (who served in the cabinets of four presidents). Bundy was also a 1940 Yale grad who had been a member of Skull and Bones and an editor of the *Yale Daily News*. There is some evidence that Griswold may have lobbied the *Atlantic* to commission Bundy to write that review; there is definitive evidence that Bundy worked with Griswold when writing the piece. Buckley later wrote that Bundy's article was "adopted unofficially by Yale as its showcase defense," and indeed the university ordered two thousand reprints of the article to distribute to alumni and benefactors. This maneuvering proved important because Bundy's review became, for conservatives, an emblem of the arrogance of the liberal establishment.

Referring to the economic textbooks that Buckley had attacked as collectivist, Bundy quoted passages that praised free enterprise or characterized an economic goal of equality as "fundamentally inconsistent with the American focus on the advantages of aggressive private initiative based on income incentive." These portions of Bundy's piece are fair and quite damning to Buckley's book. Bundy, however, was not content with demonstrating that Buckley was wrong. He attacked Buckley's integrity and honor. "I find that the book is dishonest in its use of facts, false in its theory, and a discredit to its author and the writer of its introduction," Bundy wrote. "What [Buckley] has done is to take the flimsiest of evidence or no evidence at all, and ignore whatever goes against his thesis," he continued. Buckley denounced four economic texts as being slavishly devoted to Keynesian theory, wrote Bundy, "whereas in fact all four contain major differences from Keynes's position." Bundy did not bother to support that statement with evidence. "The error is unimportant," Bundy continued, "except that it shows Mr. Buckley's ignorance of what he is denouncing."

Bundy stated that "quotations and misquotations are given whatever meaning Mr. Buckley chooses to give them and not the meaning their authors intended." Accusing one of distorting another's words is a serious charge, and accusing one of misquoting another is even more serious. Fundamental fairness required that Bundy specifically identify such instances, but he did not do so. Bundy did not, for example, point to a single instance where Buckley misquoted someone. Bundy suggested that Buckley's unidentified errors were not the result of carelessness or ignorance alone. Buckley's "method is dishonest," wrote Bundy. William F. Buckley Jr. was, Bundy declared, "a twisted and ignorant young man."

Why did Bundy and Yale take Buckley's book so seriously? Why did they not simply ignore it? "*God and Man at Yale* has the somewhat larger significance that it is clearly an attempt to start an assault on the freedom of one of America's greatest and most conservative universities," Bundy mysteriously wrote.

"Most remarkable of all," wrote Bundy, "Mr. Buckley, who urges a return to what he considers to be Yale's true religious tradition, at no point says one word of the fact that he himself is an ardent Roman Catholic." Buckley complained that Yale was insufficiently Christian; he never urged that Yale teach Catholic precepts. Why then was Buckley required to identify himself as a Catholic? "In view of the pronounced and well-recognized difference between Protestant and Catholic views on education in America," Bundy continued, "and in view of Yale's Protestant history, it seems strange for any Roman Catholic to undertake to define the Yale religious tradition." There may be differences between Catholic and Protestant views about higher education, and it would have been fair to argue that the particular model that Buckley was advocating was a Catholic model that was inconsistent with Yale's traditional Protestant model. Even if that had been the case, however, Bundy's focus should have been on the substance of Buckley's arguments, not on what Bundy called Buckley's "special allegiance." After all, had Buckley been wrong about Yale's traditions, he would have been just as wrong had he been Protestant or Catholic. By making an issue of Buckley's religious affiliation, and without relating it to a substantive point, Bundy implied that a Catholic had no business criticizing Yale. His subtext appeared to be that Yale is a Protestant institution, and only Protestants could understand, or truly belong at, Yale.

Frank D. Ashburn, headmaster of the Brooks School and a trustee of Yale University, wrote a piece for the *Saturday Review of Literature* that rivaled Bundy's for hyperbolic vehemence. *God and Man at Yale*, Ashburn said, "has the glow and appeal of a fiery cross on a hillside at night. There will undoubtedly be robed figures who gather to it, but the hoods will not be academic. They will cover the face." Henry Regnery also felt the sting of establishment anger. The University of Chicago had awarded Regnery a contract to publish its prestigious Great Books series; now, because the Regnery name had been besmirched by publishing *God and Man at Yale*, the University of Chicago canceled the contract.[55]

Looking back from today's perspective, these attacks on Buckley may seem inconsequential. But at the time Buckley was a twenty-six-year-old whose first book had been published by what was then a fly-by-night publisher. Even at the time Buckley must have realized that Yale had blundered: The extraordinarily vicious attacks in prominent magazines of literature and culture would only stimulate further interest in *God and Man at Yale*. But this did not fully compensate for the pain. He was severely stung. It is quite clear from Buckley's reminiscences about the incident, written decades later, that his wounds never completely healed.

Buckley demanded, and got, from the *Atlantic* the right to reply, which he did in the December issue. Buckley's main object was to show that Bundy had not carefully read *God and Man at Yale* and had overlooked or misrepresented key passages. Buckley should have stopped there but he wound up replying in kind. "'Fascist,'" Buckley wrote, "has been used carelessly to describe persons and points of view; but it fits with unusual precision Mr. Bundy's advocacy of irresponsible, irreproachable education by an academic elite."

The Bundy-Ashburn attacks are infamous within conservative circles. Nearly every history of the conservative movement refers to them, as do the special introductions to the twenty-fifth and fiftieth anniversary editions of *God and Man at Yale*. Conservatives consider these attacks on the young Bill Buckley to be evidence of the hubris and perfidy of the Eastern Establishment. Bundy and Ashburn came from patrician families; both were graduates of Groton. Buckley had challenged one of the Establishment's favored institutions (Yale) and its one true faith (liberalism), and the Establishment responded with a concerted program of character assassination.

The Bundy-Ashburn attacks surely struck a familiar note with Will and Aloïse. The underlying message was the same as the one transmitted in more subtle ways by their aristocratic neighbors, namely, that the Buckleys were pretenders. "Much of what came was unexpected," Bill Buckley himself wrote of the incident. "I should have known better, of course," he continued, "for I had seen the Apparatus go to work on other dissenters from the Liberal orthodoxy." As William A. Rusher, who would later become publisher of *National Review*, put it, Buckley learned "that in 1951 serious attacks on an intellectual establishment as powerful as modern liberalism could expect the Full Treatment."

Conservatives believed then, and still believe today, that the Eastern Establishment would never have so libeled one of their own. As conservatives see it, liberals look down on them for their ideology and for their class and therefore feel free to treat them with contempt. Buckley, moreover, was guilty of rank betrayal: The Establishment had taken him to its breast by admitting him to Yale—and within Yale to the hallowed precincts of Fence Club, Skull and Bones, and the *Yale Daily News*—and then he ungratefully denounced Yale and the Establishment's fundamental values. He was owed no consideration.

Buckley, Rusher, and other conservatives also saw Yale's attack on Buckley as paralleling two earlier events: Boston Brahmin lawyer Joseph N. Welch's demolition of Senator Joseph McCarthy during the Army-McCarthy hearings ("Have you no sense of decency, sir, at long last? Have you left no sense of decency?"), and liberals choosing to believe upper-class Alger Hiss rather than the middle-class Whittaker Chambers during their dueling testimonies before Congress and the courts. Both liberals and conservatives saw the historical events as morality plays—but different morality plays. To liberals, they were morality plays about evidence, burden of proof, fair play, and in McCarthy's case, demagoguery. To conservatives, they were morality plays about class, ideology, and patriotism. Yale's attack on the young William F. Buckley Jr. confirmed that worldview.

Despite the attacks on him—indeed, in large measure *because* of the attacks on him—a young Bill Buckley had achieved a significant degree of visibility. Now he set out to put that asset to use.

CHAPTER 2

Choosing the Path

North Korea invaded South Korea on June 25, 1950, eleven days before Bill and Pat were married in Vancouver. Spearheaded by 150 Soviet T-34 tanks, the invaders overran Seoul within a few days. By September, they had driven most of the way to the Korea Strait, pushing American and South Korean forces—fighting under the flag of the United Nations—to the brink of a Dunkirk-style evacuation. But a heavy influx of additional troops, artillery, and antitank weapons bolstered UN forces, and they began to hold their own. Then UN forces turned the tide with a daring amphibious landing behind North Korean lines at Inchon, masterminded by General Douglas MacArthur. At MacArthur's urging, President Harry S. Truman then made a fateful decision: He ordered UN troops to cross the Thirty-eighth parallel into North Korea and pursue the retreating enemy troops to the Yalu River, which constituted the border with China. Truman's goal was to destroy the North Korean army and reunite all of Korea under anticommunist Syngman Rhee, but his decision provoked China into joining conflict. Chinese troops poured into Korea.[1]

MacArthur had previously advised Truman that there was little danger of Chinese intervention, and initially he was dismissive of the new threat. But as tough Chinese troops pushed back UN soldiers in brutal hand-to-hand fighting, a panicked MacArthur blamed Washington. First he complained that Washington was providing inadequate support; then he complained he was being restrained from taking necessary military action. MacArthur, a popular hero of World War II, publicly demanded permission to escalate the conflict. He wanted to blockade Chinese ports and bomb targets inside China, with atomic weapons if necessary. Truman resisted these demands. Republicans took Mac-Arthur's side. Starting what would be a long-running refrain, Republicans accused Truman of being "soft on communism." The tactic reaped political benefits for Republicans, who won additional congressional seats in the 1950 midterm elections. In a California contest for an open United States Senate seat, a young congressman named Richard M. Nixon defeated his opponent, Congresswoman Helen Gahagan Douglas, by arguing that Douglas had often voted the same way as a New York congressman who always voted the Communist Party line. Douglas, Nixon declared, was "pink right down to her underwear." In Ohio, Robert A. Taft decisively won a reelection to the Senate notwithstanding charges by his Democratic opponent that Taft's isolationist position of opposing NATO had been a boon to the Soviets.[2]

Despite being the target of incendiary rhetoric accusing him of being soft on communism, Truman continued to resist MacArthur's demands to widen the war. Recognizing that fighting on the Korean Peninsula was going to be long and bitter, on December 15, 1950—about a month after the midterm elections, and while Buckley was writing *God and Man at Yale*—President Truman made a televised address in which he called for full mobilization. "Our homes, our nation, all of the things we believe in are in great danger," he told the nation. Making what would be an often-repeated Cold War mistake of perceiving all communist countries as a monolith, Truman went on to say, "This danger has been created by the rulers of the Soviet Union."

William F. Buckley Jr. did not want to be recalled for Korea. His college adviser, Professor Willmoore Kendall, suggested that Buckley join the Central Intelligence Agency—a draft-avoidance route that was popular with Yale grads. Buckley agreed, and Kendall arranged for him to be interviewed by the CIA's covert branch. As it happens, the person who interviewed Buckley in a CIA safe house in Washington, D.C., was James Burnham, who was then clandestinely working with the CIA and would later become Buckley's second-in-command at *National Review*. Buckley was accepted and spent three months training in covert work during the summer of 1951. After his training, Buckley was then assigned to Mexico City, where his station chief was E. Howard

Hunt, who later became notorious as one of the Watergate burglars.*
Buckley's chief assignment was to try to help promote anticommunism
in student organizations. Bill found the work less than exciting. Moreover, publication of *God and Man at Yale*, and Yale's attack on the book,
occurred while he was in Mexico. Defending himself from afar made
him yearn to be back in the States where he could enter the fray more
effectively. In February 1952, therefore, he resigned from the CIA.

Shortly after Bill returned to the States, Will wrote a letter of advice
to his son about his future. Bill had made it known he wanted to find
some way to become a spokesperson for conservatism. "If you are going
into politics, or if without going into politics, you want to continue to
discuss political questions, you should spend a couple of years in study,"
Will advised. Will recommended a year or two at Oxford or Cambridge. "The English have an innate mastery of politics and government
which is not reflected in their stupid incursion into Socialism," he told
his son.[3] Henry Regnery also advised Bill to pursue graduate study.
Regnery suggested studying economics under Friedrich A. Hayek, the
expatriate Austrian economist at the University of Chicago who had
created a stir with his iconic 1944 libertarian work *The Road to Serfdom*.
There were other possibilities as well. Bill applied to the graduate school,
to pursue an advanced degree in political science, and to the law school
at Yale, and was accepted by both. But he was not sure he wanted to
pursue graduate study.

Bill had been mulling over what to do next for a while, even before
writing his book. During his senior year in college, a friend had invited
Bill home for a weekend and introduced him to his father, Archibald
MacLeish, the renowned poet, playwright, and former librarian of
Congress who ultimately won three Pulitzer Prizes. Bill, always willing

---

*Bill and Pat became lifelong friends with Hunt and his wife. After Hunt was arrested
for Watergate, he told Buckley enough about his work for the Nixon Whitehouse to
make Buckley suspect that Hunt and fellow Watergate burglar G. Gordon Liddy had
been instructed to assassinate Jack Anderson, an investigative journalist whom Nixon
considered an enemy. Buckley, who placed a high premium on friendship and loyalty,
helped pay Hunt's lawyers. After anguished consideration, Buckley decided that he
was not certain enough about the assassination plot to report that to authorities. He
recused himself at *National Review* on all editorial decisions regarding Watergate,
however.

to get advice from the best, asked MacLeish what he thought about pursuing graduate work. "That would be very good, it would be very helpful in causing you to know what you think," the distinguished writer told the young man. Surely MacLeish, who himself had earned a law degree from Harvard, was taken aback when Bill replied, "No, I know what I think. The question is whether this will be helpful to me as a salesman. Will this credential help me in getting heard?"[4]

After returning to the States, Bill decided that graduate work was of little benefit, either for educational or credential-building value. Instead, he would immediately pursue a career in conservative journalism. After considering offers from both of the then-existing conservative journals of opinion—*American Mercury* and the *Freeman*—he accepted a position of associate editor with *American Mercury*, which had the larger circulation. The magazine was headquartered in New York, and Bill and Pat—who were then expecting a child, Christopher—purchased a home in Stamford, Connecticut. The fifteen-room house was on Wallack's Point, which juts into Long Island Sound. A rolling lawn descended to shore. The home was convenient not only for commuting into New York City, but also for sailing, for which Bill would develop a great passion. Money was not then, nor would it ever be, an issue for Bill and Pat, both of whom were children of superrich parents. Will had already established trust funds for his children, and with his father's permission, Bill raised the down payment on the home by liquidating $65,000 (the equivalent of more than half a million today) of principal from his fund.[5] Bill and Pat would live happily on Wallack's Point for the rest of their lives.

Buckley's tenure at the *American Mercury* was not long or happy, however. As was the case with his dad, Bill found that working for someone else was not his style. Within months—when *American Mercury*'s editor declined to publish an article that he wrote titled "The Plight of the Liberals"—he resigned. Although the *Freeman* renewed its job offer, Bill decided instead to begin work on a new book. After discussing several possibilities with Henry Regnery, Buckley decided to collaborate with his brother-in-law, Brent Bozell, who was then at Yale Law School, on a book that would defend Senator Joseph McCarthy from his critics.

* * *

Joseph McCarthy strode into the national limelight on February 9, 1950, in a speech to the Women's Republican Club of Wheeling, West Virginia. "Today we are engaged in a final, all-out battle between communism and atheism and Christianity," he told the club.[6] If America were to lose this struggle, he continued, it would be "because of the enemies within." Who were these traitors? Not immigrants or minorities, but those with the "the finest homes, the finest college education, the finest jobs in Government we can give. This is glaringly true in the State Department. There the young men who were born with silver spoons in their mouths are the ones who have been the worst." Then McCarthy made the claim that made the speech famous. He held up a sheet of paper that he claimed contained the names of 205 people who were working in the State Department despite the fact that they were known by Secretary of State Dean Acheson to be communists. McCarthy never produced such a list. Nor did he reveal that he had calculated the number by subtracting the number of employees who had been discharged for security reasons from the number about whom issues had been raised in preliminary security screenings—issues that included alcoholism, gambling, homosexuality, entertaining in their homes whites and blacks at the same time, or having been described as "a bit leftist" in their political views.

McCarthy made this speech less than three weeks after a jury found that a former State Department official named Alger Hiss had been a Soviet spy—an event that surely suggested to McCarthy that he could gain political mileage hunting communists in governmental agencies. McCarthy was unable to document his charges, but that did not slow him down. He simply changed his allegations, and quickly expanded his repertoire by denouncing people as disloyal because of their associations—often decades old or attenuated—with so-called communist-front organizations or with others who had associations with such organizations. Most responsible observers considered his methods little more than smears and character assassination.

For reasons that scholars debate to this day, the leaders of the Republican Party failed to repudiate McCarthy. Eisenhower was privately appalled but publicly silent.[7] Robert A. Taft uncharacteristically egged on McCarthy, publicly suggesting that McCarthy should "keep talking and if one case doesn't work out, he should proceed with another."[8] On

June 1, 1950, however, the highly regarded Republican from Maine, Margaret Chase Smith, rose on the floor of the Senate and in her quiet voice made an impassioned speech. By not reigning in McCarthy, Smith said, the Senate was allowing itself to be "debased to the level of a forum of hate and character assassination sheltered by the shield of congressional immunity." Six other liberal Republicans joined this so-called Declaration of Conscience. The following month a Senate Foreign Relations Subcommittee chaired by Senator Millard E. Tydings, a Democrat from Maryland, issued a report stating that McCarthy's allegations constituted "the most nefarious campaign of half-truths and untruths in the history of this republic" and was "an effort to inflame the American people with a wave of hysteria and fear."[9] It was just about this time that North Korea invaded the South, and McCarthy was a beneficiary of the invasion. Suddenly America was in a shooting war with communists, and MacArthur was also accusing Washington of being soft on communists. Even though most Americans had unfavorable opinions of McCarthy, some feared he might be right about the Establishment seeking to protect hidden communist agents and sympathizers, and politicians became more reticent about taking him on.

Even so, most commentators would have considered defending McCarthy a fool's errand. What possessed Buckley and Bozell to take on this project? They recognized that McCarthy was crude, careless, overzealous, and sloppy, if not reckless and demagogic. Yet something had drawn the brothers-in-law to McCarthy. While others saw McCarthy as a persecutor, Buckley and Bozell saw him as a man who was himself being persecuted—by the same Eastern Establishment that had attacked Buckley for *God and Man at Yale*. Buckley and Bozell's decision to defend McCarthy needs to be placed in greater context.

On August 3, 1948, Whittaker Chambers, a forty-seven-year-old senior editor at *Time* magazine, testified before the House Committee on Un-American Activities, popularly known as HUAC. His testimony shocked the nation. Chambers said that in the 1930s he had been a functionary in an underground communist apparatus and helped operate a secret cell that had infiltrated the American government. He named the seven members of the cell. One was Alger Hiss. Hiss, who was then president of the Carnegie Endowment for International Peace, had previously held a number of influential government positions. Three years earlier he had been a high-ranking aide within the State Department, high enough to join the entourage that accompanied President Franklin D. Roosevelt to the Yalta Conference. At Yalta, Roosevelt had made certain agreements with Joseph Stalin and Winston Churchill relating to postwar reorganization of areas seized by the Allies from Germany and Japan, as well as to the formation of the United Nations. Voices on the political right argued that Roosevelt conceded too much to Stalin at Yalta. Some darkly accused Roosevelt of "selling out" American interests. If Chambers's testimony was true, it meant that an aide in the American delegation at Yalta had been—at least some years before Yalta, and perhaps still—a secret communist agent. For conspiracy buffs, there was even a famous photo of the so-called Big Three at Yalta with Alger Hiss in the background.

Alger Hiss immediately sent HUAC a telegram, in which he said, "I do not know Mr. Chambers and, so far as I am aware, have never laid eyes on him. There is no basis for the statements about me to your committee." Hiss asked for permission to appear before HUAC himself, and did so two days later, amid high drama. Hiss was more persuasive than Chambers. Chambers was an overweight, rumpled, and lugubrious man who mumbled. As an admitted communist underground operative, he had a history of lies and deception. Hiss, by contrast, was handsome, urbane, and impeccably tailored, and notwithstanding the trying circumstances in which he found himself, he was self-confident, cheerful, even humorous. He denied Chambers's accusations categorically, and seemed genuinely puzzled about why Chambers had made them. He said he was disappointed that Chambers wasn't present. When Representative Karl Mundt of South Dakota, chairman of the committee, asked Hiss whether he participated in drafting parts of the Yalta agreement, Hiss answered, "I think it is accurate and not an immodest statement to say that I did to some extent, yes." By the end of the day, Hiss won over most observers, including most of the committee. Mundt told Hiss that he wanted "to express the appreciation of the Committee for your very cooperative attitude, and for your forthright statements."

This was a bitter pill for HUAC, which had hoped that the Chambers-sparked investigation would improve its own dire political fortunes. While HUAC's ostensible purpose was to ferret out communists in government, many believed its real objective was to discredit the New Deal by creating suspicions about government agencies.[10] In 1938, HUAC's chairman, Congressman Martin Dies of Texas, charged that the "gigantic bureaucracy" of the New Deal was filled with "hundreds of left-wingers and radicals who do not believe in our system of private enterprise." Thus Dies and HUAC attempted to lump together everyone on the political left—communists, radicals, socialists, and liberals—implying that they were all cut from the same cloth, and all treasonous. Dies infamously charged that there were "not less than two thousand outright Communists and Party-liners still holding jobs in government," and specifically included within these ranks three men who served in President Roosevelt's cabinet. HUAC had largely failed to back up those wild-eyed charges, however. It was skilled at generating newspaper headlines and a flop at finding communists, and by 1948 its membership included some of Congress's greatest dolts. HUAC members had believed Whittaker Chambers would help it deliver the goods—that he would provide firsthand evidence of real communists in government. But after they heard Alger Hiss, they feared Chambers would bring them to grief. "We're ruined," one member remarked when the committee gathered privately after its session with Hiss.

In his swearing contest with Whittaker Chambers—in which each man claimed, under oath, to be telling the truth—Hiss enjoyed another advantage. Chambers had come from a well-educated but impoverished and dysfunctional family. He had attended Columbia University but never graduated. He had started at *Time* on a bottom rung and climbed up on merit alone. Hiss, by contrast, was figuratively a card-carrying member of the Establishment. He was an alumnus of Johns Hopkins University and Harvard Law School, where he had become a protégé of Felix Frankfurter. After law school, he had clerked for Oliver Wendell Holmes. His friends included the distinguished jurist Jerome Frank and Secretary of State Dean Acheson. Hiss's pedigree made some members of the Establishment almost incapable of disbelieving him, even as evidence supporting Chambers emerged. This evidence included sixty-five retyped or recopied State Department documents that Chambers alleged Hiss had given to him, four pages of which were in Hiss's own handwriting.*

No one was more sensitive to this aspect of the episode than Whittaker Chambers. In his autobiography, *Witness*, published some years after his testimony, Chambers wrote that Hiss had "put down roots that made him one with the matted forest floor of American upper class, enlightened middle class, liberal and official life." In another spot in his book, Chambers described an incident when he is accosted by "a young socialite of an old and good family, and an M.A. or a Ph.D." who "with the voice of Bryn Mawr but the snarl of a fishwife" demands, "How dare you, how dare you call us Communists?" Chambers wrote, "It was no use to explain to her that what I had said was, not that she and others like her were Communists, but that they were non-Communists who were letting the Communists lead them by the nose." In what would become his most-quoted line in *Witness*, Chambers said, "The simple fact is that when I took up my little sling and aimed at Communists, I also hit something else. What I hit was the forces of that great socialist revolution, which, in the name of liberalism, spasmodically, incompletely, somewhat formlessly, but always in the same direction, has been inching its ice cap over the nation for two decades."[11]

Thus did Chambers conflate class, liberalism, socialism, and communism. Chambers was suggesting that liberalism was the quasi-official ideology of the upper class, and that it had become a façade behind which communists were advancing a socialist revolution. Liberalism, in other words, was not controlled by liberals. It was surreptitiously controlled by communists, and liberals were too blind to see that they were pushing a Trojan horse toward the gates of Western civilization. This theme ran throughout *Witness* like an underground river that visibly

---

*Because the statute of limitations had run out on his acts of espionage, Hiss was indicted for lying to Congress when he denied having been a Soviet spy. The first trial ended in a hung jury, but a second jury convicted Hiss. Although debates long raged over who told the truth, the present-day consensus among historians is that Alger Hiss was in fact a Soviet spy. E.g., G. Edward White, *Alger Hiss's Looking-Glass Wars: The Covert Life of a Soviet Spy* (2005); Allen Weinstein, *Perjury: The Hiss-Chambers Case*, rev. ed. 1997). See also Sam Tanenhaus, *Whittaker Chambers: A Biography* (1998); Susan Jacoby, *Alger Hiss and the Battle for History* (2010).

breaks the surface only now and then. Chambers was a brilliantly evocative writer, and his theme was all the more powerful because it was
suggested, implied, and alluded to rather than stated expressly.

Witness was a sensation. *Saturday Review* published the first chapter
as a special feature, and sold half a million extra copies of that issue
on newsstands. The book was a national bestseller. It is gripping—
throughout all of its 799 pages—and when the book was published in
1952 the Chambers-Hiss case was still a hotly debated melodrama. *Witness*, moreover, is far more than a spy story; it is, in its own way, a
manifesto for a particular worldview. It became one of the half-dozen
books that most influenced the development of modern American conservatism. It is so powerfully written, in fact, that some people, such as
the journalist Robert D. Novak, credit it for converting them to conservatism. Buckley was one of the people on whom *Witness* left a mark. "I
was shaken by that book," he remarked. "I wasn't shaken into a position
I hadn't already occupied, but if possible I felt more passionate about the
responsibilities of people who dissented against a particular trend in
Western history."[12]

The book's central thesis—conveyed through a variety of devices—is
that the world was facing a single, unified struggle between the forces of
good and evil. *Witness* is akin to a nonfiction *Lord of the Rings*. In J. R. R.
Tolkien's trilogy (published in 1954 and 1955), the struggle is between
the forces of good—comprised of hobbits, elves, dwarfs, and men—and
the forces of evil, consisting of orcs and other unholy creatures unified
and controlled by the Dark Lord Sauron. *Witness* portrays a similar
struggle, with the forces of good being Christianity and Western civilization and the forces of evil being atheistic communism. As Chambers
saw it, the fate of the earth hung in the balance. "At every point," he
wrote, "religion and politics interlace, and must do so more acutely as the
conflict between the two great camps of men—those who reject and
those who worship God—becomes irrepressible. Those camps are not
only outside, but also within nations." Moreover, as throughout most of
Tolkien's trilogy, the atmosphere of *Witness* is melancholic and gloomy,
as the forces of evil appear all but certain to overwhelm those of the
good. Near the beginning, Chambers related what he told his wife
when he decided to leave the Communist Party: "You know, we are
leaving the winning world for the losing world."

When the HUAC committee members first heard Alger Hiss, they feared they had smashed themselves upon the rocks by presenting Whittaker Chambers to the nation. They dumped the mess into the lap of a junior member of the committee named Richard M. Nixon, making him chair of a subcommittee tasked with determining which of the two witnesses was telling the truth. Nixon helped develop evidence that showed that Chambers was telling the truth, and made himself into a prominent national politician in the process. Joseph McCarthy saw the same kind of opportunity—although, unlike Nixon, he thought making accusations without doing the hard work of determining their validity was enough. Nevertheless, McCarthy did sense how to play on the same chords of class and suspicion as did Chambers.

The note of class resentment surely resonated with Bill Buckley. The Establishment had socially shunned his parents and viciously attacked him for *God and Man at Yale*. In addition, Buckley and Bozell could identify with McCarthy because they were all Catholics. (Bozell converted to Catholicism shortly before entering Yale.) Catholics generally saw McCarthy in a more positive light than did the public at large. A Gallup Poll taken at the height of his popularity showed that 56 percent of Catholics—as compared to only 46 percent of Protestants and 12 percent of Jews—supported McCarthy.[13]

Why were Catholics more pro-McCarthy than others? Catholics saw McCarthy as one of their own. "To be Catholic in the 1950s," writes historian Patrick Allitt, "was to be aware of oneself as a member of a minority group, set apart from the rest of society by a pattern of beliefs, ritual actions, liturgical practices, food taboos, and even a distinctive view of the nation's history in Western civilization."[14] In addition, Catholics as a group were more vehemently anticommunist than the public at large. They had a greater tendency to see the Cold War as an apocalyptic struggle between good and evil. Communism's belief in atheism, and its desire to extinguish religious belief and destroy the church, had special salience. Again, as Allitt puts it, Catholics "saw themselves as champions of Western civilization, the heritage of Christendom, and drew from their religious faith and tradition principles they believed could alone draw that civilization back from the brink of catastrophe."[15] Moreover, because they had long felt the sting of discrimination and disdain from the ruling Protestant aristocracy, Catholics were more ready than most to believe the worst about the elite. Historian David H. Bennett has written that "McCarthy's persona was that of the perfect champion of every man against the polished elites who were betraying America from their positions of privilege."[16] And because they believed in original sin and the inherently imperfect nature of man, many Catholics were more forgiving of the flawed messenger in service of a noble cause.

In addition, because of their theology and training, some Catholics were more supportive of orthodoxy and less enamored with dissenting ideas. Whereas liberal Protestants and Jews had greater faith that truth would prevail in the marketplace of ideas, conservative Catholics were more concerned about people being misled. They were more apt to worry about dissenting ideas—especially those expressing viewpoints favored by potential enemies of the nation—weakening national unity and will. Hunting for subversives and expressing intolerance of subversive ideas made more sense to them.

Catholic leaders such as Francis Cardinal Spellman and Monsignor Fulton J. Sheen were zealous anticommunists who often accused Washington of being soft on communism. The Knights of Columbus, a Catholic fraternal organization with six hundred thousand members, energetically supported efforts to remove communists and other radicals from positions of responsibility. Even liberal Catholic politicians often reacted differently to McCarthy than did their non-Catholic counterparts. Robert F. Kennedy served on McCarthy's staff, and John F. Kennedy never criticized McCarthy during their time in Congress together. JFK even expressed the view that "McCarthy may have something."[17]

Responsible analysts across the ideological spectrum today agree that, in fact, McCarthy had nothing, and, moreover, that he was exploiting fears about a problem that no longer existed. In the 1930s, some Americans in government—such as Alger Hiss—had become enamored with communism and betrayed their nation. As George Kennan put it, communist infiltration "really existed and assumed proportions which, while never overwhelming, were also not trivial."[18] But when Stalin made his pact with Hitler in 1939, scales fell from the eyes of these Americans. They no longer saw Stalin as the leader of a great utopian experiment but as a cynical and expedient dictator, and they recognized that totalitarian regimes, whether of the left or right, were totalitarian regimes. With few exceptions they turned against the Soviet Union and communism. Whittaker Chambers was the quintessential example of the genre, although through embarrassment and fear many, unlike Chambers, did not publicly confess their sins. There continued to be spies, of course, and always will be. But if we can draw a distinction between communist infiltration of American government by significant numbers of people with compromised loyalties and espionage by a relatively few spies, it is fair to say that the problem of infiltration largely ceased to exist by the time McCarthy made his speech in Wheeling, West Virginia. Historian Paul Johnson writes that by the time of McCarthy's speech "most of the real Communists in public service had been detected, dismissed, indicted, convicted or imprisoned."[19]

When Buckley and Bozell sent him the manuscript of their McCarthy book, Henry Regnery knew that he had a problem. The draft was 250,000 words—three times longer than he had expected. Even worse, it read like a legal brief. The heart of the book was a detailed exegesis of McCarthy's most prominent accusations and the evidence supporting or contradicting them. Regnery told the authors they had to cut 75,000 words. Buckley was already bored with the project. "Eighteen months of research and writing is a long enough time to spend seeking out an eighth allegory in Dante's *Inferno*; it is a very very long time to spend on the question whether Esther Brunauer was ever a member of the Joint Anti-Fascist Refugee League," he later remarked.[20] Buckley hired William S. Schlamm to do the edits. "Willi," a former communist who had emigrated from Austria, was a columnist for the *Freeman*. Schlamm made the edits, and also wrote a prologue for the book.

McCarthy and His Enemies: The Record and its Meaning was released by the Henry Regnery Company in March 1954. The timing was not fortuitous. That same month CBS began broadcasting a series of devastating investigative reports about McCarthy by Edward R. Murrow on Murrow's TV program *See It Now*. CBS invited McCarthy to appear on the show to respond. McCarthy asked that Buckley appear on his behalf instead. CBS declined to accept a surrogate, and McCarthy appeared in his own defense in April. He was his own worst enemy. Surly and bombastic, he called Murrow—one of the most respected journalists in America—"the leader and cleverest of the jackal pack which is always found at the throat of anyone who dares to expose individual Communists and traitors," confirming for viewers that he was as demagogic as previous shows had depicted. Two months later a Boston lawyer named Joseph Welch skillfully lured McCarthy into fully disgracing himself on national television during the Army-McCarthy Senate hearings. Even McCarthy realized that he had been effectively discredited. He responded by accelerating the pace at which he was drinking himself to death, dying of cirrhosis of the liver three years later.

Because it reached the bookstores just as McCarthy imploded, few people read *McCarthy and His Enemies*. Most people assumed that the book was a full-throated defense of McCarthy, but that was not quite correct. Their careful sifting of the evidence led Buckley and Bozell to concede that McCarthy's charges were sometimes unsupported, or worse. "It is clear that he has been guilty of a number of exaggerations, some of them reckless; and perhaps some of them have unjustly damaged the persons concerned beyond the mere questioning of their loyalty. For these transgressions we have neither the desire to defend him nor the means to do so," the coauthors wrote. Regarding McCarthy's allegations concerning newspaper columnist Drew Pearson, they wrote, "Drew Pearson definitely *was* smeared by McCarthy." In spite of that, they argued that "*McCarthy's record is nevertheless not only much better than his critics allege but, given his métier, extremely good.*"[21]

Buckley and Bozell tried to portray their view of McCarthyism as representing merely a difference in emphasis: They believed that the danger of communist subversion was so great as to warrant rooting out anyone in government with questionable views or associations while liberals placed a greater emphasis on protecting civil liberties. They did not conflate liberalism with communism, as had Chambers; and they said they were questioning the judgment, not the loyalty, of liberals. "The fact that a vigorous security program is geared to the national interest, while the kind Liberals want is not, raises interesting questions about the wisdom and vision of Liberals; but not about their loyalty," they wrote. "The issues involved in hard-hitting loyalty programs are issues that separate Americans from Americans, not Americans from Communists."[22]

Yet they immediately qualified that view. "It is, in any case," they wrote in the very next sentence, "a pretty precarious business to impute pro-Communism to someone on the basis of that person's stand on a single issue." In other words, we won't accuse you of being a communist sympathizer based solely on your position about loyalty programs, but we may well do so based on our evaluation of a more complete sampling of your political opinions. At one point, for example, the coauthors defended McCarthy's attack on Adlai Stevenson, the Democratic candidate for president two years earlier. McCarthy, they said, never attempted to connect Stevenson with communism. "McCarthy reached, not for a red paint brush," they wrote, "but for a list of some of Stevenson's top advisers: Archibald MacLeish, Bernard DeVoto, and Arthur Schlesinger, Jr."[23] (This, of course, is the same Archibald MacLeish from whom Buckley had sought advice about whether to go to graduate school.) McCarthy's point, Buckley and Bozell said, was not that these men were communists; it was that "they were Liberals—atheistic, soft-headed, anti-anti-Communist, ADA Liberals" and that "this was sufficient reason for rejecting the candidate for whom they were serving as" puppet masters.

Although the authors state that this is the point of what McCarthy was saying, the words they use to describe liberals appear to be their own. Either way, it is a description that—if it does not paint liberals red—at least paints them pink. The description first indiscriminately characterized liberals as atheists, with the unspoken suggestion that in this respect liberals were just like communists. (The coauthors offered no evidence that most, or even many, liberals were atheists, and could not have done so as more than 90 percent of Americans reportedly believed in God.[24]) The adjective "soft-headed" implied that liberals were warmhearted, or at least permissive, toward communists. The adjective "anti-anti-Communist" was particularly sly. It implied that liberals were unreasonably hostile to communist hunters. Moreover, because everyone learned in mathematics classes that multiplying a negative number by another negative number yields a positive number, the term "anti-anti-Communist" nudged one toward the view that liberals are procommunist. The adjective "ADA" completed the job. Americans for Democratic Action was the staunchly anticommunist liberal group founded during the New Deal by Eleanor Roosevelt, Walter Reuther,

John Kenneth Galbraith, Arthur Schlesinger Jr., Reinhold Niebuhr, and Hubert Humphrey. Mentioning ADA implied that the comments were meant to apply to all liberals, even those who claimed to be firmly anticommunist.

Buckley and Bozell argued that one of the goals of McCarthyism was to stigmatize those who espoused communist ideas. They called this the "new conformity," and they endorsed it. Once again, they claimed to want to draw a distinction between communism and liberalism. It is, they said, "only *Communist* ideas that are beyond the pale."[25] But, once again, they fudged. They acknowledged that the description of liberals might be perceived as excluding liberals from the "limits of tolerable opinion," but they suggested there was no need to worry as people as celebrated as MacLeish, DeVoto, and Schlesinger were in no danger of being read out of the community. Then they added an ominous warning: "Some day, the patience of Americans will at last be exhausted, and we will strike out against Liberals, not because they are treacherous like Communists, but because with James Burnham, we will conclude 'that they are mistaken in their predictions, false in their analyses, wrong in their advice, and through the results of their actions injurious to the interests of the nation.'"[26]

The authors, moreover, were not just subtly questioning the patriotism of liberals, but of the American government. The central thesis of their book was that while McCarthy the man was sometimes irresponsible, McCarthyism served the country well. "McCarthyism," they wrote, "is primarily the maintenance of a steady flow of criticism (raillery, the Liberals call it) calculated to pressure the President, Cabinet members, high officials, and above all the political party in power, to get on with the elimination of security risks in government."[27] This implied that the president, the secretary of state, and other high government officials did not genuinely wish to eliminate security risks. Why else would it be necessary to pressure them—through the sometimes reckless methods of Joseph McCarthy—to root out communist spies and sympathizers? And because McCarthyism began during the Truman administration and was raging on under the Eisenhower administration, Buckley and Bozell were suggesting that neither of these presidents—from different parties, with different secretaries of state—were trustworthy.

Buckley and Bozell fully understood the radical nature of their argument. McCarthy's method, which they endorsed, was, they said, "in many respects as revolutionary as the Communist movement itself."[28] Because of its legalistic style and unpropitious timing, *McCarthy and His Enemies* did not get as much attention as *God and Man at Yale* enjoyed, and because of its radicalism, the attention it received from the mainstream press was unfavorable. The book, however, reinforced Buckley's reputation as an enfant terrible of the right. He was not someone who shirked difficult questions, was reluctant to take hard-edged positions, or offend the Establishment. And despite the clever blurring of lines, Buckley and Bozell knew where the lines were and said enough to claim they had not crossed them. Patrick Allitt reflects the consensus view when he says that *McCarthy and His Enemies* was "the only defense of McCarthyism that was even partially intellectually plausible."[29]

However, Buckley had now positioned himself in a way that would have long-term consequences. He had adopted an attitude that would become increasingly problematic as conservatism rose to power and others less subtle sought to emulate him. And in questioning the patriotism of two presidents, even obliquely, he had positioned himself dangerously close to conspiracy theorists and paranoids. In the future, he would find it vital to more clearly separate himself from the kooks.

For the moment, Buckley could enjoy his growing notoriety. Around the time of their book's release, he and Bozell were invited back to their alma mater to debate two Yale Law School professors, on the subject of McCarthy and McCarthyism. At first glance, this may have appeared to be a mismatch of grown-ups versus kids. The professors were thirty-seven and fifty-seven, respectively, while Buckley and Bozell were in their twenties. But, of course, Buckley and Bozell had been a star debating team. According to the *Yale Daily News*, the former debaters trounced the professors.[30]

Buckley was becoming known as a galvanizing speaker. When he was invited to address the National Republican Club in New York later that spring, the hall in which the event was held, which seats one thousand people, was full—and another thousand people listened to his speech over loudspeakers across the street in Bryant Park. His brashness was on display the following year when he was invited to debate James Wechsler, a liberal columnist and editor of the *New York Post*, at

Harvard University. When he rose to speak before a large audience in Lamont Library, Buckley remarked that he was glad to see that Professor Arthur Schlesinger Jr. was in the audience. Schlesinger, of course, was a distinguished historian who had won his first Pulitzer Prize some years earlier, as well as being a prominent liberal. Grinning, Buckley added, "His many books would be dangerous if they weren't so boring."[31]

Buckley wanted to start a conservative magazine.[32] He knew that during the New Deal, the *Nation* and the *New Republic* played important roles in developing and defining liberalism. Conservatives needed the same thing, but both *American Mercury* and the *Freeman* were too troubled to be useful. While brother-in-law Brent went to Washington to join Senator Joseph McCarthy's staff (after briefly sampling law practice in San Francisco), Bill went to work for one of his father's companies, Catawba Corporation, in Manhattan. Both father and son knew this was a temporary resting place; Bill was not interested in a career in business. But over the four months or so that he worked closely with his father, the two grew exceptionally close.[33] Meanwhile, Bill looked into purchasing either the *Freeman* or the national conservative newspaper *Human Events*, but he did not succeed in persuading the owners to sell—at least not to a twenty-nine-year-old.

Willi Schlamm, the man whom Buckley had hired to edit *McCarthy and His Enemies*, also wanted to start a conservative magazine. Schlamm, then fifty, had experience. He had edited left-wing magazines in Austria and Czechoslovakia before fleeing to the United States to escape Hitler's invading armies. He had written for the *New Leader*, worked for Henry Luce at Time, Inc., and was then writing a column for the *Freeman*. Schlamm knew that starting a new magazine required money, and that Buckley came from a family with resources. In the summer of 1954, Schlamm invited Bill and Pat to his and his wife's home in Vermont, and during the visit Schlamm proposed to Bill that they start a new conservative journal together. Buckley agreed. Schlamm told Buckley that to avoid the kind of internecine warfare that was then destroying the *Freeman*, Buckley should own all of the voting stock in their new venture, thereby giving him total control. Buckley agreed with that suggestion too—something that turned out to be of great consequence not only to the magazine but also to the conservative movement as a whole, and something Schlamm would come to regret.

Buckley's first task was to raise money. His father contributed $100,000 to the new venture (the equivalent of more than three quarters of a million dollars today). But much more was required. To Bill, going hat in hand to potential supporters was distasteful. He did not then realize that this was going to be a never-ending responsibility. He did not expect that it was an iron law that opinion journals must lose money, and he expected his magazine to become self-sustaining. But even after becoming the most successful journal of opinion in history, *National Review* would still have to go begging for contributions. Had Buckley known this then, it may have given him pause. As a laissez-faire conservative, he believed the magazine should not only be self-supporting but profitable, and he expected to reach that goal within two years.

The estimate was that the magazine would need $550,000 to sustain itself until it went into the black. Despite his dislike for it, Buckley was good at raising money. He was charming, and he was selling a cause in which he passionately believed. He worked every angle he could think of: He approached friends and business associates of his father; he contacted wealthy members of the political right across the country; he asked Brent Bozell to arrange for Joseph McCarthy to send letters to his friends and supporters asking them to support the new magazine.[34]

Buckley and Schlamm had planned to publish the first issue of their magazine in April 1955, but Will Buckley underwent cancer surgery that month and suffered a stroke during the operation. Bill's attention was diverted; the start date was postponed. Fund-raising was also a problem. By the fall of 1955, Buckley had raised $290,000 in addition to his father's contribution. Early benefactors of the magazine included Roger Milliken, president of Deering-Milliken & Co., the nation's largest textile manufacturer; Lemuel R. Boulware, a vice president at General Electric Company; Texas oilman Lloyd H. Smith, and Jeremiah Milbank Jr., a New York financier whose grandfather made a family fortune by investing in condensed milk, who had been a Yale classmate of Bill's brother John.[35] But this left Bill more than $100,000 short, and discouraged. He considered postponing the venture further, but Willi Schlamm urged proceeding anyway. He told Buckley that once the magazine acquired twenty-five thousand readers, its subscribers would not let it fail—a prediction that turned out to be correct.

Buckley's other major focus was recruiting editors and writers. The magazine would rise or fall on the prominence and talent of the people it published, and the trajectory of the new conservatism would be determined by the people Buckley selected. Buckley very much wanted Whittaker Chambers to join the venture.[36] Chambers was not only a hero to the right; he was one of the finest writers of the day. At first Chambers agreed. Buckley was thrilled. But soon thereafter the mercurial Chambers balked. Buckley and Schlamm, who believed he had a special rapport with Chambers as they both were former communists and had been colleagues at Time, Inc., worked mightily to keep him on board. Both wrote and telephoned frequently. Buckley and Pat hosted Chambers for a couple of days at their home in Stamford, after which Buckley and Schlamm tried to close the deal with Chambers at a meeting at the Barclay Hotel in Manhattan in November 1954. Chambers refused to commit. They kept trying over the course of the next year, making their final plea just before the first issue of *National Review* was released, driving all the way down to Maryland to visit Chambers at his farm. Chambers said no. Buckley thought the problem was that Chambers—a devoted supporter of Richard Nixon—thought *National Review* editors preferred Senator William F. Knowland for the presidency. Eisenhower had suffered a heart attack, and many thought he might not run again in 1956. Chambers's concerns actually ran deeper. Buckley had privately said that he intended "to read Dwight Eisenhower out of the conservative movement." Chambers suspected that even if Eisenhower and Nixon ran again in 1956, *National Review* intended to create a Knowland-McCarthy third-party candidacy. When Chambers raised this concern, Buckley and Schlamm tried to reassure him that was not their intention.

Chambers was not convinced. But that was only part of the problem. Biographer Sam Tanenhaus writes that at this point in his life Chambers had become suspicious of "crackpotism."[37] Chambers was genuinely fond of Buckley personally and relished his company, but he worried that Buckley, Schlamm, and the band they were assembling at *National*

Review were extremists. Their pro-McCarthyism troubled him. When a year or so earlier Buckley had asked him to write a promotional blurb for *McCarthy and His Enemies*, Chambers had refused. What he told Buckley at the time was that McCarthy's "flair for the sensational, his inaccuracies and distortions, his tendency to sacrifice the greater objectivity for the momentary effect, will lead him and us into trouble." But this euphemistically reflected his views. Chambers considered McCarthy "a raven of disaster"—demagogic, even fascistic.[38]

Buckley was so upset by Chambers's refusal to join *National Review* that he offered to resign as editor in chief if that would cause Chambers to change his mind, to no avail. Buckley never fully understood Chambers's decision. "What is it that you want to hear from me, because I doubt very much it is at war with anything I actually want to say," he asked Chambers in frustration. Chambers knew better. His brand of conservatism and Buckley's brand were at odds. Although Chambers did not label himself a traditional conservative—or even a conservative for that matter, he called himself "a man of the Right"—his sensibilities had much in common with traditional conservatism. Chambers realized that Buckley and his coeditors were not traditional conservatives but radicals who wanted to repeal the New Deal. For better or worse, the New Deal had been widely accepted and was now woven into the national fabric. A responsible conservative would not now seek to rip the fabric apart. Still "a dialectician," as he described himself, Chambers believed that the responsible conservative did not reject history. Attempting to resist change would cause conservatives to sink "to futility and petulance."[39] Rather, following the example of Disraeli, whom Chambers admired, conservatives should "remain in the world" and "maneuver within its terms."

In mid-1957, the mail brought Buckley wonderful news: a letter from Chambers saying that he was then willing to write for *National Review*. Buckley believed this was because Eisenhower and Nixon had been reelected. Perhaps Joseph McCarthy's death on May 2, 1957, was a factor; perhaps Chambers did not find *National Review* as extreme as he feared; perhaps Chambers simply yearned to write again. Chambers wrote for *National Review* over the next two years, and during a span of four months in 1958 he even spent four days a month at the magazine's office in Manhattan, attending editorial meetings, writing editorials and short articles, and enjoying dinners with Buckley and the other editors. Chambers resigned permanently late in 1959. He had decided to go back to college.

Buckley also had some difficulties recruiting Russell Kirk, author of one of the intellectually richest and most highly regarded of conservative treatises, *The Conservative Mind*.[40] Buckley, himself, needlessly created some of those difficulties. Four months before *National Review* published its first issue, Buckley reviewed a new book by Russell Kirk titled *Academic Freedom* for the *Freeman* magazine. If Buckley wanted to develop a professional relationship with Kirk, this was an assignment Buckley should have declined: Kirk favored academic freedom, and as we know from *God and Man at Yale*, Buckley did not. At least, Buckley should have written a respectful review. But, in fact, Buckley's review was blistering. "No one could conceivably refer to his book as a reasoned statement of a coherent position on academic freedom," he wrote.[41] He accused Kirk of making "a major analytical blunder" in assuming that all teachers—some of whom are not scholars engaged in public debate—need to be protected by tenure. He concluded by stating that "consistent hunks [of Kirk's book] can be justly quoted to defend virtually every consistent position" in the controversy over academic freedom.

When the review was published, Buckley belatedly realized that he wanted to recruit Kirk for *National Review* but might have made that impossible. Buckley rushed a copy of his review to his and Kirk's mutual friend and publisher, Henry Regnery. "I enclose a copy of my review of Russell Kirk's last book, which you won't like, nor will he," Buckley wrote. "But I hope you both understand that it is done in context of a deep respect and friendliness for Russell Kirk. We simply happen to disagree fundamentally on this whole business of academic freedom," Buckley explained.[42] Regnery quickly replied, "You were right that I didn't like your review of Russell's book. He was here when it came in, and since you said you were going to send it to him, I handed it over to him. He read it without comment."[43]

Buckley's review was only part of the problem. The same issue of the *Freeman* included a far more serious attack on Russell Kirk by Frank Meyer, a libertarian whom Buckley had also recruited for *National*

Review.[44] Meyer's piece was an attack on the Burkeans, who were then being called the "new conservatives."* Meyer identified Kirk as the most significant member of that group and targeted him especially. The very title of Meyer's article, "Collectivism Rebaptized," was an insult. Meyer argued that by valuing community over individuals, Kirk and the new conservatives were espousing a philosophy congenial to statist systems with controlled economies, such as Nazi Germany and Soviet Russia. Kirk was fond of societies of "authority and order," said Meyer, and while they may have worked in ancient Greece or medieval Europe, in a modern world "with the technological facilities for power and centralization" such societies would "move inevitably to totalitarianism." Meyer's article must have burst into flames in Kirk's hands.

Because Buckley's and Meyer's articles were both published in the same issue of the *Freeman*, and made some similar criticisms—both Buckley and Meyer accused Kirk of muddled and internally inconsistent reasoning, for example—one might wonder whether their attacks had been coordinated. Moreover, someone sent copies of the *Freeman* issue containing both pieces to a group of people who were considering funding a new journal to be edited by Kirk.[45] Kirk believed that the responsible parties were Frank Meyer and Frank Chodorov, publisher of the *Freeman* and a radical libertarian. While Buckley may have written his book review at Chodorov's invitation, Kirk was not convinced that he was otherwise a conspirator in an anti-Kirk plot.[46]

Immediately after hearing from Regnery, Buckley wrote to Kirk (whom he did not know well), repeated his line about writing the review in a context of "deep friendliness and admiration," and deftly suggested that Kirk invite him to his home in Mecosta. "I would very much appreciate your giving me a ring next time you are in town," Buckley wrote. "Perhaps, in the meanwhile, I shall see you in Michigan. How does one get to Mecosta? By bicycle?"[47]

Kirk did not respond. How else to reach out to Kirk? A letter was sent from Will Buckley inviting Kirk to visit the family at Great Elm. Kirk declined, explaining he had no money for travel, but he added an

---

*In addition to Kirk, the "new conservatives" included sociologist Robert A. Nisbet, political scientist Clinton Rossiter, and historian and poet Peter Viereck, all of whom will be discussed later.

important postscript: "Please tell your son, if you see him soon, that I shall be very glad to entertain him at Mecosta whenever he can come."[48] Bill seized the opportunity and made the trek to Mecosta. Kirk proudly showed Buckley his library, the two repaired to a local tavern named Doyle's, and after conversation and libation—and, undoubtedly, considerable dollops of Buckley's charm—Kirk agreed to write a regular column for *National Review*.[49] However, Kirk did not agree to be listed on the magazine's masthead. Despite Buckley's subsequent attempts at suasion, Kirk remained firm. "Though I may manage to endure appearing between the same covers with Chodorov and Meyer, I won't be cheek by jowl with them on the masthead," Kirk told Buckley.

What makes Buckley's recruiting of Kirk for *National Review* interesting—indeed brilliant—is that Kirk championed a form of conservatism that Buckley quite distinctly did not favor. Buckley was himself a libertarian, even if he had not yet so described himself.[50] He was also what we today call a neoconservative and a religious conservative. Kirk's Burkeanism was incompatible with all three philosophies. Buckley talked about *National Review* providing a forum for debating—and perhaps reconciling—different views of conservatism, but in fact Buckley and Kirk's visions were irreconcilable.

If Kirk had not joined the magazine, he would likely have been an opponent. In many ways, he would have been a formidable adversary. He was erudite, thoughtful, and an excellent writer. He moved readers: His regular column for *National Review* probably generated more letters than any other.[51] By bringing Kirk within the *National Review* family, Buckley turned a potential adversary into an ally. Buckley's decision was more likely intuitive than deliberately Machiavellian, but either way, it was a brilliant move.

Buckley saw conservatism as synonymous with both individualism and libertarianism. In *God and Man at Yale*, Buckley never used the term "conservative." He spoke instead of "individualism," which he contrasted with the evil of "collectivism." Kirk, by contrast, believed that the genuine conservative "always stood for true community, the union of men, through love and common interest, for the common welfare." Kirk rejected individualism root and branch. "Individualism is social atomism; conservatism is community of spirit," he wrote.[52] This is a bedrock difference.

First and foremost, Burkeans and traditional conservatives honor the traditions of their culture and nation. (I use those terms synonymously.) In this, they draw upon the philosophy that Edmund Burke articulated in *Reflections on the Revolution in France*. The central theme of Burke's great work might be summarized this way: Civilization depends upon the rule of law. The rule of law is constructed from more than a constitution and statutes; it is interwoven into the very fabric of society. That fabric is comprised of institutions, which have evolved over time and are the product of our ancestors' accumulated wisdom and experience. All institutions are imperfect and in need of constant care, improvement, and perhaps even reform. But we cannot precipitously sweep them aside and replace them with what at the moment seems better without ripping the social fabric into shreds and destroying the rule of law. Our brightest minds cannot design entirely new institutions superior to the old. Mortals are unequal to the task. Wisdom is the product of experience— not abstract theory—and the wisdom embedded in institutions and law is not always evident to us. Even more importantly, newly created institutions will lack authority. We grant institutions authority, in significant part, because they were bequeathed to us by our ancestors. We honor them because of their history and traditions. In addition, institutions have particular classes of people who are devoted to them, as the best lawyers are devoted to the law, clerics to the church, scholars to their disciplines and universities. These people see themselves as taking part in a sacred, intergenerational covenant. They are responsible to preserve what their predecessors painstakingly fashioned, to ensure their institutions serve society in the present day, and to preserve and improve them for future generations. Indeed, society itself is an intergenerational covenant. "Society," Burke wrote, "becomes a partnership not only between those who are living, but between those who are living, those who are dead, and those who are to be born."

Burkeans and traditional conservatives are, in a sense, societal Darwinists (as opposed to social Darwinists) who believe our institutions— governmental and private—have evolved over time to serve us well. Things that have not served society well have been discarded; things that worked well have been retained and refined. Because our lives are too short to allow the individual to acquire great knowledge, we must stand on the shoulders of our ancestors and work with contemporaries

to assemble a collective wisdom. All of this is summed up by the apho-
rism The individual is foolish but the species is wise.[53]

Although Burkeans do not favor change for change's sake alone, they
are not opposed to all change. They recognize that change is necessary
because societies must adapt to new circumstances. Paradoxically,
therefore, preservation requires change. But because we cannot always
be sure why things have come to be as they are, we cannot always predict the consequences of change, and change should be made cautiously.
As Burke put it, "We must all obey the great law of change. It is the
most powerful law of nature, and the means perhaps of its conservation." Kirk added that "conservatism never is more admirable than
when it accepts changes it disapproves, with good grace, for the sake of
a general conciliation."[54]

Burke, however, did not merely accept change as something that was
necessary for preservation. He did not believe that he lived in a perfect
world, and he recognized improvements were possible. He was a reformer; indeed, at times he advocated radical reform. In 1792, for example, Burke proposed a detailed program to eliminate slavery in the
British West Indies, even though it had become an integral part of the
plantation system and abolition would require severe shocks to the economic and social systems.[55] Still, he sought, as carefully as possible, to
anticipate problems. His forty-two-point program would have immediately and dramatically improved the lot of the slaves, prepared them for
emancipation, and then emancipated them. It included elaborate programs for housing, social services, and education. Burke thought not
only about how individual former slaves could become economically
self-sufficient, but also about how they could build strong families and
communities. Every community, for example, needs leaders, and Burke
would have sent the brightest black children (or at least the brightest
boys) to London for first-rate college educations. He considered the
needs of the former slave owners as well. Burke's proposal was not
adopted, but it is a fine example of the Burkean method nonetheless: a
readiness to undertake reform, even radical reform, to reduce suffering
and improve society, combined with an effort to foresee and ameliorate
the deleterious effects of those changes.

Russell Kirk argued in *The Conservative Mind* that the following
passage contained Burke's most important contribution to political

philosophy: "Whatever each man can separately do, without trespassing upon others, he has a right to do for himself; and he has a right to all which society, with all its combinations and skill and force, can do in his favour. In this partnership all men have equal rights; but not to equal things." The passage combines both the negative and positive visions of liberty. People are entitled to be left alone to do what they wish, but in pursuing their own objectives they are obliged not to infringe on the rights of others. But Burke immediately balances that negative view of liberty—the right to be left alone—with the positive view: Individuals cannot do everything for themselves and need assistance from the community.

It is the community's responsibility—and on its behalf, government's responsibility—to provide some equality in opportunity. But there is no entitlement to equality in outcomes. People, after all, are entitled to enjoy the fruits of their own labor. How much assistance may the needy reasonably demand? How much should people be required to contribute to the welfare of others? Burke was a pragmatist. He eschewed abstract principles; he believed in applying judgment to particular circumstances. "How far economic and political leveling should be carried is a question to be determined by recourse to prudence," Kirk writes, describing Burke's thinking.

This departs widely from the rugged individualism and hard-edged libertarianism that Bill Buckley inherited from his father. Libertarians are individualists while Burkeans are communitarians. Libertarians believe individuals should be unshackled to achieve what they can and that society's wealth is the sum total of individual achievement. Communitarians believe that no individual truly achieves alone. Everyone stands on the shoulders of those who have come before—those who created the nation in which he lives, the institutions that nurtured him, the schools that educated him. Moreover, our success depends on the social structure in which we live and work. The entrepreneur could not succeed without all that society provides: a transportation system, a monetary system, police and fire protection, and on and on. As communitarians see it, the entrepreneur benefits not only from his own education but also from the education of his customers because without successful customers he would have no market for his goods.

In coming to their views, both Buckley and Kirk were influenced by their backgrounds. While Buckley saw himself standing on the shoulders of his parents, he saw his father's success as the product of self-reliance. In Bill's eyes, his father had made his fortune in a foreign land convulsed by revolution, and had done so purely on his own initiative and abilities. Government was not only of no help—there had not even been police protection—but because of corruption it had been an active hindrance. Moreover, Bill, who had been educated at home and private institutions, did not perceive how government or community made a difference in his own life. Russell Kirk's background was different. He was raised in Mecosta, Michigan, a small town that his great-grandfather helped settle in 1879 and where Kirk chose to spend his own life. Mecosta was quite unlike the affluent precincts of Sharon, Connecticut. Mecosta was a relatively impoverished place where everyone knew and helped one another. Russell Kirk's father was a railroad engineer who never attended high school and had his job reduced to half-time and half salary during the Depression. Russell attended public schools. At the urging of his high school principal, he applied for—and received—a scholarship to what is now Michigan State University. He earned a master's degree in history at Duke University on a fellowship. After serving in the army during World War II, Kirk—with veteran's benefits provided by the GI Bill and a grant from the American Council of Learned Societies—pursued further graduate work at St. Andrews University in Scotland, from which he received a doctorate in humane letters in 1952.[56]

For Buckley, capitalism and freedom were inseparable. "It is a part of the conservative intuition that economic freedom is the most precious temporal freedom, for the reason that it alone gives to each one of us, in our comings and goings in our complex society, sovereignty," he wrote. On these matters he was an absolutist. The true conservative, he believed, respected the "omnicompetence of the free marketplace."[57] Kirk did not believe capitalism was an absolute good. Moreover, whereas Buckley valued individualism, Kirk valued community. Kirk was a fan of conservative sociologist Robert A. Nisbet's vision of the new laissez-faire. "The old *laissez-faire*," Kirk wrote, speaking about Nisbet's theory, "was founded upon a misapprehension of human nature, an exaltation of individuality . . . to the condition of a political dogma, which destroyed the spirit of community." Happily that would be replaced by a new laissez-faire that, said Kirk, would "commence not with the abstract Economic Man or Citizen" but instead "recognize the basic social unit the *group*: the family, the local community, the trade union, the church, the college, the profession. It will seek . . . diversity of culture, plurality of association, and division of responsibility."[58] In an admiring biography of Robert A. Taft, Kirk repeatedly stressed Taft's express rejection of a pure laissez-faire, and Taft's advocating for government regulation to prevent monopolies, unfair competition, and, as Taft put it, other "injustices that may result from a completely free market." Kirk also favored government regulation of business to protect the environment.[59]

All of this translated into profound differences in policy preferences. Buckley, for example, decried Social Security. He argued it was a redistributionist program—taking from some in order to give to others—which he saw as inherently evil. Buckley also argued that the Social Security system was wrong because it was compulsory and thus diminished freedom.[60] Kirk, however, plainly agreed with Robert A. Taft, who favored Social Security, along with the minimum wage and federal aid to education, housing, and health care, in order to assist a fraction of the population (which Taft estimated at 20 percent) that would fall too far behind without a helping hand. It was the children of this group who most concerned Taft and Kirk. If their families and communities fell too far behind, they would lack meaningful opportunity. Kirk approvingly quoted Taft's argument that these programs were not socialistic. "The philosophy of socialism is to raise all to the average, which necessarily will bring all others down to the same dead level and take all life out of the system," Taft said. These programs created not a uniform average—only a floor in the essentials of education, health, housing, and food.[61]

Buckley and the traditional conservatives also had profoundly different views about foreign relations. Buckley and *National Review* considered America's policy of containing communism and preventing a third world war through a balance of power to be timid and defeatist, and advocated rolling back communism through subversion, covert action, and open confrontation backed by military superiority. When America's effort in Vietnam floundered, *National Review* would continually advocate the application of greater force. Kirk, by contrast, was skeptical about what could be achieved through military force. He admired Taft for believing that force should truly be a means of last resort. Taft's "natural conservatism made him a man of peace," Kirk wrote.[62] In this too, Kirk was true to Burke's legacy. When the American colonies became rebellious over what they perceived to be mistreatment by their home country, and England responded by seeking to suppress insubordination, and then insurrection, through force, Burke cautioned England about the limits of force.[63] "The use of force alone is but *temporary*," Burke declared. "It may subdue for a moment; but it does not remove the necessity of subduing again; and a nation is not governed which is perpetually to be conquered." While Buckley and *National Review* believed in projecting American values across the globe, Kirk was deeply concerned about American imperialism.[64] "Imperialism is one aspect of man's ancient expansive conceit," he wrote. Kirk warned against America's "crusading democratic sympathies," and against a new American imperialism that he believed was "economic rather than military, perhaps more cultural than economic."[65]

Kirk is best known for arguing that what mattered were "the permanent things"—a phrase he borrowed from T. S. Eliot. The permanent things were what endured, inspired, and gave life meaning: religion, tradition, community, literature, poetry, art. They were bound up in the covenant among generations about which Burke spoke; they were the things of value that one generation bequeaths to future generations. For Kirk there was something mystical about the permanent things. The permanent things, he said, "are not creations of men merely."[66]

Kirk's call to honor the permanent things resonated with those who were concerned about growing materialism. Life and politics, said Kirk, should be concerned with more important things than "another piece of pie and another pat of butter."[67] Kirk not only talked the talk of antimaterialism, he walked the walk—arguably to an extreme. Using his great-uncle's L. C. Smith typewriter, Kirk wrote, filled him with a "profound sense of continuity, and the consciousness of living among things that do not perish," which helped convince him "that Creation is good." Buckley was surprised to learn that Kirk did not own a phonograph. While Buckley was deeply religious and considered the permanent things more precious than the trinkets that could be purchased with money, he respected those who accumulated wealth—as one might expect for the son of someone who made a fortune. Buckley, moreover, delighted in living the lifestyle of a rich and famous man. He wrote with glee about skiing in Switzerland, owning a sailing vessel that was large enough to accommodate a piano, and having his limousine lengthened. This was exactly the kind of lifestyle that Kirk found appalling.

Their differences were so profound that on one level it is surprising Kirk and Buckley agreed to collaborate. What is perhaps even more surprising is that Kirk became a star in the new conservative constellation. He was one of the most popular contributors to *National Review* even though his philosophy was out of step with the magazine as a whole. Barry Goldwater and Ronald Reagan both claimed to be influenced by his work even though their libertarianism was incompatible with Kirk's traditional conservatism. Movement conservatives today consider *The Conservative Mind* one of the half dozen canonical works of their political faith even though it is fundamentally at odds with the other five.* No wonder that in 1962 political scientist Clinton Rossiter was skeptical that those who claimed to be Russell Kirk's admirers had actually read Kirk's writings.[68]

On the subject of religion, Kirk stood in the middle, between Burke to his left and Buckley to his right. Because religion became important to both *National Review* and the conservative movement, it is useful to briefly describe something about the relative positions on Burke, Kirk, and Buckley on the topic.

Burke's approach to religion was liberal and ecumenical. He found religion to be a source of inspiration. He believed religion filled people with an appreciation for enduring values and called on them to live for the greater good of the community. Burke read the Bible but took much

---

*The six works, in chronological order, are: F. A. Hayek, *The Road to Serfdom* (1944); William F. Buckley Jr., *God and Man at Yale* (1951); Whittaker Chambers, *Witness* (1952); Russell Kirk, *The Conservative Mind* (1953); Barry Goldwater, *Conscience of a Conservative* (1960); Milton Friedman, *Freedom and Capitalism* (1962). While I am unaware of any survey identifying these as the canonical texts of modern conservatism, my readings of conservative literature persuade me that this would be the likely result if such a survey were taken. For reasons discussed later, I do not classify Ayn Rand as a conservative.

of it metaphorically. He believed religion offered not answers—especially not to questions about public policy—but enrichment that comes from wrestling personally with the allegories and teachings. He warned that those who were not willing to do the hard work for themselves, to sort out what should be taken literally and what figuratively, might succumb to "dangerous fanaticism."[69] Burke did not believe that any of the great religions—Eastern or Western—offered greater theological or ethical truths than others. He thought their central tenet was the same: the Golden Rule. Although he was at least nominally a Christian, in the great volumes of his writings and speeches he never mentioned Christ's name. He often referred to God but used ecumenical terms such as "Supreme Ruler" or "Governor of the Universe."

Religion, by contrast, was an integral feature of Russell Kirk's political philosophy. Kirk had come from a vaguely Christian family that sent him to Sunday school for a while but did not attend church themselves, and did not object when he stopped attending Sunday school. In adulthood, however, a yearning for something more grew slowly within Kirk's breast.[70] In his thirties, Kirk started to read theologian John Henry Newman. That in turn led him to seek formal instruction in Catholicism from a priest. What stimulated him was intellectual curiosity about the big questions: How should we live our lives? How are we to know whether religious claims are true? What Kirk was seeking, and what he found in Catholicism, were authoritative answers to those questions. At forty-six, he was formally received into the Catholic Church.

Kirk had come to see Christianity as part of the bedrock of Western civilization, and thus integral to conservatism. The first canon of conservative thought, he declared, was belief in "a transcendent order, or a body of natural law." "Political problems, at bottom, are religious and moral problems," he continued.[71] Kirk considered the Judeo-Christian tradition fundamental to conservatism, and he took a literal approach to the Bible.[72] He was Christocentric in his writings, although Kirk's biographer, W. Wesley McDonald, plausibly argues that it was moral vision rather than Christian dogma per se that was central to Kirk's philosophy.[73] We do not know whether Kirk believed that only Christians— or perhaps Christians and Jews—could be genuine conservatives, that is, whether he believed members of Eastern religions could not be conservatives because they came from different traditions, or whether nonbelievers could not be conservatives because they did not accept a "transcendent order" and all that flows from such a belief. One suspects, however, that Kirk would have considered those to be difficult questions.

We do know that William F. Buckley Jr. believed that an atheist could not be a conservative. That question was put to Buckley in 1958 by Max Eastman, another of Buckley's big catches for *National Review*. Eastman—like James Burnham, Frank Meyer, William S. Schlamm, and Whittaker Chambers—had been a communist who underwent a conversion to anticommunism during the Second World War and embarked on a new career extolling capitalism and denouncing communism. Eastman's anticommunism was so strong that it extended to praising Joseph McCarthy and HUAC. Eastman's name had cachet: He wrote regularly for *Reader's Digest*, the magazine with the largest national circulation. Eastman agreed to be listed on the *National Review* masthead and to periodically contribute articles to the new magazine. But Eastman differed from other members of the *National Review* family on an essential point: He was an atheist. This Buckley knew. Moreover, Buckley knew that Eastman could be flippantly dismissive of religion. At a baccalaureate address to a Catholic college in 1952, Buckley had denounced a statement by Eastman that it was "silly that two-legged fanatics should run around trying to look after a God whom they at once consider omnipotent and omniscient."[74] But initially Buckley was willing to overlook atheism for a marquee contributor such as Eastman, at least as long as Eastman avoided religion in the magazine.

Religion became a problem in the relationship between Eastman and the magazine nonetheless. Surprisingly, it was Eastman who raised it. In January 1958, he wrote a letter to Buckley in which he expressed his growing discomfort with the *National Review*. It is "much more predominantly a religious magazine than I foresaw," he wrote. "I doubt," Eastman wrote, "if you realize how many statements that it makes with so much confidence [that] seem shockingly false, and moreover misleading of mankind, to a person to whom the whole Christian theology is a primitive myth."[75] Eastman, of course, had understood that Buckley was a devout Catholic, but he had not anticipated how central *National Review* was going to make religion to political conservatism. "Both Willmoore Kendall and Peter Meyer—and Russell Kirk too, if I remember rightly—in laying down the main tenets of 'conservatism,' have read me out of the brotherhood on three of four counts." (Eastman was quite right to be unsure about Kirk; it was probably not merely Eastman's memory that was fuzzy.) Eastman did not resign from the magazine, but he was in effect asking Buckley: Would you read me out of the brotherhood too?

Buckley apparently did not answer. In November, Eastman wrote again. This time he resigned. "It was an error in the first place to think that, because of political agreements, I could collaborate formally with a publication whose basic view of life and the universe I regard as primitive and superstitious."[76] One of the final straws had been a statement in the magazine by Buckley himself that "the struggle for the world is a struggle, essentially, by those who mean to unseat Him [God]." Eastman had a few other complaints as well. He did not like the magazine's ad hominem style. He gave Buckley two examples: "a snooty slap" the magazine had taken at Yugoslavian statesman and political philosopher Milovan Djilas, and a "vicious jibe" at cellist Pablo Casals, whom Eastman considered a staunch opponent of totalitarianism. But religion was the major issue. Buckley did not try to talk Eastman out of resigning. "I must reproach myself, rather than you," Buckley wrote to Eastman. "I should hate for you to think that the distance between atheism and Christianity is any greater than the distance between Christianity and atheism. And so if you are correct, that our coadjutorship was incongruous, I as editor of *National Review* should have been the first to spot it and act on it." In a later letter to Eastman, Buckley clarified his views further: "I believe atheists can be perfectly good anti-Communists. I think atheists don't make altogether convincing conservatives."[77]

Yet for all they had in common about the centrality of religion and their devotion to Catholicism, there were profound differences between Kirk and Buckley on religion as well. Buckley, typically, had inherited his religion. It was something that he accepted gladly and greatly enriched his life. Yet it was something he never questioned. Late in life Buckley wrote a book about his religious belief, *Nearer, My God: An Autobiography of Faith*. The book describes Buckley's religious upbringing and conveys his passion for his faith and church. One thing is missing: the question of whether God exists or why Buckley believes God exists. It appears to be a question with which Buckley has never wrestled. Like so much in his life, Buckley knew what he thought; there was no need for further questioning. Kirk, by contrast, thought a great deal about religion. He came to Buckley's faith—Catholicism—through study and reflection. This reflects a difference in temperament. And that difference in temperament is the basis for what was a subtle yet profound difference between Buckley and Kirk on religion. For Buckley, religion provided certitude. It filled him with joyous confidence. Religion, by contrast, filled Kirk with awe and wonder about the mysteries of God and the universe—and thus with a sense of humility.

Why, considering their fundamental differences, did Buckley decide to recruit Kirk for *National Review*? And why did Kirk accept the invitation? Both men understood that conservatism was then up for grabs. Four years later, in his book *Up From Liberalism*, Buckley described conservatism as "disordered and confused," acknowledging that "there is no commonly-acknowledged conservative position today." A battle was about to be fought over the future of conservatism and their natural positions placed these two men in opposing camps. Kirk made it clear in his famous statement to Buckley that he would not be "cheek by jowl" with libertarians and that Kirk had no interest in working out an accommodation between the competing visions. Yet Buckley did ask Kirk to join *National Review*—and Kirk did accept.

Their relationship was symbiotic. From the time he resigned his appointment at Michigan State University in 1953, Kirk struggled to support himself by writing and lecturing. It is the nature of the business of public intellectuals and political pundits that lecturing is more lucrative than writing, and thus writing principally becomes a means for establishing one's reputation. Kirk continued to write books—*Prospects for Conservatives* (1954), *Academic Freedom* (1955), *Beyond the Dreams of Avarice* (1956), *The American Cause* (1957)—as well as articles for both scholarly journals and popular magazines. But nothing was as successful as *The Conservative Mind*, and Kirk quickly learned the importance of the lecture circuit. Working with speaker's bureaus, he thrust himself forward as a public lecturer and debater. But it was difficult. "All this writing and talking, it turned out, could not suffice to make ends meet, even for a frugal Scot," Kirk wrote in his memoirs.[78] For a period of time, he was forced to supplement his earnings by teaching part-time at C. W. Post College on Long Island.

Kirk knew that he had to maintain his reputation as one of the nation's premier conservative intellectuals, particularly among groups that engaged speakers. Writing a regular column for *National Review* was the ideal vehicle. Indeed, had he not been part of *National Review*'s constellation, he ran the risk of having others outshine him. The marriage of convenience worked. As *National Review*'s circulation grew, the reputations of regular contributors, including Kirk, grew too. Speaker bureaus were able to book lectures and debates for him on more than two hundred college campuses during the 1950s. He debated such well-known personalities as Arthur M. Schlesinger, Michael Harrington, Hubert Humphrey, Norman Thomas, and Eugene McCarthy. Kirk's speaking continued to grow in the 1960s.[79]

Buckley and *National Review* received corresponding benefits from the association: As one of the most prominent conservative thinkers of the day, Kirk enhanced *National Review*'s prestige. Kirk turned out to be one of the magazine's most popular writers, and his column helped the magazine build circulation. But Buckley received a second benefit as well: Kirk was understandably reluctant to bite the hand that fed him. Buckley made it easier for Kirk to stay on the sidelines. Kirk's regular column, From the Academy, was to be principally about educational policy, a subject near to Kirk's heart but not a topic that would decide the future of conservatism.

Although Kirk never appeared on *National Review*'s masthead, From the Academy appeared regularly in the magazine until 1980 when, at age sixty-two, he stopped writing his column for the magazine. The association was of great benefit to *National Review* and to Kirk personally—but traditional conservatism lost a forceful advocate. Kirk largely confined himself to educational policy, with occasional comments on culture. His championing of traditional conservatism and his criticism of libertarianism were muted. In Kirk and Buckley's respective memoirs, one can find small hints of the ambivalence in the relationship on both sides. About Kirk, Buckley writes, "Russell I considered indispensable to the health and prestige of *National Review*, and his name is indissolubly linked to the journal; but living in Michigan, he was never part of our administrative apparatus."[80] For his part, Kirk, who somewhat strangely wrote his memoirs in the third person, said, "Kirk had little in common with some of the people on *National Review*'s lengthy masthead—on which he declined to have his name appear . . . In the course of twenty-five years' association, Kirk visited the shabby offices of *National Review* not more than six or seven times—and then usually on business with the publisher, William Rusher."[81] Garry Wills, who was part of the *National Review* family from 1957 to 1968, reports that unlike Frank Meyer (who also worked from a distant home rather than at the magazine's offices), Kirk's connection with *National Review* was never truly close.[82]

There was a moment then, in the mid-1950s, when conservatism stood at a fork in the road. Before it lay two paths: the Burkean road advocated by the new conservatives, and the libertarian path favored by Frank Meyer and, more importantly, by William F. Buckley Jr. Would history have been different if Kirk and the new conservatives stood shoulder by shoulder and fought for the future of the conservative movement? Why did this not happen?

Individually, the new conservatives were formidable. The original new conservative and the person who coined the term was Peter Viereck, a historian at Mount Holyoke College. Viereck was an unusual man.[83] He was a direct descendant (through an extramarital affair with an actress) of Kaiser Wilhelm I of Prussia. His father, George Sylvester Viereck, was proud that royal blood ran in his veins. George Sylvester had been born in Germany and although he settled in New York City and worked as a writer for the Hearst newspapers, he forever remained loyal to the fatherland. Enamored with Hitler, he became a Nazi propagandist, was convicted of conspiring with the Third Reich, and spent four years in federal prison. Peter hated everything his father stood for. He had no truck with the "royalty nonsense," as he put it, and he despised fascism. He graduated from Harvard College and went on to earn a Ph.D. in European history at Harvard before joining the army during World War II. Because of his father's activities, Peter was barred from serving in the Office of Strategic Services, yet he wound up analyzing Nazi propaganda for the army's psychological warfare branch. In how many other families was the father a Nazi propagandist and the son a decoder of Nazi propaganda for the Allies? After the war, Viereck became a professor specializing in modern Russian history—but he was also an accomplished poet, winning the Pulitzer Prize for poetry in 1949.

Viereck first proposed "a Burkean new conservatism" in an article in *Atlantic Monthly* when he was still a student at Harvard in the 1930s, and he continued to press the case in articles in *Harper's* and other magazines. After the war, he readapted his articles into a book titled *Conservatism Revisited*. In this thin volume—published in 1949, six years before Kirk's *The Conservative Mind*—Viereck declared that Edmund Burke "deserves to be the model for modern conservative leadership." Much of what Viereck said presaged (and surely influenced) what Kirk would say later. "The core and fire-center of conservatism, its emotional élan," Viereck wrote, "is a humanist reverence for the dignity of the individual soul."[84] As did Kirk, Viereck believed that flawed human beings had to rely on the civilizing influence of ancient traditions, the rule of law, "the public and private submission to ethics," and, most importantly, religion. "The churches, Protestant, Catholic, or the closely related Jewish, draw the fangs of the Noble Savage and clip his ignoble claws," he wrote. He worried that industrialization was creating people with schooling, social standing, and wealth but who were also prideful, believed that might made right, and had become morally illiterate—"Neanderthalers with a high I.Q." He considered Burke's teachings about ordered liberty a fundamental tenet. Without order, cries for liberty were merely "a disguise for the ambitions of some selfish group," he wrote.[85]

Like Kirk, Viereck was a communitarian who was offended by libertarian romanticizing of the individual pursuit of wealth in an environment of pure laissez-faire. The new conservatism, he said, "fights on two fronts. It fights the atomistic disunity of unregulated capitalism. It fights the merely bureaucratic, merely mechanical unity of modern socialism." He surely amazed others who called themselves conservatives by arguing that trade unions were among the most important conservative institutions of the time. Quoting *A Philosophy of Labor* by Frank Tannenbaum, Viereck argued that the "clustering of men about their work" was a humanistic antidote to the isolation of modern man.

All of this creates a large chasm between Viereck's new conservatism and Buckley's conservatism. But perhaps the most profound difference was the way the two men viewed liberalism. To Buckley, liberalism was un-American. Buckley's antagonism for liberalism was, in part, something that he inherited from his father and that was intensified by the personal attacks on him following publication of *God and Man at Yale*. It was also partly something he learned from Whittaker Chambers and the other ex-communists at *National Review* who saw the entire political left—from liberalism to communism—as fundamentally socialist, collectivist, and statist.[86] Viereck saw liberalism and conservatism as complementary: two halves of the American tradition. Both valued individual liberty, though they had somewhat different approaches of pursuing it. What made America was the balance provided by both.[87]

By himself, Viereck was not an entirely satisfactory champion of a political philosophy. He was too idiosyncratic. Some readers may have found him highfalutin. The conservative model Viereck devoted the most attention to in *Conservatism Revisited* was not Edmund Burke, John Adams, or some other historical figure to whom American readers could easily relate but Prince Clemens Metternich of the Hapsburg empire. But Viereck was not the only writer beckoning conservatives toward the Burkean path.

Another new conservative, Clinton Rossiter, was an extraordinarily compelling writer. Handsome, urbane, and brilliant, Rossiter was one of the nation's most prominent political scientists. He held the only university chair—reserved for a scholar who transcends disciplines—at Cornell University. Rossiter's voice carried beyond the halls of academe. His writing was fluid and graceful, easily accessible not only to scholars but to the public at large. In the mid-1950s, Rossiter was at the height of his career. His 1953 book, *Seedtime of the Republic*, won three awards, including the prestigious Bancroft Prize in history. Three years later he wrote *The American Presidency*, a work that has been translated into more than thirty languages and to this day remains a definitive work on the American presidency. In 1955, between these two works, Rossiter wrote *Conservatism in America: The Thankless Persuasion*, which received the Charles Austin Beard Memorial Prize.

Paradoxically, considering it was written by a professional academic, *Conservatism in America* is brisker and even more evocative than Kirk's *The Conservative Mind*. Kirk's book was his doctoral thesis. He had to write it with an eye toward satisfying his dissertation committee that it was a work of high scholarship. As a result, as well written as it is, *The*

Conservative Mind is quite dense. It covers dozens of conservative thinkers and writers—arguably too many. Its becoming a national best-seller was a surprise. Rossiter, by contrast, wrote *Conservatism in America* when he had nothing to prove. He could afford to write a popular book, and that was clearly his intent. *Conservatism in America* was published by Random House and found a sizable audience.

Although he did not use the term "new conservative," Rossiter described a philosophy, grounded in Edmund Burke, similar to that described by both Peter Viereck and Russell Kirk. "The Conservative, contrary to popular belief, is not an extreme individualist," he wrote. "His distrust of unfettered man, his devotion to groups, his sense of all the complexity of the social process, his recognition of the real services that government can perform—all of these sentiments make it impossible for him to subscribe whole-heartedly to the dogmas and shibboleths of economic individualism: laissez-faire, the negative state, enlightened self-interest, the law of supply and demand, the profit motive."

Rossiter agreed with Kirk that conservatives place a special importance on institutions—family, church, neighborhoods, occupational or professional groups—and put the interests of the community before those of the individual. He agreed with Kirk as well that conservatives have a special reverence for history, in which they see the hand of God at work, and that religion—and more specifically, the Judeo-Christian tradition—lies at the core not only of conservative thought but also of American democracy. As Rossiter put it, the "mortar that holds together the mosaic of conservatism is religious feeling." Rossiter's tone about religion was similar to Kirk's; that is, he suggested that religion fills conservatives with a sense of the grandeur of life, not that it provides answers to political questions. Rossiter agreed with Kirk as well on the special importance of education. He quoted John Adams, who famously said, "Education makes a greater difference between man and man, than nature has made between man and brute."

Rossiter exhorted conservatives to follow their better instincts. "Principle—the conscience-stricken recognition that the Negro should not have to beg and fight for the ordinary rights of an American—will surely make its claims upon the minds of many conservatives," he wrote. Most of all, he cautioned conservatives to avoid extremes. "When a conservative once decides, as many articulate conservatives seem to have decided in explosive America, that the best of all possible worlds was here yesterday and is gone today, he begins the fateful move toward reaction and ratiocination that turns him from a prudent traditionalist into an angry ideologue."[88]

Rossiter quoted Peter Viereck quite a number of times. He gave Russell Kirk an even more prominent place in his book, making it clear that he admired much of Kirk's thinking. For his part, Kirk wrote a favorable review of *Conservatism in America*.[89] "A historian of politics like Rossiter is just the man to write a book" dissecting conservatism, Kirk wrote, adding that "Rossiter's book should itself do something . . . to give permanence to the present conservative mood in the nation." There were some things about Rossiter that gave Kirk pause. On education, Rossiter recommended steering a middle course between traditionalists and progressives such as John Dewey. Kirk, who uncompromisingly believed in tradition and rigor in education, thought Rossiter had mistaken "the disputed middle for the golden mean."

Although Rossiter rejected the idea that statecraft could be successfully practiced by applying business methods to government, he thought that conservatives should locate the center of gravity of their philosophy in the business community and the professions. America needed an aristocracy, and this was where it had to be developed. Both Rossiter and Russell Kirk worried that the fires of base materialism were growing in America—it was the fifties, and in this concern they were not alone—and they both recognized that business fanned these destructive flames. Rossiter, however, was optimistic that business leaders could be taught to serve the public interest. "We are far from developing what one might call, with some reservations, a spirit of *noblesse oblige* in American business," he wrote. "Yet we may look forward hopefully to a steady growth in the number of businessmen who are genuinely concerned about the welfare of their workers, alert to the social implications of their decisions, sobered by the thought that they wield public rather than private power, and anxious to prove that American capitalism is servant rather than master of American democracy." Conservatism, Rossiter believed, had a role in turning business leaders into statesmen.

For Kirk, this was decidedly an unconservative view. It was utopian. Conservatism held that man was flawed, and good intentions were not going to purge avarice and self-interest from either the human breast or the machines of industry. Moreover, Kirk was just as fearful about the Leviathan of business as he was about the Leviathan of government; an overconcentration of power in either realm threatened the republic. Kirk agreed that America needed an aristocracy. Indeed, a belief that the nation needed an aristocracy—an elite filled with a sense of noblesse oblige that would serve as the nation's ballast—may be a fundamental tenet of conservatism. But while Rossiter leaned toward a meritocratic aristocracy, Kirk placed faith in family lineages. He believed that people had to be born and bred to the sense of duty, and that it took generations to fashion worthy aristocrats. Moreover, he believed families should be connected to the land. He criticized Rossiter for rejecting what Rossiter called "country-house Conservatism." There is both country-house liberalism and country-house conservatism, Kirk said, and both may be valuable if balanced one against the other. "Does Rossiter really think that it did Jefferson harm to live in Monticello, or that Roosevelt sank into reaction through living in Hyde Park?" he asked. To Rossiter, Kirk's mind-set was archaic. Kirk, he said, sounded like "a man born one hundred and fifty years too late and in the wrong country."[90] Anyone who might suspect that this would upset him did not know Russell Kirk. In his memoirs, Kirk wrote about himself: "His was no Enlightenment mind . . . It was a Gothic mind, medieval in its temper and structure."[91]

Kirk stated in his review of *Conservatism in America* that "Rossiter is truly a conservative—though showing traces, now and then of a lingering liberalism." It was a statement with considerable significance. Hard-edged conservatives were calling Rossiter an imposter and *Conservatism in America* a Trojan horse.[92]

Among those attacking Rossiter was James Burnham, who would become Buckley's second in command at *National Review*. In a scathing review of Rossiter's book, Burnham attacked not only Rossiter but Burkeanism—and, by extension, Kirk too. "Feudalism never existed in America," Burnham wrote. "Therefore, there is no historical basis for a true Burkean conservatism, which rests on traditional aristocracy."[93] Burnham was also clearly upset that Rossiter suggested that liberals and conservatives should not be enemies. Rossiter said that conservatism had a "high duty to maintain its historic links with American liberalism," and vice versa. "The American, like his tradition, is deeply liberal, deeply conservative," Rossiter wrote. "If this is a paradox, so, too, is America."[94] Burnham was not willing to concede that liberalism was a genuine or valuable part of the American tradition. And Burnham thought Rossiter revealed himself as a liberal by declaring that "immoderation" was not conservative and that therefore Joseph McCarthy was no conservative, and by stating that some of the best conservative thinking was coming from progressives such as Walter Lippmann, Reinhold Niebuhr, and Adlai Stevenson.[95] Rossiter, said Burnham, was Arthur M. Schlesinger's twin.[96]

Rossiter's belief in tradition, community, the social fabric, and institutions, as well as the importance of understanding history, made Rossiter a Burkean through and through. But although he saw conservatism and liberalism as a partnership, he viewed conservatism as the junior partner. "Our commitment to progress means that liberalism will keep its role as pace-setter in the arena of politics, and that conservative doers will continue to spend far too much time fighting the reformers and then adjusting to their reforms," he wrote.[97] Thus, he believed that liberalism provided society with its momentum, and the conservative mission was to moderate and consolidate the progress. That is why the contemporary thinkers Rossiter so admired—Lippmann, Niebuhr, and Stevenson—were liberals who sought to improve society yet do so prudently, guided by careful studies of history.

Frank Chodorov was also blasting *Conservatism in America*. In a private letter, Chodorov sought to persuade a prominent conservative that the new conservatives, including both Russell Kirk and Clinton Rossiter, were in fact liberals.[98] Kirk rejected the key principles of libertarianism or individualism, which he said were limited government and the free economy, Chodorov declared. But it was not Kirk alone who bothered him; it was the combination of Kirk and Rossiter that upset him. "I would never have become exercised over this matter," he wrote, "if it were not for a book called 'Conservatism in America' by Clinton Rossiter. Mr. Rossiter welcomes Kirk's brand of conservatism because it fits in very nicely with Mr. Rossiter's 'liberalism.'" Chodorov recounted that two student clubs had sprung up at Harvard University—one calling itself the Conservatives and the other, following Russell Kirk, calling itself the New Conservatives. Chodorov sent a blind copy of his letter to William F. Buckley Jr.

Kirk realized his defense of Rossiter placed him on thin ice with Buckley and the group Buckley was assembling at *National Review*. In his July 1955 letter to Will Buckley—the one to which he added a post-script inviting Bill Buckley to come and visit him in Mecosta—Kirk crossed the Rubicon. "I have never called myself a New Conservative, and no one ever has called me that to my face," he wrote. And in a later letter to Bill Buckley, Kirk seemed to go out of his way to mention that neither Viereck nor Rossiter was on the board of the new journal that Kirk was planning to edit.* Kirk was signaling that he would not ally himself with the Burkeans in a struggle for the future of conservatism, at least as long as he wrote for *National Review*.

Kirk might have been surprised to know that Rossiter and Buckley were making tentative but strained overtures to each other. They met at least once. After *National Review* was about three months old, Rossiter sent a letter to Buckley in which he said, "*The National Review* continues to interest, amuse, and anger me, and what more can I ask of a magazine? I don't get this reaction from any other journal these days." Buckley immediately wrote back, asking permission to use the statement for promotional purposes. Rossiter consented, though somewhat testily, "you may use my ridiculous two sentences," he replied.[99] But their relationship never progressed much further—and for good reason.

When, in 1955, Clinton Rossiter wrote the original edition of *Conservatism in America*, he sounded like a man who considered himself a conservative and was advocating the Burkean vision. "For the record," he declared in the introduction, "I write as one who is himself caught up in the current revival; who is alarmed by the confusion of thought, excess of emotion, and irresponsibility of action that have thus far attended it; and

---

*Kirk's journal began publication in 1957 as a quarterly under the name *Modern Age*, a name that Kirk considered ironical as the journal was to be "in sardonic defiance of the fads and foibles of the twentieth century." Kirk edited the journal for only two years. He said that under his stewardship, the journal "obtained a surprisingly friendly reception from unconservative quarters," which, no doubt, Meyer and Chodorov would have taken as further confirmation that Kirk was not a true-blooded conservative. Although it never achieved wide circulation, *Modern Age* is still being published—today by the Intercollegiate Studies Institute, an organization founded by Frank Chodorov. Russell Kirk, *The Sword of Imagination*, 191 ("sardonic defiance"), 195 (resignation as editor).

who believes that a high-minded conservatism is America's most urgent need for the years ahead." But Rossiter deleted those words from a revised edition published in 1962. Instead, he included a new preface in which he denied that he was or had ever been a conservative, even a Burkean conservative. He claimed he was merely a political scientist who sought to describe conservatism. He admitted to admiring Burke warmly (among other ideological mentors, including Adams) but suggested that he was unable to classify himself ideologically.

Rossiter's change of heart was understandable. So much had changed over the intervening seven years. Conservatism had previously stood at a fork in the road; now Rossiter watched as it followed Buckley down the other path. After lingering awhile at the crossroads, even Russell Kirk had decided to quietly follow Buckley. Rossiter had been left behind. Rossiter was reduced to shouting last words of advice to figures receding in the distance. He begged them to see that the "ultra-conservatives" they were following were, in fact, radicals. The "Goldwaters must be made to see the impossibility of reversing history" and the "Buckleys made to see the essential radicalism of their total war on the New Orthodoxy," he wrote in his revised edition.[100] Limited war on liberalism was certainly authorized, but deep contempt for liberalism was "reckless, imprudent, and indeed 'unconservative.'" Some conservatives had not succumbed to this (he named Viereck). Some had (he named Kirk).

In 1962, the same year that Rossiter claimed he had never been a conservative, Peter Viereck added fifty-eight pages to his book, *Conservatism Revisited*. He styled this addition Book II, *The New Conservatism—What Went Wrong?* Viereck did not repudiate his conservatism, but he lamented that the lot of the new conservative was to be accused of "being really a liberal at heart, hypocritically pretending to be a conservative." He also vigorously attacked Russell Kirk. But his principal criticism was that Kirk talked the talk but did not walk the walk. Kirk evoked the "true humanistic conservatism" of conservative figures of the past but failed to follow their examples. Where, for example, were Kirk and other conservatives on such worthy humanistic causes such as desegregation? Viereck urged conservatives to reread Burke's speeches against the slave trade and reminded them that John Adams was one of America's first champions for Negro rights. In a similar vein, Viereck accused Kirk of arguing for the preservation of pseudotraditions that appealed to him and rejecting genuine traditions that didn't—as he did by romanticizing utopian dreams of an aristocratic society while rejecting New Deal liberalism. Kirk, Viereck said, was guilty of an "unhistorical appeal to history" and a "traditionless worship of tradition." "In contrast," he continued, "a genuinely rooted, historically-minded conservative conserves the roots that are *really there*." Viereck completed his assault by essentially accusing Kirk of cowardice. Kirk had summoned mock courage in denouncing Robert Welch—founder of the John Birch Society—but had remained studiously silent about Joseph McCarthy, who had the ability to strike back.[101]

Both Clinton Rossiter and Peter Viereck left the battlefield after publication of their revised works. After a few years, Viereck stopped writing about politics altogether. Rossiter continued to write important works of history and political science—until, according to the *Cornell Alumni News*, he was terribly shaken by events that "he could not jibe with his view of the ability of American institutions to deal with new forces and pressures."[102] That, of course, is a quintessentially Burkean way of looking at things. The events that so rattled Rossiter were Vietnam, the assassination of Robert Kennedy, and the occupation of Willard Straight Hall at Cornell University in 1969 by armed members of the Afro-American Society. As one of the most prominent members of the Cornell faculty, Rossiter was very much involved in that last incident. Rossiter first took the position that the university should press disciplinary charges against the armed protestors, but he reversed himself when thousands of students and some faculty threatened to take over other buildings unless the university unilaterally dropped all charges. Both Cornell and Rossiter were heavily criticized for the decision to drop disciplinary charges, and Rossiter—a man who highly valued collegiality—was anguished when two colleagues in the political science department permanently stopped speaking to him.[103] The anger directed at him throughout the wider community was further driven home when Rossiter lost elections for the University Faculty Senate and a faculty seat on the Board of Trustees. On July 10, 1970, Clinton Rossiter took his own life.

The fourth new conservative was Robert Nisbet. Nisbet entered the debate in 1953—the same year that Russell Kirk published *The Conservative Mind*—with his first book, *The Quest for Community*.[104] Nisbet was then a thirty-nine-year-old sociologist at Berkeley. His central thesis was that human beings found meaning for their lives within communities—the family, village, church, guild, labor union, or professional association—but that this rich tapestry of associations was weakening, and as a result people were suffering from cultural disintegration, dislocation, and feelings of insecurity and alienation.[105] Nisbet quoted Dostoevsky, who said that the "craving for *community* of worship is the chief misery of every man individually and all humanity from the beginning of time"; that is, man sought to find something that everyone within the community could "believe in and worship" together.[106] Communities did not exist to provide people with psychologically satisfactory homes; they existed to do things, to perform functions. The family, for example, was originally the primary unit of economic production and consumption.[107] The growth of the modern state, however, led increasingly to a centralization of functions. As the state did more, other communities did less; as the functions of these communities diminished, their salience diminished. The relationship between the individual and the state was becoming increasingly direct and more important. The state became the primary guarantor of the individual's rights, and the individual came to think of his primary institutional relationship as that of citizen. But the citizen-state relationship was too remote and impersonal to be satisfying. "The individual not only does not feel a part of the social order," wrote Nisbet, "he has lost interest in being a part of it."[108] The result was apathy, boredom, even hostility.

By placing such emphasis on the fabric of social institutions, Nisbet was adopting a Burkean perspective. He had studied Burke, and acknowledged his debt to him as well as to other thinkers who emphasized the importance of community, including Alexis de Tocqueville, theologians Reinhold Niebuhr and Martin Buber, and—surely to the horror of many conservatives—John Dewey.[109] *The Quest for Community* was a bit of an odd work for a professional sociologist; it was more political philosophy than sociology. The writers that Nisbet discussed most, whether favorably or unfavorably, were political philosophers such as Plato, Hobbes, Locke, Rousseau, Marx, Lenin, and Walter Lippmann.

Nisbet's book was a counterpoint to *The Road to Serfdom*, the libertarian manifesto published nine years earlier by F. A. Hayek.[110] Hayek was an economist who had been born and raised in Austria and educated at the University of Vienna. He left Vienna in 1931, as Hitler and the Nazi Party were beginning to rise to power in Germany, to accept a position at the London School of Economics. Hayek began writing the *The Road to Serfdom* in London a month after the German blitz against Britain started, and he completed it as the Allies were preparing to invade Normandy. It was an instant sensation. *Reader's Digest* published a condensed version that sold six hundred thousand copies in the United States, and the unabridged version continues to sell well to this day.

Hayek's book attempted to illuminate what he believed led to the rise of totalitarianism. The answer, he argued, was central planning over the economy. Planners may have the best of intentions. They may seek to use reason and science to organize an efficient, well-functioning economy. But economic choices are all about values: Should we have more automobiles or more cans of soup, more televisions or more typewriters? The question was whether people should make these choices for themselves. Comprehensive economic planning would eventually require an economic dictator to make fundamental choices for the society. Hayek argued that "individuals should be allowed, within defined limits, to follow their own values and preferences rather than somebody else's."[111] Laissez-faire was therefore the system of individual freedom. "Money is one of the greatest instruments of freedom ever invented by man," wrote Hayek, because it offers "an astounding range of choice," not only to the wealthy but to the poor as well.

Hayek also thought that any collectivist system would inevitably give rise to cries for greater equality. It was simply not possible in a collectivist system to advocate for any other principle of distributive justice. Efforts for greater equality, however, would incite the lower middle class to seek more at the expense of the established middle class and unsuccessful professionals to seek more at the expense of successful professionals. It was the resentments of these groups, Hayek argued, that provided much of the fuel and many of the recruits for fascism and National Socialism.

By modern standards, Hayek was a rather moderate libertarian. He emphasized the need for "a legal system designed both to preserve competition and to make it operate as beneficially as possible." He advocated regulatory mechanisms to prevent fraud, deception, and monopolies, and said there was a strong case for government providing "some minimum of food, shelter, and clothing, sufficient to preserve health and the capacity to work," and organizing a comprehensive system of social insurance for sickness and accidents. Nevertheless, the principal theme of his work tied together freedom, democracy, and capitalism. They were, as Hayek saw them, interdependent.

Nisbet took issue with Hayek's making economics the fulcrum of the effort against a drift to totalitarianism. Sure, a free market system was superior to a controlled economy, said Nisbet, but a free market system was neither the natural order nor a bulwark against totalitarianism. Nisbet was concerned about ideology that elevated the individual at the expense of the community, and he saw laissez-faire as doing just that. The purpose of laissez-faire was to create conditions under which individuals could prosper. As previously mentioned, Nisbet wanted a new laissez-faire designed to create conditions under which social groups would prosper.[112] A healthy society contained a vibrant pluralism of social institutions. A system that let that pluralism wither was in danger of drifting toward totalitarianism, for when occupational, cultural, social, and religious groups grew weak, all that was left was the individual and the state. Labor unions were among such groups. Labor unions, Nisbet wrote, "have been powerful forces *in support* of capitalism and economic freedom," and have been among the first targets for destruction in totalitarian nations.[113]

Nisbet was not in favor of a weak government. To the contrary, he argued that a strong central government was essential to ordered liberty.[114] The evil to be avoided was what he called "omnicompetent government." Nothing drove government more in that direction than war. "The power of war to create a sense of moral meaning is one of the frightening aspects of the twentieth century," he wrote.[115] Wars were national crusades. Within an "intoxicating atmosphere of spiritual unity," the enemy became a symbol of total evil. With everything mobilized for a single purpose, society succumbed to a "stifling regimentation and bureaucratic centralization." Perhaps with an eye to speaking to libertarians, Nisbet observed that war created conditions in which capitalist societies adopted socialist reforms such as equalization of wealth, progressive taxation, nationalization of industries, and "death taxes."

Although Nisbet did not consider himself a conservative when he wrote *The Quest for Community*, its distinct Burkean flavor caused others to categorize him as a new conservative. Shortly after writing the book, Nisbet read Russell Kirk's *The Conservative Mind*, with which he found himself largely in accord. Kirk and Nisbet became mutual admirers, and as mentioned, Kirk took up Nisbet's cry for a new laissez-faire. In *Conservatism in America*, Clinton Rossiter praised *The Quest for Community* as "a relentless yet good-tempered exposure of both the sociological and ideological fallacies of run-away individualism."[116]

Shortly after writing *The Quest for Community*, Nisbet left Berkeley to assume the deanship of a new liberal arts college at the University of California at Riverside. After ten years of administrative work, he returned to the classroom, first at Riverside, then at the University of Arizona, and later at Columbia. In 1978, he left academia for the work of a political think tank, becoming a resident scholar at the American Enterprise Institute in Washington, D.C. He remained a prolific writer until his death in 1996, at age of eighty-two, leaving behind him more than twenty books and 150 articles. He remained until the end a Burkean and an opponent of libertarianism. He became an ever-more-fierce critic of the military-industrial complex, and he saw war—including the war in Vietnam—as a tool for expanding the power of the state and acquiring empire. He considered the politicization of religion, especially by right-wing fundamentalists, a danger to the republic. He thought that conservatism had become corrupted by its quest for political power. After Ronald Reagan left office, Nisbet wrote, "In large measure conservatism has become, within a decade or two, an ideology seeking to capture democratic absolutism rather than secure from it social and moral authority distinct from political power."[117]

Even as it raged, few people were aware of the battle between Buckley-ism and the new conservatism. It was inside baseball, something only the players themselves understood. Buckley, however, fully appreciated the significance of his victory. In 1963, he observed that the followers of Clinton Rossiter and Peter Viereck had been successfully sidelined. They were, he wrote with obvious satisfaction, "bound to enter the ranks of eccentricity."[118] Today the new conservatism is forgotten. Even most of the intellectuals in the conservative movement itself are unaware that this struggle ever took place.

Why did Buckleyism prevail? How did Buckley pull it off? Why was the struggle so short and decisive? The answer has little to do with the competing ideas themselves. The answer has to do with leadership.

It is ironic that the new conservatives—notwithstanding their philosophical emphasis on community over individualism—were loners. Despite the commonalities of their views, Kirk, Viereck, Rossiter, and Nisbet never united to collectively promote the Burkean vision. It is doubly ironic that William F. Buckley Jr. was exactly the opposite; he was philosophically an individualist but built a community at and through *National Review.*

Like a good general, Buckley's first stratagem was to divide and conquer. With charm and a juicy carrot, he peeled away Russell Kirk, the new conservative with the greatest credibility within conservative ranks. Buckley's pilgrimage to Mecosta was itself flattering to Kirk. Buckley was rich, handsome, Yale educated, confident, socially skilled, exuberant, and exciting. Kirk was introverted, awkward, and shy. Kirk's defense mechanism was to look down on those whom he found threatening. Had Buckley not worked hard to acquire interpersonal skills in the army, Kirk might have found him overwhelming and threatening. But Buckley had learned how to take stock of other people, sense what they needed, and provide it. He could dial his buoyancy to just the right level. Kirk describes him on that visit as "the convivial young gentleman from New York."[119] Buckley allowed himself to be suitably impressed by Kirk's library, by the local tavern, by Kirk himself. The last part was especially easy because Buckley, in fact, genuinely admired Kirk. The juicy carrot, of course, was the engagement at *National Review.* It is no wonder that Kirk found both Buckley and his offer irresistible. In one way, Buckley needed Kirk as much as Kirk needed Buckley: For the sake of the magazine and the conservative movement, he very much wanted—perhaps even needed—to bring Kirk into the tent. Yet it was never a relationship between equals. Partly because Kirk's mind leaned toward the feudalistic, it may not be outlandish to say that their relationship was a bit akin to prince and vassal. In any event, Kirk remained loyal—to the point of swallowing his criticisms of libertarian and neoconservative ideas, which he detested—for more than a quarter century.

None of the new conservatives had anything like the organizational and political skills—or the single-minded dedication to a cause—that

Buckley possessed. Rossiter, Viereck, and Nisbet were all academics, with all that implies. They were interested in ideas and animated by the classroom. Kirk also was foremost a scholar. They lived in places like Ithaca, New York; South Hadley, Massachusetts; Riverside, California; and Mecosta, Michigan. Viereck and Rossiter wanted the new conservatism to prevail, but neither considered that cause to be his principal ambition. When the going got tough, Viereck retreated into poetry and Rossiter retreated into denial. Buckley, however, considered the conservative cause to be his life's mission, and he believed that the fate of his nation might depend on his success. The new conservatives were all talented and formidable individuals—but they were individuals. They never cohered as a group, and there is no evidence that they ever considered doing so. None saw himself as a general leading an army to war. Buckley saw himself in just that way. He knew that he was not going to prevail over the new conservatism—or more importantly, liberalism—alone. He was, moreover, not merely a leader, but an extraordinary leader.

In 1981, the year after he left *National Review*, Kirk regained his voice about the conflict between traditional conservatism and libertarianism. In an article in *Modern Age* titled "Libertarians: The Chirping Sectaries," Kirk let loose.[120] What, he asked, did conservatives—by which he meant traditional conservatives—and libertarians have in common? They both "set their faces against the totalist state and the heavy hand of bureaucracy," he wrote. But they have nothing else in common. "Nor will they ever," he added. "To talk of forming a league or coalition between these two is like advocating a union of ice and fire." It was as if a dam of twenty-five years had burst. Kirk did not merely dislike libertarianism; he disliked libertarians. "The representative libertarian of this decade is humorless, intolerant, self-righteous, badly schooled, and dull," he declared.

Kirk's substantive arguments were more thoughtful. He argued that while society's first need is for order, libertarians sacrificed order for abstract notions of liberty. Kirk said that libertarians believe that society revolves around "self-interest, closely joined to the nexus of cash payment," but that conservatives see society as "a community of souls, joining the dead, the living, and those yet unborn" and cohering "through what Aristotle called friendship and Christians call love of neighbor." Kirk maintained that while the "libertarian takes the state for the great oppressor," the conservative believes, in Burke's words, that government "is a contrivance of human wisdom to provide for human *wants*." The libertarian, said Kirk, believes the "world is chiefly a stage for the swaggering ego," while "the conservative finds himself a pilgrim in a realm of mystery and wonder, where duty, discipline, and sacrifice are required." In the eyes of the conservative, he said, the libertarian is impious.

"It is of high importance, indeed," he concluded, "that American conservatives dissociate themselves altogether from the little sour remnant called libertarians." It was a ringing call to arms—but in a journal with a tiny circulation, and in 1981. It was much too little, much too late. The course of modern conservatism had long been set.

CHAPTER 3

Civil Rights

The conservative movement was born on November 19, 1955, the publication date of the first issue of *National Review*. The publisher's statement, signed by William F. Buckley Jr., then still just shy of his thirtieth birthday, set forth what have become the most famous words in the history of modern conservatism. *National Review*, he declared, "stands athwart history, yelling Stop, at a time when no one is inclined to do so."

Readers quickly grasped that this was not merely a magazine. What they held in their hands was a cry for a crusade—a battle for the future. The crusaders were to be iconoclasts, people who found themselves out of place in America. It was, moreover, not to be a crusade by everyone who called himself a "conservative." Buckley sought to appropriate that term for a narrowly defined group. Conservatives would no longer include people who sought to conserve and improve upon the then-existing American model—people, we might imagine, such as the late Robert A. Taft. Although Buckley only implied this, his meaning was plain enough. He wrote, "Conservatives in this country—at least those who have not made their peace with the New Deal, and there is serious question whether there are others—are non-licensed nonconformists." Undertaking the crusade was going to be risky, "a dangerous business in a Liberal world." The crusaders would be attacked—"suppressed," "mutilated," "ignored," and "humiliated" were the words Buckley used—not only by liberals, but also by "the well-fed Right, whose ignorance and amorality have never been exaggerated for the same reason that one cannot exaggerate infinity." Thus, Buckley and his coeditors threw down two gauntlets: one against liberals, who they conceded controlled both government and the press; the other against conservatives cut from a different cloth. "Radical conservatives" were the true crusaders, and those on the "well-fed Right" were not allies but adversaries. The crusade would begin with a fight for the soul of conservatism.

The magazine's first issue also included a statement of principles. Reading the list from today's perspective gives us the opportunity to look back in time and identify seeds that over time would develop into formidable organisms. As the decades would roll on, the conservative movement would become a coalition of three diverse groups: libertarians, neoconservatives, and social conservatives. Only one of these—libertarians—existed as an identifiable group when *National Review* published its inaugural issue. Yet more than half a century later, each of the three groups can look back and find a central tenet of its philosophy in the magazine's original statement of principles.

The first principle began: "It is the job of centralized government (in peacetime) to protect its citizens' lives, liberty and property. All other activities of government tend to diminish freedom and hamper progress." This is a classic statement of libertarian doctrine, which holds that government should be limited to three functions: protecting citizens against violence or fraud, providing a justice system to resolve disputes, and protecting the nation against foreign invasion. Another of the *National Review* principles stated: "We consider 'coexistence' with communism neither desirable nor possible, nor honorable; we find ourselves irrevocably at war with communism—and shall oppose any substitute for victory." This reflects the neoconservative view that accommodations with ruthless adversaries provide false security. There is ultimately only victory or defeat. Social conservatives can find a key sentiment of their philosophy in a principle warning of the "cultural menace" from "intellectual cliques which, in education as well as the arts, are out to impose upon the nation their modish fads and fallacies." Social conservatives could find another important hint of their philosophy in another principle that described communism as "satanic utopianism," thereby reflecting the view—previously reflected in *God and Man at Yale*—that the contest between Western democracies and communism was part of a larger, transcendent struggle between good and evil.

The heart of the magazine would be a collection of regular one-page columns, or as the magazine referred to them, "departments." L. Brent Bozell wrote one titled National Trends. President Eisenhower had suffered a heart attack not quite two months earlier. Although Ike was recuperating well, his condition fueled speculation that he would not run for reelection the following year. Bozell's piece in the first issue reported on a plan supposedly being developed by leaders of right-wing organizations to capture the 1956 Republican presidential nomination, provided Eisenhower did not run for reelection. Bozell suggested the favorite conservative candidate would be Senator William F. Knowland. And, in fact, although Bozell did not reveal this, Buckley and his co-editors were privately urging Knowland to run.[1]

Willmoore Kendall, former professor of political science at Yale who had become a friend and mentor to Buckley, wrote a weekly column called The Liberal Line, which was to be devoted to keeping a "watchful eye" on the "huge *propaganda machine*" of the liberal establishment. Watching the liberals was apparently a considerable task because another column appearing in every other issue, The Printed Word by Karl Hess, was also to be devoted to reconnoitering the liberal press. Meanwhile, a third column, On the Left, would explore what domestic communists—and their "fellow travelers and dupes"—were up to. This carried the by-line C.B.R., whose identity was not disclosed. The author was actually Ralph de Toledano, an associate editor at *Newsweek*, which forbade its editors to write for other magazines. James Burnham wrote a column titled The Third World War, in which he would analyze the geopolitical struggle with communism. The magazine reported that Willi Schlamm was ill, but would soon begin contributing two weekly columns, Foreign Trends and Arts and Manners, and Frank Meyer would write a monthly column devoted to academic journals. In the inaugural issue, a newsletter titled "From Washington Straight" by Sam M. Jones appeared just inside the front cover. The magazine promised that F. A. Voigt would soon begin a regular newsletter from London, and an unnamed "special correspondent" would provide occasional reports from behind the Iron Curtain. There would also be periodic columns about the law, business, labor, and the United Nations. Book reviews would appear at the back of the issue. In the inaugural issue, the lead book review was by John Chamberlain, the well-known journalist who had also helped boost *God and Man at Yale* by writing a foreword for the book.

What about Russell Kirk? From the Academy—described by the publisher as a column "about doings in the academic stratosphere"—was relegated to page twenty-five of the inaugural issue, at the back of the issue and just before the theater and book reviews. It was to alternate every other week with a column by Buckley titled From the Ivory Tower. Kirk's first column was typical of what was to follow: It commented on a speech by Robert M. Hutchins, the former chancellor of the University of Chicago, about how, if he were able to do it over again, Hutchins would reorganize that institution. Educational policy was certainly not an unimportant subject, and what Hutchins said he wished he had done—provide more personal interaction between teacher and student and avoid "self-defeating excesses in specialization" in the faculty—understandably seized the interest of the man who resigned his academic position because he was dismayed by "Behemoth University." Buckley was endorsing the importance of critiquing higher education by making it the subject of his own column. In a few years, however, Buckley would instead be addressing issues central to politics and policy in a thrice-weekly syndicated column, On the Right. Perhaps surprisingly, Kirk's column was to become one of the magazine's most popular features and continue in the same vein for twenty-five years, outlasting every one of the other original columns.

Buckley worked at gathering momentum for *National Review*'s launch. He ran a display ad for the new journal in the *New York Times* shortly before the first issue came off the press. The ad proclaimed that "*National Review* proposes to revitalize American conservatism" and would publish "news that many periodicals suppress." The magazine signaled its distance from the now disreputable likes of *American Mercury* and the *Freeman* by promising to be both "exciting and responsible" and provide "honest controversy and civilized debate." Readers were invited to try *National Review* for fifteen weeks for two dollars or become a charter subscriber for one year for seven dollars.

With possible assists from Clare Boothe Luce—the famous writer, former member of Congress, ambassador to Italy, and wife of *Time*'s publisher, Henry Luce—and Ralph de Toledano, *Time* and *Newsweek* ran short articles about the new magazine in their November 21 issues. *Time* reported that the first issue was being sent to ten thousand charter subscribers and thirty thousand people who received promotional copies. Another ten thousand copies were destined for newsstands. Where did all the charter subscribers come from? Wealthy benefactors sponsored gift subscriptions. Roger Milliken sponsored more than twelve hundred subscriptions during the magazine's first few months, and Lemuel Boulware also underwrote gift subscriptions.[2] Buckley maintained a strict policy that all gift subscriptions had to be paid for. Just as the first issue was going to press, Frank Meyer requested that a gift subscription be sent to a particular individual. Buckley sent him a terse reply. "We are very rigid about free subscriptions. We give them only to people whom we are whorishly courting, such as Andre Malraux and T. S. Eliot," Buckley explained. He then drove home the conservative point that there is no free lunch. If the individual for whom Meyer had requested a gift subscription could not afford to subscribe, "I shall myself pay for her subscription, and would appreciate your letting me know as to this."[3]

National Review's arrival on the political landscape provoked attention. Within six months, three liberal journals—*Harper's*, *Commentary*, and the *Progressive*—published critiques.[4] None was complimentary. The piece in *Harper's* was by John Fischer, the magazine's editor, and was given prominence by being the lead piece in The Editor's Easy Chair near the front of the magazine. In three blistering pages, Fischer said, among other things, that he found the new conservative journal to be devoted to conspiracy theories, suffering from a persecution complex, inconsistent, utopian, dreadfully earnest, and "like most of the extremist little magazines . . . aimed primarily at an audience of True Believers." Contrasting *National Review* and Robert A. Taft, Fischer concluded the magazine was not genuinely conservative but, in fact, radical. Murray Kempton, who wrote the piece for the *Progressive*, principally complained that the new conservative magazine was boring. The title of his piece, in fact, was "Buckley's National Bore."

Social critic Dwight Macdonald, writing in *Commentary*, liked *National Review* even less. It was, Macdonald said, poorly written, journalistically amateurish, and—worst of all—dull. Macdonald was not surprised; after all, *National Review* was edited by a young man with a clear but shallow mind who might make an excellent journalist if only "he had a little more humor" and "knew how to write." "The tongue is his instrument of expression," Macdonald observed, "not the type-writer." Among other things, the magazine was long-winded. Nor did the collection of writers and editors assembled by *National Review* impress Macdonald. The magazine was staffed largely by unknowns, he sniffed. Among those he did recognize were Chamberlain and Kirk—both of whose names, he astutely observed, were on the original masthead but then disappeared "perhaps because they preferred to take responsibility only for their own contributions." Macdonald also believed that *National Review* was not truly conservative. He found it ideologically antiliberal and nothing more. Macdonald quoted the magazine as saying that segregation was "a problem that should be solved not by the central government, but locally—in the states—and in the hearts of men." "A true conservative," wrote Macdonald, "appeals to the laws, or if desperate, to tradition, but certainly not to the 'hearts of men.'" "This," he declared, "is demagogy." The one bright spot in the otherwise bleak landscape was Russell Kirk, who provided the "only consistently humane and civilized voice" in the magazine. But this was insufficient to redeem a magazine otherwise so bereft. The bread and butter of journals of opinion are ideas. Ideas, however, were just what *National Review* lacked, and it did not have an encouraging future.

These pans only helped *National Review*, especially with its target audience. No one expected liberals to be objective critics, and hard-core conservatives relished getting under liberal skins. Besides, if *National Review* was so maladroit and tedious, why bother writing—in each case, at some length—about it? Like Yale's attack on *God and Man at Yale*, these articles only succeeded in stimulating greater interest in the new magazine. Buckley took full advantage of the attention. He wrote a six-page response titled "Reflections on the Failure of 'National Review' to Live Up to Liberal Expectations," giving as good as he got, and concluding that "we shall continue to be grateful for counsel from our allies. Liberals, however, should submit their recommendations in self-addressed, stamped envelopes."[5]

History would prove that the critics spectacularly underestimated *National Review* and its young publisher. First, while their philosophy may not have been conservative as that philosophy was previously understood, Buckley and *National Review* were redefining the term. Second,

Buckley and *National Review* were—especially to their target audience—
anything but boring. As we shall soon see, there was, however, one area
on which Macdonald touched a nerve—the subject of race.

Buckley recruited two other talented people to serve in key roles at *National Review*. The first was his sister Priscilla. After graduating from
Smith College in 1943, Priscilla had gone to work as a "rewrite" person
for United Press International in New York City. Her job had been to
turn fact-dense newswire reports into interesting scripts of five to fifteen minutes in length that radio disc jockeys could read on the air.[6]
Serving more than five years in that job, she had mastered the art of
making a piece just so many words in length, of writing strong sentences and interesting pieces, and of working efficiently under deadline.
She had also worked briefly as a news editor for a Camden, South Carolina, radio station. And, like Bill, she also had worked awhile for the
CIA, though Priscilla had been posted in Washington and not involved
in covert work. Priscilla then returned to UPI as a general correspondent. She was working in its Paris bureau when, in February 1956, Bill
called and asked her to join the staff of his new magazine. Priscilla flew
home and promptly began work. She found it difficult, however, to raise
the issue of salary. It was months later, after the bookkeeper asked Buckley why his sister did not appear on the payroll, that Priscilla started
getting paid—and Bill set her salary at the modest rate she received when
she first began working for UPI, twelve years earlier.[7]

For her first three years, Priscilla wrote articles under her own name
and much of the short, unsigned pieces commenting on current events
in the For the Record section in the front of the magazine. One of the
readers she impressed was Whittaker Chambers, and he suggested to
Bill that he make Priscilla managing editor when the position became
vacant. Bill asked his sister whether she would take the job. She agreed
to accept under one condition: She wanted six weeks of vacation per
year to indulge her passion in traveling. Priscilla served as managing
editor from October 1959 until 1985. She was calm, cheerful, and efficient.
She not only kept the trains running on time, she helped difficult personalities work together. Everyone was fond of Priscilla, and many confided
in her. When her brother sought her counsel, Priscilla typically sided with

James Burnham and the pragmatists. She was conservative through and through, but a moderate conservative. In her memoirs, Priscilla remarked that *National Review* attracted great writers as well as "other valiant and energetic right-wingers, some of whom, however, bordered on kookery."[8]

Buckley also had good fortune recruiting William A. Rusher to serve as *National Review*'s publisher. Rusher, born in Chicago and educated at Princeton and Harvard Law School, started his career as an associate lawyer in a leading Wall Street firm. He was right wing by instinct, and the political world attracted him. He took a leave of absence from his law firm to serve as special counsel to a New York State Senate committee. That in turn led to his resigning permanently from the law firm to become associate counsel for the U.S. Senate Internal Security Subcommittee. There, he met Brent Bozell, who was working for McCarthy, a member of the committee. Through Bozell, he briefly met Buckley. When political fortunes caused Rusher's position with the Senate to come to an end, Rusher, thirty-four years of age, returned to New York City to look for another job practicing law. He asked Bill Buckley to lunch to find out whether the Buckley family oil business could use a lawyer.[9] He was surprised when Buckley made him a different proposition: How about becoming publisher of *National Review*?

Buckley needed help with the business side of the magazine. Willi Schlamm had just left. The relationship between Buckley and Schlamm had quickly turned unpleasant. Schlamm had expected Buckley to defer to his more experienced professional judgment, but Buckley took the reins with full confidence—and as Schlamm had himself suggested, Buckley held all of the corporate voting stock and had full authority to run the magazine as he wished. After a period of childish acting out, Schlamm decided to go his own way. Although Schlamm's leaving was a relief, it made Buckley realize that he couldn't handle both the editorial and financial responsibilities. And so, at lunch with Rusher in mid-1957, Buckley asked him to become publisher of the magazine. It is not clear why Buckley thought Rusher, who had no experience with magazines whatsoever, would make a good publisher. And Rusher did not immediately say yes. Leaving the law was not an easy decision. But he wanted to become involved in the conservative movement, and Buckley sweetened the deal by telling Rusher that he would also have the rank of a senior editor and be consulted on major editorial decisions. Eleven weeks later, Rusher accepted Buckley's offer. Buckley's instinct had been right. Rusher was an extremely effective publisher, who helped guide *National Review* through precarious finances in its early years, and remained publisher until 1988. He was a participant in major editorial decisions. He typically leaned hard right—often harder right than Buckley himself—but he was not an extremist. Rusher also was active in the conservative movement in many ways, and often served as the magazine's ambassador to Republican politicians. Rusher was also a major force in the draft Goldwater movement.

National Review came on the stage at a time when America was trying to absorb *Brown v. Board of Education*. *Brown* had been a unanimous decision, not because all members of the Supreme Court agreed with it, but because Earl Warren persuaded them that for the good of the nation the court should speak with one voice. Looking back from more than six decades later—when the court's most socially tender decisions are routinely decided 5-4, with sniping between the majority and dissenting opinions—Warren's feat seems remarkable. But the 1950s were a time when many of the nation's leaders (not all, to be sure) were better able to separate patriotism from partisanship.

It wasn't immediately clear how the nation would react to *Brown*. The court first decided that desegregated schools were unconstitutional, and said it would take up the question of implementation later. The day after the court announced its first decision, President Eisenhower told the District of Columbia that the nation's capital should set the example and comply without waiting for court orders.[10] Governor James E. "Big Jim" Folsom of Alabama said, "When the Supreme Court speaks, that's the law." Arkansas's governor, Francis Cherry, declared, "Arkansas will obey the law. It always has." In a later opinion, the court decreed that desegregation must proceed with "all deliberate speed." The phrase was deliberately vague, yet many school districts immediately made arrangements to comply. Within two years, 723 school districts—most of them in border states—had desegregated.

Before long, things turned ugly. Eight blacks were lynched in the South during 1955. The most famous incident involved fourteen-year-old Emmett

Till, a Chicago boy who, while visiting relatives in Mississippi that August, made the fatal mistake of whistling at a white woman who sold him candy in a grocery store. Had this happened to a Southern boy, there might have been little publicity, but when Emmett's body was returned home, Chicago newspapers turned it into a cause célèbre. In September, reporters from around the nation descended on Sumner, Mississippi, for the trial of two men arrested for Emmett's murder. They were stunned at what they observed at the trial. At the courthouse, the country sheriff greeted black spectators with "Hello, niggers." In his summation, a defense lawyer told the jury, "I am sure that every last Anglo-Saxon one of you has the courage to free these men." Jurors took an hour to come back with an acquittal. "If we hadn't stopped to drink a pop, it wouldn't have taken that long," one juror mockingly declared. Less than two months later, on December 1, 1955, Rosa Parks was arrested for refusing to move to the back of the bus in Montgomery, Alabama. Her arrest ignited a boycott of city buses, and the ad hoc group organizing the effort had the usual prescience to select a twenty-six-year-old preacher named Martin Luther King as its leader.

Thus—two weeks after *National Review* started publishing—one of the most significant events in the civil rights movement began. The Montgomery bus boycott was a war on two fronts. One was in the courts. NAACP lawyers appealed Rosa Parks's conviction in the state courts and instituted a separate action in federal court to declare Montgomery's segregated bus system unconstitutional. Meanwhile, a grand jury indicted King and others for organizing a boycott "without just cause." The second front was in the streets. The boycott became a protracted economic war lasting eleven months. The city commissioners served public notice of where they stood by publicly joining the White Citizens' Council. Then the bombings began. King's house was bombed first. The home of E. D. Nixon, another black preacher and boycott leader, was bombed next. When the Alabama White Citizens' Council held a rally in Montgomery, ten thousand people attended.

The question the nation faced was not only about segregation; it was also about the rule of law. Would the nation's leaders declare that the law of the land had to be obeyed, as governors Jim Folsom and Francis Cherry had? Or would they permit the instruments of the law—its courts, prosecutors, juries, and police—to be turned against the law itself? Just as Martin Luther King's trial for organizing a boycott without just cause was getting under way in Montgomery, Senator Walter F. George of Georgia rose on the floor of the United States Senate to read a statement signed by nineteen senators and seventy-seven members of the House of Representatives. Known as the Southern Manifesto, the statement decried the Supreme Court's decision in *Brown v. Board of Education* as "a clear abuse of judicial power" and commended "those States which have declared the intention to resist forced integration by any lawful means." Only three senators from the South declined to sign the manifesto—Lyndon Johnson of Texas, and both of the senators from Tennessee, Albert Gore Sr. and Estes Kefauver, who would become Adlai Stevenson's running mate later that year.

Thus did the leaders of the South turn away from the sentiment that the law of the land, as interpreted by the Supreme Court, had to be respected and obeyed. As a strictly political decision, they were not wrong: Defending segregation and railing against the evils of Northern aggression turned out to be more popular. When he ran for reelection in 1956, Francis Cherry was defeated by archsegregationist Orval Faubus. When Jim Folsom ran again for governor, he was defeated by his former friend and campaign manager, George Wallace, who told the voters that Big Jim turned out to be "soft on the nigger question."[11]

On September 23, 1957, President Eisenhower, who was not enamored with *Brown v. Board of Education*, but believed that it was his duty to enforce the law nonetheless, dispatched one thousand paratroopers from the elite 101st Airborne Division to Little Rock, Arkansas, where nine black students were attempting to enroll in a previously all-white high school. Eisenhower acted after a mob—numbering in the thousands and screaming, "Lynch the niggers!"—overran police barricades. Eisenhower simultaneously ordered the Arkansas National Guard into federal service. He federalized the guard not because he intended to use it to preserve order but because Governor Faubus, defying orders of the federal courts, previously called out the National Guard to *stop* the black students from attending the school.

The civil rights movement presented conservatives with a challenge. Conservatives instinctively resist dramatic social change and, in addition, are skeptical about change prompted by government edict. Change should ideally come organically. But wise conservatives also recognize that change is inevitable. No society can remain frozen. Edmund Burke famously said, "A state without the means of some change is without the means of its conservation."[12] In the summer of June 1780, the radical Protestant Lord George Gordon whipped mobs into a frenzy because Parliament modestly relaxed discriminatory restrictions on Catholics, causing riots that left buildings burned and hundreds dead. Burke argued that Parliament was partly to blame—not because it brought about social change too hastily—but because it did so too slowly. Parliament had spent forty years deliberating about whether to remove some of the long-standing injustices imposed on Catholics. As Burke saw it, Parliament's hesitation further ingrained and intensified fear and prejudice against Catholics.[13]

A similar view would hold that the Supreme Court caused social upheaval not by acting too rapidly when, in 1954, it declared segregated schools to be unconstitutional but by waiting so long to do so. The Fourteenth Amendment's guarantee that no state shall "deny to any person within its jurisdiction the equal protection of the laws" was made part of the Constitution eighty-six years earlier. The Supreme Court's previous decision that this could be accomplished by "separate but equal" facilities was a sham—not a means of providing equality but a pretense for denying it. If that had not been abundantly clear when the Supreme Court enunciated that doctrine in the 1896 case of *Plessy v. Ferguson*, it had at least been undeniably clear for decades. In 1945, for example, for every dollar per pupil that South Carolina spent in white schools, it spent only thirty-three cents per pupil in black schools. In Mississippi the ratio was even lower: roughly twenty-two cents to the dollar.[14] Indeed, as everyone fully understood, the entire purpose of segregation was inequality—to hold blacks in an inferior position and deny them both equal opportunity and equal dignity as human beings.

Conservatives also had to wrestle with the rule of law issue. The Supreme Court had spoken. Its decision was the law of the land, and the law of the land is entitled to respect. Ordered liberty depends on society's deep and abiding respect for the rule of law. Anything that destroys that respect threatens ordered liberty. This does not mean that one cannot disagree with the law—whether imposed legislatively or judicially—or seek to change it. But for conservatives especially, disagreement must be expressed responsibly, in a manner that does not do unnecessary damage to the esteem of the courts. This is very much how President Eisenhower viewed *Brown v. Board of Education*.

These were not the views *National Review* chose to adopt. It wasted little time denouncing the court's decision in the harshest of terms. In an editorial that expressed its corporate position, *National Review* called *Brown* "one of the most brazen acts of judicial usurpation in our history, patently counter to the intent of the Constitution, shoddy and illegal in analysis, and invalid in sociology."[15] Considering the express words of the Fourteenth Amendment, it was not self-evident how *Brown* "patently" ran counter to the intent of the Constitution, and the editorial did not explain how it did so. The editorial endorsed a proposal in Virginia known as the Gray Plan, adding that libertarians generally should find themselves in agreement with that plan, regardless of how they felt about segregation. It was interesting that here *National Review* had chosen to address its readers as libertarians rather than conservatives.

Under the Gray Plan, if a federal court ordered the schools of a city or county to desegregate, the local school board could decide for itself whether to do so or instead close all of its public schools. The state would provide tuition grants to students, white or black, who wished to attend private schools, regardless of whether their schools were integrated or closed, so that no student would be forced to attend an integrated school. To make this part of the plan possible, voters amended the state constitution by referendum to permit public funds to be used for private schools. Proponents characterized the Gray Plan as a compromise measure, arguing that it allowed some localities to integrate and others not. The more extreme positions, they said, called for either all of the schools to be integrated or none of them to be integrated.[16]

Several months later, *National Review* ran a second article about the Gray Plan, this titled "The Right to Nullify" by Forrest Davis.[17] Davis praised both the Gray Plan and the Southern Manifesto signed by more than one hundred "statesmen," and saw the latter as a responsible means of implementing the former. "The South, its governors, legislators and Citizens' Councils, is [sic] striving to find a way around the Court's finding 'by,' in the language of the Manifesto 'any lawful means.'" How many readers gasped at Davis's including Citizens' Councils among those admirably striving for a way around the court's ruling? Many, if not most, Citizens' Councils were repackaged White Citizens' Councils, which in turn were repackaged Ku Klux Klan chapters. Should not a careful editor have excised this reference?

Davis considered the Gray Plan "a plausible compromise" that "put tax monies available for public education at the disposal of parents rather than the existing dual school systems." If implemented, the plan might result in valuable experimentation that could wind up improving education. Davis did not argue this was the purpose of the plan; it was a byproduct, though potentially a valuable one. He described the Gray Plan as "an ingenious device with which to nullify" *Brown v. Board of Education.* The theory to which Davis alluded was that states had a right to nullify unjust laws by the federal government or to "interpose" themselves between the federal government's attempt to enforce such laws and its citizens.

The Gray Plan was not, in fact, immediately adopted. In a special legislative session in the summer of 1956, the Virginia General Assembly instead enacted a more extreme approach known as "massive resistance," which required that schools subject to desegregation orders be closed. Schools in Norfolk and other large districts were closed pursuant to the plan. When, in 1959, the Virginia Supreme Court declared the massive resistance legislation to be unconstitutional, the legislature repealed that legislation and adopted a program that resembled the Gray Plan. Under this approach, formally called "freedom of choice," localities that were ordered to desegregate their schools had the option of complying or of closing their public schools entirely. The battle over this approach was most intense in Prince Edward County. When a federal court ordered the county to desegregate its schools, county supervisors closed the schools entirely—and they remained closed for five years. For the first school year, the county provided no support of any kind to schools or students. A private foundation operated schools for white students only. It also offered to establish separate schools for black students, but the black population of the county declined that offer, choosing instead to challenge the now-privatized segregated school system in the courts. During the first academic year, Prince Edward County gave no financial support to the new private schools, but in its second year of operation students received tuition grants of up to $250 from both the state and the county. In addition, the county enacted an ordinance providing property tax credits of up to 25 percent for contributions to private schools in the county.[18]

In February 1956, Sam M. Jones wrote another article about Southern resistance to school desegregation.[19] "Southerners will not accept the edict that the races *must* mix, in schools or elsewhere," he declared. "And it won't be shoved down their throats, even with federal bayonets." Luckily, in Jones's view, the South had found a champion in Senator Strom Thurmond of South Carolina. Along with several other Southern leaders, Thurmond was going to defend the cause of segregation at the 1956 Democratic National Convention. "If the Convention nominates a Liberal," wrote Jones, "there is every reason to believe that the States' Rights movement will be reactivated immediately."

The same issue that contained Jones's paean to Thurmond also ran an editorial about Autherine J. Lucy's attempt to enroll in the University of Alabama. This editorial pioneered what would become a standard technique: taking care to go on record denouncing segregationist violence while implying that because such violence was predictable, the real instigators were the integrationists who provoked it. "The reaction of the student body—the mob violence, the hoodlumism—is a disgrace," the editorial carefully stated. "However," it continued, "the nation cannot get away with feigning surprise at the fact that there was a demonstration by students, nor even that the demonstration became ugly and uncontrolled." The editorial did not say who claimed to be surprised that there was violence. Nor did it explain why—if an ugly, violent demonstration was to be expected—public officials should not have been expected to provide adequate police protection so that the demonstration did not, in fact, become "uncontrolled." Thus did the editorial subtly shift blame to the victim. Its message was: Yes, of course, what the rioters did was unforgivable—please don't accuse us of excusing them—but Lucy and the integrationists who sent her to the University of Alabama bore greater responsibility for the violence. The editorial went on to warn that this was "only one of many such incidents whose occurrence we had better get used to if we intend to enforce the Supreme Court's decision at bayonet point." The ultimate blame, therefore, rested with the Supreme Court, for it had tipped over the first domino. "The Supreme Court elected to tamper with organic growth," it explained. "It must, under the circumstances, accept the fatherhood of social deformity."

A February 1956 editorial took a different approach: The South's resistance to school desegregation was truly about federalism. This piece was a transparent attempt to provide conservatives with cover for opposing desegregation; they could do so not because they favored segregation but because they believed such decisions should be made locally. Resistance to *Brown* was not about race relations; it was a transcendent issue about the structure of the republic. The editorial made matters worse by laughably overstating its position. "Support for the Southern position rests not at all on the question whether Negro and White children should, in fact, study geography side by side; but on whether a central or a local authority should make that decision," it proclaimed.[20] *Not at all?* If the reader wondered whether the editorial writer had let *not at all* slip into the sentence without much thought, the editorial's penultimate sentence made it clear that was not the case. "Segregated schooling, we repeat, is not the issue," it read.

Suddenly, in the spring of 1956, this spiraling descent into dogmatism was interrupted by three short pieces about the Montgomery bus boycott. The first ran as part of a new feature that continues to this day in *National Review*: a section at the beginning of each issue, titled The Week, composed of short notes and observations. The entry read in full:

> There doesn't seem to be any doubt about the fact that the forty Negro leaders in Montgomery, Alabama, have conspired to boycott the bus company, and evidently there is a law against that kind of thing in Alabama. It is a bad law, in our opinion; it is difficult, in these days of centralized political power, to make effective protest. In free societies, change should be brought about as a result of social, not legal pressure; and it is the kind of pressure the Alabama Negroes are in the process of exerting.[21]

This was followed by two other pieces, which although also short, were editorials and therefore more significant.[22] The city of Montgomery was refusing to allow Negroes to operate their own bus company because it claimed the city could not support two bus companies, the first editorial piece explained. But Montgomery could support two bus companies; it just couldn't have two for the price of one—and that was irrelevant. "We believe that the force of law ought not to be used by the federal government to force integration. And we believe the force of law ought not to be used by the states to deprive Negroes of the right to protest, or the right to compete with established institutions of business." If blacks were willing to pay the cost of a second bus company, they should be permitted to do so; and "for the segregation they cherish, white people must be prepared to pay the whole cost—twenty cents a ride, instead of ten, if need be." *National Review* reiterated this position in a second editorial when the boycott ended.

Here was a principled conservative position. Social change should come organically. It should not be brought about by government edict, but it should not be impeded by government either. Protests and economic pressures are part of the process of organic change. It is influenced by people's desires and behaviors. People may advocate for change, and they may also associate with others to organize their lives differently. The extent to which they affect society at large depends on a host of factors, including whether they can sustain the way in which they choose to live and whether others join them. The editorial was therefore consistent with Burkean philosophy. Moreover, it was consistent with libertarianism as well because it deemed a government-protected monopoly to be illegitimate.

Who or what produced these more enlightened articles is lost to history. These, however, were the anomalies. During the same period of time, *National Review* continued to lambaste the Supreme Court for its desegregation decisions. Indeed, not only did it reiterate its criticisms of sloppy reasoning and judicial activism but it also remarked "that is not altogether clear whether a moral issue is at stake."[23] And the magazine also praised the Senate for filibustering to death legislation that would have imposed on the South "extreme measures of racial integration."[24] Just before the 1956 presidential election, Buckley wrote a signed article setting forth his reflections on the choice before the voters.[25] His central theme was that Dwight Eisenhower and Adlai Stevenson were Tweedledee and Tweedledum. If each were made absolute monarch of a small island, Buckley speculated, their kingdoms would look very much alike. They would both have golf tournaments, the young publisher quipped. And they would both have racial intermarriage.

By raising intermarriage, Buckley was employing a strategy favored by segregationists. Although, especially in the North, Americans were increasingly in favor of equal rights for black citizens, intermarriage still made them nervous. As late as 1963, 90 percent of white Americans said they would object if their teenage daughter wanted to date a black person.[26] *National Review* kept raising the specter of intermarriage— or miscegenation as segregationists preferred to call it. In a July 1957 interview of Senator Richard Russell of Georgia, the magazine's principal voice on race, Sam M. Jones, asked two questions on the topic: "Do the people of the South fear political domination by the Negro or miscegenation or both?" "Do you believe that school integration would be a step toward mass miscegenation in the South?" Russell's answers were, respectively, "both," and "yes, a long insidious step toward it."[27]

The following month *National Review* published what was to become its most infamous piece about race, an editorial titled "Why the South Must Prevail."[28] Though the piece was not signed, in accordance with the magazine's policy for editorials expressing the corporate position of the magazine, Buckley had written it (as some readers may have guessed from his distinctive style).[29]

> The central question . . . is whether the White community in the South is entitled to take such measures as are necessary to prevail, politically and culturally, in areas in which it does not predominate numerically? The sobering answer is *Yes*—the White community is so entitled because, for the time being, it is the advanced race. It is not easy, and it is unpleasant, to adduce statistics evidencing the median cultural superiority of White over Negro: but it is a fact that obtrudes, one that cannot be hidden by ever-so-busy egalitarians and anthropologists. The question, as far as the White community is concerned, is whether the claims of civilization supersede those of universal suffrage . . . *National Review* believes the South's premises are correct . . . it is more important for any community, anywhere in the world, to affirm and live by civilized standards, than to bow to the demands of the numerical majority.

The editorial also declared, "The great majority of the Negroes in the South who do not vote do not care to vote, and would not know for what to vote if they could."

From the vantage point of more than half a century later, what probably shocks most is the rank racism of portraying blacks to be inferior and incapable of responsible citizenship. But just as significant is the willingness to throw over fundamental precepts of the nation—democracy, the rule of law, and the Constitution—for desired political and social ends. It is totalitarians who cry that the laws need to be suspended to save civilization.

Let us pause, however, to try to consider the editorial, as best we can, from *National Review*'s point of view. The editors would claim that their position was mandated by reality. "Look," we can imagine them saying, "we don't like the facts any more than you do. But the facts are that Negroes are, as a group, more impoverished and poorly educated than whites. Their literacy rates are lower. We deplore this unhappy reality as much as you do. But as conservatives we cannot ignore facts—even unpleasant facts. We are not saying that Negro inferiority is innate. We are only saying that it is the reality today, and unless and until Negroes become prepared for the responsibilities of citizenship, it is essential that in the South, where in places they outnumber whites, they not take control through the ballot box." Even if the editors were wrong in many ways, at least can we say that they were making a genuine effort to deal with reality? The answer is no. Even assuming for the sake of argument that the editors were right about the facts, and even putting aside fundamental questions about what it means to live in a democracy and under a constitution and rule of law, the editors' imagined defense is destroyed by the editorial.

> The South confronts one grave moral challenge. It must not exploit the fact of Negro backwardness to preserve the Negro as a servile class. It is tempting and convenient to block progress of a minority whose services, as menials, are economically useful. Let the South never permit itself to do this. So long as it is merely asserting the right to impose superior mores for whatever period it takes to effect a genuine cultural equality

between the races, and so long as it does so by humane and
charitable means, the South is in step with civilization.

The editorial suggests that the South's moral claim to disenfranchise
black citizens would be extinguished if whites were to engage in that
conduct for selfish reasons instead of seeking to advance toward, or at
least waiting for, cultural equality between the races. But, of course,
everyone conversant with the facts knew that the South was not working for, or even just patiently waiting for, cultural equality. It was, for
example, notoriously employing sham literacy tests and intimidation to
prevent even well-educated blacks from voting while allowing illiterate
whites to vote. Moreover, the Southern states were working actively to
impede black progress and preserve cultural inequality, and had been
doing so since the beginning of the Jim Crow era, some seventy years
earlier. Gross underfunding of black schools was but one device to suppress black progress. Segregationists and their allies suspended disbelief
so as not to have to concede that the objective of Jim Crow, as the editorial itself put it, was to permit whites to exploit blacks as menial labor—
and so did *National Review*. The editorial deploys techniques that
pretend to confront facts while in fact avoiding them. It scoffs, for example, at "ever-so-busy" anthropologists without setting forth what
they had to say and refuting it. Dismissal by derision became a staple of
the magazine.

There was no philosophical reason for conservatives to oppose civil
rights. Even if one were to argue that the libertarian position naturally
favored allowing the owners of private businesses such as hotels and
restaurants to serve only those they chose, one could not have argued
that libertarianism—or conservatism of any stripe—justified inferior
black schools and the rest of Jim Crow. It was the presidential campaigns of Barry Goldwater in 1964 and, most especially, Richard Nixon
in 1972 that exploited resentment over civil rights and caused the South
to shift from the Democratic to the Republican Party, but it was *National Review*'s raw position on race in the late 1950s that made that
possible by placing conservatives in opposition to civil rights. And *National Review*'s position flowed not from any preexisting conservative
philosophy but from Buckley's personal background.[30]

Not everyone at *National Review* agreed with Buckley. In fact, two weeks after the magazine ran "Why the South Must Prevail," Brent Bozell publicly took on his brother-in-law.[31] "This magazine has expressed views on the racial question that I consider dead wrong, and capable of doing grave hurt to the promotion of conservative causes," he wrote. The magazine had permitted him a full page to make his case, for which Buckley and *National Review* deserve credit. Bozell's central point was easily stated: "There is a law involved, and a Constitution, and the editorial gives White Southerners leave to violate them both in order to keep the Negro politically impotent." *National Review* had, in effect, said the law and Constitution must "go hang," and by so doing had called into "question how seriously *National Review* takes the law and the Constitution." Bozell made his charge specific by observing that the Fifteenth Amendment—which prohibits states from denying or abridging a citizen's right to vote on account of race—applied, and although the editorial had failed to mention the amendment, Bozell observed that the magazine's familiarity with it "may be assumed."

The magazine responded in the same issue in a one-paragraph editorial comment, titled "A Clarification," also anonymously written by Buckley. Buckley did not back off. He reemphasized—and, if anything, intensified—*National Review*'s position. He repeated that *National Review* believed that majority rule must give way to "the right of the few to preserve, against the wishes of the many, a social order superior to that which the many, given their way, might promulgate" and that it was "responsible" for Southerners "to refuse to enfranchise the marginal Negro," which he defined as the Negro voter who would tip the scales of an election.[32] That was, in fact, what the South was doing; discrimination against blacks at registrars' offices tended to vary in proportion to the size of the black population.[33] He observed that Southerners regarded the Fourteenth and Fifteenth Amendments to the Constitution to be "inorganic accretions to the original document, grafted upon it by victors-at-war by force." His implication was that *National Review* considered these amendments less than fully legitimate. (He did not mention the Thirteenth Amendment, which abolished slavery.) Finally, Buckley added what some have suggested was a concession—a moderation of the position taken in the original editorial.[34] Buckley wrote, "The South should, if it determines to disenfranchise the marginal Negro, do so by enacting laws that apply equally to blacks and whites, thus living up to the spirit of the Constitution, and the letter of the Fifteenth Amendment." There were two problems with Buckley's reply. First, if the South determined "to disenfranchise the marginal Negro" and devised a technique for that specific purpose, it would violate the Fifteenth Amendment regardless of whether it applied the technique equally to white and black voters. Second, the South's then-existing voting laws were, on their face, race neutral, but it applied those laws to disenfranchise only black voters. Buckley and *National Review* were sticking with a fantasy.

Even the best conservative histories tend either to deny *National Review*'s early racism or suggest that it was an aberration—a momentary lapse in an otherwise decent and principled opposition to the civil rights movement. For example, in the book that many conservatives consider the authoritative history of their movement, George H. Nash writes, "The conservative leadership strenuously adjured any notions of innate black inferiority. No ranting, vulgar racism besmirched *National Review*."[35] In his memoir, longtime senior editor Jeffrey Hart concedes that racism stained the pages of the magazine. He quotes at length from a 1960 *National Review* editorial, which stated in part that "in the Deep South the Negroes are, by comparison with the Whites, retarded ('unadvanced,' the National Association for the Advancement of Colored People might put it) . . . Leadership in the South, then, quite properly, rests in White hands."[36] But although Hart is repelled by the editorial, he suggests it is an anomaly. "Everyone has a bad day," he says.

When it came to race and civil rights, however, *National Review* repeatedly had bad days. One of the journal's favorite authorities on race was sociologist Ernest van den Haag. In 1964, *National Review* featured on its cover—with large block letters reading NEGROES, INTELLIGENCE & PREJUDICE—a rather strange five-page article presented in Q&A format as though Van den Haag were both interviewer and interviewee. Stranger still, Van den Haag and the fictitious interviewer ostensibly play a cat and mouse game in which the interviewer repeatedly presses Van den Haag to be more specific, and Van den Haag coyly declines to do so.[37] The piece begins with the question of whether differing results in intelligence tests among ethnic groups are due to heredity or environment. Van den Haag tells the interviewer that "we do not know whether the differences that tests find occur because of differences in cultural opportunities or because of differences in native intelligence." The interviewer presses his subject: "But what about a practical guess?" "I'm reluctant," Van den Haag replies. "I feel uneasy about guessing." The interviewer persists. Van den Haag says it is "very possible but not certain" that much of the difference in average results between white and Negro children is due to innate differences, and that he "should be inclined to believe" that is the case. The interviewer asks again, "What then is your conclusion?" That question is an artifice to allow Van den Haag to then pretend to decline to answer a question he has, in fact, just answered.

This game is repeated several times. Van den Haag suggests that blacks are intellectually inferior to whites while disclaiming that is his conclusion.[38] "What about the lower cultural performance of Negroes in their native habitat?" the fictitious interviewer asks. Van den Haag replies that in terms of cultural achievements "such as the invention of a written language, or of the wheel, the creation of a literature, of arts and humanities, of mathematics, the rule of law, or medical progress," Negroes compare unfavorably with other racial groups. "It does not follow that a bio-genetic explanation is correct," he cautions. He then adds, "But I see no reason—other than fashion—to discard the possibility of differential genetic distribution of talents among ethnic groups as a possible partial explanation."

The pseudointerview also deals with whether black students will do better in segregated or integrated schools. In *Brown v. Board of Education*, of course, the Supreme Court held, based in part on sociological studies by Kenneth Clark, that segregated schools were inherently unequal because they made black students feel inferior. Van den Haag tells his interviewer this is poppycock. The evidence on which the Supreme Court relied "has been clearly shown to be wrong" and if the court were to follow valid evidence it would reverse itself. "The learning ability of Negro children *on the average* is not as responsive at present as that of white children to the stimulation given by average white schools," he explains. "We don't know whether it will ever be . . . Therefore, Negroes and whites should be educated separately—unless there is evidence in specific cases that the learning of neither group suffers from congregation and that neither group objects."

Finally, the interviewer asks his last question: "Do you have any conclusions?" "No," replies Van den Haag. "I'd like you to draw your own."

Van den Haag contributed articles to *National Review* for forty-five years. When he died in 2002, Buckley wrote an obituary describing him as "most awfully learned" and presided over his memorial service.[39]

Van den Haag's views were typical for *National Review*. Both Buckley and the magazine consistently took the position that black people, whether in America or elsewhere, were inferior, whether genetically or by virtue of deficient culture and education, and that they were not up to the responsibilities of citizenship. In his 1959 book, *Up From Liberalism*, Buckley repeated at greater length the view that whites in the South were entitled to "prevail politically" by denying the franchise to the marginal Negro voter because "the claims of civilization (and of culture, community, regime) supersede those of universal suffrage."[40] In a 1961 *National Review* article about Africa by Peter Duignan and Lewis Henry Gann, one learned that wherever in the "Dark Continent" European settlement occurred, both economic progress and true liberty expanded for blacks.[41] South Africa had the most mature economy, and thus nowhere were conditions less suitable for a black uprising. The authors did not bother mentioning that the relatively tiny white population ruled the nation through a system of apartheid; apparently they thought blacks in South Africa considered that of little consequence. In an article that same year, J. D. Futch referred to Africa and Asia as "the black and yellow continents" and "the savage and heathen worlds," and their inhabitants as "barbarians."[42] By turning over nations to "bushmen" with "no capacity to govern themselves," the Western powers were opening the door to Soviet subversion and power, he said. In a 1963 article titled "I *Know* About Negros and the Poor," Robert J. Dwyer informed *National Review* readers "that most poor people in America are poor today because they want to be. They make themselves the way they are by being lazy, uneducated, sick, undependable." And in his 1963 book, *Rumbles Left and Right*, Buckley gave what he declared to be the conservative solution to the race problem in the South: "There is no present solution to it." There was no solution because the ends did not justify the means. The means—"the drastic proposals that are being put forward with an end to securing the rights of the Negro"—included depriving states of the right to establish voting qualifications. The ends were coming without governmental action because "never in the history of nations has a racial minority advanced so fast as the Negroes have done in America." No one should be taking Martin Luther King's word for the fact that blacks were unhappy. Dr. King was "more sensitive, and so more bitter, than the average Southern Negro."[43]

Another favorite *National Review* authority on race, civil rights, and state's rights was archsegregationist James J. Kilpatrick. In the 1950s, Kilpatrick was the opinion page editor for the *Richmond News Leader* and an ardent advocate of massive resistance. Resurrecting John C. Calhoun's pre–Civil War theory of "interposition," Kilpatrick argued that in extraordinary cases the states had the right—indeed, the duty—to interpose themselves between their citizens and unconstitutional federal laws, such as those mandating desegregation.[44] Kilpatrick was far more sophisticated than Ernest van den Haag. His tightly reasoned arguments revolved around theories of constitutional law and political science. Kilpatrick would later become one of the most widely syndicated newspaper columnists in the country and a regular on the CBS show *60 Minutes*, where, as pugilist for the conservative point of view, he sparred with a liberal counterpart at the end of each week's broadcast. He was skilled at live debate—so skilled, in fact, that when he debated Martin Luther King on television in the fall of 1960, members of the executive committee of the Student Nonviolent Coordinating Committee (SNCC) believed that Kilpatrick delivered a drubbing to their hero.

During the Little Rock crisis, Kilpatrick wrote an article for *National Review* in which he sided with Governor Orval Faubus over President Eisenhower.[45] "Manifestly, race-mixing of certain schools now leads to knifings, dynamiting, and other forms of violence," he wrote. As Kilpatrick saw it, the "question thus raised so formidably in Little Rock is whether the rights of nine pupils override the rights of 1,900 pupils, whether admission to a desegregated school is a right superior to the right of a community to peace and order." Once again, a *National Review* author was suggesting that the ultimate threats to law and order were not violent mobs but the integrationists who provoked them.[46]

Kilpatrick framed the issue as balancing the rights of nine students against those of nineteen hundred students although, of course, the nine black students represented all black pupils in Little Rock's segregated schools—and indeed across America. It was as if these other black students were somehow invisible to Kilpatrick—a point he himself sur-prisingly suggested in a piece he wrote for *National Review* four years later.[47] The South, he then wrote, was changing. Thousands of South-erners were "beginning to see the Negro in a way they never saw him before." It was, Kilpatrick said, like getting new glasses and for the first time seeing clearly shapes that had previously been blurred. The civil rights movement was forcing him to confront issues, such as genuinely unequal schools, he never thought about before. "A sense of the Negro point of view, totally unrecognized before, stirs uneasily in the con-scious mind," he wrote. It was, he admitted, an unsettling experience.

Were things getting better or just different? Kilpatrick seemed un-sure. The sharpened sense of black grievances was also sharpening the white Southerners' sense of their own grievances. Buses were integrated, but fewer people were riding them. Lunch counters were integrated, but more people were eating in private clubs. Token integration of public schools was stimulating a revival in private schools. "I sometimes won-der," he wrote, "if my children will not know in the South a society far more deeply separated than the society in which I was reared, in which the races are neither friends nor enemies, but only strangers." These were honest concerns about serious problems. One would have loved to see Kilpatrick wrestle with finding conservative approaches to improving race relations and providing more equality of opportunity.

But Kilpatrick fell back to providing arguments and devising strate-gies for resisting integration. In 1963, Kilpatrick penned a dense and extensive attack on President Kennedy's then-proposed civil rights bill for *National Review*.[48] He argued that six of the bill's seven major provi-sions were unconstitutional. The voting rights provision, for example, would have prohibited literacy tests for voters who successfully com-pleted sixth grade and required that literacy tests for other voters be in writing and available to registrants upon request. Kilpatrick argued that the provision infringed on the right of states to establish their own vot-ing requirements. "I have no patience with conspiracies or chicanery or acts of intimidation to deny genuinely qualified Negroes the right to vote," he claimed. Yet he argued that all that was necessary to bring fairness to polling places was to enforce existing laws—a position pa-tently refuted by history and the practical impediments to litigating in-dividual cases. As Kilpatrick surely knew, despite herculean efforts, the

Department of Justice was making little headway in efforts to compel registrars to treat voters alike. Existing law was simply not equal to the task. Under the Civil Rights Act of 1957, the department had to provide the court with evidence of individual blacks who had been denied registration, individual whites of equal or lesser competence who had been registered, and enough instances in each category to prove not merely discrepancies but a pattern of discrimination.[49] Even a single case was difficult to bring because blacks were terrified of Ku Klux Klan reprisals if they appeared as witnesses in such lawsuits. Moreover, cases could only be brought on a county-by-county basis, and there were 1,157 counties in the eleven states of the former Confederacy.

Six months before Kilpatrick's attack on Kennedy's civil rights bill, readers of *National Review* encountered Brent Bozell's review of Kilpatrick's book, *The Southern Case for School Segregation*. "Kilpatrick acknowledges without blinking that the root cause of the war [over civil rights] is the South's belief that the Negro race is innately inferior to the white race," wrote Bozell.[50] The presumption of black inferiority was, in Kilpatrick's view, supported by the Negro's "bleak historical record as a civilization-builder" and his "crime and illegitimacy rates that do not seem to change with improved environment." Black demands for equal treatment were ungrateful and counterproductive. Somewhat curiously, in light of his other articles, Bozell seemed to endorse Kilpatrick's thinking. "The Negro can force his way into the white man's house by breaking down its walls," wrote Bozell in the conclusion of his review, "but he will have destroyed thereby the white man's capacity for hospitality, and thus his own dream of true integration."

In 1965, Kilpatrick wrote another article attacking the voting rights bill then before Congress.[51] "For the better part of a century," he conceded, "much of the South has engaged in systematic, deliberate, ingenious and effective devices to deny the colored citizen his constitutional right to register and to vote." But there were extenuating circumstances. Most Southern blacks were "genuinely unqualified for the franchise." Kilpatrick acknowledged that blacks would not have been illiterate if they had been provided decent schools, but said that "rightly or wrongly, some realistic account must be taken of life as it is and not of life as perhaps it ought to be." Kilpatrick was appalled that the voting rights bill would only affect states that had previously employed literacy tests or qualification devices *and* in which less than half of eligible adults were registered to vote or voted in the 1964 presidential election, a set of criteria that he believed had been devised to capture most of the South while excluding Lyndon Johnson's Texas. Kilpatrick argued that the bill was overly broad and unnecessarily infringed on the rights of the states to determine voting requirements. Besides, federal interference was entirely unnecessary. Things were taking care of themselves. As "the Negro's education and his income improve," Kilpatrick explained, "new doors open to him, the South's urban places beckon, and here he votes as other men do."

Kilpatrick's views reflected those of the *National Review* generally. A series of editorials praised Orval Faubus for his actions during the Little Rock crisis. The editorials also denounced Dwight Eisenhower for being a "prisoner of the nation's most dangerous and extreme Liberal ideologues" and "power-hungry enough" to trample upon the division of authority between the federal and state governments, and they implied that the black students who sought to attend Little Rock Central High School were in cahoots with communists.[52] An article by Brent Bozell took a different tack. Bozell thought Faubus's claim that he originally called out the National Guard because he feared violence seemed phony from the start. Why, if that were the case, did Faubus order the National Guard to remove the students from the campus rather than ordering them to escort them into the school and protect them? But Bozell criticized Faubus for collapsing on the central issue—asserting Calhoun's right of interposition and refusing, come hell or high water, to knuckle under to federal pressure, even if that meant refusing to comply with orders of the federal courts. Bozell argued that the most important principles at stake were preserving "the states' constitutional powers against federal encroachment" and "contesting the proposition that the Supreme Court is the final arbiter of what the Constitution means." Because Faubus lacked the stomach for a real fight, he let the South down.

National Review argued that the states' rights were intertwined with freedom. "We believe that if there is such a thing as a mechanical safeguard to freedom, it is political decentralization," it explained in an early editorial. But while that may be a fine statement of abstract political philosophy, it sounded less than fine in the context of the civil rights struggle, where the Southern states were denying genuine freedom to their black citizens.

National Review's positions on desegregation and states' rights had long-term ramifications. The magazine—and with it conservatism as a whole—drifted to the view that the states were wiser and "closer to the people" than the federal government, and that state authority was primary while that of the federal government was merely derivative.[53] What were the consequences of Buckley and *National Review*'s positions about race, civil rights, and states' rights? In one respect, *National Review*'s opposition to civil rights was good for *National Review*. Just as *Playboy* thrived by packaging photographs of naked women together with serious articles by respected authors, *National Review* thrived by wrapping racism with ostensibly highbrow arguments about constitutional law and political theory, thereby appealing not only to self-confessed racists but to those who disliked the civil rights movement but believed themselves to be untainted by racist impulses. The latter was a large group in the 1950s and 1960s—not because those in it were mean-spirited but simply because they had been raised in racist times. This was hardly the only reason for *National Review*'s success, but it was almost certainly a factor. By no means does this mean that Buckley crafted that editorial position for tactical reasons. As we shall soon see, Buckley was willing to take editorial stands that he believed were right on the merits even when that position ran against *National Review*'s financial benefit.

We are all prisoners of our upbringings. It cannot be otherwise. Sometimes we are able to break our constraints and see the world through different eyes, but sometimes our prisons are simply too ingenious. Unable to perceive a greater reality, we are like fish in an aquarium that bump their noses against the glass. In February of 1965, in what should have been an auspicious occasion for him, Buckley—at the height of his powers, and in a setting all but tailor-made for him—bumped his nose against the glass. The event was a debate at Cambridge University. As the oldest and one of the most prestigious debating forums in the world, the Cambridge Union Society was accustomed to sponsoring events at which personages of special skill and status debated great issues of the day, yet even for the Union this debate, which commemorated its 150th anniversary, was special. The Union had selected a topic related to the civil rights struggle in America, which all the world was then witnessing on its television sets. The motion to be debated was "The American Dream is at the expense of the American Negro." Arguing for the motion was novelist, essayist, playwright, and civil rights activist James Baldwin, one of the most admired writers of the day. Baldwin was born and raised in Harlem, and his specialty was describing the psychological effects of racism. Arguing against the motion was William F. Buckley Jr., then the lesser known of the two. More than seven hundred Cambridge undergraduates crammed into the hall, taking up not only every seat but also every inch of floor space, and another five hundred watched the debate from other campus locations on closed-circuit television. The debate also received considerable attention outside of Cambridge University. On March 7, 1965 (which coincidentally turned out to be the so-called Bloody Sunday in Selma, Alabama), the *New York Times* published a nearly full transcript of the debate, and American public television broadcast the entire debate later in the year. Some watching that broadcast would have noticed that only two black faces could be seen in the chamber—those of Baldwin and of actor Sidney Poitier, who is seated in the audience.[54]

Buckley enjoyed considerable advantages in this form of combat. Baldwin was a writer of rare and powerful talent, but he was, after all, a writer. Buckley's circle of activities was wider, and he was an accomplished speaker and debater. Buckley understood the customs of the venue: A debater should wear formal attire rather than a business suit; a debater should formally address the president of the Union rather than appeal to the audience at large; a debater may or may not accept questions or comments from persons in the house seeking to be recognized. However, he suffered a significant disadvantage as well: He was arguing the more difficult side of the motion.

Baldwin argued first. At the outset of his remarks, he laid a trap for Buckley. Beginning in calm, measured tones, Baldwin said the proposition before the house was "horribly loaded" and depended on one's "system of reality." The Alabama sheriff, he said, truly believed the Negro had to be "insane to attack the system to which he owes his entire identity." Baldwin then proceeded to describe what it is like for a black child, around the age of five, or six, or seven, "to discover that the flag to which you have pledged allegiance, along with everybody else, has not pledged allegiance to you. It comes as a great shock," Baldwin continued, "to see Gary Cooper killing off the Indians and, although you are rooting for Gary Cooper, that the Indians are you." Finally, Baldwin addressed the motion before the house. The American economy, especially those of the Southern states, was built by cheap black labor. With rising passion, he personalized his argument, speaking for generations of slaves and exploited freed blacks. "I picked cotton; I carried it to market; I built the railroads under someone else's whip for nothing. For nothing." The audience had witnessed a masterful performance—one that was extraordinarily eloquent, moving, and persuasive. The crowd rose and gave Baldwin long and lusty applause—something that was rare, if not unprecedented, in the history of the Union.

Buckley had his work cut out for him as he rose to address the house. Despite his considerable skill, Buckley fell into Baldwin's trap by immediately becoming the very example of the person who considered Baldwin "insane to attack the system to which he owes his own identity." Buckley began his remarks—on the heels of the standing ovation for Baldwin—by attacking the writer personally. He attacked Baldwin as a phony and a pretender. He called Baldwin a "posturing hero" who won adulation by showering contempt on American society. It was necessary, said Buckley, to deal with Baldwin "as a white man" and say to him that the "fact that you sit here, carrying the entire weight of the Negro ordeal on your own shoulders, is irrelevant to the argument we are here to discuss. I am treating you as a fellow American," Buckley continued, "as a man whose indictments of our civilization are unjustified, as an American who—if his counsels were listened to—would be cursed by all of his grandchildren's grandchildren." Buckley even accused Baldwin of affecting a British accent for the evening, for which Buckley was immediately booed.

To what indictments was Buckley referring? He did not specify. Baldwin had stated that "the Southern oligarchy . . . was created by my labor and my sweat and the violation of my women and the murder of my children." He added, "None can challenge that statement. It is a matter of historical record." This was Baldwin's harshest indictment of American society, and he had been correct that it was undeniable.

"What should James Baldwin be doing other than telling us to re-
nounce our civilization?" asked Buckley. But the audience had not heard
Baldwin say anything that could be so construed. Buckley had said he
was going to deal with James Baldwin not as a black man but as a white
man and a "fellow American," thereby revealing that he considered only
whites to be fellow Americans. This paradigm probably existed un-
examined and unconscious within Buckley's mind, but the audience
could not help but see Buckley as an example, right before their eyes, of
a man unwittingly trapped in a "system of reality."

Referring to two vignettes Baldwin had related in his book *The Fire
Next Time*, Buckley asked the audience what it would have America do
about a New York police officer who accosted the thirteen-year-old James
Baldwin in Midtown Manhattan, demanding, "Why don't you niggers
stay uptown where you belong?" or about a Chicago bartender who refused to serve the adult James Baldwin on the pretext that Baldwin was
obviously underage. Buckley presented these as rhetorical questions,
implying that there was no political solution to the bias in men's hearts.
But, of course, there were political responses to such acts—sanctions that
could be imposed for such acts by police officers, a civil rights law that
made it unlawful to discriminate against people in places of public accommodation. The audience may have inferred—quite accurately—that
Buckley opposed such responses. Indeed, on the one occasion Buckley
accepted a comment from the audience, an undergraduate declared, "Mr.
Buckley, one thing you can do is let them vote in Mississippi." "I think
actually what is wrong in Mississippi is not that not enough Negroes have
the vote but that too many white people are voting," Buckley replied. It
was the one time the audience laughed with him. Buckley did not take
the time to explain that this was not merely a clever line but his considered
view.

The audience voted 544 to 164 in favor of the motion, namely, that the
American dream is at the expense of the American Negro. Buckley
later told Garry Wills that although this was the worst drubbing he ever
received in debate, it was also the "most satisfying debate" he ever
had.[55] The debate, explained Buckley, "was planned as an orgy of anti-
Americanism," and Buckley had been advised that his best approach
was to acknowledge that criticism of America was warranted. "But I

didn't give them one gaw-damn *inch*! They were infuriated . . . But I walked out of there tall, so far as self-respect goes."

Buckley also wrote about his debate with Baldwin in *National Review*.[56] He believed his mistake was to assume that the audience was familiar with James Baldwin's writings and were "unaware that Mr. Baldwin's indictment of our society is total." But, in fact, the undergraduates at Cambridge may have read *The Fire Next Time* more carefully than did Buckley, for that work—notwithstanding all of the unpleasant truths it tells about America—is infused with patriotism and pleas for reconciliation. In a letter to his nephew, which comprises a portion of that book, for example, Baldwin writes:

> Please try to be clear, dear James, through the storm that rages about your youthful head today, about the reality which lies behind the words *acceptance* and *integration*. There is no reason for you to try to become like white people and there is no basis whatever for their impertinent assumption that *they* must accept *you*. The really terrible thing, old buddy, is that *you* must accept *them*. And I mean this seriously. You must accept them and accept them with love. For these innocent people have no other hope. They are, in effect, still trapped in a history which they do not understand; and until they understand it, they cannot be released from it . . . For this is your home, my friend, do not be driven from it; great men have done great things here, and will again, and we can make America what America must become.[57]

At the twilight of his life, *Time* magazine would ask Buckley over a career spanning half a century and involving all the great debates in American politics if he had taken any positions he had come to regret. "Yes," Buckley answered. "I once believed we could evolve our way up from Jim Crow. I was wrong: federal intervention was necessary."[58] He also observed elsewhere that "indifference to the rights of minorities can mutate, and during the century has done so, to genocide."[59]

CHAPTER 4

"The Loonies"

Word was circulating among important conservatives that Robert Welch had written a document that—because it was extremely sensitive—he was making available, with utmost care, only to a select number of individuals. Some of those who read the document considered it of vital importance to the republic, and asked Welch to send copies to friends they trusted. Others who read it thought Welch had lost his mind. Both reactions caused the grapevine connecting top conservatives to vibrate with rumors. The document was said to be about Dwight D. Eisenhower. Some called it "The Politician"; others called it "The Black Book." When, in November 1958, Buckley heard about the document, he was intrigued. He immediately wrote to Welch at the offices of Welch's magazine, *American Opinion*—the one Willi Schlamm was now working for—in Cambridge, Massachusetts. "Dear Bob," wrote Buckley, "If you have an extra copy of your manuscript on Ike that I have heard about from several people, I'd be awfully pleased to have a look at it."[1]

Robert Welch, born in North Carolina in 1899, is said to have been a child prodigy. He graduated from high school at age ten and from the University of North Carolina at age sixteen. He attended the U.S. Naval Academy at Annapolis, but when the United States entered World War I he left the academy to enlist in the navy. After the war, Welch entered Harvard Law School, where, like Buckley at Yale, he was appalled to discover that the faculty—especially Felix Frankfurter—was not devoted to a pure laissez-faire vision for the American economy. In disgust,

Welch left Harvard and started his own candy company. Four years later, he invented a confection known as the Sugar Daddy, and company sales roared. After a tussle with colleagues, he became vice president of another candy company operated by his brother, the James O. Welch Company, which eventually produced Junior Mints and Milk Duds, among other candies. Robert became well known in national business circles, serving on the board of directors of the National Association of Manufacturers for seven years, beginning in 1950. But as time went on, he became less interested in business and more interested in politics. He supported Robert A. Taft for the GOP presidential nomination in 1952. That same year Welch wrote a book, *May God Forgive Us*, about how communist subversion was shaping public opinion, which like Buckley's *God and Man at Yale* was published by the Henry Regnery Company. Two years after that he wrote another book, *The Life of John Birch*, also published by Regnery. John Birch had been a Christian missionary in China when the Second World War broke out. He joined a U.S. air force group organized in China by Lieutenant Colonel Jimmy Doolittle. Ten days after Japan surrendered and World War II ended, Birch led a mission to see where Chinese communist forces were positioned, and he was captured and killed by the forces he was reconnoitering. Welch considered him the first American casualty of World War III.[2] In 1957, Welch left business to devote himself exclusively to the anticommunist cause, and started his own magazine, which he originally called *One Man's Opinion* and later renamed *American Opinion*.[3]

Welch and Buckley were not close friends, but they weren't strangers either. Henry Regnery, who had published books by both men, had introduced them years earlier, and Welch had been one of *National Review*'s original investors, albeit not a major one (he had contributed a total of $2,000, the equivalent of about $15,000 today).[4] Welch replied to Buckley's letter immediately.[5] He was glad to send along the manuscript. He would have sent it to Buckley earlier but he wanted to talk to him about it first and the opportunity to do so hadn't arisen. The manuscript was not intended for publication. He had been sending it only to "a limited number of good friends and outstanding patriots, who could be depended on to treat it with the confidence requested, and to take reasonable precautions to safeguard the document while it was in their possession," and would mail it to Buckley the next morning by registered mail, return receipt requested. Welch asked Buckley to take it home immediately, and cautioned him against absentmindedly leaving it on the train. Two days later, the two-hundred-plus-page manuscript arrived. It had been reproduced by photo-offset, and held together with a black cover by plastic comb binding. The first page, in the nature of a letter to the reader, said that this was the third version of the manuscript. The first, much shorter draft had been circulated to about thirty of the author's "best-informed friends," in 1954, and a longer version was given to about sixty friends two years later. This version too was being sent only to friends who had been "very carefully selected—for reasons which will become obvious." Each copy was individually numbered, and the number of Buckley's copy had been handwritten in a space for that purpose. The reader was further advised that the copy was on loan and "for your eyes only." "But I shall not ask for it back in a hurry," Robert Welch explained, "because if anything happens to me I should like to have a goodly number of copies safely out in other hands."

After writing Welch a brief note acknowledging receipt and assuring him that "I shall observe all the precautions you urge upon me," Buckley took the manuscript home and read it.[6] The reasons for all of the precautions were obvious. Welch argued that Dwight David Eisenhower, then president of the United States, was an agent of the international communist conspiracy and secretly working to allow the conspiracy to slowly take full control of the country. As part of this treasonous scheme, Eisenhower had appointed communists and their agents and fellow travelers to many high-level government positions. "Eisenhower and his Communist bosses and their pro-Communist appointees are gradually taking over our whole government, right under the noses of the American people," wrote Welch.[7] The conspiracy was already well developed. The Supreme Court was "strongly and almost completely under Communist influence" and the Executive Department was "to a large extent, an active agency for the promotion of Communist aims."[8] Other members of the conspiracy included General George C. Marshall ("a conscious, deliberate agent of the Soviet conspiracy"); Secretary of State John Foster Dulles ("I personally believe Dulles to be a Communist agent"); CIA Director Allen W. Dulles ("the most protected and untouchable supporter of Communism, next to Eisenhower himself, in Washington"); and Justice William J. Brennan Jr. ("Brennan's pro-

Communist leanings were so clearly established in his record that we do not believe he could possibly have been confirmed for the Supreme Court . . . before the Eisenhower-Communist machine had worn down, browbeaten, and completely demoralized so much of the anti-Communist strength.")[9]

One of the central features of the work was to collapse together, without distinction, dedicated communist agents, fellow travelers who deliberately worked with the conspiracy for personal advancement, others who aided and abetted the conspiracy because they were sympathetic to some or all of its aims, and stooges who were manipulated into doing the conspiracy's work because they were too naïve to know better. Welch could have argued this was necessary as the conspiracy was secret and he could not be sure which individual fit into which category. Yet he placed under the umbrella of treason—chapter seventeen was, in fact, titled "The Word Is Treason"—communists and liberals. About Chief Justice Earl Warren, for example, Welch wrote, "Warren is probably not a Communist, although the ardent advocacy of him for the Presidency by Eleanor Roosevelt, Joseph Rauh, Jr., and many of their ilk, makes one wonder. As does the sharp turn taken by the Court, in support of rabidly pro-Communist measures, since Warren became Chief Justice."[10] About President Eisenhower's economic adviser, Arthur F. Burns, Welch wrote, "It is quite probable that the job of 'economic adviser' has been merely a cover-up for Burns' liaison work between Eisenhower and some of his bosses in the Establishment."[11] Is the "Establishment" the communist organization or the liberal Eastern Establishment? Welch implies that this is a distinction without a difference. In similar fashion, Welch lists as conspirators or fellow travelers—the reader is often unsure which, or even whether there is a difference—the secretaries of defense, labor, and the interior; the solicitor general of the United States; the U.S. ambassadors to Russia, India, France, West Germany, and Italy; Senators Jacob Javits (R-NY), Margaret Chase Smith (R-ME), and Clifford P. Case (R-NJ); W. Averell Harriman, then governor of New York—not to mention mystery writer Rex Stout, and Albert Einstein, who, wrote Welch, "had been run out of Germany and had come to America, not because he was Jewish, but because of his pro-Communist activities," which he continued "in this more complacent country, with increasing boldness, to the day of his death."[12] The book also included the 1958

American Opinion scoreboard—an annual feature of the magazine that
estimated the degree of communist control for each of the 105 nations.
American Opinion experts conservatively estimated that as of June 1, 1958,
the United States was 20–40 percent under communist control. By 1962,
this estimate would rise to 50–70 percent.[13]

At about the same time that William F. Buckley Jr. was reading this
remarkable manuscript in his study in Stamford, Robert Welch was
reading aloud another document to eleven carefully selected friends in
Indianapolis. He had asked them to meet him there to hear him out
about forming a society to help America resist communist domination.
For two days, Welch read this group his statement about why the nation
needed this society, what it would do, and how it would operate. Another audience would have found this a mind-numbing experience—
Welch tended to plod through a prepared text in monotone—but these
eleven men had come from around the country because they shared
Welch's belief that the nation was in peril, so we may assume they were
riveted. And surely all of them had read "The Politician." Welch told
the group he wanted to name the new organization the John Birch Society, taking as its namesake the man Welch had written a biography
about.

Welch told the group that it would be necessary to fight fire with fire,
and the John Birch Society would adopt some of the same methods that
the communists were using. Obviously, communists would try to penetrate and subvert the society. Therefore, while the Communist Party
was organized into secret cells, the John Birch Society would be organized into semisecret chapters. The organization would be monolithic,
and Welch would exercise full plenary power over all of it, making all
decisions and appointing all chapter leaders and staff. The size of the
organization and its revenue, the location of chapters, and other critical
information would be secret. The society would also adopt some other
communist techniques such as working in part through front organizations. There would be a council—presumably the eleven in attendance
would make up the core of that group—but Welch would select its
members and its role would be only advisory. According to Welch, the
founding group made one demand upon him: "The Politician" was not
to become a publication of the John Birch Society. As Welch put it,
"The founders of the Society . . . disavowed the document, and the

COUNCIL of the Society . . . made it clear that this was a purely personal problem of my own, with which they wanted nothing whatsoever to do in any way."[14] It is not entirely clear why council members would draw the line with "The Politician." *The Blue Book of the John Birch Society*—the transcript of Welch's two-day speech, which became the bible of the society—does not mention Eisenhower but is just as radical nonetheless. Welch told his audience that they had "only a few more years before the country in which you live will become four separate provinces in a world-wide Communist domination ruled by police-state methods from the Kremlin. The map for their division and administration is already drawn." The plan had been devised decades earlier by Lenin. "We shall not have to attack" America, Lenin told his comrades; "it will fall like overripe fruit into our hands." The communists were now in "virtual control" of many slices of national life, from the United States Army to the mass media. The "door of betrayal is known to be wide open and nobody—in Congress, in the executive branch, in the Pentagon itself—nobody dares to try to close it," Welch declared.[15]

After reading "The Politician," Buckley wrote a letter to Welch telling him that in Buckley's view Welch was mistaken in his analysis. Their principal point of difference was that Buckley did not believe that one could infer from the fact that the communists were winning that American leaders wanted them to win. Buckley added that he considered Welch's analysis "curiously" optimistic. If Welch's view was correct, then eliminating Eisenhower "would be a critical step in setting things right," but Buckley believed that things would probably get worse when Eisenhower left the White House. "And the reason for this," wrote Buckley, "is that virtually the entire nation is diseased as a result of the collapse of our faith." Welch wrote back, telling Buckley that of the people who had read "The Politician," he was the only one not persuaded by its hypothesis.[16] Apparently, Buckley's letter made Welch think that perhaps Buckley's was not one of the sets of hands in which the "The Politician" should be residing. He asked Buckley to return the manuscript, and Buckley did so. Nevertheless, the relationship between the two men remained overtly cordial. They agreed to meet and talk about Welch's theories personally when Welch found himself in New York City, although it is not clear whether they ever did so.

The distance between the coauthor of *McCarthy and His Enemies* and the author of "The Politician" was not great. Both men believed that communist infiltration into American government was deep and extensive and that many of the nation's leaders were aiding and abetting the conspirators, if only as a result of naiveté. Buckley thought that although Eisenhower was a good man, he was nevertheless "a miserable President" who was lethargic, indecisive, and ignorant in the face of the communist threat.[17] Welch agreed with Buckley that getting rid of Eisenhower would not cure what ailed America. In *The Blue Book*, Welch told his flock that defeating the communists would not be enough unless America also rid herself of the cancer of collectivism. The bedrock of both Buckley and Welch's worldviews was that just when America needed to be more determined, disciplined, and righteous to prevail against her enemies, she was becoming decadent and self-indulgent.

Although these two men were only a few notches apart on an ideological spectrum, they were separated by the stark line of rationality. Welch had crossed over into an alternative universe in which the communists were so clever and powerful that the most likely explanation for almost any event was that the communists had secretly engineered it. Buckley realized this, and Welch realized how Buckley perceived him. The two men remained carefully civil to one another however. A month after the founding of the John Birch Society, Welch wrote a letter to Buckley to tell him about it. "But at present," Welch wrote, "it is completely 'off the record,' and we want no publicity for it, or mention of it, of any kind." Perhaps in the nature of a small peace offering after having told Buckley to return "The Politician," Welch enclosed a seventy dollar check for ten gift subscriptions to *National Review*.[18] Buckley wrote back, professing delight at hearing the news about the John Birch Society, inviting Welch to let him know when his new organization was "prepared for a little publicity," and reminding Welch to stop in when he was next in New York.[19] But both men knew this was merely a kabuki dance.

Buckley thought it wise to inoculate himself against Welch. The same month he told Welch that he was delighted to learn about the John Birch Society, Buckley published an article by the well-known journalist Eugene Lyons slamming *American Opinion* for a Welch-penned article about Boris Pasternak's Nobel-winning novel, *Doctor Zhivago*.[20] Welch had discerned that the Soviet censorship of the book was a sham—a devious ploy to create wider interest in what only appeared to be an anticommunist work but was truly procommunist. Lyons never mentioned Welch by name in this three-page review, but he made it clear that Welch's article—which Lyons called a "grotesquerie" and "sheer fantasy"—was "only the latest in a long array of myths" peddled by *American Opinion*. Lyons's piece was carefully done. He set forth the passages from the novel that Welch claimed were procommunist, explaining how these were the views of particular characters and how Pasternak effectively refuted those views. He also set forth powerfully anticommunist passages from the novel. "The implication that any anti-Communist book which wins a very large readership is really poison is hyperbolic nonsense," wrote Lyons. Buckley gave Welch advance warning about Lyons's piece—suggesting that some friendly controversy between them now and then would be a good thing; although considering Lyons's take-no-prisoners approach, it would have been madness to think Welch would consider the article friendly controversy. Welch assured Buckley that "I shall not mind in the least" his publishing Lyons's piece, and that it would not affect Welch's high regard for either Lyons or Buckley.[21]

Welch had begun to recruit for the John Birch Society by holding seminars about the communist threat across the country. These were essentially repeat performance of the Indianapolis meeting and were open by private invitation only. Welch and his aides carefully selected people whom they thought would be receptive to their message and willing to join an organization to combat communist influence in America. Both Buckley and Bill Rusher were invited to attend one of these seminars in New York City—and then were disinvited because, the bemused Buckley observed, the organizers "ran out of chairs."[22]

Suddenly something occurred that alarmed Buckley. In May 1959, Welch started an ad hoc group called the Committee Against Summit Entanglements (CASE), which published full-page ads in one hundred newspapers—including some of the nation's largest such as the *New York Times* and the *Chicago Tribune*—beseeching President Eisenhower not to attend a summit meeting with Soviet Premier Khrushchev. The ad explained that summits were a bad idea because the "President of the United States is seriously handicapped, in bargaining in any such conference with a man like Khrushchev." For anyone who believed the thesis of "The Politician," of course, this was eyewash; bargaining was beside the point if the president did what his communist bosses told him to do. In actuality, CASE was a recruiting vehicle for the John Birch Society. People were asked to send contributions to CASE and sign petitions asking the president not to exchange visits with Khrushchev, which enabled Birch recruiters to collect tens of thousands of names and addresses of potential new members. Buckley was not a member of the CASE board; he had never been invited. But when Buckley read the names of CASE's national board—ballyhooed in its advertisements—he was shaken. Its masthead included financial backers of *National Review*, as well as prominent people within the political right whom Buckley was courting, including economist Ludwig von Mises, Dean Clarence Manion of Notre Dame Law School, and Senator Barry Goldwater of Arizona. CASE's ads made no mention of the John Birch Society—indeed, the society was still a public secret—and not everyone on CASE's board was a Bircher. Barry Goldwater, for example, was not. But Welch was CASE's chair, most members of the JBS council were on the CASE board, and the two organizations had the same address. In a footnote to a later edition of *The Blue Book of the John Birch Society*, Welch boasted that CASE was the society's first "large national front."[23]

Meanwhile, as Buckley was surely aware, other people within the *National Review* family were becoming Birchers. In fact, the magazine's masthead then included at least five people who became members of the John Birch Society, including two who were members of the society's council. Moreover, a number of the magazine's financial contributors—including Roger Milliken, its largest backer—were also becoming Birchers.[24] All of this gave Buckley pause. Maybe an adversarial relationship with Robert Welch was not a good idea. Buckley reached out for help to a mutual friend who was on the mastheads of both *National Review* and CASE. "A glance at the masthead of the Committee Against Summit Entanglements indicates to me an operative boycott of *National Review* editors," began Buckley's letter to his friend.[25] "I undertake to say this," he continued, "to prove I have a nose for conspiracy, the impression to the contrary notwithstanding." This line, which had too much edge to be accepted as good-natured humor, betrayed Buckley's ambivalence; he was of two minds about mending fences with

William F. Buckley Jr. holds a copy of his first book, *God and Man at Yale*, in 1951, the year of the book's publication. Photograph © Bettmann/CORBIS.

Whittaker Chambers in 1948.
Photograph by Fred Palumbo of the *New York World-Telegram & Sun*, courtesy of the Library of Congress.

Robert Welch, founder of the John Birch Society, reading from his controversial manuscript *The Politician*. Photograph courtesy of the Library of Congress.

Professor Clinton Rossiter of Cornell University, one of the so-called "new conservatives" who advocated a Burkean vision rather than Buckley's approach. Photograph courtesy of Caleb Rossiter.

Senator Robert Taft, the figurehead of American conservatism before Buckley's movement, seen here in 1940. To Taft's right is a portrait of his father, former president and chief justice William H. Taft. Photograph courtesy of the Harris & Ewing Collection, Library of Congress.

Frank S. Meyer. Meyer—a libertarian, and Russell Kirk's nemesis—was the magazine's reviews editor and one of several regular columnists. Photograph courtesy of Wikimedia Commons.

The dust jacket of the first edition of *God and Man at Yale*. The flap copy describes Buckley as "a Christian and an individualist." Photographs courtesy of Yale University Library, Manuscripts & Archives.

(Continued from front flap)

"academic freedom." He believes that responsible men and women must energetically defend and encourage whatever values they cherish. He believes that any attempt to preserve our civilization which does not take into account the influencing of students is doomed to failure.

As a Christian and an individualist, Mr. Buckley takes his *alma mater* Yale as a case in point. He demonstrates the secularist and collectivist impact of Yale education, and points out the large number of faculty members dedicated to overthrowing those features of our civilization which Yale's supporters wish to preserve. Why, asks Mr. Buckley, should the alumni be called upon to support an institution which is destroying the values they believe in?

The issues are drawn. This challenging book sets forth the sound but much neglected viewpoint that, the highly touted canons of "academic freedom" notwithstanding, the American people are entitled to shape their own destiny, which means they are entitled to supervise their own schools.

WILLIAM F. BUCKLEY, JR., graduated from Yale in 1950 with a brilliant—and somewhat stormy—record. His explosive editorials as chairman of the Yale *Daily News* roused the Yale campus in a manner that will long be remembered. Called everything from a "brilliant journalist" to "the most dangerous undergraduate Yale has seen in years," he was perhaps most generously described by a fellow classmate: "He had a gift for debating and . . . writing; he made no excuses for his convictions; he did an enormous amount to stimulate political interest on the campus."

In addition to his activities on the News, Buckley was also a leading member of the Debating Society, and one of the team that scored a victory over Oxford on the subject of "Socialism vs. Capitalism." He was Class Orator, member of the Elizabethan Club, Fence Club, Torch Honor Society, and Skull and Bones.

God and Man at Yale · Buckley

Russell Kirk. The retiring intellectual Kirk was propelled to prominence at a young age, much like Buckley, by the publication of his *The Conservative Mind* in 1953. Though Buckley successfully recruited Kirk to write a regular column for *National Review*, Kirk refused to appear on the masthead. Photograph courtesy of Annette Kirk.

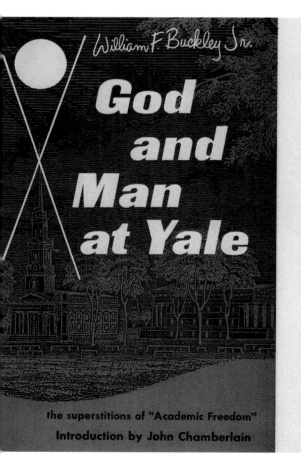

William F. Buckley Jr.

God and Man at Yale

the superstitions of "Academic Freedom"

Introduction by John Chamberlain

$3.50

GOD AND MAN AT YALE

The Superstitions of "Academic Freedom"

BY WILLIAM F. BUCKLEY, JR.
Introduction by John Chamberlain

Must the American people support schools whose students are taught to disparage American traditions and institutions? Is the alumnus entitled to insist that the college or university he supports encourage a respect for God and for individual freedom, if these are the values he wishes to further?

The academic "liberal" says no. He insists that the educational overseer has no right to discriminate against any teacher who supports doctrines alien to his own, and that any attempt to do so is in violation of "academic freedom."

William F. Buckley, Jr., a recent graduate of Yale, vigorously and eloquently indicts this theory of

(Continued on back flap)

The cover of the first issue of *National Review*. Courtesy of *National Review*.

NATIONAL
REVIEW

20 Cents
November 19, 1955

A WEEKLY JOURNAL OF OPINION

Peace — with Honor
WILLIAM F. KNOWLAND

They'll Never Get Me on That Couch
MORRIE RYSKIND

I Raised Money for the Ivy League
ALOISE HEATH

Articles and Reviews by · · · · · · JOHN CHAMBERLAIN
JAMES BURNHAM · RUSSELL KIRK · FRANK S. MEYER
WILLMOORE KENDALL · FREDA UTLEY · C. D. WILLIAMS

Barry Goldwater, the hard-right 1964 Republican presidential candidate.
Photograph courtesy of Lyndon Baines Johnson Presidential Library.

Campaign materials for Buckley's 1965 run for mayor. Photograph courtesy of Yale University Library, Manuscripts & Archives.

A 1965 shot of Buckley at his campaign headquarters explaining his views on New York City business tax rates. Photograph courtesy of Yale University Library, Manuscripts & Archives.

Pamphlet from 1965 mayoral campaign highlighting Buckley's opposition to a civilian review board for New York City's police. Photograph courtesy of Yale University Library, Manuscripts & Archives.

Find Out Why Wm. F. Buckley Jr. Supports New York City's Police

Read for yourself what The Conservative Party Candidate says about the Civilian Review Board —

(text inside)

Buckley and his opponent John V. Lindsay await a question at a debate during the 1965 mayoral campaign. Photograph courtesy of Yale University Library, Manuscripts & Archives.

Welch. Buckley explained that he did not want to write to Welch directly, as it could lead to an embarrassing confrontation. "Still, I feel I ought to know if war has been declared and wonder if you could give me your advice?" Buckley also suggested that perhaps the friend could write to Welch on Buckley's behalf.

The man to whom Buckley was appealing was, in many ways, unusual. His name, Revilo P. Oliver, was a palindrome. It had been given to him by a father who loved linguistics. Oliver was a professor of classics at the University of Illinois. His home study had twelve typewriters, each with a typeface for a different language, modern or ancient. Perhaps unbeknownst to Buckley, Oliver was one of the dozen men (including Welch) who founded the John Birch Society in Indianapolis, and he was on its council. Buckley did know, however, that Oliver was the vilest sort of bigot. Oliver disparaged a wide assortment of ethnic groups, especially Jews, and did so in Buckley's presence and in correspondence with Buckley. In April 1956, Oliver became an official associate and contributor to *National Review*. His specialty was book reviews. Four years later, Buckley expelled Oliver—not for holding racist or anti-Semitic views—but for revealing them publicly. In a speech, for example, Oliver said that Cuba was "largely populated by mongrels." To preserve its own good name, *National Review* could not publish pieces by such authors, even if their articles for the magazine were carefully scrubbed. Buckley sought to preserve his friendship with Oliver even after excommunicating him. Oliver went on to write regularly for *American Opinion*. His articles for that magazine, among other things, praised an anti-Semitic book, denied that the Holocaust occurred, and declared that "there is in the human species some biological strain of either atavism or degeneracy that manifests itself in a hatred of mankind and a lust for evil for its own sake." Presumably, Jews and communists shared satanic genes. In 1964, the Warren Commission called Oliver to testify about his theory—set forth in an article in *American Opinion*—that President Kennedy's communist handlers assassinated him because he was going to "turn American." Eventually, Oliver decided that Welch himself had sold out to the international communist conspiracy, left the John Birch Society, and affiliated with an organization of Holocaust deniers.[26] He remains, posthumously, a hero to white supremacists and neo-Nazis. But, of course, most of this was still in the future when Buckley asked Oliver to serve as an intermediary between him and Welch.

Buckley could not have been pleased when he received Oliver's four-page reply. The tone was frosty. Oliver made clear his loyalty to Welch: "I have the highest esteem and regard for Mr. Robert Welch, and I am always glad to be associated with him in any undertaking." Although Oliver said that he did not believe Welch regarded Eugene Lyons's article "as a declaration of war or even a border incident"—which was consistent with what Welch had told Buckley—Oliver added that he, himself, considered the Lyons incident unfortunate, and he waxed at length about how displeased he was about internecine conservative warfare. Nevertheless, Oliver contacted Welch, who wrote a five-page letter to Buckley of his own. Welch assured Buckley that there was no reason why he had been omitted from CASE. "To tell the truth, I simply didn't think about it," Welch explained. This time around, however, Welch admitted to being annoyed by the Lyons article, which had gone beyond disagreement and held up "to complete and sarcastic ridicule a theme to which we [sic] had given careful and considered argument." Moreover, Buckley had gone even further by making the piece the cover article of the issue, and by not later publishing even one of the many dissenting letters to the editor that Welch knew *National Review* had received. Welch admitted that his annoyance over the incident had probably stopped him from sponsoring more subscriptions to *National Review*. However, said Welch, this was the kind of minor incident that should best be forgotten; and although Welch could not promise anything, the John Birch Society—"about which we still want absolutely no publicity for a while"—might soon be in a position to obtain subscriptions for *National Review*. Why the John Birch Society would wish to do so when it has its own quasi-official magazine, *American Opinion*, Welch did not say.

The denouement of the episode was that William F. Buckley Jr. became a member of CASE's national board, and thereafter his name appeared on its masthead and in its newspaper advertisements. In the first skirmish between Buckley and Welch, Welch prevailed. As Robert Welch—or even the coauthor of *McCarthy and His Enemies* himself—might have put it, by lending his name to its front organization, William F. Buckley Jr. became a dupe or fellow traveler of the John Birch Society. But a first skirmish does not always determine a war's outcome.

Buckley looked for a way to assume a separate leadership role on the summit issue—and had a brainstorm: *National Review* would hold an antisummit rally at Carnegie Hall in September. He assigned the organizational chores to Bill Rusher, who brought his own mastery of the theater of public relations to the Carnegie Hall project. At a press conference announcing the event, Buckley threatened to dye the Hudson River red when the Soviet premier entered New York. Twenty-five hundred people—wearing black armbands to symbolize their grief for the victims of communism—turned out for the event. Buckley had arranged eleven speakers. Striking just the right balance vis-à-vis Welch, Buckley included both Clarence Manion—one of the eleven men who had met Welch in Indianapolis and a member of the council of the John Birch Society—and none other than Eugene Lyons. The last speaker at the podium that night was Buckley, who delivered what would become one of his most famous speeches. His theme was that the nation had profaned itself by inviting a ruthless communist dictator to its shores. But it was not what he said that made Buckley's speech great; it was how he said it. It had a cadence that, combined with Buckley's distinctive accent and syntax, gave it special power. Buckley borrowed imagery from the likes of *Gulliver's Travels* and *One Thousand and One Arabian Nights*. "The damage Khrushchev can do to the United States on this trip is not comparable to the damage we have done to ourselves," Buckley began. In one section of the speech, he intoned:

> I deplore the fact that Khrushchev travels about this country—
> having been met at the frontier by our own prince, who arrived
> with his first string of dancing girls, and a majestic caravan of
> jewels and honey and spices; I mind that he will wend his lordly
> way from city to city, where the Lilliputians will fuss over his
> needs, weave garland through the ring in his nose, shiver when
> he belches out his threats, and labor in panic to imperil his ap-
> petites. I mind that Khrushchev is here; but I mind more that
> Eisenhower invited him.[27]

Buckley, then thirty-three, outshone better-known speakers. Buckley, of course, was already a conservative celebrity. But this event introduced another dimension of him—his power as a speaker, and his charisma—to conservatives who had previously known him as an author and an editor of the four-year-old *National Review*. If there was a moment when Buckley became *the* leading conservative in the nation, it may have been at Carnegie Hall during the evening of September 17, 1959.*

An uneasy truce between Buckley and Welch ensued. They largely ignored one another. Meanwhile, both of their organizations flourished. By 1961, *National Review*'s circulation was fifty-six thousand.[28] The John Birch Society was even more successful. Welch was a skilled salesman and organizer. Observers estimated that by 1961 the John Birch Society had sixty thousand members, a full-time salaried staff of fifty-eight, and—through membership dues, books sales, magazine subscriptions, and contributions—annual revenue of about $1.6 million (the equivalent of about $11 million today).[29] The society was predominantly made up of older middle- and upper-class businessmen and professionals, skilled laborers, and housewives. For the first year and a half, Welch built up the group quietly, neither seeking nor receiving publicity.

The John Birch Society received its first burst of publicity in August 1960. During the Republican National Convention in Chicago, columnist Jack Mabley wrote an exposé about Welch, the society, and "The Politician" in the *Chicago Daily News*. The cat was out of the bag; a few other newspaper stories followed. Welch reacted by drawing a distinction between his unpublished manuscript—or long letter to friends—and the John Birch Society, which Welch said had nothing to do with "The Politician." But in light of the fact that Welch was the absolute leader of the John Birch Society, as well as the nature of the society's views as expressed in its official literature, it was difficult to persuade people that the distinction was meaningful. *Time* magazine ignited a national explosion of publicity when it published a disparaging article about Welch and the John Birch Society in its March 10, 1961, issue. The John Birch Society "might seem a tiresome, comic-opera joke," wrote

---

*Buckley did not receive accolades from Whittaker Chambers, however. Buckley had portrayed Khrushchev as a ruthless murderer. In a private note, Chambers told Buckley that Khrushchev was not Stalin. Khrushchev was not a monster—and it did the conservative cause a disservice to say that he was.

Time, if it did not have secret cells in thirty-five states and its members were not harassing teachers and principals for alleged communist influence in their schools or warning homeowners about suspected communists in the neighborhood.

A few weeks later, Thomas H. Kuchel (R-CA) rose on the floor of the Senate and denounced the John Birch Society in an impassioned speech. Birchers came to Kuchel's attention when they sent thousands of letters to him telling him that Chinese communists were massing in Mexico in preparation for an invasion of the United States. After sending a form reply that there was no evidence of communists, Chinese or others, gathering in Mexico, Kuchel found himself labeled a "Comsymp." The term was new to him, but it got his goat. Kuchel told the Senate what Welch had said about Eisenhower, and expressed outrage that such "spleen" should be poured over someone like the former president. Birchers, of course, knew what to think: Kuchel, after all, had first entered the Senate nine years earlier when he was appointed to an open seat by none other than then-governor Earl Warren. Welch had two responses to Kuchel's attack—one clever, one foolish. Cleverly, Welch asked the Senate Internal Security Committee to investigate the John Birch Society and, with rhetorical flourish, promised that "none of our members will plead the Fifth Amendment." Foolishly, Welch claimed that he never held the opinion that Eisenhower was a communist agent. Newspapers and magazines reported Welch's claim, and then punished him with quotations from "The Politician."

It was not clear whether the explosion of publicity was going to be good or bad for the John Birch Society. Shortly after Kuchel's speech, Welch spoke to a sellout crowd of more than six thousand in Los Angeles. It was clear that the John Birch Society had become a national issue—and conservatives had to explain where they stood on it. Barry Goldwater was the first to stake out a position. The John Birch Society had thrived in Arizona. Goldwater knew that its ranks included prominent citizens and some of his own most dedicated supporters; so he decided to ignore Welch but express admiration for the people in the society. "A lot of people in my home town have been attracted to the society, and I am impressed by the type of people in it. They are the kind we need in politics," Goldwater said.[30]

The editors at *National Review* were in a bind. They knew that some backers and readers were members of the society, but they did not know how many. Buckley and his team were in the dark about just how grave a wound they might inflict upon the magazine by denouncing Welch and his society. Moreover, Buckley was also discovering that even within his inner circle not everyone was as repulsed by Welch's conspiracy theories as was he. While Bill Rusher conceded that Welch was peddling nonsense, he thought that many Birchers accepted Welch's theories as more figurative than literal—a poetic cry of distress about the grave state of affairs.[31] Rusher also thought that Buckley was jealous that Welch, rather than *National Review*, was leading a successful conservative membership organization, and that, in fact, this was upsetting Buckley more than was Birch doctrine. Frank Meyer argued that *National Review* had to disassociate itself from the John Birch Society, but he thought it should be done in a way to give as little offense as possible to society members.

Buckley finally decided to take an approach similar to Goldwater's. In the spring of 1961, he wrote a three-page article titled "The Uproar." It appeared under Buckley's byline but in the editorial section of the magazine so that it was apparent he was speaking for the journal.[32] In a question-and-answer format designed to simulate a conversation between editor and readers, Buckley said that he did not consider the John Birch Society to be totalitarian. "I consider it reasonable that a man who founds an ad hoc organization . . . should have as much dominance over its affairs as he considers to be in the best interests of the organization's objective," he wrote (not mentioning that he, himself, had just as much authority over *National Review*). Buckley said he did not understand the complaints that the society thrived on secrecy because its literature about its beliefs and programs was widely available. Buckley disclosed the entirety of his relationship with Welch, including Welch's investment in *National Review*, and said that he admired Welch's "personal courage and devotion to his cause." However, said Buckley, he and *National Review* did not believe that the communist conspiracy was in control of the government—a thesis, he added, that was not merely stated in "The Politician" but permeated the society's membership bulletins and magazine. "The point has come, if Mr. Welch is right, to leave the typewriter, the lectern, and the radio microphone, and look instead to one's rifles," wrote Buckley. "Things are bad, I certainly agree. But we are not in Czechoslovakia in February 1948."

Buckley told his readers that the John Birch Society was being so widely attacked because certain elements of the media were taking advantage of Welch's views "to anathematize the entire American right wing." And although he did not say so, this was the principal reason Buckley had decided to act. To avoid being tarred with the same brush, *National Review* had to draw a clear distinction between itself and the John Birch Society. He sought to conclude the piece on a semiconciliatory note. *What was the future of the John Birch Society?* he imagined readers asking. "I hope it thrives," he answered, "provided, of course, it resists such false assumptions as that a man's subjective motives can automatically be deduced from the objective consequences of his acts." This was, of course, internally inconsistent. Buckley had just finished saying that the society was built on those false assumptions. Saying that he hoped the society would thrive provided it gave up those assumptions was like saying he hoped the Daughters of the American Revolution would thrive provided it would be open only to male descendants of Civil War veterans. But it was optics, not consistency, that mattered. The trick was to step cleanly away from the John Birch Society without alienating its members. Would this work?

Robert Welch may not have been thrilled, but he was grateful. "Despite the differences of opinion between us, which remain and are stressed, I think the article is both objectively fair and subjectively honorable," he wrote to Buckley, adding, "and I want you know it is deeply appreciated."

This precarious truce could not last. The future of the conservative movement was at stake. It was not long before their followers dragged both men into a tug-of-war. With Buckley's help and encouragement, one hundred conservative students from forty-four colleges had assembled at Great Elm in September of 1960 to found Young Americans for Freedom (YAF). Buckley was their inspiration. The manifesto they adopted that day, called the Sharon Statement, reflected his beliefs, and *National Review* more or less controlled the group. Buckley was pleased with the organization and believed it was important for the future of the conservative movement. But some of YAF's leaders, including Scott

Stanley Jr., a law student at the University of Kansas, had become
Birchers. Politics makes strange bedfellows, and Stanley and the Birchers united with others who were either loyal to Governor Nelson Rockefeller of New York or upset that oldsters at *National Review* exercised so
much influence over the organization to seize control of YAF.[33] Bill
Rusher spent part of his 1961 Labor Day weekend frantically helping
Buckleyites crush the attempted coup. Meanwhile, Buckley was helping a group form the Conservative Party of New York. Their goal was to
imitate the success of the state's Liberal Party, which had been formed
in 1944.[34] The Liberal Party rarely ran candidates of its own. It generally
endorsed candidates of the major parties who most closely reflected its
viewpoint. This was more often Democratic candidates, but the Liberal
endorsement was a boon to liberal Republicans such as John Lindsay
and Jacob Javits, providing them with a ballot line for voters who could
not bear to "vote Republican." The Liberal Party could also act as a
spoiler by nominating its own candidate when both of the major parties
nominated conservative candidates. This would bleed votes away from
the Democratic candidate, punishing the Democratic Party for not
nominating a liberal. In the wake of the 1960 election, conservatives
decided it was time to form their own party. Their strategy—most
emphatically—was not to compete with the Republican Party. Rather,
conservatives wanted to take control of the Republican Party, and a
state conservative party would give them an instrument to pressure the
Republican Party to nominate conservative candidates.[35] But in November 1961, just as the new Conservative Party was being launched,
the *New York Times* reported that it was infested with Birchers. This
gave the Republican Party a stick with which it would try to club the
embryonic effort to death. Buckley's initial effort had not been successful. The John Birch Society had been effectively discredited to the public at large—not as much by Buckley as by the mainstream media—but
it had not been effectively discredited on the political right. Like a
cancer, it was continuing to grow and threatening the life of the conservative movement.

Barry Goldwater asked Buckley to meet with him privately at the
Breakers Hotel in Palm Beach, Florida, in January of the following

year. The request was made through William Baroody, a skilled political operative who was also head of the American Enterprise Institute, a conservative think tank in Washington, D.C. It was all rather mysterious. The meeting was to take two days—and no one outside the small group of attendees was to know about it. Buckley was told that Russell Kirk and Jay Hall, a public relations executive at General Motors who was a Goldwater confidante, would also be present. Goldwater wanted Brent Bozell to attend as well, but Bozell was in Spain. Little was said about the purpose of the meeting other than that Goldwater wanted the group's advice. There was public speculation at the time that Goldwater was considering running for the Republican presidential nomination two years down the road, and Buckley assumed that would be the topic of the meeting. But soon after the meeting got under way, Buckley realized he was wrong. Goldwater wanted to talk about the John Birch Society.[36]

Goldwater had good reason to want to draw a bright line between himself and the John Birch Society—and to reach out to Bozell and Buckley for help—but he knew he was dealing with political nitroglycerin. In 1960, Goldwater published a slim but powerfully written political manifesto titled *The Conscience of a Conservative*. The book became an instant classic within conservative circles, and it made the junior senator from Arizona the foremost conservative politician in the nation. The ghostwriter for the book was Brent Bozell. Bozell had been commissioned to write the book, not by Goldwater, but by a small group that wanted to make Goldwater into a contender for the 1960 Republican presidential nomination. The leader of that group was Clarence Manion. The member of the group that secured Goldwater's consent for the project was Frank Brophy, one of Phoenix's largest landowners and wealthiest citizens. Brophy was not shy about his membership in the John Birch Society, and he would later become a member of its council. Other members of Manion's small group included Spruille Braden and Adolphe Menjou, both Birchers, as well as Robert Welch himself. Bozell, in fact, announced that he completed the manuscript at a council meeting of the John Birch Society, whereupon one council member from Wichita immediately purchased twenty-five hundred copies.[37] (Buckley, surely, would not have been happy about Bozell associating closely with Birchers, but he and his brother-in-law were drifting apart. In 1963,

Brent had resigned as an editor of *National Review*, and he and Trish followed an increasingly radical path.[38])

Backing Goldwater for president was semiofficial Birch dogma. In *The Blue Book of the John Birch Society*, Welch declared that he knew Goldwater, that Goldwater was a great American who came nearest to being the leader America needed, and that he hoped Goldwater would become president.[39] Goldwater, therefore, was vulnerable to being portrayed as the Birch candidate. Moreover, Goldwater was endangered not only by close connections with Birchers, but—as was the case with Buckley and *National Review*—by how close his ideas were to Birch doctrine. *The Conscience of a Conservative* argued that America was endangered by "collectivists"—communist and noncommunist—who, through the instrument of welfare programs were pursuing "their ultimate goal" of subordinating "the individual to the State." The collectivists "understand that private property can be confiscated as effectively by taxation as by expropriating it," and that "the individual can be put at the mercy of the State . . . by divesting him of the means to provide for his personal needs and by giving the State the responsibility of caring for those needs from cradle to grave." The plain consequences of all this were that the state would be "able to deal with its citizens as wards and dependents" and "rule as absolutely as any oriental despot." How was it that America found itself sliding down the slippery slope of collectivism? "In part, we were swindled," wrote Goldwater. All of this vaguely suggested that the collectivists were not merely mistaken. By talking in terms of what the collectivists "understand" and what "their ultimate goal" was, and using terms such as "swindled," Goldwater implied collectivists—in which he included liberals—intended all of those pernicious consequences. Moreover, when Goldwater talked about the communist threat in his book, he argued that because the communist was bent on world conquest, "unless you contemplate treason—your objective, like his, will be victory. Not 'peace,' but victory."[40] This echoed the *National Review* doctrine that the United States should abandon containment policy and adopt instead a policy of seeking to roll back communism. But by injecting the word "treason," Goldwater suggested that those who favored containment had less than honorable motivations. Among those who favored containment, of course, was the man who was president of the United States when Goldwater's book was published, namely, Dwight David Eisenhower. This is not to suggest that Goldwater thought for a moment that Eisenhower was a communist. He did not. But when Brent Bozell wielded his pen, Goldwater's rhetoric was reckless. He insinuated that those who held different views—those who favored Social Security, or welfare programs, or containment policy—were less than honorable, less than fully patriotic.

At the time of their meeting in Florida, Goldwater was contemplating running for president two years hence. Being a presidential candidate would invite much greater scrutiny than he previously received. He was standing far too close to the John Birch Society for comfort. He had to find a way of delicately moving further away, hopefully without infuriating Frank Brophy or Clarence Manion. Goldwater mentioned none of this to the group in Palm Beach. He simply allowed William Baroody to broach the question: What should be done about the John Birch Society?

Russell Kirk—by his own admission the least politically savvy person in the room—spoke first. Welch and the Birchers were crackpots, he said. They should be clearly labeled as such because they would burden the conservative movement until they were excommunicated. Goldwater groaned. "Every other person in Phoenix is a member of the John Birch Society," he told Kirk. Many of them were the prominent citizens. Did anyone know of Frank Cullen Brophy? Goldwater asked. Buckley did know Brophy: He had tried unsuccessfully to get Brophy to invest in *National Review*. Goldwater said that he did not want to denounce people like Frank Brophy. Buckley volunteered to take the lead in holding Welch up to ridicule. He would do so in *National Review* and in other writings and speeches. Moreover, he would criticize the society as a whole unless and until Welch recanted on his "operative fallacy," which to Buckley was that subjective intentions could reasonably be deduced from objective consequences. Goldwater liked that approach, and it was agreed that was how the group would proceed.

The next month *National Review* ran a six-page editorial entitled "The Question of Robert Welch." It began by quoting Russell Kirk to the effect that Welch, although a likeable and honest man, had become "the kiss of death" for the conservative movement, and Barry Goldwater as saying that Robert Welch should resign as head of the John Birch Society, and that if he refused to do so, the society should reorganize under different leadership. The magazine argued that Welch was damaging the anti-communist cause by "distorting reality." It quoted Welch's statement in "The Politician" that he firmly believed Eisenhower to be "a dedicated, conscious agent of the Communist conspiracy," along with Welch's views that the CIA was procommunist and NATO was a hoax. "Woe unto the man who disagrees with Mr. Welch," said the editorial. "He is 1) an idiot, or 2) a Comsymp, or 3) an outright Communist." John Birch Society chapters could do much to advance conservative aims, the editorial concluded, "but only as they dissipate the fog of confusion that issues from Mr. Welch's smoking typewriter."[41] In its next issue, *National Review* ran six letters to the editor about the article—the first by Barry Goldwater, who said that he did not believe that Welch's views "represent the feelings of most members of the John Birch Society" and reiterated that he thought Welch should resign.

Goldwater, however, was wrong when he said that Robert Welch did not reflect the views of most members of the John Birch Society. There was never a serious effort within the ranks to replace Welch nor was there any mass exodus of members. Moreover, the society continued to grow. Three years further down the road it would have eighty thousand or more members, a paid staff of 220, and annual revenues of $6 million (the equivalent of $39 million today). It would also have its own publishing company (Western Islands) and operate 350 bookstores selling Birch books and literature across the country. *American Opinion* magazine would boast a paid circulation of forty thousand.[42]

In the end—and to his undoing—it was Barry Goldwater who accommodated himself to the John Birch Society. Some of his advisers begged him not to do it. Nevertheless, when he accepted his party's nomination for president in July 1964, Goldwater stood before the Republican National Convention and declared, "I would remind you that extremism in the defense of liberty is no vice." Cheers shook the Cow Palace in San Francisco. Goldwater had to wait more than forty seconds before he could deliver the companion line: "And let me remind you also that moderation in the pursuit of justice is no virtue!" The audience leaped to its feet. Everyone understood that Goldwater had just said that the John Birch Society was okay by him. Richard Nixon, who had introduced Goldwater, grabbed his wife Pat's arm to keep her from rising with the crowd.[43] Why Goldwater chose to do this after having tried, albeit halfheartedly, to separate himself from the John Birch Society will forever remain something of a mystery. Perhaps he found it too difficult to turn his back on the likes of Clarence Manion and Frank Cullen Brophy. Perhaps it was orneriness: If Rockefeller and other liberal Republicans were going to insist that he unequivocally repudiate the John Birch Society, then by golly he was going to do just the opposite. Perhaps it was loyalty to the foot soldiers who helped him win the nomination. Whatever it was, Goldwater surely understood the magnitude of his words. The John Birch Society had been a major issue in the struggle for the Republican presidential nomination, and it remained a source of bitter confrontation throughout the convention. In his keynote address, Senator Mark Hatfield of Oregon denounced the society. Goldwater delegates did not hear him however; they had been instructed not to attend his speech. The next day, when Governor Nelson Rockefeller of New York rose to speak in favor of a resolution repudiating "irresponsible extremist groups" including the John Birch Society, the boos were deafening. "God save the Union," Senator Tom Kuchel (R-CA), GOP minority whip, exclaimed when the motion failed. In his book, *The Making of the President 1964*, Theodore H. White endorsed the view that the 1964 Republican National Convention represented the end of the reign of pragmatism in the Republican Party.[44]

Goldwater went on to suffer one of the worst electoral defeats in modern history. While the John Birch Society itself was one of many issues, it was part and parcel of a larger theme: Was Goldwater reckless or loony? Was Goldwater outside the mainstream of American politics? Was the Republican Party in the hands of extremists? Because of those two lines in Goldwater's acceptance speech, and the positive reaction of Republican delegates, many voters decided the answers were yes.

Buckley realized that he had failed: The John Birch Society continued to grow and threaten the image of the conservative movement. In addition, Buckley was upset that the John Birch Society was now opposing American involvement in Vietnam. Welch had decided that the war was futile; after all, it was being directed by communist agents or dupes such as Dean Rusk and Robert McNamara. Birch opposition to the war threatened to drive a wedge into conservative ranks. Buckley and *National Review* were arguing that America should not only persevere in Vietnam but also escalate the war. Most conservatives were following their lead. But increasingly intellectuals on the left—and some moderates within the Republican Party—were arguing that the war was unwinnable.[45] Those calling for escalation were repeatedly winning: Whenever it became apparent that current war efforts were not succeeding, President Johnson, after anguished reflection, escalated America's involvement. That might change if conservatives split on the war. A conservative split on Vietnam also threatened the conservative movement's commitment to the overall Cold War strategy advocated by *National Review*, namely, rolling back rather than just containing communism.

Buckley resolved to finally drive a stake through the heart of the John Birch Society. He was now writing his thrice-a-week newspaper column, On the Right, and he used both that platform and *National Review* to accomplish his objective. In August 1965, he devoted a series of three columns to the John Birch Society and then in October, *National Review* published a special twelve-page feature section titled The John Birch Society and the Conservative Movement. Part one of the special feature reviewed the background of the society and the magazine's previous positions on it. Part two reproduced Buckley's three On the Right columns. The first of the three columns set forth Birch doctrine about a host of issues—mental health, Medicare, the Kennedy assassination, civil rights, the economy, the Supreme Court, and more— all of which explained Birch doctrine with the same proposition, namely, that the communists controlled everything. Buckley also observed that *American Opinion* estimated that the United States was then 60–80 percent under communist influence.

In the second of his two columns, Buckley took the step he had previously refrained from taking: He attacked the membership of the society. He and others had always believed that a great gulf existed between Robert Welch and members of the John Birch Society, wrote Buckley, but the letters he received in reaction to his first column were troubling. He quoted passages from fifteen mean-spirited, wacky letters and reported that they were typical of six hundred letters he had received. The third of Buckley's columns was devoted to one letter—from Frank Cullen Brophy of Phoenix, Arizona, who was a member of the national council of the John Birch Society. Brophy's letter, said Buckley, "is a specimen of the utter hopelessness of communication with anyone suffering from advanced Birchitis." Brophy, for example, complained that

Buckley had criticized an *American Opinion* article about the Supreme Court. "The pro-Communist activities of the Court in recent years are so obvious that I find it hard to believe that you would find any comment to offer," wrote Brophy. Buckley observed (once again) that it was a mistake to infer intention from effect. The court may have interpreted the First Amendment in ways that granted license to the Communist Party, but decisions procommunist in effect were not necessarily procommunist by design. Yet the *American Opinion* article in question had expressly said that the Warren court was "working for" a foreign dictatorship, thus suggesting "pure and simple, that the majority of the Court are pro-Communist traitors."

Parts three and four of the special feature were signed articles attacking the John Birch Society by Frank S. Meyer and James Burnham. Part five was a series of questions and answers about the John Birch Society. Many of the questions were claims repeatedly made by Birchers—e.g., "Welch didn't actually say Eisenhower was a Communist"—followed by evidence, such as direct quotations from *The Politician*,* demolishing those claims. To the question: "Are you trying to say that the John Birch Society, as headed by Robert Welch, is a grave liability in the conservative and anti-Communist cause?" *National Review* answered simply, "Yes." The last part of the special feature was a collection of letters from prominent conservatives, including Admiral Arthur W. Radford, Russell Kirk, Senator John G. Tower of Texas, and Senator Barry Goldwater.

Prior *National Review* attacks on Robert Welch were pulled punches. This was not. It landed with full force, not only on Robert Welch, but also on the society as a whole. No longer was a distinction drawn between Welch and his followers; no longer was it suggested that while Welch was harebrained, members of the society were reasonable people. Membership in the John Birch Society was indefensible. It was an act of lunacy, and it was irresponsible because it harmed the conservative movement.

---

*I italicize *The Politician* for the first time because Welch published it as a book in March 1963. Welch said that because so many wild statements had been made about the manuscript, he was forced to publish it in self-defense so that readers could judge it for themselves.

It was one thing to be a member of the John Birch Society while prominent conservatives denounced Robert Welch and said they disagreed with Birch doctrine. It was something else entirely when figures such as Birch hero Barry Goldwater said that only a fool or a crackpot would be a Bircher. No fig leaf of respectability remained. The society went into steep decline. Recruiting new members was exceedingly difficult, and members who had never made their membership public drifted quietly away. Even highly visible members quit. Wichita industrialist Fred Koch—one of the eleven men Robert Welch invited to Indianapolis, and an original member of the JBS council—quit in 1967, saying that he considered Robert Welch too extreme.[46] Welch continued to head the John Birch Society until his death in 1985, but it was a depleted group, bereft of allies. William F. Buckley Jr. had successfully excised it from the movement.

As Buckley saw it, the John Birch Society was not the only threat to the conservative movement from the right. A different kind of threat was posed by a woman who had been born in 1905 to a wealthy Jewish family in St. Petersburg, Russia.[47] Her birth name was Alisa Rosenbaum. Her father was a chemist. When Alisa was twelve, the Red Guard—acting in the name of the people—seized her father's chemistry shop at gunpoint. The state claimed such actions were necessary for fairness and equality, but for Alisa this was a cruel lesson in how totalitarianism justifies abuse. Nevertheless, when the Bolsheviks made the Soviet universities tuition-free and open to all citizens, including women and Jews, Alisa was able to attend Petrograd State University. She studied history primarily, but also a variety of other subjects, including philosophy. Although his work was not part of the formal curriculum, Alisa read and became enamored with Friedrich Nietzsche. Along with all students, she was also force-fed a great deal of Marxist doctrine. She watched in dismay as anticommunist faculty were purged. Because she was from a bourgeois family, she herself was dismissed from the university. That policy, however, was soon reversed. She was readmitted and ultimately graduated from the institution that had been renamed the University of Leningrad.

Alisa and her family agreed that communist Russia was no place to make a life. Alisa obtained state permission to travel to the United States. She told the authorities she was going to study American film, and would be in America for a brief period. This was a ruse. She had no intention of returning. In January 1926, the family packed Alisa off to relatives in Chicago. It was a difficult farewell; they too knew Alisa was never coming back.

Alisa wanted a new name to go with her new life, and decided to call herself Ayn Rand.

In Chicago, Rand spent as much time as possible in movie theaters. She did this partly because her interest in American film was genuine and partly to improve her English. In six months, she saw 135 movies. But living with relatives was a bore, and Chicago lacked glamour. Rand decided to seek fame and fortune in Hollywood. Once there, she went to DeMille Studios to apply for a job as a screenwriter. She pitched herself to a secretary, who politely showed her the door. Then, as Rand was leaving, she serendipitously bumped into Cecil B. DeMille himself. In a story line fit for a movie, DeMille invited the awestruck young woman to take a ride in his roadster—and Rand successfully parlayed this chance encounter into a position as a junior screenwriter.

One thing led to another. Rand wrote screenplays. She met and married a handsome aspiring actor. She wrote a play. In 1934, she published an autobiographical novel titled *We the Living*. Because of Rand's intriguing background, *We the Living* got widely reviewed, often with a separate profile of the author. But Rand, who thought she knew something of communist Russia firsthand, was stunned when reviewers questioned the accuracy of her portrayal of the Soviet Union. The liberal *Nation* was dubious that "petty officials in Soviet Russia ride to the opera in foreign limousines while the worker goes wheatless and meatless."[48] Despite all the ink devoted to it, *We the Living* was not a success in the bookstores. After the first printing of three thousand copies sold out, the publisher discarded the type. The reviews convinced Rand that American liberals were misinformed—or worse. Some, she suspected, were communist sympathizers. Later she would testify about her suspicions before the House Un-American Activities Committee.

Sorely disappointed, but undaunted, Rand started work on another novel. This was to be a grand fictional elaboration of her views about human achievement and political philosophy. Her work on this project was periodically interrupted however. In 1940, she became passionately engaged in Wendell Willkie's campaign for president against Franklin Roosevelt. She worked on another play. She began reading right-wing American authors, including H. L. Mencken and Albert Jay Nock, who were then calling themselves something new—"libertarians." She wrote a futuristic novella titled *Anthem*. It was too offbeat for the American market but sold well in England. Finally, in 1943, after working on it on and off for nine years, she finished her big novel. It was big not only in its philosophical sweep but, at nearly seven hundred pages, in sheer mass as well. She had originally planned to title the novel "Second-Hand Lives," but her husband persuaded her to call it *The Fountainhead*. Though the word *fountainhead* never appears in the novel, the title was meant to refer to the source of human creativity and achievement.

The hero of *The Fountainhead* is an extraordinarily talented architect named Howard Roark. Roark's work is genuinely original. The book begins with Roark being expelled from architectural school because he insists on submitting original designs rather than kowtowing to instructors' demands that he imitate classic works. His career as a professional architect proceeds along similar lines. He insists on designing buildings as he wishes, refusing to diminish his work by incorporating suggestions from superiors or clients. His genius is valued by a few, but more often it is resented. Some "second-handers" (Rand's term for those who can only imitate) find ways to pass off his designs as their own. Despite terrible adversity, Roark remains unbowed. When he can't make a living as an architect without compromising his ideals, he chooses instead to become a manual laborer in a quarry.

While there, Roark meets Dominique Francon, the beautiful daughter of the most successful architect in New York. Her father owns the quarry in which Roark is laboring. Though Roark and Dominique first see each other only from a distance, there is immediately electricity between them. She believes him to be a common worker but summons him to her home to replace a piece of marble. Roark humiliates Dominique in small ways, which she finds erotic. Then he rapes her. Rand describes the act as follows:

> It was an act that could be performed in tenderness, as a seal of love, or in contempt, as a symbol of humiliation and conquest.

It could be the act of a lover or the act of a soldier violating an enemy woman. He did it as an act of scorn. Not as love, but as defilement. And this made her lie still and submit. One gesture of tenderness from him—and she would have remained cold, untouched by the thing done to her body. But the act of a master taking shameful, contemptuous possession of her was the kind of rapture she wanted.[49]

Many have puzzled over this scene. When questioned about it on one occasion, Rand is reported to have described it as "rape by engraved invitation."[50] Her other fiction was also infused with sex, and William F. Buckley Jr., among others, believed that Rand's popularity had more to do with sex than philosophy.[51] But is that why she included sex in her novels? It would have been rank hypocrisy for Rand to gratuitously spice her books with sex—not to mention, rape—for the purpose of making them popular; after all, the central theme of *The Fountainhead* is that a hero produces art for its own sake, not to please others. In fact, the rape scene comports with Rand's vision of the Nietzschean superhero, who transcends social mores. Dominique follows a strange path of debasing herself still further in order to eventually—through absolution and growth—become worthy of Roark. She marries the lowest kind of second-hander, a man she neither loves nor respects, who in turn permits a newspaper magnate named Gail Wynand to take Dominique as his wife in return for a commission to design Wynand's corporate headquarters.

Rand created Wynand to symbolize the man who "could have been."[52] He possessed the intelligence and vitality of a superhero but lacked the integrity. He controlled public opinion by following public opinion; he built a publishing empire by catering to public taste. When push finally comes to shove and Wynand finds himself in a furious struggle over a cause that he truly cares about, he first gambles his empire to do the right thing but ultimately folds. Wynand is a tragic figure—one of the few who sees the world for what it is and knows and respects what is right. Nevertheless, he disgraces himself—in his own eyes, though not in the eyes of the Lilliputians who surround him—by being unable to place righteousness ahead of everything else. His fate is to remain wealthy and powerful but steeped in shame.

The archvillain of *The Fountainhead* is Ellsworth Monkton Toohey. In her private notes, Rand described Toohey as "worst of all possible rats. The man who never could be—and knows it."[53] For Rand, who was still smarting from the reviews of her first book, the worst rats were critics, and she cast Toohey as an architectural critic. Toohey was a pied piper of a pernicious worldview: Magnificent architecture was not the achievement of great architects but of accumulated wisdom. Toohey preached that a famous architect stood on the shoulders of an "army of craftsmen, unknown and unsung, who proceeded him in the darkness of the ages, who toiled humbly—all heroism is humble—each contributing his small share to the common treasure of his time." Toohey was, therefore, the quintessential egalitarian, the ultimate leveler. Toohey also maintained that there was no such thing as free will. Style, he believed, was not the product of creative impulses; it was dictated by the economic structure of the times. Toohey argued "that the decadence of architecture had come when private property replaced the communal spirit of the Middle Ages." Deep within Toohey, the Red Guard resided.

At the book's climax, Howard Roark is prosecuted for blowing up a housing project. Roark had secretly designed the project but allowed another architect to take full credit for designing it in return for a promise that the project would be built exactly as Roark designed it. That promise, codified in a contract, was nonetheless broken. Roark was entitled to make the contract public, reveal that he was the principal architect of this admired project, and repudiate the modifications that he believed besmirched his original design. But that is not how Nietzschean heroes operate. Roark dynamited the project to smithereens— an act Rand portrays as noble. Although those who owned and financed the housing project were unaware of Roark's involvement, Rand suggests they were blameworthy for defacing Roark's magnificent design.

At his trial, Roark admits he blew up the project and defends his action by giving the jury a history lesson. History, he says, has always been a struggle between the creator and the second-hander. "Every creative job is achieved under the guidance of a single individual," Roark declares. All thoughts, inventions, and creations come from individuals—not from collaborations. The creator is not selfless. It is "only by living for himself" that he is able to produce "the things that are the glory of mankind." The masses do not celebrate the creator, however. They resent him. At first, they denounce his achievement. When they realize the achievement is valuable, the second-hander steals it. "From the beginning of history, the two antagonists have stood face to face: the creator and the second-hander," declares Roark. "When the first creator invented the wheel, the first second-hander responded. He invented altruism." In Roark's speech, one can hear Rand cry out against the Red Guards seizing her father's chemistry shop.

Roark recounts how he agreed to design the project in return for a particular kind of payment, namely, an agreement that the project would be built exactly as he designed it. But his work was stolen. The owners "took the benefit of my work and made me contribute it as a gift. But I am not an altruist," said Roark. Roark tells the jury that he dynamited the project as an act of loyalty to every creator who was exploited by a second-hander. The jury acquits. To complete the happy ending, Dominique leaves Wynand and marries Roark.

The Fountainhead was released in April 1943. Except for Rand herself, no one expected it to be a blockbuster. The publisher, Bobbs-Merrill Company, anticipated selling no more than ten thousand copies. After all, Rand's earlier work had received poor reviews, and Bobbs-Merrill had reason to expect much the same for *The Fountainhead*, which, despite its length and philosophical pretention, is a work of cartoonlike simplicity. For the most part, the characters are purely good or purely evil and act in ways that flesh-and-blood people rarely behave. As the *Times Literary Supplement* review put it, "Miss Rand can only create gargoyles, not characters." *The Fountainhead*'s philosophy is similarly sophomoric. Ideas are clear-cut: Individualism and selfishness are good; living for oneself alone is virtuous; altruism is a sinister plot by parasites and collectivists. Complexity of any kind—human or philosophical—does not exist in *The Fountainhead*. But the novel resonated powerfully with some readers. Perhaps simplicity was also a strength: The sharply delineated ideas are crystal clear. Some critics raved about the book. The *Providence Journal* declared that Rand had taken "a position of importance among contemporary American novelists." In a great stroke of luck for Rand, the most effusive review—indeed, the most positive review in Rand's entire career—came from the most influential outlet, the *New York Times*, which said Rand had "a subtle and ingenious mind and the capacity of writing brilliantly, beautifully, bitterly."[54]

By summer *The Fountainhead* was a national bestseller. Bobbs-Merrill worked frantically to keep printing ahead of sales. By year-end, the book had sold fifty thousand copies. Then something even more unexpected happened. For most books, popularity diminishes after a year or two. *The Fountainhead*, however, just kept doing better and better. Two years after its release, it was selling a hundred thousand copies a year. By its sixtieth anniversary, it had sold more than six million copies.[55] Even today that number keeps rising.

The novel has always been popular in high schools and colleges. It appeals to the romantic sense of alienation that resonates so powerfully with young adults. They identify with Howard Roark because he is a unique and talented person rejected by the throng of conformists surrounding him. Despite the fact that Roark is confident and self-possessed while they are insecure and awkward, Roark has something in common with such alienated adolescent protagonists as Holden Caulfield of *Catcher in the Rye* and Benjamin Braddock of *The Graduate*. Caulfield is surrounded by "phonies." Braddock is searching to find meaning in life, only to be given one word of advice: "plastics." Roark, Caulfield, and Braddock are too pure for the world, and that's exactly how adolescents see themselves. Many young people also found Rand's libertarian worldview fresh and counterrevolutionary. When it was published, *The Fountainhead* provided a rationale for rejecting the prevailing political wisdom of the day. Regardless of the political zeitgeist, *The Fountainhead* perennially provides young adults with a rationale for rejecting the harping of parents and teachers exhorting them to be more generous and considerate of others. What young adult cannot be beguiled by a philosophy that makes selfishness a virtue?

William F. Buckley Jr., however, was not beguiled. He met Rand for the first time in 1954, the year he published *McCarthy and His Enemies* and started *National Review*, at a Manhattan party, possibly at the home of J. B. Matthews. Matthews—a supporter of Joseph McCarthy, and later a member of the Council of the John Birch Society—held gatherings in his penthouse for right-wing luminaries, and both Rand and Buckley were periodic guests. According to Buckley, Rand's very first words to him were: "You ahrr too intelligent to believe in Gott."[56] Although Buckley was taken aback, his etiquette exceeded Rand's, and the two chatted amiably. He found her odd but charming. He called a few common acquaintances to learn more about her, among them Isabel Paterson.[57] Paterson was a staunch anti–New Dealer and libertarian who wrote an influential column about books for the *New York Herald Tribune*. Years earlier, Paterson and Rand had been close friends, a relationship each of them treasured because they were both irascible, egocentric personalities who did not make friends easily. But Paterson and Rand had a bitter falling out—in significant part over the issue of religion. Paterson believed that without a belief in God, it was not possible to coherently ground a belief in human rights. Rand had been outraged that Paterson suggested that she could not be both an atheist and a true believer in individualism. Undoubtedly, Paterson gave Buckley a scathing critique about what she perceived as the many flaws in Rand's philosophical views, including Rand's atheism—a subject that had already come to Buckley's attention.

On the surface, Buckley maintained a cordial relationship with Rand. They had no trouble carrying on animated conversations at social gatherings. They had much in common. They were both passionate anticommunists. They both supported McCarthyism. They both disliked Eisenhower. They were both free market purists. But what divided them transcended those commonalities. Buckley believed that the free market and the struggle against atheistic communism were intertwined with religious belief. "I myself believe that the duel between Christianity and atheism is the most important in the world. I further believe that the struggle between individualism and collectivism is the same struggle reproduced on a different level," he had famously written in *God and Man at Yale*.[58] Rand believed that commitments to the free market and anticommunism were mandated by objective reason. Man had to learn to live for himself and reject the idea "that the standard of man's ethics is set beyond the grave, by the laws or requirements or another, supernatural dimension."[59] Religion was superstition, and superstitions led people and nations astray. Morality flowed from autonomous individuals freely entering into transactions for mutual benefit. As something of a slap in the face to Christians and the cross, Rand later adopted the dollar sign as her symbol. She liked to wear a black cape adorned only with a gold dollar sign brooch. In a famous photograph, she stands so attired on Wall Street.

Under the guise of good-natured teasing, Buckley sent Rand postcards in liturgical Latin. In retrospect, she may have considered these post-cards a portent of what was to come. At the time, however, she probably didn't give them much thought. In her eyes, Buckley and his embryonic magazine were small potatoes while she was a figure of stature. Her readership kept growing. A group of devotees now surrounded her. On Saturday nights, she held a regular salon at her house for the inner circle. They laughingly called themselves the Collective. One member of the group, whom Rand nicknamed the Undertaker, was then-thirty-year-old Alan Greenspan. It would be misleading to say the Collective freely debated politics or philosophy. Rand considered her views the only correct ones, and it is probably more accurate to say that Rand instructed the group. "Check your premises," she repeatedly cautioned her acolytes. Nevertheless, the Collective provided Rand with a place to try out ideas as she was striving to fashion them into a coherent philosophy, to be called Objectivism. Her most favored acolyte, Nathaniel Branden, told her it was a mistake to ally herself and Objectivism with either conservatives or libertarians. Conservatives were not truly on "our side," he said.[60] Rand considered this a seminal moment in her thinking. She decided that Branden was right, that "conservatives as such are not on my side . . . that I'm standing totally alone and have to create my own side."

Rand let members of the Collective read sections of her work in progress. This was, for them, a signal honor. The worlds of publishing and the political right were abuzz about Rand's work on a new novel, but only members of the Collective had firsthand knowledge about the project. The publisher this time would be Random House, which had agreed to pay Rand a $50,000 advance and spend at least $25,000 promoting the book (the equivalent of more than half a million dollars today). When Rand delivered the eagerly awaited manuscript, it was 645,000 words long, the size of five average novels. Its great bulk resulted from Rand's longwinded style—*The Fountainhead* was a massive tome—combined with her goal of making this new work the definitive statement of Objectivism. The book is filled with mind-numbingly long speeches and internal monologues. In one passage, in which two characters are chatting in a cafeteria, a single paragraph of dialogue by one of the characters runs on for nearly four pages. In another spot, one character is telling another character a story. After the story unfolds in dialogue format for several pages, the character listening to the story says, "Go on." The other character does just that, without interruption, for more than ten pages. And on page 923, by which time many readers are begging for the book to end, the hero of the novel, John Galt, launches into a radio speech that continues for fifty-six pages.[61]

The editor in chief of Random House was Bennett Cerf. Cerf was himself a celebrity. Urbane and witty, Cerf was a regular on the popular television game show *What's My Line?* He had deployed his considerable savvy and charm—not to mention a great deal of money—to persuade Rand to sign with Random House; now he was counting on her book becoming a bestseller. He loved Rand's plot. He told Rand that after reading a scene in which, after much romantic tension, two characters wind up each other's arms, he rushed out of his office, exclaiming to his staff, "It's magnificent!" But how would readers react to a novel more than a thousand pages long, especially with its narrative pace repeatedly slowed by philosophical speechifying? Cerf told Rand the manuscript had to be cut. Specifically, he wanted Rand to pare down Galt's long radio speech. Much of what Galt said was repeated three or four times before, Cerf observed. "Would you cut the Bible?" Rand asked. Not a word of the novel was eliminated, but Rand acceded to Cerf's demand that her royalties be reduced by nearly half to pay for the additional printing costs.

Atlas Shrugged was published on October 10, 1957. Cerf expected mixed reviews. He turned out to be wrong—the reviews were uniformly terrible. The most damning of all was published by *National Review*. Buckley had selected someone special to write that review, someone, in Buckley's own words, "whose authority with American conservatives was as high as that of any man then living."[62] Moreover, Buckley knew this person well and correctly suspected that he would detest Rand's philosophy. Buckley's reviewer was Whittaker Chambers. Reviewing *Atlas Shrugged* was, in fact, the first assignment Buckley gave his most famous contributor after he finally agreed to write for *National Review.* Chambers did not disappoint: His piece all but burst into flames in the reader's hands. It has become, depending upon one's point of view, either the most famous or infamous book review in the history of the conservative movement. Before we get to Chambers's review, however, it is necessary to describe the central themes of *Atlas Shrugged*.

The novel has something in common with the alternative history genre. The story does not take place in the world we know; the reader infers that at some point the trajectory of history was bent. Rand does not explain why history changed course, but at some point the United States began following a less capitalistic, more socialistic path. In the United States of *Atlas Shrugged*, there are higher taxes and more governmental regulation, and both are increasing. We are told that experts favor central planning of production. Most important, there is a strengthening belief that productive members of society have a duty to support the weak and unproductive members. At one factory, management and workers voted to adopt the program that everyone work according to his ability and be paid according to his needs. One of the long speeches in the book describes the nightmare of this communist collective. Ability became a curse. The better one was at his job, the longer the hours he was made to work, and to no benefit. Compensation was determined not by one's contributions but by popular vote after workers described their needs at twice-yearly meetings. Workers strove to outdo one another in presenting their needs—how many mouths they had to feed, illnesses in the family—with as much pathos as possible. The meetings were, says one participant, "a contest among six thousand panhandlers."

But the economic results of the system are not Rand's main point. Rand understood that at bottom political philosophy is about values, morality, and human nature. Given human nature, as she saw it, the capitalistic system allowed individuals not only to thrive economically, but also to achieve their highest potential. In short, capitalism encourages people to become the best people they can become while socialism and communism force them into becoming parasites and scoundrels. Rand's main point is that socialism and communism are not merely economically inefficient; they are evil. Rand takes this to the extreme by arguing that selfishness is virtuous and altruism is wicked. Moreover—and this point becomes important both to Whittaker Chambers's review and to the history of the conservative movement—Rand defends taking things to the extreme. Moderation is evil and extremism is virtuous. "There are two sides to every issue: one side is right and the other is wrong, but the middle is always evil," John Galt declares in his radio address, presaging Goldwater's famous statement, seven years after *Atlas Shrugged* was published.

Despite what happened at one particularly progressive plant, the United States has not become communist, or even wholly socialist, as the story in *Atlas Shrugged* begins. Things are, however, trending that way. The titans of industry are having increasing difficulty. Among other things, less successful competitors are successfully lobbying government to adopt anticompetitive regulations. It is the titans of industry—a sort of circle of heroes—who comprise the ensemble of main characters. Francisco d'Anconia is heir of the world's largest copper mining company. His childhood sweetheart, Dagny Taggart, is director of operations of the nation's largest railroad, established by her grandfather. Hank Rearden built the nation's largest steel company and then invented a new metal alloy, Rearden's Metal, which is stronger, lighter, and cheaper than steel. However, the people Rearden supports don't appreciate him. On a personal level, these are Rearden's wife, mother, and ne'er-do-well brother, Philip, all of whom live high off the hog in Rearden's home, contributing nothing and resenting Rearden for his largesse. They ridicule him for being so interested in the business that supports them all. His interest is crass while theirs—social matters consume wife and mother while brother incompetently tries to raise money for altruistic causes—are worthy. One evening Philip describes how he failed that day to raise money for a group named Friends of Global Progress. Rearden has no interest in the group. From listening to his brother's vague descriptions, Rearden gathers it is "devoted to some sort of free lectures on psychology, folk music and co-operative farming." Rearden is not enamored of silly do-gooders, but to make his brother happy he offers to donate a large sum. Philip asks Rearden to donate the money in cash rather than by check so that Friends of Global Progress would not be embarrassed by taking money from "the blackest element of social retrogression in the country." Rearden has earned this disdain merely by being enormously successful. He does not exploit his workers; he pays the highest wages in the industry. Rearden wants to slap Philip's face.

Instead, he agrees to Philip's request. This illustrates a central theme: At both the personal and societal levels, those who produce are controlled by those who do not. The mechanism of control is a false sense of guilt. In *The Fountainhead*, the parasites and exploiters are called "second-handers"; in *Atlas Shrugged* they become "looters."

One man has recognized the ruse: John Galt. (Galt does not appear until page 643, but plenty of time is left for the book's major character.) Galt is a brilliant engineer. He invented a new method of producing energy, an engine powered by drawing static electricity from the air. His invention would have been a great gift to humankind and made him—or at least the company he worked for—rich. But Galt developed the engine while employed by the factory that turned itself into a communist collective. As he sat in that meeting at which the workers voted to adopt the communist program, Galt realized where the company and the country were headed. "I will put an end to this, once and for all," he said as he got up to walk out. "How?" someone asked. "I will stop the motor of the world," he answered.

Hundreds of pages earlier, readers learned that titans of industry are mysteriously disappearing. They just seem to disappear overnight. Their plants, equipment, workers, and even their capital remain behind, but their businesses flounder without their leadership. There are cascading effects of failure. Each business that fails—or continues under incompetent leadership—causes problems for its suppliers and customers. Failing businesses try to protect themselves from superior competitors by creating anticompetitive cartels protected by government. Incompetence and failure spread. The economy slows. Infrastructure deteriorates. The motor of the world—driven by the superior minds of the titans of industry—is stopping.

What happened to the titans? It turns out that John Galt secretly visited them one by one to help them realize how they were being victimized by the looters and what to do about it. He had receptive audiences. The titans were tired of being taxed to support the parasites of society. As Galt puts it, "The men who have carried the world on their shoulders, have kept it alive, have endured torture as sole payment." Galt persuaded them to go on strike. They simply withdrew their participation from the world. The title of the book comes from the idea of Atlas deciding to no longer hold up the world and instead simply shrugging. The leaders join Galt in a kind of heaven on earth: a secret valley in Colorado, dedicated to a pure laissez-faire system where everything is earned and nothing is given away or requested. This small collection of extraordinary people builds a sophisticated new society. One of them manufactures a unique and especially delicious brand of cigarettes, on which only a single symbol is stamped: the dollar sign. Another operates a bank that provides savings accounts, makes loans, and mints the only form of currency residents of Galt's Gulch accept (gold coins, of course).

Galt's followers live by the following oath: "I swear by my life and my love of it that I will never live for the sake of another man, nor ask another man to live for mine." The oath was a practical application of Rand's three basic premises, which she later set forth in a work of political philosophy. Her first premise is that a person exists, and that the only thing sacrosanct for the individual is his or her own life. Second, individuals should value whatever perpetuates or enhances their existence. Third, individuals must rely exclusively on logic to determine what is in their self-interest.[63]

Galt preaches the libertarian view that government should be limited to protecting citizens from criminals and foreign invaders and to maintaining a judicial system to protect property, enforce contracts, and settle disputes. Anything else—public schools or services of any sort—is a form of theft. "You regard as 'in the public interest' any project serving those who do not pay," says Galt. "Public welfare is the welfare of those who do not earn it," he continues. Standard libertarianism holds that it is appropriate for government to provide police, courts, and national defense because those services benefit everyone, but in her nonfiction works of political philosophy Rand argued that in a "fully free society" taxation to support even those limited government functions would be voluntary.[64] She offers a government-run lottery as an example of voluntary taxation. Rand even suggests for consideration a system in which one making a contract would have the option of purchasing from the government the right to enforce that contract in the courts. Purchasing this right would not be required, but contracts not so insured would not be legally enforceable.

There is no room in Rand's philosophy for religion. She based her philosophy on the existence of the individual and endorsed atheism. But she went much further. *Atlas Shrugged* denounces religion in stark and brutal terms. Galt calls religion "superstition" and clerics "mystics." Religion, he says, is a "protection racket" that first makes people feel guilty about pleasure and then sells them consolation and a place in heaven. Man's highest virtue is not his soul, his spirit, or his capacity to love; it is his ability to produce wealth. Though Galt never mentions Christianity, he attacks its most fundamental tenets. He denounces faith and declares humility a sin and pride a virtue. He calls original sin (a doctrine of especial importance to Catholic teachings) a "monstrous absurdity." As a final blasphemy, Rand replaces the sign of the cross with the sign of the dollar. The last sentence of *Atlas Shrugged* reads: "[Galt] raised his hand and over the desolate earth he traced in space the sign of the dollar."

Whether or not Rand thought about it, whether or not she cared when she declared war in these terms on religion—on Christianity, and Catholicism especially—she declared war on William F. Buckley's vision of conservatism. She and her followers should have expected the strongest possible counterattack. But she might not have anticipated that Whittaker Chambers would declare, "From almost any page of *Atlas Shrugged*, a voice can be heard, from painful necessity, commanding: 'To the gas chamber—go!'"[65]

How did Chambers reach that conclusion? He starts by observing that the essence of Rand's message is philosophical materialism. Any consistent materialism must reject God and religion, says Chambers. The problem inherent in any materialistic system is that it leads easily to hedonism, or as Chambers puts it, "the pursuit of happiness, as an end of itself, tends automatically, and widely to be replaced by the pursuit of pleasure." Any philosopher worth her salt who wants a philosophy nobler than that must find some solution to the problem. Rand's solution was to call on man to be heroic. The protagonists in her novel are truly heroes—extraordinary people who are smarter, more creative, and more capable (not to mention more beautiful) than run-of-mill human beings. In complex societies, says Chambers, people are tempted to have "some species of Big Brother" solve their problems and supervise them. The species of Big Brother that Rand seems to be calling for is an aristocracy of geniuses, or perhaps an aristocracy of talents, but Chambers argues that the age of aristocracies is over and "the impulse toward aristocracy always emerges now in the form of dictatorship." This brings

Chambers to his final point: "Out of a lifetime of reading, I can recall no other book in which a tone of overriding arrogance was so implacably maintained . . . Its dogmatism is without appeal . . . Dissent from a revelation so final (because, the author would say, so reasonable) can only be willfully wicked." Reason will ultimately dictate that the only way to deal with that kind of willful wickedness is Hitler's way.

Chambers's review created an explosion on the political right. Rand was sufficiently furious to make the incredible claim that she never read Chambers's review.[66] She held Buckley responsible for it, however, and would never again attend a party to which he was invited. Her acolytes made no pretense about not reading Chambers's review. They bombarded *National Review* with angry letters, many of which the magazine happily published. One letter complained that the magazine had been unfair by assigning the review to a former communist, ignoring the small fact that Chambers had become the quintessential anticommunist.

Buckley claimed that he had not purposefully selected Chambers to write a negative review of *Atlas Shrugged*, even as he boasted that "Chambers did in fact read Miss Rand right out of the conservative movement."[67] And, indeed, many conservatives considered Rand excommunicated. However, although Whittaker Chambers had the full measure of stature on the American right that Buckley claimed for him, there were several problems with his review. First, it was too subtle for many readers. They understood, of course, that Chambers was condemning Rand in the most emphatic terms, but not everyone understood exactly why. One reader who wrote a personal letter to Buckley about Chambers's review was T. Coleman Andrews. Andrews was a former commissioner of the Internal Revenue Service and the presidential nominee of the States' Rights Party in 1956. He would also become a member of the Council of the John Birch Society. "Oh, boy! What a review!" he exclaimed. "But, to tell you the truth," he confided, "Mr. Chambers was so far over my head in most of the review that I really didn't understand what he was talking about."[68]

A second problem with Chambers's review was that it was over-the-top. Many readers considered Chambers's gas chamber line unfair and in bad taste, especially since he was attacking a woman of Jewish heritage. It also distracted from Chambers's most trenchant criticism: that *Atlas*

Shrugged is unrealistic because its characters are entirely good or bad. The novel, says Chambers, is the classic fable of "The War between the Children of Light and the Children of Darkness." This point deserved more prominence even though some readers might accept the characters as archetypes and *Atlas Shrugged* as allegory, and believe Rand successfully used those devices to illuminate central truths.[69] There is peril in drawing lessons from such unlifelike fiction.

Chambers's review succeeded to an extent. The *National Review* family understood that Rand had been excommunicated from the movement. In those circles, it would no longer be acceptable to say that one came to conservatism through reading *Atlas Shrugged*. Chambers's review may even have cost Rand some readers, but it was like pulling a bucket of water out of the Atlantic Ocean. *Atlas Shrugged* was on the *New York Times* bestseller list for seven months. Within five years, it sold one million copies.[70] Countless readers have reported being profoundly moved by the novel. In 1991, the Library of Congress and the Book-of-the-Month Club cosponsored a survey that asked people what books most influenced their lives. *Atlas Shrugged* came in number two, after the Bible.[71]

Of course, Buckley's primary interest was not suppressing Rand's total readership; it was suppressing her influence within the conservative movement, especially her views about the illegitimacy of religion, reason trumping authority, and the virtues of pride and selfishness. Despite his boast that Chambers had effectively excommunicated Rand from the movement, Buckley knew that Chambers had only partially succeeded. Rand's works had a profound effect on young people, and she continued to have strong—and from Buckley's perspective, troubling—influence on young members of the conservative movement. This was most visible within YAF. When YAF was established at Great Elm in September 1960, Rand's admirers were strong enough to successfully fight off a proposal to name the organization Young Conservatives.[72] But Buckley-style conservatives clearly had the upper hand. The second line of the Sharon Statement reads, "We, as young conservatives, believe," after which follows an even dozen beliefs the organization considered fundamental. The first of these is "that foremost among the transcendent values is the individual's God-given free will, whence derives his right to be free from the restrictions of arbitrary force." Nevertheless, Rand's influence remained significant within YAF. The organization's first national chairman, Robert M. Schuchman, was a Rand devotee. According to an MIT student who joined YAF four years later, most of the key people he encountered considered themselves Objectivists.[73]

In 1962, Rand—together with her favorite acolyte (and lover) Nathaniel Branden—began creating a community of Objectivists by launching the *Objectivist Newsletter*.* In the first issue, Rand proclaimed, "We are *not* 'conservatives.' We are *radicals for capitalism*." That same year, Branden and his wife, Barbara, published a biography of Rand. In 1963 and 1964, Rand published two nonfiction collections of her Objectivist philosophy: *For the New Intellectual*, which was comprised of key philosophical speeches by characters in her novels, including John Galt's radio speech; and *The Virtues of Selfishness*, which reproduced short essays that had been previously published in the *Objectivist Newsletter*. All three of these books sold briskly. Indeed, within just the first four months of its release, *The Virtues of Selfishness* sold more than four hundred thousand copies.[74] In 1966, Rand and Branden converted their newsletter into a magazine named the *Objectivist*, which soon had a paid circulation of twenty thousand. Rand's popularity seemed to grow ever stronger on college campuses.

Clearly, Chambers's review hadn't killed Objectivism. In its October 3, 1967, issue, *National Review* launched a second attack on Rand. The magazine's cover portrayed an Ayn Rand stained-glass window. Rand held a little flag that read "St. Ayn"; a flowing ribbon at the bottom read "The Movement to Canonize Ayn Rand," and a dollar sign sun streamed shafts of color throughout the window. Inside was a five-page story, titled "The Gospel According to Ayn Rand," written by associate editor M. Stanton Evans. Trying not to repeat Chambers's mistakes, Stanton wrote a less inflammatory piece. He began by generously listing

---

*Branden was twenty-four and Rand was forty-eight when, in 1954, they began their affair. Rand insisted that because it was rational for them to have a romantic relationship, they inform both of their spouses and insist upon their consent. Rand's husband, Frank O'Connor, had an easier time accepting the affair than did Nathaniel's wife, Barbara, although both tried. When, in 1968, Branden broke off the affair, and Rand learned that he had fallen in love with a third woman, she became enraged and ejected him from her organization—which, Rand's critics argue, demonstrates that even Rand could not live by philosophy.

a number of subjects on which, Stanton said, Rand was right, which he listed as her understanding of the "secular conditions of freedom," "her excellent grasp of the way capitalism is supposed to work," her "trenchant anti-Communism," and her political realism. Stanton was vague on the last point but appeared to be referring to Rand's having urged readers of her newsletter to support Goldwater's presidential campaign. But praise was prelude to the hatchet. He devoted most of the article to expounding on the numerous ways that Rand was "depressingly wrong." Here Evans tried a new tack: suggesting that Rand had things in common with liberals. Because Rand had no spiritual support for her belief in freedom, she fell back on atheistic humanism. "This is, in all its major points, the standard left-liberal fare with which we have been regaled for years," said Evans. Making Rand out as some kind of confused liberal was a clever way of tarnishing her in the eyes of right-wingers.

Evans argued that Rand failed at defining appropriate limits on freedom. "Guided only by the physical imperatives of survival, a man might do almost anything—including a number of things destructive to the Randian regime of freedom," Stanton observed. The individual, guided only by reason to enhance his survival, might decide to go on welfare, become a bureaucrat, or even a looter. Therefore, Rand is forced to reintroduce various moral restraints on behavior. But her restraints have no a priori basis; Rand simply decrees them. Thus Rand contradicts her own philosophy that individuals should reject all authority and act on the basis of pure reason alone. Moreover, even with her restraints, she is lost. "Miss Rand correctly denounces 'altruists who would neglect wife and children to mollycoddle strangers—although cases of this sort are, on the record, comparatively infrequent," notes Evans. "She has nothing to say about the egotist who neglects his wife and child to feed his appetites—a case much more common." The first part of Evans's critique does not quite hit the mark. Galt's oath (which Stanton never mentions in his article) includes two parts, the second of which states the individual will never ask another man to live for his sake. This is an entirely logical corollary to the proposition that one should never live for the sake of another. The individual simply recognizes that other individuals also exist, and it grants them, as human beings, the same dignity and rights the individual claims for herself. The logical deductions that flow from that corollary can go a long way in prohibiting antisocial behavior.

One is almost persuaded to say that Rand has simply articulated a somewhat different version of the golden rule—until, that is, one considers Evans's telling example of the individual who neglects his family to satisfy selfish desires. The golden rule tells us that neglecting your children is wrong but Galt's oath does not.

But none of that analysis decisively set apart Rand's philosophy and acceptable conservative and libertarian thought. In his final and most important point, Evans made Christianity the boundary. Evans said Rand's fundamental error was rejecting Christianity. The last third of the Evans article is a paean to Christianity, which he said was the only system of belief predicated on something more than mere survival. By attacking "the Christian culture which has given birth to all our freedoms" Rand stood with the collectivists who would destroy freedom.

Evans's approach had the advantage of clarity, but there were disadvantages to suggesting that only Christians could be first-class citizens in the conservative movement. Jews, among others, would feel less than fully welcome. Years earlier, Buckley and the other editors might not have thought much about keeping a welcome mat out for the Jews. They were a demographically tiny and predominately liberal group. But two years before Evans's article, three prominent Jewish intellectuals—Irving Kristol, Nathan Glazer, and Daniel Bell—founded a journal named the *Public Interest* that was espousing a "neoconservative" philosophy. Not long after that Buckley appointed a Jew, sociologist Will Herberg, to be the first religion editor of *National Review*. Herberg had been arguing that conservatives recognize a more ecumenical moral foundation. "Conservatives, true to the classical tradition of our culture, whether Hebrew or Greek, of course affirm the doctrine of higher law as the very cornerstone of their moral, social and political philosophy," he had written in *National Review*. Herberg suggested this was more than sufficient to distinguish a religious or spiritually based morality from value systems based on "some form of legal positivism, cultural relativism, and moral pragmatism," which were often favored by liberals.[75]

Herberg was something of a welcome mat to Jewish conservatives. Now Evans was pulling in the opposite direction. Buckley's permitting Evans and Herberg to express such different viewpoints in *National Review* illustrates one of the reasons why Buckley was the leader of a movement and Rand was the leader of a cult. A movement must transcend any individual. It must allow room for differences of opinion while still maintaining definition. It is a difficult balancing act but one at which Buckley was skilled. Buckley was willing to exclude people such as Robert Welch and Ayn Rand. But within rather broad parameters, Buckley allowed—indeed encouraged—robust discussion and debate, including disagreement with some views he held strongly. Buckley also respected and nurtured others who possessed strong voices and leadership skills of their own. Rand was just the opposite. For her, there was only one acceptable viewpoint: her own. She brooked no dissent, insisting on being the sole and absolute authority on all matters within the Objectivist universe. While Buckley recruited and nurtured other strong and talented people within both the *National Review* family and the larger conservative movement, Rand wanted only devotees. One witness to this at a very early stage was Murray N. Rothbard.[76] Rothbard, who was then studying for his doctorate in economics at Columbia and was enamored with libertarian economist Ludwig von Mises, had many ideas in common with Rand. Indeed, Rothbard would later say he considered *Atlas Shrugged* "one of the very greatest books ever written, fiction or nonfiction." Rothbard attended a number of gatherings of the Collective in 1954. He found that Rand's "total system is a soul-shattering calamity." She was indeed charismatic, but it was a kind of charisma that overwhelmed her devotees, leaving them "almost lifeless, devoid of enthusiasm or spark, and almost completely dependent on Ayn for intellectual sustenance." When one member of the Collective ventured to express some disagreement, Rand attacked him unmercifully. Moreover, Rand denied that her philosophy owed any debt to other thinkers or philosophic traditions (except for Aristotle). She was also displeased by those who claimed they owed her an intellectual debt but did not fully embrace Objectivism. When, in the 1970s, a robust libertarian movement claimed to be following her ideas, she was unmoved. Libertarians, she said, were nothing more than "scum" and "plagiarists."[77] She was also so intent on maintaining strict proprietary control over her work and ideas that she became angry when others used the Objectivist label without her consent. "Objectivism is not a movement and is not to be regarded as such by anyone," she declared.[78]

*   *   *

In the evening of August 28, 1969, William F. Buckley Jr. sat on a stage
in St. Louis, waiting to give the opening address to the annual convention of Young Americans for Freedom.[79] YAF was the organization
founded at Great Elm nine years earlier. It was now a large organization
with college chapters throughout the country. Its rally, five years earlier,
for Goldwater's presidential campaign at Madison Square Garden drew
an audience of more than eighteen thousand. But as soon as YAF's
ninth annual convention was declared formally in session, and before
Buckley could be introduced, a demonstration erupted in the hall. A
delegation of free market anarchists from California was demanding
that their chapter president, Pat Dowd, be seated on the stage—a position of prominence that conference organizers had carefully reserved for
conservatives. It was outrageous that a small band of dissidents should
obstruct proceedings. "We want Buckley! We want Buckley!" thousands
of voices shouted. But they were rattled by hundreds of voices yelling
back, "We want Hess! We want Hess!" They were referring to libertarian
Karl Hess, whose request to speak on the floor of the convention had
previously been denied.

This was the beginning of a rebellion. A coalition of libertarians and
anarchists were going to challenge the conservative YAF leadership. As
delegates arrived in the hall, the rebels were putting in their hands the
most recent issue of a semi-monthly newsletter entitled the *Libertarian
Forum*, which under the heading "Listen, YAF" featured an open letter
to the delegates by editor Murray N. Rothbard.[80] Rothbard had written,
"This letter is a plea that you use the occasion of the public forum of
the YAF convention to go, to split, to leave the conservative movement
where it belongs . . . Leave the house to your false friends, for they are
your enemies." The conservative movement was "being run by a gaggle
of ex-Communists and monarchists," he continued. Rothbard was both
a libertarian and an anarchist, a combination that in those turbulent
times was becoming popular. These free market anarchists—or anarcho-
capitalists, as some liked to call themselves—had adopted as their symbol a black flag (the traditional banner of anarchism) with a gold dollar
sign emblazoned on it. While YAF's convention was being planned, the
rebels had sought to put Hess—one of *National Review*'s original contributors, and Barry Goldwater's principal speechwriter during his 1964
presidential campaign—on the list of speakers addressing the convention.

But Hess was now persona non grata within the conservative establishment. He was now Washington editor of *Libertarian Forum* and the leader of a rebel YAF contingent calling itself the Anarcho-Libertarian Alliance. Hess waited outside the hall, promising to speak to whoever would listen under the famous St. Louis arch as soon as the opening session ended—or to debate Buckley there, if Buckley accepted his invitation.

Buckley was confined to his seat for half an hour while the debate over seating the anarchist on the stage raged on. Eventually the anarchist was given a place on the stage, and Buckley rose to address the group. At a press conference earlier in the evening, a reporter had asked Buckley whether there was a split within YAF and, if so, how serious it was. Buckley had pooh-poohed the notion of rebellion, arguing that the band of dissidents was minuscule. Now he devoted the first half of his speech to attacking Rothbard and Hess. Over the next couple of days, the coalition of libertarians and anarchists sought significant changes in YAF policy and doctrine. Among other things, they wanted to delete "young conservatives" from the second line of the Sharon Statement. They also wanted YAF to call for an immediate withdrawal from Vietnam and endorse both draft resistance and the legalization of marijuana—positions then anathema to conservatives. They were, in the end, soundly defeated on all scores. But for the first time libertarian strength was measured. About three hundred of the twelve hundred delegates—25 percent—fell into the libertarian camp.

Some of the libertarians heeded Rothbard's call to leave YAF. The YAF establishment was glad to see them go, and dissenting chapters that did not resign were purged. Within a few months of the convention, twenty-four chapters either resigned or were expelled in California alone. The chapters that remained were composed of conservatives and libertarians who were willing and able to make common cause.

Buckley never softened on Ayn Rand. When Rand died in 1982, he wrote an uncharitable obituary for *National Review*.[81] He talked about how Chambers had trashed *Atlas Shrugged*, how Rand had purportedly cried at a dinner party because Ludwig von Mises had told her she was being foolish, and how Rand's principal disciple claimed he had been cast out because he rejected Rand's sexual advances. He noted that Russell Kirk opined that Rand's novels sold so well because of their sex scenes. But Buckley closed his obituary on a substantive note. After objecting one final time to her declaring that God did not exist, Buckley said that by declaring altruism to be despicable and self-interest noble, Rand risked "giving capitalism that bad name its enemies have done so well in giving it."

Ironically, however, Rand has been a powerful recruiter for a movement from which Buckley tried to excommunicate her (and one she claimed to detest). Year after year, decade after decade, *The Fountainhead* and *Atlas Shrugged* have converted young people into laissez-faire purists. Some of these converts came to consider themselves conservatives; others came to consider themselves libertarians. Through these two books, Rand may be responsible for recruiting more people into the broad conservative movement than anyone else. As her biographer, Professor Jennifer Burns, wrote in 2009, "For over half a century Rand has been the ultimate gateway drug to life on the right."[82] For its part, to this day *National Review* continues to publish articles denouncing Rand and her work.[83]

CHAPTER 5

The Cold War

When William F. Buckley Jr. established *National Review*, he needed a commentator with recognized expertise to specialize in foreign affairs. It was an especially important role, because conservatives considered the Cold War the most important issue of the day. Buckley set out to recruit James Burnham for that role.

Burnham was, in many ways, different from other top editors at *National Review*. He was fifty-five when Buckley recruited him—twenty-five years older than Buckley, and more than twenty years older than either managing editor Priscilla or publisher Bill Rusher. Burnham was among more than half a dozen former communists within the early *National Review* family, but that would have been difficult to deduce had one not known it. The experience seemed to have left him unscathed. He did not suffer melancholy, as did Whittaker Chambers; he was not plagued by anger, as was Willi Schlamm; he lacked the eccentricities of the nocturnal Frank Meyer. When tumult overwhelmed others, Burnham remained composed, logical, and cogent. Fifteen years earlier, his book *The Managerial Revolution* had made him something of a celebrity, yet he wore fame as lightly and naturally as his expertly tailored suits. Indeed, you could not have survived a cocktail party in the early 1940s without being conversant with the book's theme.[1] *The Managerial Revolution* had made Burnham such a prominent futurist that magazines and newspapers such as *Reader's Digest*, *Life*, and the *New York Herald Tribune* published condensed versions of his next books. So in many ways it is easy to understand why Buckley considered Burnham to be a catch. Yet for several reasons, Burnham was a strange choice.

For one thing, Burnham had no formal training in foreign affairs. At both Princeton and Oxford, he had studied neither international relations nor political science but rather English literature. At Oxford, in fact, he had studied under J. R. R. Tolkien. NYU had initially engaged Burnham to teach in its English department, but before Burnham took up the position NYU's needs changed and it reassigned him to the philosophy department. It was the Depression, and in the face of shrinking enrollments it was not uncommon for universities to have instructors teach in more than one area. Burnham wound up straddling both literature and philosophy. His academic specialty, aesthetics, was at the interface of the two disciplines, and at one point Burnham simultaneously chaired the comparative literature and philosophy departments. Although he most often taught courses such as Thought and Literature of the Renaissance and Principles of Aesthetics, Burnham occasionally ventured into the realm of political philosophy. One term, for example, he taught the course Philosophies of Power. But neither as a student nor as a teacher did Burnham ever specialize in political science.

Another thing that made Burnham a curious choice as *National Review*'s guru on foreign policy is that he was a former communist. In 1933, Burnham had joined the American Workers Party. When, the following year, the AWP merged with the Communist League of America, Burnham became a devoted Trotskyite. He held a seat on the political committee of the new organization, the Socialist Workers Party; he wrote a regular column for its newspaper, *Socialist Appeal*; and he also coedited a Trotskyite journal called *New International*. Indeed, Burnham became a regular correspondent of Trotsky, and one of Trotsky's most trusted American supporters.

Burnham was an unlikely Trotskyite. In 1934, Burnham and his wife, Martha, were living in a tony apartment in the Sutton Place section of New York City. One evening, Max Schactman—Burnham's Socialist Workers Party comrade and *New International* coeditor—turned up at the Burnhams' door with galley sheets that he and James needed to review immediately. Schactman found an elegant dinner party in progress and Burnham in formal wear. Burnham excused himself from his guests and repaired with Schactman to a separate room, where they stooped over the galleys on behalf of the proletariat. When the work was done, Schactman dashed off into the night with the corrected galleys and Burnham returned to his dinner party. Schactman later remarked that he was quite sure that James Burnham was the only Trotskyite who owned a tuxedo.

During this period, Burnham advocated extreme—even kooky—ideas. In his newspaper columns, Burnham argued that while Franklin Delano Roosevelt feigned concern for the common people, he was actually working for big business, wealthy bankers, and munitions manufacturers. Eventually, Burnham claimed that FDR was an agent for the sixty wealthiest families in the United States, who secretly controlled the American plutocracy. Roosevelt was determined to take America to war to increase capitalist profits, and both political parties were committed to a "capitalist dictatorship."

In 1939, Burnham denounced the Soviet invasion of Poland as an act of imperialism. This breached Trotsky's dictum that the Soviet Union had to be supported unconditionally, and in 1940 the Socialist Workers Party expelled Burnham along with other dissidents. Burnham and the other purged Trotskyites formed a new communist group, the Workers Party, but after only a few months, Burnham submitted a letter of resignation. His reason for resigning was classic Burnham, grounded in his self-image as an objective empiricist. Burnham declared that historians, anthropologists, and economists had now shown Marxist theories to be false. So, based on the facts, he had changed his mind. Burnham was no longer a communist or a socialist.

Burnham's communist period could not be easily dismissed as a brief flirtation or youthful foolishness. He had been a hardworking communist for seven years, until age thirty-five, and not merely as a follower but a leader. Why was a conservative journal so populated with former communists? Ex-communists comprised one of the magazine's cofounders, its literary and religion editors, and with Burnham, its foreign policy guru. Still others—including Whittaker Chambers, the man most famous for being a former communist—wrote for the *National Review*. Buckley suggested that these men became conservatives because they knew firsthand the threat communism posed to America and the West, but there is another explanation: These were men who craved ideology. After becoming disillusioned with communism, a psychological need impelled them to attach themselves to another ideology—even one diametrically opposite to the one they were leaving.

There was still something else that made Burnham a strange choice as *National Review*'s foreign policy expert: Although his books about foreign affairs were popular successes, they had been critical flops.

In the book that made him famous, *The Managerial Revolution*, Burnham argued that power in industrial nations was flowing away from capitalists and into the hands of a new ruling class of technocrats—"managers" in industry, government, and the military, who collectively would control the economy. Even in the capitalistic democracies, production would no longer be determined by the hidden hand of the free market but through central planning. Moreover, the new ruling class would extend its power throughout all aspects of society, controlling not merely production but—through a "fused political-economic apparatus"—politics and culture as well. The result would be that collectivism and totalitarianism would supplant freedom everywhere, at least for the foreseeable future. While democracy and freedom might eventually reemerge in a mature managerial state, that was a distant prospect. The managerial revolution was already well under way in Germany with the rise of the Third Reich, in the Soviet Union with the rise of Stalinism, and in the United States with the rise of the New Deal. Though Burnham conceded that the New Deal was not Nazism or Stalinism, he maintained that "in terms of economic, social, political, and ideological changes from traditional capitalism, the New Deal moves in the same *direction* as Stalinism and Nazism."

Burnham went on to argue that the managerial revolution would drive toward a single global nation. However, "insuperable" obstacles—administrative, technological, ethnic, and cultural—stood in the way of merging the entire world into a single state, and therefore a small number of superstates would emerge. Probably, there would be three: the United States, which would absorb the Western hemisphere and become the "receiver" of the bankrupt British Empire; Germany, which would take over the European continent; and Japan, which would control all of Asia. Because Russia was too primitive to develop into a superstate, its western half would be absorbed by the European superstate and its eastern half by the Asian superstate.

It is easy to see why Burnham's book was both a bestseller and panned by critics. Burnham's view of the future was chilling and compelling. Even readers who did not fully buy Burnham's predictions found them provocative. Burnham purported to be a rigorous analyst, synthesizing history, technology, economics, and politics, and his view of the future was intriguing. *The Managerial Revolution* offered an additional attraction for those who despised the New Deal, which Burnham did not attack on ideological grounds but associated with totalitarian systems purely for socioscientific reasons.

The problem with *The Managerial Revolution* was that it was claptrap. Burnham had no idea what he was talking about. Burnham was, to be sure, a man of genuine erudition. He was someone who could read the memoirs of Pierre-Étienne Flandin, France's foreign minister when Hitler occupied the Rhineland in 1936, in French. And he worked hard at thinking carefully and systematically. However, he was not a historian, political scientist, sociologist, or economist, and he lacked a social scientist's understanding of just how difficult—or impossible—it is to predict the future. The reviewer for the *New York Times* said that once the major premise was granted, Burnham presented a closely reasoned scenario, but added that "I stall at the premise, and wouldn't grant it to someone who knows twice as much as Mr. Burnham." Many reviewers also criticized the book for its deterministic absolutism, that is, its premise that the course of history was governed by iron laws and the future was preordained. Some book reviewers would observe that Burnham's absolutist view of historical determinism had much in common with, well, Marxism.

Burnham was, and would always remain, the quintessential anti-Burkean. Burke believed that the complexity of the world is great, human reason—despite its considerable powers—is limited, and the former often outstrips the latter. This did not lead Burke to throw up his hands; it led him to proceed with humility, caution, and constant mindfulness about the possibility of unintended consequences. Burnham, by contrast, believed that if one purged himself of sentimentality and applied rigorous analysis to the hard, cold facts, one could understand the dynamics of the human enterprise well enough to set a course for a desired objective with confidence—or at least with a much higher degree of confidence than a Burkean would consider wise. Burnham, in fact, had much in common with Ayn Rand. Rand's mantra was "check your premises," Burnham's was avoid "sentimentality," and both believed in the power of objective reasoning. But Burnham's biographer, Daniel Kelly, suggests that Burnham was not the strong empiricist that he considered himself. Although Burnham genuinely intended to reason empirically and believed he was doing so, Kelly concludes that Burnham "tended to argue as much from ideological premises as from observation," and "sometimes seemed deaf to the demands of empirical reason," even when he purported to be reasoning empirically.[2]

Burnham's next two books—both written during World War II— were something of a bridge in his career, taking him from purportedly dispassionate analyses of sociopolitical trends toward a passionate concern about the dangers of totalitarianism. The first, *The Machiavellians*, was published in 1943. Burnham claimed that like Machiavelli, he was a realist who went where the facts took him. And the facts showed that managerial elites were moving nations toward "democratic totalitarianism" or "Bonapartism." Bonapartism, said Burnham, was already ensconced in Nazi Germany, fascist Italy, and the Soviet Union—and it was making great strides in the United States under Franklin D. Roosevelt's leadership. The reviews were largely negative.

Burnham's vision of the future was even darker in *The Struggle for the World*, published in 1947. Burnham opined that atomic war between the United States and the USSR was "very probable" and would likely break out within the next four or five years. Although the United States alone possessed the atomic bomb, it was only a matter of time before the USSR had it too. The "entire history of war and society" showed that fear of retaliation was not an effective deterrence, and war was inevitable. Burnham devoted considerable time to describing the enemy. Communism was a "monolithic structure" with "steel discipline," he wrote. The communist had a single passion—a "will to power" from which "neither wife nor child nor friend, neither beauty nor love nor pleasure nor knowledge cherished for its own sake" could divert him.

Burnham's next book, *The Coming Defeat of Communism*, published in 1949, was brighter. Burnham now said warfare was unlikely. Conventional warfare would be too costly in lives lost, and although U.S. superiority might make a preventive nuclear strike strategically sensible, the American people were too "confused" to accept it. Therefore, Burnham now advocated that the West adopt communism's own strategy of "political-subversive" warfare. This would consist of propaganda and material aid to anticommunist leaders such as Charles de Gaulle and anticommunist organizations such as the Catholic Church, worker organizations, liberation groups in Eastern Europe, and Muslim groups hostile to the Soviet Union. In Burnham's later writings, this strategy would become known by the term "polwar."

Like Burnham's previous books, *The Coming Defeat of Communism* earned generally negative reviews. Burnham now had an established record as a seer with a cloudy crystal ball, which reviewers pointed out. Nevertheless, *The Coming Defeat of Communism*—together with a 1953 follow-up, *Containment or Liberation?*—had an enormous influence on the development of the modern conservative movement.

These were the early days of the Cold War, and a great debate was under way about how America should deal with the challenge of communism and the Soviet Union. In its July 1947 issue, the influential journal *Foreign Affairs* published a trenchant article titled "The Sources of Soviet Conduct." While the magazine identified the author only by the pseudonym "X," it was an open secret that X was George F. Kennan. Kennan had worked for the State Department for twenty years and was recognized as one of America's most knowledgeable experts on the Soviet Union. Kennan had not originally written the piece as a magazine article. The document was originally a fifty-three-hundred-word memorandum that Kennan cabled from Moscow, where he was deputy head to the U.S. Mission, to Secretary of State James Byrnes. It is best known to history as "the long telegram." Secretary of the Navy James Forrestal, who was advocating a hard-line Soviet strategy within the high counsels of the Truman administration, urged Kennan to publish the dispatch to help bolster the hard-line position in the general debate.

In the piece, Kennan presented a sober assessment of the "political personality of Soviet power." Under Stalin's leadership, he wrote, "tremendous emphasis had been placed on the original Communist thesis of a basic antagonism between the capitalist and Socialist worlds." Some of this flowed from Marxist ideology, which saw capitalism as exploitative. And some flowed from Soviet experience with "great centers of military power, notably the Nazi regime in Germany and the Japanese

Government of the late 1930s, which did indeed have aggressive designs against the Soviet Union." This meant, wrote Kennan, "that there can never be on Moscow's side any sincere assumption of a community of aims between the Soviet Union and powers which are regarded as capitalist."

Kennan advocated a calm and resolute long-term strategy. Because Marxist-Leninist ideology postulated that capitalism was doomed and that communism would inevitably prevail, American strategists should not make the mistake of believing that the Soviet leadership had "embarked upon a do-or-die program to overthrow our society by a given date. The theory of inevitability of the eventual fall of capitalism has the fortunate connotation that there is no hurry about it." Kennan argued that "the main element of any United States policy toward the Soviet Union must be that of a long-term, patient but firm and vigilant containment of Russian expansive tendencies." Although the Soviets would seek to project their influence outward, and could not be charmed out of their eventual goal of overcoming capitalistic systems, "the Kremlin is under no ideological compulsion to accomplish its purposes in a hurry." Lenin had taught that communist leaders should pursue their goals with "great caution and flexibility," and therefore "the Kremlin has no compunction about retreating in the face of superior force." The bottom line was that "the Soviet pressure against the free institutions of the Western world is something that can be contained by the adroit and vigilant application of counterforce at a series of constantly shifting geographical and political points, corresponding to the shifts and maneuvers of Soviet policy."

Kennan was not advocating a permanent stalemate. He believed that there was a strong likelihood that Soviet power "bears within it the seeds of its own decay." Time was therefore on America's side. Kennan also believed it important that the United States demonstrate to the world that it was a nation "coping successfully with the problems of its internal life and with the responsibilities of a world power." He also wanted America to display "a spiritual vitality" that would provide a stark contrast to a Soviet system laboring under significant cultural and economic disadvantages, with rulers who maintained power through a secret police and other mechanisms that Stalin himself termed "organs of suppression." Although Kennan did not think that American policies

could themselves precipitate an early fall of Soviet power, he was arguing that through containment and leading by example America would
"promote tendencies which must eventually find their outlet in either
the breakup or the gradual mellowing of Soviet power."

Containment strategy was considered a hard-line approach at the
time. Senator Robert Taft worried about a strategy that would "give the
Russians the impression, justified at least to themselves, that we are ringing them about with armies for the purpose of taking aggressive action
when the time comes" or that would "make permanent the division of
the world into two armed camps." Taft consequently opposed creating
NATO in 1949.[3] James Burnham, however, was attacking containment
strategy as too soft. To him, the most important question was "Does the
United States *choose* to win?" He called containment a "guarantor of
ultimate defeat." Burnham advocated waging political-subversive warfare not merely to contain but to "roll back" communism. Burnham
worked hard to promote his alternative theory in the "circles that count."
He spoke to public affairs groups, gave interviews, participated in radio
forums, and adapted excerpts from *The Coming Defeat of Communism* for
periodicals ranging from the *Annals of the American Academy of Political
Science* to *Reader's Digest*.

Burnham succeeded in making rollback the principal alternative to
containment strategy. One newspaper described the debate in an article
titled "Burnham vs. Kennan." Notwithstanding Taft's concerns, rollback became popular with hard-line conservatives in the Republican
Party. Echoing James Burnham, the 1952 Republican National Platform
denounced containment as "a negative, futile, and immoral policy." The
platform, however, was deliberately ambiguous about just how far a Republican administration should go in attempting to liberate Eastern
Europe. On the one hand, it accused Democratic administrations of
abandoning "friendly nations such as Latvia, Lithuania, Estonia, Poland and Czechoslovakia to fend for themselves against the Communist
aggression which soon swallowed them." It promised that a Republican
administration would "make liberty into a beacon light of hope that will
penetrate the dark places" and "revive the contagious, liberating influences which are inherent in freedom" that would "inevitably set up
strains and stresses within the captive world which will make the rulers
impotent to continue in their monstrous ways and mark the beginning

of their end." On the other hand, a careful reader of the platform would search in vain for liberating influences more aggressive than giving the Voice of America "real function." Moreover, the platform stated that the "supreme goal of our foreign policy will be an honorable and just peace. We dedicate ourselves to wage peace and to win it." The platform also had a McCarthyite tinge. It accused Democrats of "shielding traitors in high places" and proclaimed, "There are no Communists in the Republican Party."

Eisenhower found much in this platform he did not like. He believed in containment, and he was repulsed by Joseph McCarthy. However, to unite the party and rally the conservative wing behind him, he had no choice but to announce his fidelity to the party's platform. This alone was not enough. In a speech to the American Legion—one of the organizational pillars of right-wing foreign policy—shortly after the Republican convention, Eisenhower declared that the United States should never accept the "permanence" of Soviet control over Eastern Europe and should use its "influence and power to help" the enslaved nations throw off the "yoke of Russian tyranny." Meanwhile, Nixon was sounding similar themes on the campaign trail, such as calling Adlai Stevenson an alumnus of the "cowardly college of communist containment." In the grand tradition of politics, these were rhetorical flourishes designed to allow audiences to hear what they wanted. But rhetorical chickens come home to roost.[4]

A few months before publishing *The Coming Defeat of Communism*, Burnham took a leave of absence from New York University and moved to Washington. Although Burnham told NYU he was taking a leave to pursue government work, he presumably did not tell the university exactly what kind of work he was pursuing. In the summer of 1949, Burnham secretly became a consultant for the CIA's Office of Policy Coordination. The OPC had been established the preceding year and given a deliberately misleading name: It was not a policy group at all but rather the agency's division of covert operations. It was formed in late 1948, but for years its existence was secret, even though it quickly became the largest part of the agency.[5] Although Burnham had finished writing *The Coming Defeat of Communism* before joining the OPC, what Burnham advocated in that book—polwar—was precisely what the OPC was doing. Moreover, the OPC saw its mission not merely in terms of containing communism but in rolling it back. (George Kennan was involved with the formation of the OPC, and in classified memoranda Kennan was himself advocating that the agency engage in "guerrilla warfare" and "organized political warfare" and that it covertly support "all-out liberation movements."[6]) There is, therefore, reason to suspect that Burnham's views about polwar and rollback may have been influenced by an earlier relationship with the agency. In any event, Burnham lived in Washington and worked for the OPC for four years, and it was during this period—in June 1950 to be exact—that Burnham interviewed a recent Yale graduate named William F. Buckley Jr. for a position with the OPC.

One of Burnham's covert jobs was to help establish and support a liberal, anticommunist organization named the American Committee for Cultural Freedom (ACCF). Many well-known liberals—including Sidney Hook, Lionel and Diana Trilling, Reinhold Niebuhr, Arthur Schlesinger Jr., Norman Thomas, Dwight Macdonald, Mary McCarthy, and Henry Luce—joined the ACCF or participated on its projects, most of them, presumably, unaware of its CIA connection. Burnham served on the executive board of the ACCF and worked to guide it in directions the OPC considered useful. When the ACCF ran into financial difficulty, Burnham secured grants for it from the Fairfield Foundation, which in fact was a CIA front.[7]

From 1949 to 1953, most of Burnham's time was spent on OCP projects—much of it related to the ACCF—but he also continued to write and lecture. He elaborated on his views about polwar in several articles and then, in 1953, in a book titled *Containment or Liberation?* Burnham argued that polwar should include not only propaganda and helping people escape from behind the Iron Curtain but subversion and sabotage as well. Burnham also argued that containment was doomed to fail—an argument he would continue to make for decades. As Burnham succinctly put it elsewhere, because containment is "purely negative, it had to win every individual engagement in order to work; it excluded the attempt to achieve a positive gain, and any loss was and remained a loss; but it is impossible to win every time."[8] Burnham also objected to containment strategy because it had nothing to say about people imprisoned behind the Iron Curtain. Burnham wanted to attack the foundations of Soviet power. He made an arguably below-the-belt attack on Kennan: After conceding that Kennan was undeniably anti-Soviet on an intellectual level, Burnham added that Kennan's writings failed to reflect "a hatred of communism." To the extent that Burnham had a legitimate point, it was that Americans needed to be passionately motivated to win the death struggle with communism. Nevertheless, Burnham was questioning Kennan's commitment to the ultimate triumph of the West over communism.

Kennan did not then reply to Burnham's arguments, but in his memoirs Kennan observed that the argument that containment could not succeed failed to appreciate Kennan's claim that Soviet power would gradually mellow. Burnham's argument also implicitly rejected the view, expressed later by Ronald Reagan, that communism was "a temporary aberration which will one day disappear from the earth because it is contrary to human nature."[9] Kennan and Reagan both believed that time was on the side of the West—either because the Soviet Union's truculence was bound to diminish or because the communist system was bound to collapse. With the benefit of hindsight, we know that both Kennan and Reagan turned out to be right. It may be unfair to judge even a self-proclaimed prognosticator such as Burnham through hindsight. Nevertheless, it is worth observing that Kennan and Reagan both possessed a confidence about America that Burnham—and others who constantly preached her doom—lacked.

Containment or Liberation? failed to impress many book reviewers. Robert Strausz-Hupé, one of the leading geopolitical thinkers of the day, found it filled with errors and marred by "partisan sniping." Truman's foreign policy had been shot at by "better marksmen" than Burnham, said Strausz-Hupé. Writing in the *New Republic*, Arthur Schlesinger Jr. was even harsher. He dismissed *Containment or Liberation?* as "an absurd book written by an absurd man." It was, he said, "a careless and hasty job, filled with confusion, contradiction, ignorance, and misrepresentation." Nevertheless, *Containment or Liberation?* alarmed George Kennan. Burnham was not an extremist but a mainstream thinker of some repute, his book was well written, and, Kennan feared, a significant number of people—including people of influence—might find it persuasive.[10]

Up till this point in his career, Burnham remained in good standing on the political left. He was a stalwart of the liberal, anticommunist

ACCF. He wrote frequently for left-wing journals such as *New Leader*
and *Partisan Review*, and served on the editorial advisory board of the
latter. He had begun to draw favorable attention in conservative circles
and started also to contribute articles to *American Mercury* and the *Freeman*, but his liberal credentials were largely intact.[11] But in 1952, something possessed Burnham to start attacking fellow liberals viciously and
personally. In March, a battle erupted within the ACCF as to whether
the organization should condemn Joseph McCarthy. Some members of
the board, including Arthur Schlesinger, wanted to condemn McCarthy
as a demagogue. Others, including Max Eastman, argued that the dangers of communist espionage exceeded the dangers posed by McCarthy's
tactics, and condemning McCarthy would do more harm than good.
There was a heated meeting. Burnham sided with the pro-McCarthy
faction. But Burnham not only attacked those holding opposing views
personally—he did so publicly, in the pages of the *Washington Post*. A
few months later, Burnham took indiscretion to a higher level in an article for *American Mercury*. Burnham, who was supporting Eisenhower
for president, said that Adlai Stevenson, the Democratic candidate for
president, was temperamentally among the group of liberals who created an atmosphere in which "pro-Communist points of view and individual Communist agents have flourished." Burnham blamed these
liberals for Yalta and for the communists coming to power in China.
And for good measure, Burnham attacked Arthur Schlesinger Jr. and
Americans for Democratic Action (ADA) too. Schlesinger was working on Stevenson's campaign, and ADA—which Schlesinger helped
found in 1947 along with Eleanor Roosevelt, Hubert Humphrey, Reinhold Niebuhr, and John Kenneth Galbraith, among others—was the
nation's premier liberal, anticommunist organization. Its anticommunist bona fides were beyond reasonable question. "We reject any association with Communists or sympathizers with communism in the
United States as completely as we reject any association with fascists or
their sympathizers," ADA declared in its first statement of principles.[12]
In fact, some criticized ADA for being so anticommunist that it had
been slow to oppose McCarthyism—though by this time it had spoken
out against McCarthy, and thereby earned Burnham's disfavor.[13] In his
American Mercury article, Burnham called ADA "a pretentious outfit of

nostalgic New Dealers looking for a new depression to save the country from, and specializing in anti-anti-Communism."

"James Burnham has committed suicide," said Philip Rahv, one of the founders of *Partisan Review* and a central figure in liberal intellectual circles. *Partisan Review* demanded Burnham's resignation from its editorial advisory board, and the ACCF expelled him from its executive board.[14] This ended Burnham's usefulness to the CIA. Even prior to this, Burnham's relationship with the agency had begun to sour. Burnham was criticizing the agency for not prosecuting polwar with sufficient energy, and some agency officers internally criticized Burnham as too hard-line; one even considered Burnham "a fascist." At about this juncture, Joseph McCarthy's aides asked the CIA for information relating to its foreign propaganda efforts. The agency feared that it might become a target of McCarthy's Senate committee—and was concerned that Burnham might be furnishing McCarthy with ammunition. In June 1953, Burnham left the agency. Presumably he was fired.

There was no reason to return to New York. After a two-year leave of absence had expired in 1951, Burnham had resigned his position at NYU. Moreover, Burnham's professional suicide had effectively extinguished his and his wife Marcia's social lives.[15] The Burnhams retreated to a large farmhouse they owned in Kent, Connecticut. Burnham, however, did not become a gentleman farmer. He accepted an invitation from Henry Kissinger, who was then a Ph.D. candidate at Harvard, to speak at a seminar in international relations at Harvard in July of 1953. More importantly, in 1954—the same year that Buckley and Bozell published *McCarthy and His Enemies*—Burnham published *The Web of Subversion: Underground Networks in the U.S. Government*. The general theme of *Web* is captured by its title: Like a spider in the dark, the Soviet Union had spun a web of spies, saboteurs, and collaborators throughout the federal government, and especially within the armed forces. Burnham made his argument through dozens of case histories, most of which he drew from transcripts of congressional hearings. He concluded some people in the web "were not consciously disloyal" and did not understand the consequences of what they were doing. Their Soviet manipulators were slyly exploiting the innocent concern for civil liberties on the part of these unwitting collaborators, which caused the collaborators to invoke their Fifth Amendment rights rather than provide investigators with the information necessary to eradicate the web. Burnham argued for legal reforms designed to make it easier for investigators to penetrate this shield. The courts, for example, should interpret the Fifth Amendment more narrowly and more readily admit evidence from government wiretaps. Congress should lengthen the statute of limitation for espionage and related crimes. And the federal government should not employ people who invoked their Fifth Amendment rights in response to national security inquiries. Arthur Schlesinger did not like *Web* any better than *Containment*, but the mere fact that Schlesinger's review appeared in *Saturday Review*, then one of the largest circulation magazines in the nation, reveals that Burnham was still prominent. *Web of Subversion*, however, had more success with other reviewers. In stark contrast to *Containment*, critics often praised *Web* as a careful and balanced work. *Newsweek* and the *Chicago Tribune* gave the book high praise, and at year's end the *New York Times* placed it on its list of the twenty-four best nonfiction books of 1954.

Burnham was now a man of the right, if not entirely by choice, then by necessity. He was toying with the idea of starting his own right-wing journal (both *American Mercury* and the *Freeman* had become unacceptable venues for his work) when the young William F. Buckley Jr. came calling with a proposal that he join *National Review*, which was then still in the planning stage. Burnham leaped at the opportunity. They agreed that among other duties Burnham would write a regular column for the magazine about foreign policy. It would be titled The Third World War. Burnham would remain at the magazine for more than twenty-three years, until a stroke forced him to retire in 1978. Burnham was not merely a contributor to the magazine; he became Buckley's most trusted colleague and the unofficial second-in-command at the magazine. Burnham was, as previously mentioned, the grown-up in the group. And he acted like a grown-up. He remained calm when others became ruffled. He was careful and meticulous. He identified flaws in arguments. He took an interest in every aspect of the enterprise, from typography to the positions the magazine took in unsigned editorials.

Buckley particularly valued Burnham's intellectual methodology, which was to eschew sentimentality and reason objectively and analytically, or at least appear to do so. In his memoirs, Buckley wrote, "Beyond any question, [James Burnham] has been the dominant intellectual influence in the development" of *National Review*.[16] And in his memoirs about the magazine, Jeffrey Hart wrote, "From the beginning, James Burnham was absolutely central to *National Review* and remained increasingly so" until his retirement.[17]

Not everyone was as impressed with Burnham. Others—Frank Meyer and Bill Rusher especially—didn't trust him. They believed that Burnham was not a full convert to the conservative cause. Burnham gave them good reasons to doubt him. He was always pulling in the direction of making the magazine less conservative, less ideologically pure, or as Burnham put it, less sectarian. He wanted to stress good writing and strong analysis and to reach out to readers beyond conservative precincts. In a speech at *National Review*'s tenth anniversary dinner, Burnham said that the magazine should move away from "the sectarian and doctrinaire clannishness that is natural enough in the early stages of every political movement" and "become more flexible, more generous, more intelligent and more humane." Needless to say, true believers at the dinner did not welcome being told that they were not intelligent and humane enough. Burnham took some positions that were unorthodox for conservatives: He supported Medicare for example. Most disturbing of all was Burnham's taste in politicians: Burnham supported Eisenhower over Taft in 1952, he never warmed to Goldwater, and his favorite politician—whom he repeatedly urged *National Review* to endorse for the presidency—was Nelson Rockefeller. As Priscilla Buckley observed, Meyer and Rusher considered Burnham's support of Rockefeller nothing less than treasonous. When Buckley left for summer vacations in Switzerland and Burnham took unofficial control of the magazine, Meyer and Rusher often tussled with Burnham over editorial decisions—what position the magazine should take in unsigned editorials, what articles it would publish—and sent urgent letters of complaint to Buckley. But Buckley never lost faith in Burnham. He thought about giving Burnham the title "executive editor" to formally designate him as the second-in-command (a move Priscilla supported) but ultimately decided against doing so because he feared that would upset Meyer and Rusher even more.

In the main, Burnham was a moderating influence on both Buckley and *National Review*. He tried to sand down the magazine's roughest ideological edges. But there are at least two areas in which this was not the case.

One was race. Burnham too was a prisoner of racist stereotypes. He saw black people as intellectually inferior. Although he sometimes expressly denied that was his view, he revealed prejudices in writing in numerous ways. In his book *Suicide of the West*, for example, Burnham carries on a mock discussion between himself and a liberal. The liberal tells Burnham that "the races of mankind do not differ in intellectual or moral capacity." "I mention," Burnham writes, "that most scholars in the field . . . seem to agree that at any rate the Australian bushman and the African pigmies are somewhat defective in these respects, however admirable in others." Burnham goes on to say that "I point out to him that Negroes in the United States have not attained levels of intellectual eminence in as high a proportion to their numbers as whites." Burnham informs the liberal that the comparison holds true when restricted to members of the two races that have received the same amount of schooling.[18] Burnham displays this kind of racist stereotyping again and again.[19]

The other area on which Burnham was not a moderating influence happened to be his specialty, namely, the Cold War.

The first world crises to occur after *National Review* began publication—Soviet suppression of an uprising in Hungary, and the coordinated Israeli-British-French attempt to seize control of the Sinai and the Suez Canal—both came to a head in the fall of 1956, but each was stimulated by events earlier that year.

Soviet Premier Nikita Khrushchev unintentionally planted the seeds of the Hungarian crisis when, on February 25, 1956, he stunned fourteen hundred delegates to the Congress of the Soviet Communist Party with a speech that laid bare Stalin's crimes of cruelty and terror and called for a program of de-Stalinization in both the Soviet Union and Eastern

Europe. Khrushchev also suggested that capitalism and communism were not incompatible, and that he favored peaceful coexistence with the West. The speech was intended to be secret, but the CIA obtained a transcript. The Eisenhower administration privately provided the transcript to the *New York Times*, and the *Times* published it on June 5. Totalitarian regimes often risk disorder when they attempt liberalization, and that rule held firm in this instance. The Polish Communist Party reacted to Khrushchev's speech by sweeping Stalinists out of power and reinstalling Wladyslaw Gomulka—who had been a victim of one of Stalin's purges—as head of their party. Riots broke out between hardliners and reformers. Khrushchev was furious. This was more destabilization than he intended. At first he threatened to send in Soviet troops to remove the new government, but after discussions in Warsaw he relented and permitted the new government to remain. Seeking to avoid a replay of this scenario in nearby Hungary, Khrushchev arranged to have the Stalinist leader there, Mátyás Rákosi, removed and brought to Moscow, under the guise of Rákosi stepping down for health reasons. But once again, liberalization caused disorder. Hungarian "freedom fighters" rushed into the streets of Budapest, demanding that Imre Nagy, whom the Soviets deposed a year earlier, be reinstalled as premier.

Egyptian president Gamal Abdel Nasser planted the seeds for the second crisis when, on July 26, he nationalized the Suez Canal. His move was not motivated solely by nationalism; it was entangled in Cold War politics. Britain and the United States had promised to help finance and build the Aswan Dam, but retracted that promise when Egypt recognized Red China and purchased arms from Soviet-bloc Czechoslovakia. British prime minister Anthony Eden cabled Eisenhower that Nasser's nationalization of the canal was unacceptable, but Eisenhower replied that Nasser was within his rights to exercise "the power of eminent domain" in his own country. This caused Britain, France, and Israel to plot to seize both the Sinai Peninsula and the canal without the consent or knowledge of the United States. Israel would seize the Sinai Peninsula, and England and France—purporting to save the canal and international shipping from warring armies—would use Israeli-Egypt fighting as a pretext to seize the canal. They expected Eisenhower to be upset, but what could he do? They were confident America would not turn against its allies. Besides, November 6 was the day of the presidential election, and Eisenhower would have his hands full.

On October 23, Imre Nagy was returned to the premiership of Hungary. He said that Soviet troops would leave Hungary and he promised a new government would pursue a policy of "democratization." Unbeknownst to Eisenhower—and perhaps even to Allen Dulles, then head of the CIA—Radio Free Europe, and other stations controlled by the OPC (the covert operations division within the CIA that had employed James Burnham) began urging Hungarians to fight the Soviets. The broadcasts told freedom fighters to sabotage railroads and cut telephone lines, and instructed them on how to make Molotov cocktails and use the homemade bombs against Soviet tanks. The broadcasts also erroneously accused Nagy of being a Soviet stooge, and claimed Nagy had invited Soviet troops to return to Hungary.[20] Thousands of Hungarians heeded the call to insurrection. Despite Nagy's reassurances to the people, rioting continued. At a meeting of the National Security Council on October 26, Allen Dulles informed Eisenhower that Soviet troops were reentering Hungary. Eisenhower told Allen Dulles not to do anything that would give the Soviets reason to believe that the United States would come to the aid of the freedom fighters. Eisenhower was concerned that Soviet fears might tempt them "to resort to extreme measures," and he did not want to increase those fears.

On October 28, Israel launched a surprise attack in the Sinai. Britain and France issued an ultimatum: Unless there was a cease-fire between Israel and Egypt, with both sides withdrawing ten miles from the canal and permitting British and French forces to occupy key positions along the waterway, they would seize the canal by force. Israel immediately agreed.

In the early morning of October 31, the Soviet Union announced it would withdraw its troops from Hungary and not interfere in that country's internal affairs. A few hours later in New York, Ambassador Henry Cabot Lodge told the General Assembly of the United Nations that the United States was introducing a resolution calling on Israel and Egypt to agree to a cease-fire and for all UN members—i.e., Britain and France—to refrain from the use of force. Meanwhile, British aircraft began bombing Egyptian targets, and Nasser set out to block the Suez Canal by sinking thirty-two ships in it. In the evening, Eisenhower addressed the nation on television. He announced that the United States would give economic assistance to a new, independent government in Hungary, but that while the United States wanted to be friends with new governments in Eastern Europe it would not regard them as military allies (i.e., not bring them into NATO).

On November 1, Nagy announced that Hungary was withdrawing from the Warsaw Pact, declaring neutrality, and appealing to the UN for assistance. Two days later, the Soviet Union sent two hundred thousand troops and four thousand tanks into Hungary.[21] Hungarian freedom fighters greeted the Soviets with Molotov cocktails. Four bloody days of fighting raged in Budapest. More than a thousand Soviet troops and twenty thousand Hungarians died in the fighting. Freedom fighters wondered why America had not come to their aid.[22]

On November 2, 1956, the United Nations adopted a U.S.-sponsored resolution calling for an immediate cease-fire in the Middle East and for sending a UN peacekeeping force to the area. Britain and Israel declined to honor the resolution. On November 5, British and French soldiers invaded the Suez Canal zone. The Soviet Union sent messages to Israel, Britain, and France stating it was ready to resort to force to help Egypt defend itself, and it sent a separate message to Eisenhower proposing a joint Soviet-American military action to restore peace in Egypt. This was a precarious moment. The Soviets were "both furious and scared," Eisenhower told his advisers, and that "makes for the most dangerous possible state of mind." It was important "to be positive and clear in our every word, every step." Eisenhower issued a public statement that if Soviet troops were sent to the Middle East the United States would resist them with force. Privately he instructed that "every outpost of our armed forces is absolutely on their toes . . . If those fellows start something, we may have to hit 'em—and, if necessary, with *everything* in the bucket."

Tuesday, November 6, was election day. Eisenhower received more than 57 percent of the popular vote and carried every state but seven (six of them in the Deep South). Britain agreed to accept the cease-fire in Suez, and the UN peacekeeping force moved into position. But breaking a promise of safe-conduct, the Soviets arrested and executed Imre Nagy.

Historians applaud Eisenhower's performance during this period. He stood against old-school colonialism and imperialism, even when practiced by allies. Stephen E. Ambrose, for example, writes, "Eisenhower's insistence on the primacy of the U.N., of treaty obligations, and of the rights of all nations gave the United States a standing in world opinion it had never before achieved."[23] Speaking of Eisenhower's full tenure as president, John Lewis Gaddis calls Eisenhower "the most subtle and brutal strategist of the nuclear age."[24] Eisenhower recognized that nuclear war would be catastrophic and that limited nuclear war was impossible. The balance Eisenhower "exquisitely but terrifyingly" struck, according to Gaddis, was to insist that the United States prepare *only* for nuclear war. Nuclear weapons became the ultimate deterrent, and temptations to engage in conflicts that could escalate into armageddon were avoided.

Right-wing bombast about rollback and liberation profoundly affected the Hungarian crisis. Although we do not know to what extent Burnham's writings directly influenced OPC head Frank G. Wisner to initiate take-up-arms Radio Free Europe broadcasts, those broadcasts—and other liberation rhetoric by American politicians—encouraged the uprising. The Hungarians thought they had been promised help "by Radio Free Europe, and by [Secretary of State John Foster] Dulles' many references over the years to liberation," writes Stephen Ambrose.[25] Rollback-liberation rhetoric in American politics may have influenced Soviet action as well. Khrushchev was genuinely interested in some form of liberalization. As events in Poland showed, he was willing to make significant concessions. But as disorder spread from Poland to Hungary, the Soviets had reason to fear that if they allowed the crisis to continue too long the United States might actively support insurrection. Soviet analysts studied what American leaders said. They undoubtedly read Eisenhower and Nixon's campaign speeches, Dulles's many speeches advocating liberation, and the Republican platform (Soviets tended to place too much weight on party doctrine). They likely read Burnham too. Even the CIA—which asked him for permission to parachute arms to the freedom fighters—thought that the president might aid the freedom fighters. But, in fact, Eisenhower always considered American intervention in Hungary out of the question. "He knew it, had known it all along, which made all the four years of Republican talk about 'liberation' so essentially hypocritical," Ambrose writes.[26]

During the crises, James Burnham and *National Review* were, unsurprisingly, urging Eisenhower to pursue liberation strategy. Early in the crisis in Eastern Europe, *National Review* published an unsigned editorial (apparently written by Burnham) that stated, "If the Eisenhower Administration is in any degree serious about that 'liberation' of Eastern Europe about which it has so often spoken, then it should be ready for action along at least two indispensible lines." First, should Poland "*in deed and not merely in slogan*, move away from Moscow," the United States should provide economic assistance to help make Poland economically viable. Second, Eisenhower should declare that a Soviet attack against Poland would "be deemed by the United States *a casus belli.*"[27]

After the Soviet Union brutally crushed the uprising in Hungary, *National Review* endorsed a proposal by Senator William F. Knowland of California, who was then Senate minority leader, that the United States bar the Soviet Union from the United Nations and suspend diplomatic recognition of the Soviet Union and its satellites.[28] *National Review* did not say exactly how the United States would go about barring the Soviet Union from the United Nations. Since the United States had no legal authority to do that—and, in fact, all of the nations of the world acting collectively lacked authority to bar a member of the Security Council from the UN over that member's veto—the United States would have to physically bar the Soviets from the UN, presumably by expelling the Soviet ambassador to the United Nations—and, indeed, all Soviet diplomats—from the United States.

Who would have been punished more by suspending diplomatic recognition of the Soviet Union—the United States and the West, or the Soviet Union? And who would have been punished more by destroying the United Nations in this fashion: the Soviet Union or the United States? For Robert Welch and the Birchers—who wanted to "Get the US out of the UN, and the UN out of the US"—the answer to that question was easy. The United Nations was a threat to American sovereignty and a base for communist espionage and infiltration within the American homeland. *National Review*, however, was not quite so clear. It made a proposal that would have effectively destroyed the United Nations without defending—or even acknowledging—that result.

During the same course of events, *National Review* published a separate three-page editorial about the situation in the Suez (again apparently written by Burnham).[29] Unsurprisingly, *National Review* viewed the matter through a Cold War lens. Britain and France understood the situation perfectly: "They saw that Nasser's ravenous ambition and unbounded unscrupulousness were driving him into the hands of the Soviet Union." The situation, therefore, was all about keeping the strategically important Suez Canal out of Soviet hands, which was a matter of necessity for the West. Indeed, the first portion of the editorial was subtitled "The British and French Choose to Survive." What about colonialism or imperialism? "We should make it immediately clear that we are not in league with Israeli imperialists, and we would not consent to Israel's exploitation of the Suez crisis for national aggrandizement," the editorial declared. Apparently, in *National Review*'s judgment, Nasser's attempt to unite the Arab world behind his leadership—his emergence as "the popular, dragon-slaying hero of the Arab masses," as the editorial put it—while forming an alliance with the Soviet Union, presented an existential threat to Britain and France but not Israel. (In a later editorial, also apparently written by Burnham, the magazine said, "Our government cannot feed every hungry Egyptian, clothe every ragged Bedouin, educated every illiterate Yemenite and soothe every fanatic Jew—nor is it our government's business to do so." But the United States government should ensure that an enemy did not gain control of Middle East oil or acquire "positions of strength on land or sea" in the region.[30]) In any event, *National Review*'s position was that Israel should leave the Sinai, Britain and France should keep the canal, and the United States should support Britain and France in that endeavor.

These two crises were watershed events in American foreign policy. Henceforth, there was no more rhetoric about rollback or liberation from the Eisenhower administration. Burnham and *National Review* thought the Eisenhower administration betrayed valued allies in the Middle East—not only by abandoning them but by actively opposing them—and the cause of freedom in Eastern Europe. As they saw it, the United States had adopted a policy that gave too high a priority to avoiding confrontation with the Soviet Union.[31]

In March 1958, Ernest van den Haag published a three-page article in which he laid out some unique ideas about resisting communist aggression.[32] Democracy, he argued, was by itself not an effective principle for rallying the West against the communist challenge. Democracy was nothing more than a set of procedural rules for regulating competition for political power—and "an empty box," as he put it. However, democracy's great advantage was that, unlike communism, it was compatible with religion. Religion had power. Religion could command passion and "hold people more fully and permanently than the Communist faith." However, democracy was weakening "itself unnecessarily by weakening religion mainly through excessive distribution of education." Education confused people by confronting them with a "multiplicity of ideas and ideals." Some people were able to work their way through the confusion and find a "more elegant version" of what they used to believe. But education had a negative effect on "the great mass" of students; it increased their skepticism and weakened their religious faith. This caused them to become anxious and frustrated, and made them easy prey for proselytizers of dangerous secular faiths. Thus, argued Van den Haag, "the weakening of religion both weakens the fabric of democratic society, and deprives democracy of its strategic long-range weapon against the secularized faith of Communism." The solution? Education should be limited to the truly able. "Education, after all, was meant for those capable of being educated, not for those who at most can be led astray by it," explained Van den Haag. This might be accomplished by teaching in Latin, or at least in "literate English."

Later in the year, the Soviet Union launched its first intercontinental ballistic missile and then, in short order, two Sputniks, the first artificial satellites. The second weighed more than a thousand pounds and carried a dog named Laika. America panicked. The Soviets had gotten ahead in technology, especially the strategically critical area of rocketry. One person who was not panicked was President Eisenhower. From photographs taken by secret high-altitude U-2 reconnaissance flights over the Soviet Union, he knew that America remained well ahead in strategic weaponry. He could not tell the nation what he knew without compromising those flights, but he did his best to project a reassuring calm. Nonetheless, the conventional wisdom was that America was behind—and the reason was that America had fallen behind in education, particularly in the sciences. From coast to coast, a cry went out for a strong push to improve the nation's educational system. Perhaps because Van den Haag's wisdom was still fresh in its mind, *National Review* was not so easily stampeded. "The main sin of the Liberals," it wrote in an unsigned editorial, "has been to seize upon the Sputniks in order to justify such things as a demand for a complete overhauling of the American system of education at fantastic federal expense and the sort of 'crash' rocket programs that would resemble mounting a horse and riding off in all directions at once." What was needed instead was "a firm resolve to stand up to Moscow's heightened campaign of psycho-political terror."[33]

On November 8, 1960, John F. Kennedy defeated Richard M. Nixon for the presidency. The election was practically a dead heat: Kennedy captured 49.7 percent of the popular vote to Nixon's 49.6 percent. Less than three percentage points had separated the candidates in seventeen states, including California, Illinois, Michigan, New Jersey, and Pennsylvania. Geographic preferences were different then: The Republican ticket composed of Nixon and Henry Cabot Lodge carried California, Oregon, Washington State, Wisconsin, and Vermont while the Democratic ticket of Kennedy and Lyndon Baines Johnson carried most of the South. Little had separated the two candidates on foreign policy. Both were ardent cold warriors. Both accepted the doctrine of containment. Moreover, both implicitly accepted "domino theory," which analogized nations to a row of dominoes: If one nation fell to the communists, it would topple the adjoining nation. From the time President Eisenhower first described this theory to the nation in 1954, it became accepted wisdom. During the campaign, Nixon and Kennedy sparred over where the perimeter should be drawn—where, in essence, to prop up the first domino. Both Kennedy and Nixon promised to defend the large island of Formosa, about seventy-five miles from mainland China, held by Chang Kai-shek and the Chinese nationalists. Nixon said he would defend the tiny islands of Quemoy and Matsu, about five or six miles from mainland China, which Chang Kai-shek also held, and he accused Kennedy of being weak in not making the same pledge.

When Kennedy and Eisenhower met at the White House on the day before Kennedy's inauguration, Eisenhower reiterated the domino theory. "If Laos should fall to the Communists, then it would be a question of time until South Vietnam, Cambodia, Thailand and Burma would collapse," he told Kennedy.[34]

There was a problem much closer to American shores: Cuba, only ninety miles from Florida. The American government did not know what to make of Fidel Castro when he and revolutionaries overthrew the corrupt and repressive Cuban dictator, Fulgencio Batista, two years earlier. The CIA originally thought Castro was a democratic revolution-ary, and the agency's officer in charge of Caribbean operations proudly called himself a "Fidelista." When Castro visited the United States in April of 1959, Vice President Richard Nixon spent three hours with him. But by the end of that year, it had become clear that Castro was a communist. Richard Bissell, head of the CIA's covert operations, sent Allen Dulles, the agency's director, a memorandum recommending the "elimination" of Castro. Dulles crossed out the word "elimination" and penned in "removal from Cuba."[35] On March 17, 1960, Dulles and Bis-sell met with Eisenhower and Nixon in the White House and proposed a plan for toppling the Castro regime. The CIA would train sixty Cu-ban exiles in jungle warfare techniques and surreptitiously insert them into the island, where, supported by propaganda beamed to the island by radio, they would lead an uprising against Castro. Dulles and Bissell assured the president that the plan would bring down Castro within eight months, and that the CIA's involvement would be kept secret.

Eisenhower told Dulles and Bissell to proceed, but from that mo-ment on the CIA began expanding the plan. Sixty trained soldiers would not be enough. In short order, the agency was training five hun-dred Cuban exiles at a CIA base in Guatemala. That number increased to fifteen hundred, even as CIA analysts concluded that a three-thousand-man force would not be enough. The agency was beginning to realize that an invasion was not going to spark an uprising against Castro. Castro, in fact, enjoyed strong loyalty; he had, after all, rid Cuba of a brutal dictatorship. Dulles and Bissell, however, did not choose to share with Eisenhower or Nixon the problems with the op-erations. They apparently believed that once an invasion was under way, they would persuade the president to send American aircraft and ma-rines to support Cuban exiles fighting on the beaches. Nixon was canny enough to insist that the operation be delayed until after the U.S. presi-dential election in November.

Just before he was to turn the reins over to Kennedy, Eisenhower re-ceived a report he had commissioned about the CIA. The report said

that the agency's covert operations, including its political and psychological warfare activities, had not been worth the monies expended for
them, and, moreover, they had distracted the agency from intelligence
gathering and analysis. The report said Allen Dulles was not capable of
managing both intelligence and covert actions. At his last National Security Council meeting, Eisenhower confronted Dulles with the report.
Dulles insisted all was well. The president became angry. The structure
of the American intelligence was faulty, Eisenhower declared. For eight
years, Eisenhower had failed to successfully reform the agency, and now
he was going to "leave a legacy of ashes" to the next president.

Kennedy, however, did not know the CIA was untrustworthy. About
a week after the election, Dulles and Bissell briefed Kennedy on the
plan to land a force of fifteen hundred Cuban exiles at the Bay of Pigs in
Cuba and thereby spark a national uprising against Castro. They did not
tell the president-elect that CIA analysts believed the force of Cuban
exiles would fail unless they were supported by U.S. armed forces.
When they met at the White House on the day before Kennedy's inauguration, Eisenhower urged Kennedy to support "guerrilla operations
in Cuba" but stressed he had not approved final plans of an operation.
Castro, in fact, knew more about what the CIA was planning than did
either Eisenhower or Kennedy. His intelligence service had penetrated
the group of exiles working with the CIA. Liberals Kennedy consulted—
Arthur Schlesinger Jr., Chester Bowles, Adlai Stevenson, and J. William
Fulbright—cautioned the president against an invasion, but Kennedy
listened to the advisers he considered tougher, including Dulles, Bissell,
and national security adviser McGeorge Bundy. The CIA was telling
Kennedy that except for a few sorties by disguised U.S. aircraft, piloted
by Americans pretending to be defectors from Castro's air force, the
invasion would be conducted entirely by Cuban exiles. To assure himself that was so, Kennedy telephoned Marine Colonel Jack Hawkins, an
amphibious landings expert who had been sent to Guatemala to review
preparations by the invasion. Hawkins told the president that the exile
force was "truly formidable" and that its "officers do not expect help from
U.S. armed forces."

The issue of the *National Review* that went on the stands on the day
of the invasion included a two-page editorial about what to do about
Cuba.[36] Cuba "occupies a spot of prime strategic importance for the

defense of the Americas," the magazine declared. "The present Cuban regime is intolerable." A policy of not intervening in the internal affairs of other nations "presupposes that those nations do not jeopardize our own national security and basic interests . . . Otherwise intervention becomes a government's duty, granted the power to intervene—and we have the power," the editorial continued. Did that mean sending in the marines? Perhaps, but that was not yet necessary. The United States should first undertake a "propaganda and psychological campaign" and support Cuban opposition elements that, said the magazine, had "recently begun underground operations in Cuba." This was one time the United States government was taking a more right-wing course than *National Review* recommended. But both the government and the magazine were laboring under the assumption that Castro was unpopular on the island because he was communist.

History has recorded that the Bay of Pigs invasion was an utter disaster. The invaders were pinned down as soon as they disembarked from their landing craft. They found themselves mired in swamps and cut off from the jungle by a large military force that included fifty-four tanks and was personally led by Fidel Castro. The CIA twisted Kennedy's arm to permit airstrikes by navy jets from the USS *Essex* aircraft carrier, then fifty miles away.* After repeatedly saying no, Kennedy relented and permitted six futile sorties by U.S. Navy fighters. At one point in the engagement, a Cuban warplane fired a rocket into a freighter that was carrying munitions for the invading force, igniting 145 tons of ammunition and three thousand gallons of gasoline. The explosion created a mushroom-shaped cloud half a mile high; a CIA commando on shore thought Castro had used an atomic bomb. The invasion ended in less than three days. More than a hundred invaders were killed and more than a thousand were captured. There was no uprising on the island.

Kennedy was distraught for allowing himself to be misled. He feared he destroyed his credibility with the American people. At a press conference shortly before the invasion, he told the nation that under no

---

*Without Kennedy's authorization, four Alabama National Guard pilots flew two B-26 bombers from a CIA base in Nicaragua. Both planes were shot down over Cuba and all four pilots killed. Cover stories were devised to conceal the pilots' participation in the invasion, even from their own families.

circumstances would U.S. armed forces intervene in Cuba. Despite official disavowals, it was obvious that the invasion had been supported by the American government. Kennedy was stunned that his approval rating went up after the Bay of Pigs. "The worse you do, the better they like you," he ruefully remarked.[37] *National Review* was not so forgiving. "The weakness we showed last week was of our own making," the magazine said in an editorial. "Anyone looks ridiculous who lies, deceives—and is ineffectual." The Soviet Union never looks ridiculous, the magazine said, because although it lied, deceived, murdered, killed, and enslaved, "the assertion of the will, and the harnessing of history to that will, is the business of men."[38] To the liberal mind, the Bay of Pigs was seeking to emulate the Soviets too much.

The Bay of Pigs settled nothing. The Kennedy administration still considered the Castro regime unacceptable. The administration developed a clandestine campaign—code-named Operation Mongoose—to weaken the Castro regime through propaganda and sabotage, to develop insurgency on the island through infiltration, and to make the exiled Cuban community into a more potent force. The CIA sought to make an arrangement with the Mafia to assassinate Castro. None of these efforts bore much fruit.[39]

Meanwhile, *National Review* clamored for further efforts to remove Castro. Less than three months after the Bay of Pigs, *National Review* published an article by Anthony Harrigan, a frequent contributor, titled "How to Save Cuba."[40] It read as if the Bay of Pigs had never happened. Harrigan argued that the United States might eventually have to send in the marines, but not yet. First, the United States should encourage a Cuban liberation movement composed of Cuban exiles. "The basic American assumption," Harrigan wrote, "must be that the Cuban people will join the liberation forces when they land on the island." By the end of the year, *National Review* was advocating a complete military blockade of Cuba. Early in 1961, it published a five-page article titled "A Foreign Policy for America," by Barry Goldwater. "We . . . should make it clear in the most explicit terms that Communist governments are not tolerated in this hemisphere—and the Castro regime, being such a government, will be eliminated," Goldwater declared.[41] Goldwater recommended an economic embargo against Cuba and, if that was not successful, a naval blockade. A blockade would precipitate riots in the capitals of Brazil, Venezuela, and Mexico, which, Goldwater said, "we would ignore."

Someone else agreed with domino theory, at least insofar as believing that communism might somehow spread from Cuba to other Central or South American nations: Nikita Khrushchev.[42] Khrushchev and his aides were amazed that communism had sprung up spontaneously in Cuba while the Soviets were having a devil of a time selling nations in Eastern Europe on the benefits of communism. Castro seemed like a romantic figure to them—"a genuine revolutionary," one Soviet official declared after meeting the Cuban leader. The Soviets also understood the Bay of Pigs settled nothing. Hard-liners in America were demanding that the communist infection in their hemisphere be removed, and the post–Bay of Pigs activities by the United States were consistent with planning a second invasion. Cuba had to be defended, but how? Khrushchev's answer was nuclear weapons—in Cuba. Moreover, Khrushchev thought that placing ballistic missiles in Cuba was tit for tat; the United States had Jupiter medium-range ballistic missiles on the Soviet Union's doorstep in Turkey. In fact, several years earlier, when Khrushchev complained about the American missiles in Turkey, Eisenhower remarked to his aides that Khrushchev was well within his rights to call the missiles a provocation, and that for the Soviet Union, American missiles in Turkey were the equivalent of Soviet missiles in Cuba or Mexico.

For months, American intelligence was aware of unusually large shipments from Soviet to Cuban ports. Large objects from those ships were placed on open-bed vehicles, covered with tarpaulins, and trucked to remote areas in the jungle. Significant numbers of Soviet technicians were also arriving on the island. What were the Soviets up to? Some within high government councils worried that these shipments might be ballistic missiles, but others assured the president that was highly unlikely; the Soviets had always kept their nuclear weapons under tight control within Russia. In an effort to press the president to take action, officials within the CIA and the State Department were leaking this information to selected politicians and journalists. One of the people they were feeding it to was Senator Kenneth Keating, a liberal Republican from New York, who took to the floor of the United States Senate and, sounding very much like Winston Churchill in the days leading up

to World War II, recited details about the Soviet buildup on the island. "What are the Soviets planning to do with their new island
fortress?" Keating asked. "What are they going to build with all that
new equipment? What will the army of technicians be required to
maintain?" When he was asked about this at a press conference in
August, the president said that, in fact, the Soviets were sending large
quantities of supplies and more technicians to Cuba, but there was no
information that more Soviet troops were on the island. But Keating
kept up the pressure. In a Senate speech on October 10, Keating claimed
that construction was under way in Cuba on launching sites for ground-
to-ground, intermediate-range missiles. "Keating is a nut," Kennedy
remarked to *New York Times* columnist James Reston. In fact, Keating
was making a claim that was not warranted according to the president's
best information.

But what were the Soviets really up to? To find out, high-altitude
U-2 reconnaissance aircraft were photographing locations of interest on
the island. On October 15, 1962, film from a U-2 overflight was developed at the National Photographic Interpretation Center. It revealed
mobile missile launchers and medium-range Soviet ballistic missiles,
some of which were capable of delivering nuclear warheads as far as
Washington, D.C. The missiles did not appear to be operational, but
CIA analysts estimated that they would be ready to fire within one
to two weeks. Photographs from subsequent overflights also revealed
intermediate-range ballistic missiles; with the exception of Seattle,
Washington, every large American city was within their range. American officials did not see nuclear warheads but assumed they were on the
island. What no American official even guessed, however, was that
Khrushchev had given Soviet field commanders the authority to launch
the missiles if they were under attack. For the next week, a special
group of fourteen men, designated by Kennedy, privately debated
United States options while the president maintained a normal schedule
so as not to alert the press, or the Soviets, that something was up.

In the *National Review* issue on the stands that week, James Burnham criticized Kennedy for allowing a communist government to exist
on Cuba. Kennedy was abrogating the 139-year-old Monroe Doctrine,
Burnham groused. (That doctrine states that the United States would
deem any attempt by European nations "to extend their system to any

portion of this hemisphere" to be a threat to its own peace and safety.)
Burnham argued that "Cuba's threat to the United States is real, immediate, and multiple. There were three dimensions to the threat—"psycho-political, paramilitary and military." Castro's regime was eroding American prestige throughout the world. It was also providing the communists with a base for exporting propaganda and subversion throughout Latin America. And "what possible guarantee is there that the equipment will not include, does not already include, nuclear devices?" Burnham asked.

On Monday, October 22, the White House announced that President Kennedy would address the nation that evening, but no one would say what the president was going to talk about. One hour before the president's address, Russian ambassador Anatoli Dobrynin was summoned to the State Department and handed a letter from Kennedy to Khrushchev, informing him that the United States knew about the missiles in Cuba. "I must tell you that the United States is determined that this threat to the security of this hemisphere be removed," Kennedy wrote. The letter said the United States was taking "the minimum necessary" action to remove the threat to its security, but did not say what that action was.[43] The president revealed that in his televised address to the nation. The United States was imposing "a strict quarantine on all offensive military equipment under shipment to Cuba." American warships would stop and inspect Soviet vessels bound for Cuba. This was, in essence, a blockade; the president and his advisers had chosen to use the term "quarantine" because under international law a blockade was deemed an act of war. "It shall be the policy of this Nation," the president declared, "to regard any nuclear missile launched from Cuba against any nation in the Western Hemisphere as an attack by the Soviet Union on the United States, requiring a full retaliatory strike upon the Soviet Union." The president never mentioned the Monroe Doctrine, then or at any point during the crisis. He thought a pronouncement by James Monroe in 1823 was utterly beside the point.

Twenty-seven Soviet ships were then on the high seas bound for Cuba. By the next morning, the United States Navy reported Soviet submarines were now escorting those ships, and further U-2 overflights revealed that work on the Cuban missile sites was accelerating. Khrushchev delivered a letter to Kennedy via the United States Embassy in Moscow. The Soviet

Union could not recognize the right of the United States to assert control over vessels in international waters or stop ships bound for Cuban shores. No one then knew whether war could be avoided.

To navigate through the crisis, both Kennedy and Khrushchev had to prevail against hard-liners within their own governments. Kennedy ordered that American forces be raised to DEFCON-3 alert status. On his own initiative, and without consulting the president or the secretary of defense, air force general Thomas Power ordered the Strategic Air Command to DEFCON-2 (prepare for immediate action), the highest alert short of actual war—and transmitted the order uncoded so that the Soviets knew it had been given. Meanwhile, when Secretary of Defense Robert McNamara asked Admiral George Anderson how naval vessels were going to enforce the quarantine, the admiral told McNamara to go back to his quarters. "This is none of your goddamn business, Mr. Secretary," Anderson said.

Three days into the crisis, Khrushchev sent Kennedy a long, private letter in search of a mutual solution. "If indeed war should break out, then it would not be in our power to stop it, for such is the logic of war," Khrushchev wrote. Before Kennedy and his team could devise a response, a second, more truculent letter was delivered and also made public by the Kremlin. Kennedy's advisers concluded that Khrushchev had been overruled by hard-liners in his government. History has recorded how, at Robert Kennedy's suggestion, the president decided to reply to the first message and ignore the second, thereby pursuing a course that led to final agreement: The Soviets would remove all their missiles from Cuba in return for a public pledge by the president that the United States would not invade Cuba and a private pledge to remove the Jupiter missiles from Turkey six months hence.

While most of America breathed a sigh of relief, *National Review* did not. In an editorial published while the crisis was still ongoing, the magazine briefly praised the president for giving a good speech to the nation and the world, but then it asked whether Senator Keating had better intelligence than the president. The magazine thought the president was mistaken to focus exclusively on the missiles. "Even today," the editorial said, "the most critical threat of a Communist Cuba is not from any missiles that may be there, but from the political and subversive warfare against which navies alone can do nothing."[44] Writing in the same issue, Frank Meyer warned that if the United States did not "eradicate a focus of infection so near our vitals it will spread until it destroys us." It was too late for a blockade, Meyer wrote; the situation demanded "direct action and at once."[45] In later issues and after time for further reflection, *National Review* editorials and Burnham's personal column continued to argue that removing missiles from Cuba was not enough. The United States should remove Castro from power to deprive communism of a polwar beachhead in the Americas, to free the men Castro captured at the Bay of Pigs and were still being held prisoner, and to liberate the Cuban people from the slavery of communist tyranny.[46] The consensus—then and now—is that Kennedy handled the crisis skillfully and successfully. *National Review* disagreed. "The Administration has demonstrated that it can neither understand nor cope with the shifting stresses of Soviet strategy," it concluded.[47]

Burnham and *National Review* believed the world was engaged in a death struggle between the West and the communist bloc. They saw this struggle very much in terms of what Whittaker Chambers, speaking in another context, called the children of light versus children of darkness paradigm—an existential struggle between good and evil. In conservatives' eyes, communist leaders were committed to world domination above all else. They did not care about the welfare of their own people, whom they enslaved, and if they pursued peace, it was only because they believed that they could not achieve world domination through war. Communist leaders would not make a deal with the West unless they were convinced the deal would be advantageous to them. The communists' advantage was often their duplicity—their willingness to lie and cheat and thus secretly remain free from the constraints of the agreement while the decent but naïve West foolishly shackled itself. The advantage might also be that the communist leaders knew something that Western leaders did not know. The neoconservative mind seemed never to entertain either the reverse possibility—that Western leaders might possess superior knowledge or analysis—or the possibility that some agreements might serve both sides well. *National Review* therefore consistently opposed arms control agreements, even when made by staunch anticommunist presidents such as Nixon and Reagan.[48]

In its desperation to keep America from falling into such traps, *National Review* allowed itself to become seduced by strange but convenient scientific theories. In one editorial, for example, *National Review* observed that it was "the only American magazine that consistently and continuously opposed this country's acceptance of a ban on nuclear tests."[49] What apparently separated *National Review* from all others was not only that the magazine was on to the communist ploy of trying to stimulate Americans' fears about "the frightfulness of nuclear warfare," but that the magazine also realized that the communists—"though dupes and fools"—were also exploiting irrational fears about radioactive fallout. *National Review* assured its readers that the dangers of fallout, even from all-out nuclear war, were exaggerated, and that fallout from atmospheric nuclear testing presented nothing more than "a negligible danger to mankind." (In similar fashion, Burnham dismissed concerns about pollution raised by environmentalists, and *National Review* long denied that climate change was a genuine problem.[50])

After having been expelled from *National Review* and the conservative movement for his heresies of opposing the Vietnam War and being sympathetic to demands of militant civil rights activists, Garry Wills saw internal inconsistencies in the Burnham-*National Review* view of communism. "Our very fear of the Soviet Union arose from a certitude that, in war, Russians would fight us—and do it very well," Wills wrote. "How could that be true if they were only slaves or helots yearning to escape their masters?"[51] Most members of the conservative movement, however, would continue to see communism as an evil, implacable, and unified force right up to the dissolution of the Soviet Union.

CHAPTER 6

Liberalism Falters

For half a century, the Holy Name Society of the New York Police Department (NYPD) held an annual communion breakfast. Notwithstanding its sectarian nature, this event was traditionally the largest gathering of NYPD members during the course of the year. The vast majority of New York City police officers were then Catholic—more specifically Irish Catholic—and the highest-ranking officers were virtually all Irish Catholics.[1] For that reason alone, it would have been understandable that the society selected as the speaker for its 1965 communion breakfast an Irish Catholic intellectual known for his great eloquence. But there was another reason for the society to have chosen William F. Buckley Jr. as its speaker that year. The police felt besieged. Crime was rising dramatically. Over the past decade, murders had more than doubled and robberies nearly tripled, and narcotic trafficking was increasing by leaps and bounds. Moreover, this crime surge was occurring even though the city, at great expense, had drastically expanded the police force. During his three terms, Mayor Robert F. Wagner had added seven thousand officers—a 35 percent increase—to the NYPD. Police were well aware that they looked ineffectual. To make matters worse, complaints about police brutality were also rising. It was not at all clear that there was in fact more police brutality in New York—or that there were significant numbers of instances of police brutality—but outrages conducted by police against civil rights demonstrators in the South were making citizens throughout the nation skeptical about police generally. The previous year, Theodore S. Weiss introduced a bill in city council to reshape New York City's Civilian Complaint Review Board (CCRB). The CCRB was then composed of three deputy police officers; Weiss wanted it to include civilians. Although the bill was defeated, Weiss was a popular politician (who later would be elected to Congress), and his distrust of the police's ability to investigate and punish their own stung. The Holy Name Society hoped Buckley would provide tonic for low morale. He could be counted on to extol the police and lambaste their critics.

As it turned out, Buckley's speech was a public relations disaster. Buckley chose to speak about events that occurred four weeks earlier in Selma, Alabama. On a day now known to American history as Bloody Sunday, civil rights leaders John Lewis and Hosea Williams led six hundred black demonstrators on a march to Montgomery to petition the governor for protection of black citizens who were seeking to register to vote.[2] (Although Selma's population was more than half black, registered voters were 99 percent white.) When the demonstrators crossed the Edmund Pettus Bridge just outside of town, they found their path blocked by sixty state troopers in helmets and gas masks. Even more ominously, Sheriff Jim Clark, a notoriously brutal archsegregationist, sat on horseback with a large posse of deputy volunteers, many of them KKK members. The major of the state police told the marchers they had two minutes to turn around and return to the church from which they had come. The demonstrators remained where they were. When the time expired, the state troopers surged forward, swinging billy clubs and firing tear gas canisters. Next came Clark and his posse, who bullwhipped the demonstrators and trampled them with their horses. John Lewis's skull was fractured; five women were beaten unconscious; seventy-eight demonstrators were hospitalized. Much of the mayhem was captured by television cameras.

The event shocked the nation. President Johnson called for stronger voting rights legislation in a nationally televised address to Congress. Governor George Wallace infuriated the president by declaring that if the march were attempted again he could not guarantee the safety of the marchers. When, on March 21, Martin Luther King Jr. and Ralph Bunche led more than three thousand marchers out of Selma on a renewed march, they were protected by thousands of military police, U.S. marshals, and federalized Alabama National Guardsmen. By the time the marchers stood on the steps of the state capitol in Montgomery, their ranks had swelled to twenty-five thousand. The Ku Klux Klan, however, was determined to have the last word. That night four Klan members followed Viola Gregg Liuzzo as she drove her 1963 Oldsmobile along Route 80. Liuzzo was a white woman from Detroit who, shocked by the events of Bloody Sunday, had gone to Selma to support the demonstrators. On the night of March 21, she was ferrying demonstrators back to Selma. She had just dropped off a carload of demonstrators in Selma and was on her way back to Montgomery to pick up more passengers when the Klan members shot her to death from another vehicle.

These events were still raw wounds in the national consciousness when Buckley addressed the Holy Name Society on April 4.[3] The day after his speech, the *New York Times* ran the following headline: BUCKLEY PRAISES POLICE OF SELMA/HAILED BY 5,600 POLICE HERE AS HE CITES RESTRAINT. The *Herald Tribune* ran a similar story. Buckley was stunned: The newspapers were, in effect, calling both him and the police group racists—indicting him for remarks praising what the police did in Selma and indicting the police for cheering his remarks. But he did not believe he had praised the Selma police. He called the Holy Name Society to ask whether it happened to record his speech. It had. What good fortune—he could prove the newspapers had distorted his remarks. He borrowed the tape and made arrangements to play it for the press at noon that very day. The press came and Buckley played the tape, even before he had listened to it himself. It was a moment of high drama—intensified by the tape suddenly stopping just before the germane portion of the speech. A colleague from *National Review* labored over the recorder while Buckley grew jittery watching skepticism creep across the facial expressions of the reporters. A full ten minutes went by before playing resumed. Half a minute of tape had been destroyed in the process; but luckily the key portion of the speech was intact. Buckley listened as the tape proved to his satisfaction that the articles grossly distorted his remarks, and he looked forward eagerly to corrections in the next day's editions. But he was stunned yet again. The press did not publish corrections. And, in fact, other articles started to appear that were based on the original premise. What about fair play? Was this liberal press bias?

We know that Buckley genuinely believed that his speech to the Holy Name Society was not racist. To show how unfairly he had been treated, he recounted this episode and included the entire transcript of his speech in his book *The Unmaking of a Mayor*. What Buckley in effect tells the reader is: See for yourself how shabbily I was treated. But what he instead reveals was his tin ear about matters of race and civil rights.

Buckley begins with his comments about the murder of Viola Liuzzo:

> Mrs. Liuzzo of Detroit went down to Alabama to protest conditions there . . . It was generally conceded—most specifically conceded by the Governor of Alabama—that anyone arriving in Alabama to protest the existing order under the glare of national klieg lights, precisely needed protection against the almost certain recourse to violence of the unrestrained members of almost every society, who are disposed to go to criminal lengths to express their resentment. That after all, is why the President mobilized the National Guard of Alabama—at the Governor's urging.* So the lady drove down a stretch of lonely road in the dead of night, sharing the front seat with a young Negro identified with the protesting movement, and got killed. Why, one wonders, was this a story that occupied the front pages from one end of the country to another, if newspapers are concerned with the unusual, the unexpected?

Buckley's ostensible point was about the press. Why had it lavished so much ink and airtime on this particular death? Apparently blind as to why it was newsworthy that a Detroit housewife would risk her life to help the civil rights struggle in the South—and pay the ultimate price—Buckley was suggesting that Liuzzo's murder was the proverbial dog-bites-man story. After all, it was only to be expected that the KKK might kill someone like her. But Buckley did not truly expect his audience to be interested in questions of newsworthiness. This audience was concerned about how stories such as this were affecting their image. Police in the South were often portrayed as being in cahoots with the

---

*No one reasonably believed that Governor Wallace genuinely asked President Johnson to nationalize the Alabama National Guard. Johnson nationalized the guard because Wallace would not use either it or the state police to protect the civil rights marchers.

Klan, and police in the North were often portrayed as racists as well. Buckley was saying, I stand with the police. If anyone besides the Klan should be blamed for Liuzzo's murder, it was Liuzzo herself.

Taking the audience slightly further back in time to the Edward Pettus Bridge, Buckley then reached his main point:

> What the viewer did not see was a period of time, twenty minutes long, 1200 seconds, freighted with tension, when the two camps stood facing each other, between the moment the sheriff told the demonstrators to return, which order the demonstrators refused by standing there in defiance of it, until the moment when the human cordite was touched—who threw the lighted match? We do not know—and the policemen moved excitedly, humanly, forward: excessively, yes, and their excesses on that day have been rightly criticized, but were ever the excesses criticized of those who provoked them beyond the endurance that we tend to think of as human?

Although he was careful to say that the police were "rightly criticized," Buckley was trying to mitigate the police conduct. The police, he said, acted "humanly." He also drew a kind of a moral equivalence between the police and the demonstrators. The police were guilty of "excesses," but Buckley suggested the demonstrators provoked those excesses. On this, Buckley was right. Both in Selma and later in Birmingham, civil rights leaders made strategic decisions to confront police forces led by hard-core segregationists—Jim Clark in Selma, "Bull" Connor in Birmingham—whom they expected to brutally attack nonviolent demonstrators, and do so before television cameras. But that does not establish moral equivalence between the contending forces. What seized the nation's attention was that this was a moral contrast between nonviolent demonstrators and brutal police. These fundamentals were not changed because civil rights leaders wanted the nation to witness the confrontation.

Retelling the story in his book, Buckley noted that he was wrong about the police and the demonstrators facing each other for twenty minutes before the mayhem began. He later learned that the two groups confronted each other for only three or four minutes. (Most histories put it at two minutes—the deadline given by the state trooper at the scene.) Considering how central the supposedly prolonged standoff was to his argument of pushing the police beyond human endurance, one might have expected Buckley to be more careful about the length of the standoff. It had been widely reported that the police did act not spontaneously: Their superiors ordered them to attack. In fact, with minor exceptions concerning injuries sustained by the marchers, my description of the events at the Edward Pettus Bridge comes exclusively from the issue of *Time* magazine that reported them.

Paradoxically, Buckley's speech to the Holy Name Society began one of his signal achievements: his 1965 campaign for mayor of New York City.

In his memoir about the campaign, Buckley reported that he decided to run for mayor of New York City on June 3, 1965, and a few days later resolved to keep a personal, tape-recorded diary of the campaign. That resolution lasted one day and resulted in a single diary entry. In that one entry, says Buckley, he recorded his reasons for running. Buckley does not reveal what he told his diary, other than to say he did not once mention the name John Vliet Lindsay, who had announced his own candidacy for mayor three weeks earlier. Buckley included this little fact in his memoir to refute charges that he ran because he had a personal vendetta against Lindsay.[4] It is curious that Buckley did not tell readers what he did say in that entry. Some things are, in any event, clear. First, Buckley wanted to rob a liberal Republican of victory. Second, regardless of whether he loathed Lindsay before entering the race, by the time he wrote his memoir Buckley absolutely despised Lindsay—not merely Lindsay the liberal Republican, nor Lindsay the politician, but Lindsay the man. He considered Lindsay shallow, dim-witted, and inarticulate. Buckley's disdain for Lindsay drips from every page of his book about the campaign. Regardless of what he told his diary, Buckley's race was partly about John Lindsay. But it was also about more than Lindsay. Throughout Buckley's career, one objective was always in the forefront of his mind: advancing the conservative movement. The mayoral campaign offered him a powerful vehicle for doing that. It was a rare opportunity to project conservative ideas beyond the community of people reading his magazine and syndicated newspaper. Buckley's brother

James, who served as his campaign manager, said Bill thought the race would give him an opportunity to learn more about urban problems and think about conservative approaches for them.[5]

It was Lindsay's presence in the race that guaranteed extraordinary attention. Lindsay was a rising star. When he announced he would run for mayor of New York City, three of the country's most-read magazines—*Life*, *Look*, and *Newsweek*—put him on the covers of their next issues. Part of Buckley's disdain for Lindsay surely flowed from seeing Lindsay as a favorite son of the Eastern Establishment. Lindsay had gone to the St. Paul's School in Concord, New Hampshire, one of the nation's most socially elite prep schools, and then to Yale College and Yale Law School. Lindsay's mother, from whom he derived his middle name, had descended from one of the Dutch families that founded New Jersey. His wife, Mary Anne Harrison, a graduate of the socially elite Miss Porter's School in Farmington, Connecticut, and Vassar College, was distantly related to presidents William Henry Harrison and Benjamin Harrison. John and Mary had met at the high-society wedding—John was an usher and Mary a bridesmaid—of a daughter of Senator Prescott Bush of Connecticut (the father and grandfather of United States presidents). Lindsay carried himself with a patrician's demeanor; he had a bit of starch and a dash of haughtiness. He did not smile easily, at least in public. But he radiated kinetic energy.

Historians are fond of observing that Lindsay was not truly upper class. His paternal grandfather had emigrated from the Isle of Wight, and his father had worked his way through night classes at New York University School of Law. Lindsay's parents were sufficiently well-off to send all of their five children to the most prestigious private schools in New York City and New England, but they were not positively rich. When John's father died in 1962, he left his family a mere $700,000 (the equivalent of about five million dollars today).[6] Thus, experts assure us, the Lindsay family was merely upper-middle class. This, however, was a distinction lost on nearly everyone who was not an editor of the *Social Register* or a sociologist. Buckley, who was neither, likely assumed Lindsay was a member of the aristocracy who had snubbed his family.

Lindsay had agonized about whether to run for mayor. Some thought that America's large cities had become ungovernable, and that mayoral-

ties had become dead-end jobs. In fact, being mayor of New York had
never been a good stepping stone for the politically ambitious. In the
city's long history, only three mayors had gone on to higher office—only
one of them in the twentieth century. Moreover, it was unclear whether
a Republican could win in staunchly Democratic New York. The city
had not elected a Republican since Fiorello La Guardia in 1941.

In Congress, Lindsay represented the so-called Silk Stocking District
of Manhattan, which included iconic buildings such as the United Nations and the Empire State Building; posh apartments; corporate headquarters in Midtown Manhattan, including those of the national
newspapers and broadcast networks. He was, moreover, considered
someone with great potential. At the end of his first term, fifty Washington reporters surveyed by *Newsweek* magazine rated Lindsay not only
the top freshman but the ninth-best member in the entire House of
Representatives. Because of his personal attributes—he stood six feet
four inches tall and was strikingly handsome—the district he represented, and the acclaim he acquired right out of the starting gate, people
were mentioning Lindsay as a potential president. But to position himself for a presidential run Lindsay needed a more prominent position
than being one of 435 members of the House of Representatives. This
was a problem. Lindsay was a liberal Republican, and other liberal
Republicans—Nelson Rockefeller and Jacob Javits—occupied the governor's mansion and one of the state's United States Senate seats. He did
not have a political argument for running against incumbents from his
own party who shared his political philosophy. Until 1964, another liberal Republican, Kenneth Keating, had occupied New York's other Senate seats. Robert F. Kennedy, brother of the recently slain president, had
wrestled that seat away from Keating that year. It would be a long wait to
run for that seat—Kennedy would not stand for election again until
1970—and, besides, running against Kennedy, who was one of the most
formidable politicians in the country, was not an appealing prospect.

John Lindsay's interest in running for mayor of New York City was
partly born of political necessity—but only partly. Lindsay believed the
city's problems were difficult but not intractable. He believed that he
could assemble an administration staffed by the brightest minds, and that
such a team, guided by social science from the nation's top universities,
could restore New York City to greatness—which is a way of saying

Lindsay believed in enlightened liberalism. Lindsay first privately decided against running for mayor, but that decision made him miserable. Lindsay had a strong streak of Puritanism, and he believed he was evading a crucial responsibility. He began to vacillate. Robert Price—Lindsay's key political confidante—came up with a scheme to shove Lindsay into the race. Lindsay had met Bob Price when Lindsay was president of the New York City Young Republicans—an influential group within the party's infrastructure—and Price was president of the New York University chapter. Lindsay recognized Price's brilliance and Price recognized Lindsay's political potential. During his first run for Congress, Lindsay persuaded Price, who was then in his last year of law school, to manage the campaign. Price performed so skillfully that he earned the reputation of being a political genius in the process. Now Price was determined to cut through Lindsay's ambivalence and make him run.

On Tuesday, May 11, Price had lunch in Manhattan with two of Nelson Rockefeller's key aides.[7] Price told them—without authorization from or even the knowledge of his principal—that Lindsay would run for mayor if Rockefeller contributed half a million dollars to his campaign (the equivalent of more than three million dollars today). The aides dutifully relayed this to Rockefeller, who called Price that same afternoon. Okay, said Rockefeller, he'd contribute the money, but Lindsay had to ask for it himself. Price next called a reporter at the *New York Times*. Lindsay was going to announce his candidacy for mayor and he would give the *Times* an exclusive on breaking the news—provided the *Times* agreed to do so in a three-column-wide, front-page story. There were a couple of other conditions too: The *Times* could not call anyone, including Lindsay, to confirm the story, and the *Times* had to wait until eight P.M. that evening for Price to give a final green light for the story. A bit later A. M. Rosenthal, then the paper's metropolitan editor, telephoned Price. No deal, said Rosenthal; the *New York Times* did not allow people to dictate terms for a story. Oh, well, said Price, he'd give the story to the *New York Herald Tribune* instead. Rosenthal relented. Then, for the first time, Price called Lindsay in Washington and told him to immediately fly to New York. "I'm not running for mayor," replied Lindsay, who realized what Price was about. But Lindsay flew to New York nonetheless. Price met him at the airport, where for the first time he told Lindsay what he had done. The governor's Beechcraft was waiting on the tarmac to fly them to Albany to meet with Rockefeller. Still insisting he was not going to run, Lindsay got on the plane. In Albany, Rockefeller turned on his charm to convince Lindsay to run. He promised Lindsay that the Rockefeller family would guarantee $500,000 for campaign costs. Lindsay relented. He'd run, but he had to be able to select his own running mates. Rockefeller agreed. Price called the *New York Times* and told them they could run the story. All this occurred within half a day. The next morning, Wednesday, May 12, the lead headline in the *New York Times* read LINDSAY, IN SHIFT, CONSIDERS RACE AGAINST WAGNER. But, striking a blow for journalistic independence, the *Times* ran the story two columns wide.

Liberals were thrilled by Lindsay's candidacy. Borrowing a phrase from an article about Lindsay by journalist Murray Kempton, the campaign adopted the slogan, "He is fresh and everyone else is tired." On June 10, Robert F. Wagner, who had served as mayor of New York for fifteen years, announced he would not seek reelection.

Lindsay, however, was anathema to conservatives. In the 1952 Eisenhower-Taft contest, Lindsay had been an Eisenhower loyalist. As a leader of young Republican organizations, Lindsay had traveled to Paris to urge General Eisenhower to challenge Taft for the Republican nomination. After a brief stint in a Wall Street law firm, Lindsay became executive assistant to Eisenhower's attorney general, Herbert Brownell, who, after a period of time, urged his young protégée to return to New York and run for Congress. In Congress, Lindsay voted with fellow Republicans only about one third of the time. Americans for Democratic Action rated Lindsay's voting record 87 percent liberal for his last term. Lindsay fought to disband the House Un-American Activities Committee and supported the Kennedy administration's proposal to establish a cabinet-level department of urban affairs. He worked hard for civil rights legislation, and at the 1964 Republican National Convention, he fought for a plank supporting the Civil Rights Act, which the Goldwater-dominated convention rejected by a vote of 897 to 409. After Goldwater's controversial acceptance speech, Lindsay announced that he could not support his party's presidential nominee. Conservative Republicans considered that an act of political treason.

Conservatives wanted retribution, but that was not all that was on their minds. The Goldwater nomination had intensified a struggle for control of the Republican Party. Goldwater was the first conservative presidential candidate the Republican Party had nominated since the New Deal, and notwithstanding his ignominious defeat in the general election, conservatives were determined to hold on to the party. Meanwhile, the liberal wing of the party—not merely a centrist wing, but a genuinely liberal wing—was robust. Among governors the liberal wing included Nelson Rockefeller of New York, George W. Romney of Michigan, William Scranton of Pennsylvania, Mark Hatfield of Oregon, Daniel J. Evans of Washington, and John Chafee of Rhode Island. The liberals were convinced that the margin of Goldwater's defeat—he had carried only six states and won less than 39 percent of the popular vote—demonstrated that their wing should take control of the party. The result was intraparty warfare.

Accordingly to Buckley, the idea about running for mayor flowed from a suggestion Priscilla made at a *National Review* staff meeting in May 1965. Bill had written an article for the magazine and his syndicated newspaper column. Titled "Mayor Anyone?" the piece half facetiously presented a packaged, ten-point platform for anyone interested in running for mayor of a large city. At a routine staff meeting discussing the forthcoming issue of *National Review*, editors considered what to write in a yellow streamer running diagonally across the top left corner on the cover—a device periodically used to attract attention on newsstands. This time the editors seemed stuck. After half an hour of coming up dry, Priscilla suddenly asked, "How about 'Buckley for Mayor'?" And so the streamer read on the cover of the next issue. No one was expected to take the streamer literally. Bill was registered to vote in Stamford, Connecticut, and assumed that he was ineligible to run for mayor of New York City. He had been trying to persuade William Rusher to run for mayor on the Conservative Party line. Only after Rusher said no and Bill was informed that he could become eligible did the idea of running occur to him. That, at least, is Bill's version. Rusher tells the story differently.[8] He says he had previously told Buckley he would not run, and that the streamer was a deliberate device to "show a little ankle" and put forward the idea of a Buckley candidacy.[9]

Either way, the streamer caught the eye of J. Daniel Mahoney, who three years earlier had cofounded the New York State Conservative Party with Buckley's help. In the prospectus he wrote for prospective contributors when he founded it, Mahoney said the objective of the Conservative Party would be to "bring down the liberal *apparat* in New York."[10] Fielding a candidate to divide the Republican vote and defeat Lindsay was an obvious—indeed, arguably necessary—project for the Conservative Party. Mahoney first called Frank Meyer to ask whether Buckley was, in fact, interested in running for mayor; then he called the party's counsel to find out about Buckley's eligibility. His third call was to Buckley, who denied the streamer had been in earnest, but seemed interested as soon as Mahoney told him he could make his New York City apartment his official residence during the summer and be eligible to stand for election in the fall. In short order, Buckley agreed to become the Conservative Party candidate for mayor. But Buckley stipulated that he would campaign only part-time and that his responsibilities to *National Review* would continue to come first. Mahoney reluctantly agreed to this proviso.

So that the campaign would not devour too much time, Buckley decided not to let the Conservative Party provide him with a campaign manager. Buckley wanted his brother Jim (who would successfully run for the United States Senate as the candidate of the New York Conservative Party five years later) to take the job, but he was concerned about a personal issue. Jim and John Lindsay's twin brother, David, were close friends. They had been classmates and fellow members of Skull and Bones at Yale. They were so close, in fact, that Jim had been an usher at David's wedding and was godfather to one of David's children. Bill did not want to destroy a friendship that he knew his brother cherished. Bill called Jim, who was then vacationing in Carmel, California, to ask whether he could take the job without impairing his friendship with David. Jim wrote to David. David wrote back. They agreed that Jim could serve as Bill's campaign manager and promised to consider all differences to be political and not personal. Before things were done, the campaign became personally bitter, but these two men kept their promises to each other and remained good friends.[11]

Following a little political theater—leaks to the press to stimulate newspaper articles reporting that Buckley was considering entering the race, followed by a supposedly spontaneous demonstration outside *National Review*'s offices urging Buckley to run—Buckley formally announced his candidacy at a press conference at the Overseas Press Club in Manhattan on Thursday, June 24.[12] He began with a fifteen-minute opening statement explaining why he was entering the race. He was forthright about the political reasons for his candidacy. "I am a Republican," declared Buckley. "And I intend, for so long as I find it possible to do so—which is into the visible future—to remain a Republican." The Republican nomination, however, had been given to someone who was outside "the mainstream of Republican opinion." Lindsay was running as a fusion candidate and seeking the endorsements of both the Republican and Liberal parties. Lindsay "qualifies for the support of the Liberal Party and the Republican Party only if one supposes there are no substantial differences between the Republican Party and the Liberal Party," said Buckley.

"New York," Buckley continued, "cries for the kind of attention that is not being given to it by those who coolly contrive their campaigns so as to avoid offending major voting blocks." This would become one of Buckley's main themes. He believed the city was suffering from balkanized politics. Everything was about allocating city resources and political spoils among various ethnic groups—Irish, Italian, Jewish, and so forth. Buckley thought this wrong. "To satisfy major voting blocks in their collective capacities is not necessarily to satisfy individual members of those voting blocks in their separate capacities," he observed. Buckley, however, vowed he was not going to treat voters as members of ethnic groups. He would not engage in the traditional campaign shenanigans of eating blintzes in Jewish neighborhoods, cannoli in Italian neighborhoods, and so on.

Candidates for mayor traditionally ran on ethnically balanced tickets with running mates for president of city council and comptroller. The Democratic standard-bearer, Abe Beame, ran with Frank O'Connor for city council president and Mario Procaccino for comptroller. This created a ticket with a Jew, an Irish Catholic, and an Italian. Lindsay presented himself as a fusion candidate, that is, a candidate spanning political parties. His running mates were Timothy Costello, chairman of the Liberal Party and an Irish Catholic, and Milton Mollen, a Democrat and Jew. When Buckley introduced his running mates—Rosemary Gunning for city council president and Hugh Markey for comptroller—the *Herald Tribune* ran an article with the wry headline: BUCKLEY HAS A 'BALANCED' TICKET: MARKEY, MRS. GUNNING—ALL IRISH. Buckley claimed that he had not even thought about ethnicity and religion and did not know Rosemary Gunning was Catholic until he read that article. Buckley did follow the convention of geographically balancing his ticket however: Gunning was from Queens, Markey was from Staten Island, and Buckley was from Manhattan (or Stamford, Connecticut).

After delivering his prepared remarks, Buckley spent the next fifteen minutes of his first press conference attacking Lindsay as an apostate Republican and laying out the general themes of his campaign, which he promised to elaborate on during the campaign. Then he took questions from the press.

> REPORTER: Do you want to be Mayor, sir?
>
> BUCKLEY: I have never considered it.
>
> REPORTER: Do you think that is something that at present should be considered?
>
> BUCKLEY: Not necessarily. What is important is that certain points of view should prevail. Whether you or I administer those points of view is immaterial to me, assuming you are a good administrator.
>
> REPORTER: But you are asking people to vote for you. If you win, will you serve?
>
> BUCKLEY: If elected, I will serve.
>
> . . .
>
> REPORTER: Do you think you have a chance of winning?
>
> BUCKLEY: No.
>
> . . .
>
> REPORTER: How many votes do you expect to get, conservatively speaking?
>
> BUCKLEY: Conservatively speaking, one.

Dan Mahoney and other officials with the Conservative Party were horrified. A candidate is not supposed to tell voters he has no chance of winning. They will not take him seriously. Mahoney, however, was wrong. Buckley charmed untold numbers of voters—and observers throughout the nation—with his wit and honesty. People laughed, and people were impressed. Around office water coolers and at weekend barbecues people talked about Buckley's press conference. Buckley gave everyone more to talk about when he held a second press conference a week later. "What would you do if you *were* elected?" a reporter inquired. "Demand a recount," Buckley replied. And so, from the start, Buckley seized the public's attention.

Meanwhile, four candidates were vying for the Democratic nomination. Paul Screvane, city council president and a Wagner protégé, was considered the front-runner. The other candidates were Beame, the city comptroller, and two candidates from the weak liberal reform wing of the party, Congressman William Fitts Ryan and radical lawyer Paul O'Dwyer. None of them generated much excitement. The results of the September 14 primary surprised most observers: colorless Abe Beame— five feet two inches tall—won handily. He prevailed by amassing more votes in his home borough of Brooklyn than all three of the other candidates combined.

The general election campaign was now under way. Lindsay was an exciting candidate, but Beame had a considerable asset of his own: He was the candidate of the Democratic Party in an overwhelmingly Democratic city. The first major poll showed Beame in the lead, with 45.7 of respondents saying they expected to vote for him. Lindsay followed with a disappointing 35.6 percent. Buckley ran third with 10.2—a surprisingly strong showing for a third-party candidate whom no one thought had a chance, including the candidate himself.

Buckley rolled out a series of ten detailed position papers that he wrote personally.[13] He promoted those positions in speeches, press conferences, and interviews, as well as in three debates, two on television and one on radio. Buckley argued that his policy positions flowed from a series of conservative presumptions and assumptions. Perhaps the most fundamental presumption was "that which is yours, is yours." Buckley stressed that this was a presumption—a strong one perhaps, but still just a presumption—because government has the right to take things away from you when the evidence clearly shows that it is required. Governmental finances should be simple and transparent—or as Buckley put it, "tidy"—so that it is clear who is paying for what. Government should take things equitably, that is, through "impartially designated laws unanimated by class prejudice." Private arrangements should be preferred to public arrangements. Private arrangements are less wasteful because they are "disciplined by competitive pressures." Moreover, preferring private arrangements is a means of resisting "the natural tendency toward centripetalization of power in government, which is the prime historical oppressor, and therefore needs constant domestication." Finally, jobs should be done by a lower echelon of government whenever it can do a job as well as a higher echelon of government. Buckley was vague about the rationale for the last proposition. One might infer that Buckley preferred lower rather than higher echelons of government for the same reasons he preferred private to public arrangements, namely, to promote efficiency and disperse power. However, the explanation he expressly offered was that this was in accord with Catholic social doctrine enunciated by Pope Leo XIII.[14]

Buckley's first position paper was devoted to water policy. The mid-Atlantic region had experienced a four-year dry spell, culminating in 1965 with the most severe drought in more than a century.[15] Buckley observed that under normal conditions New York City's reservoirs were adequate. And they would be adequate during even severe drought conditions if waste could be eliminated. Philadelphia had reduced water consumption by 20 percent by installing universal metering, Buckley observed. Metering provided incentive to reduce waste. But only 24 percent of New York's water use was metered. Thus, he argued, New York should institute universal metering. "When the supply is abundant (which is most of the time)," he wrote, "the price of water should be no more than the nominal cost to the city of providing it. As the reservoirs diminish, the price should rise—so as to put the premium on water conservation and encourage the location and repair of leaks." He noted that a single leaky faucet could waste one hundred thousand gallons of water per year. It would cost $85 million to institute universal metering compared to $200 million or more to build an additional reservoir. Buckley, therefore, proposed the classic conservative market-based solution, rationing water through prices when necessary. Lindsay and Beame both proposed intensive programs to investigate leaks combined with developing additional sources of water. Lindsay also proposed requiring industrial users to build water recycling systems.

Buckley also wrote position papers relating to city finances. "New York City," he declared, "is in dire financial condition, as a result of mismanagement, extravagance, and political cowardice." Politicians wanted to be able to say yes to requests for more services without telling the voters how much they would have to pay to support those services. And the costs of various services were often hidden. "Where feasible, city services should have a price tag," Buckley wrote. Politicians often subsidized new or expanded services by borrowing money, and the city was spending nearly 15 percent of its revenues to service its accumulated debt. "New York City must discontinue its present borrowing policies, and learn to live within its income, before it goes bankrupt," warned Buckley. The city had tried to reduce its deficits by raising both the sales and commercial occupancy taxes. Buckley said the most recent sales tax increase had been a dismal failure: It was expected to generate $92 million in additional revenue but brought in only $57 million. The problem, Buckley argued, was that these tax increases were counterproductive. They were driving marginal businesses either out of the city or out of business altogether, as evidenced by a loss of seventy-five thousand industry jobs over the past five years. Buckley claimed that a reduction in the sales tax, "accompanied by a restoration of confidence in New York City, could stimulate business sufficiently to generate tax revenues equivalent to the original expectations of the five-per-cent tax, and more." He also proposed scrapping the system of multiple taxes levied on business—gross receipts, sales, use, occupancy, cigarette, and amusement taxes, among others—and replacing them all with a single value-added tax. Value added was defined as a firm's gross business receipts minus the cost of all previously taxed goods and services purchased from other businesses. Because it was based on the fundamentals of cash receipts and payments, small businesses would be able to compute the value-added tax easily, often without the help of accountants and lawyers. And a single simple tax would reduce the city's costs of administering the complicated existing system.

Although the environmental movement was in its infancy and the first Earth Day was five years in the future, Buckley issued a position paper about air and water pollution. "Here is a legitimate concern of government—a classic example of the kind of thing that government should do, according to [Abraham] Lincoln's test, because the people cannot do it themselves," he wrote. He proposed building new sanitary sewers to reduce overflows of sewage and storm water during periods of heavy rains. The improvements would be financed by increases in sewer rents. He said that the flow of pollutants into the water from industrial sources should be monitored, with "offenders assessed at a set rate based on the amount of pollutants that enter the water flow." This was, once again, a market-based solution. Buckley did not contemplate enforcing discharge limits through punitive fines or injunctions. "The rates should be high enough to encourage purification measures, yet not so high as to drive the polluter from the city," he said.

As for air pollution, Buckley thought the city should first and foremost cure its own transgressions. City-owned buses were a significant contributor to the problem. In the short term, he wanted to reduce emissions by modifying engines and exhaust filters. For the long term, he proposed buying buses that ran on liquefied petroleum gas, which, he said, could be properly burned so as not to discharge noxious fumes. He wanted control devices (though he did not specify what devices) installed on other city cars and trucks—a considerable fleet including police cars, fire engines, garbage trucks, and the like. He also noted that none of the city's own municipal incinerators—which themselves accounted for nearly 20 percent of the soot in New York air—met the emission limits imposed on Consolidated Edison. These had to be modernized. The city should meet the standards applied to private industry. Here Buckley was willing to use some stricter measures: He wanted to institute a staged program to eliminate the burning of all garbage, and he wanted to prohibit the burning of bituminous coal. The largest burner of coal was Con Ed. Buckley was willing to allow the company to convert to natural gas in the short run, but only "until public attitudes have become acclimated to the use of nuclear energy as the primary power source for Con Ed operations." Although Buckley may have been unduly dismissive of the risks posed by nuclear power plants—he called them "imagined perils"—he was ahead of the curve in recognizing that air pollution could not be adequately controlled as long as energy came principally from coal-burning power plants.

Connected to Buckley's environmental platform were his proposals regarding traffic and transit. Buckley said that he had a devil of a time with this particular position paper. Though he didn't say so, he may have been perplexed by putting together a package of proposals that blend the indisputably conservative with the downright progressive. "The only way to move large numbers of people into Manhattan is by the use of rapid transit facilities," he wrote. He proposed imposing tolls to discourage private automobiles registered outside of the city from entering Manhattan. Sounding very much like Franklin Roosevelt, Buckley declared, "The key is experimentation." He proposed beginning by charging out-of-city cars one dollar and raising that toll until it was sufficient to reduce the number of cars entering Manhattan by at least ten thousand per day. (Buckley recognized the commerce clause of the Constitution might prohibit the city from imposing tolls only on out-of-city cars but was prepared to ask Congress for authority to do so.) Sounding rather like Theodore Roosevelt, Buckley proposed constructing an elevated bikeway—twenty feet wide and twenty feet high— running along both sides of Second Avenue from First Street to 125th Street. There would be six crosstown spurs and ramps for bicyclists to enter the bikeway at every block. If this first bikeway proved successful, he would construct a second one down the length of Seventh Avenue. Bikeways, said Buckley, would reduce traffic congestion while providing New Yorkers with exercise that would improve their health and give them pleasure. Sounding like the most aggressive social engineer, Buckley observed that "nothing can be done about the traffic problem except by interfering with existing habits."

Buckley, however, was against subsidizing subways and buses. "It does no service to the taxpayer to give him a ride on the subway for 15 cents and then to add taxes to his milk, bread, and cigarettes," he wrote. Buckley was fully aware of the argument that mass transit needed to be subsidized to encourage its use, and he himself had argued that commuting habits had to be changed to advance the public good. But he feared the slippery slope. He argued that "the public-subsidy principle needs to be opposed as close as possible to its roots, or else the justification becomes harder and harder to formulate for opposing it anywhere this side of the totally socialized economy built around Marxian postulates, which have proved economically inefficient and socially totalitarian." Superficially, this seems a sensible statement of conservative principles; but on a deeper level, problems arise. If it is good public policy to decrease car use and increase mass transit, why is it appropriate to tax cars but inappropriate to subsidize mass transit? Buckley, however, was particularly worried about subsidies. They were simply too politically expedient. Politicians promised voters free lunches of one sort or another all the time, and that practice was leading New York City toward financial disaster. Buckley's concern was entirely reasonable, but he failed to consider that government subsidies might be inevitable. Governments subsidize cars and trucks by building roads, for example. If there are too many cars and trucks, why should it not subsidize mass transit?

Predictably, Buckley's most controversial positions were those that touched on racial issues, including those dealing with welfare, education, and crime. In all of these areas, Buckley was heavily influenced by *Beyond the Melting Pot*, a book written two years earlier by Nathan Glazer and Daniel Patrick Moynihan.[16] Glazer was a Harvard sociologist. Moynihan, then only thirty-eight, had been a speechwriter and adviser to New York governor Averell Harriman, an assistant professor of political science at Syracuse University, and an assistant secretary of labor. Ironically, during the summer of 1965, while Buckley was citing Moynihan's work on the campaign trail, Moynihan was himself running on a competing ticket as Paul Screvane's running mate for city council president.

In their book, Glazer and Moynihan argued that the Negro community was in trouble because the Negro family was in trouble. The problem was broken homes. According to Glazer and Moynihan, the illegitimacy rate among Negroes was fourteen to fifteen times that among whites. Glazer and Moynihan argued that there was little that either government or whites could do to remedy the situation. The Negro community had to take the lead. "It is probable that no investment of public and private agencies on delinquency and crime-prevention programs will equal the return from an investment by Negro-led and Negro-financed agencies," they wrote. Glazer and Moynihan observed that this was not yet happening. The Negro middle class was not contributing much, either in money or involvement, to the effort. Nevertheless, Glazer and Moynihan believed that only institutions that were led, financed, and staffed by Negroes were likely to make a difference.

At his first press campaign conference, Buckley acknowledged that New York suffered from problems caused by a long history of racial discrimination. "The ill-feeling that exists between the races in New York is due in part to a legacy of discrimination and injustice committed by the dominant ethnic groups," he said. He wanted to find ways to address the problems, but "by sounder means than undifferentiated infusions of politically deployed cash." To many, that decoded as Buckley saying that he didn't really want to help black citizens who were disproportionately living in neighborhoods plagued with poverty, crime, and poor schools. There were, after all, few ways to address such problems without deploying money. "Family irresponsibility; lawlessness; juvenile delinquency—whatever subtle explanations there may be for the pressures that conduce to them—are nonetheless deplorable, and a matter of urgent social concern," he continued.

Unlike most cities, New York did not impose a residency requirement for welfare. Buckley claimed that as a result "thousands of persons who either do not desire to work, or who cannot work, come to New York, often with large families," even when they were leaving areas with higher employment, more available housing, and where they had families to assist them. He wanted to adopt a one-year residency requirement for welfare eligibility. He criticized the policy of reducing welfare payments by outside earnings on a dollar-for-dollar basis. This, said Buckley, resulted in "a clear economic inducement to idleness." He wanted to adjust the policy so that recipients could keep "a sufficient proportion of outside earnings so as to provide them with the incentive to seek gainful employment." Somewhat more controversially, Buckley wanted to require welfare recipients to engage in vocational training programs or work on public work projects "for which they should receive a few extra dollars per week, to take care of the cost of transportation, lunch away from home, and some pocket money for miscellaneous expenses."

About one third of the city's welfare expenditures went to the Aid to Dependent Children program. Buckley noted that two thirds of children in the ADC program were illegitimate. He was concerned that the program promoted broken homes. Payments stopped if a breadwinner came into the household, creating a financial disincentive for fathers to marry mothers or for split families to reunite. Buckley did not, however, propose a solution to this problem. He called for vigorous investigations of eligibility to reduce fraud. He claimed the District of Columbia had reduced their Aid to Dependent Children payments by one third through such methods. Yet without solving the problem of cutting off payments once a breadwinner was in the household, a vigorous enforcement program would only further discourage marriage and family reunification.

Charles Moerdler, president of the New York Young Republican Club and a Lindsay stalwart, tried to make political hay out of Buckley's failure to offer a solution. In a letter to the *Herald Tribune*, he wrote, "We recognize the reason for Mr. Buckley's unwillingness to come squarely to grips with the problem, for the only conceivable solution lies in family planning and for purely political reasons Mr. Buckley lacks the courage to speak out on that subject." He was suggesting that as a devout Catholic, Buckley had to oppose any government assistance for birth control. In reply, Buckley published a letter stating that while he "would decline myself to do something which is forbidden to me by the Catholic Church," he did not believe in interfering "with the dissemination of birth control information to persons whose religion does not forbid the use of it."

Professor Timothy Costello, Lindsay's candidate for city council president, suggested that Buckley's stinginess toward the poor made him a bad Catholic. Costello—a Roman Catholic from the liberal social action tradition—made those remarks at Fordham University and thus presumably before a predominately Catholic audience. When asked whether he disagreed with his running mate's remarks, Lindsay demurred; not being a Catholic himself he was not as familiar with Catholic doctrine as was Costello, Lindsay explained. Costello surely understood his role was to win as many Catholic votes for the ticket as possible and this was a ball he had to carry by himself. But Costello did not fully appreciate the man he was attacking. He had only handed Buckley a sword. "If I am a bad Catholic," Buckley responded, "I shall be punished by Someone I fear far more than the New York Catholic voter. To whom I say this: I don't want you to vote for me because I am a Catholic. I want you to vote for me because of the positions I take."

One of Buckley's welfare proposals, together with a twin proposal in a position paper about narcotics, created a hullaballoo. Buckley advocated "a pilot program . . . to explore the feasibility of relocating chronic welfare cases outside the city limits" and quarantining "all addicts, even as smallpox carriers would be quarantined during a plague."[17] A mother with three illegitimate children, said Buckley, cost the city a great deal of money in welfare payments, schooling costs for her children, and in some cases subsidized housing costs. And, he added, her family imposed considerable police and hospital costs on the city. Such a family needed "special opportunities, special protections, a special environment, special teaching," but it was difficult to provide those in the city where housing costs were high and "temptations are abundant." Better to move such families to "great and humane rehabilitation centers" in the country with special schools and supervision. Predictably, Lindsay and Beame vied to express the greater horror over what they both called Buckley's desire for "concentration camps." Lindsay may have won that contest by also describing Buckley's proposal as "deportation camps." Others, including Senator Jacob Javits, also denounced Buckley's proposal.

Buckley's defense of these proposals was weak. "If [Abe Beame] does not know the difference between a quarantined hospital for sick people, and a concentration camp, I suggest that he ask someone who has been in a concentration camp what the difference is," Buckley said in one of his final speeches of the campaign. Beame must "harbor deep suspicions of all doctors, and health inspectors, and statesmen" if he believes that they will then want to quarantine other groups of people, Buckley declared. But these statements were just a clever way of evading the question of what, in fact, distinguished Buckley's rehabilitation camps from concentration camps. Is it that Buckley's camps would be comfortable? Can we deprive people of liberty if we confine them in pleasant places? Is it that Buckley genuinely expected his camps to rehabilitate people—to cure them of dependency on welfare or narcotics the way hospitals cure people with physical diseases? Buckley offered no evidence to show that was possible.

Regrettably, these proposals distracted from Buckley's worthier proposals. They would be used to paint him as a dangerous extremist. Early in the campaign, Lindsay and Beame pretty much ignored Buckley. There was nothing to be gained by making a minor candidate more prominent. But as the race proceeded, it became increasingly apparent that Buckley was becoming a significant factor. He outshone both candidates in debate. Many of his policy proposals were the freshest and most interesting of all the candidates'. He was popular with certain groups—particularly the police. The police were a natural constituency for Buckley. They were heavily Irish Catholic, and saw Irish Catholic Buckley as one of their own. The policy debate made them even more passionately pro-Buckley. From his first press conference on, Buckley emphasized that nothing was more important than controlling crime. He wanted to hire more policemen. Even more significantly, he vigorously opposed adding civilians to the CCRB. He said he wanted policemen "to lust after the apprehension of criminals even as politicians lust after the acquisition of votes." The mayor, said Buckley, "should encourage the police to do their duty, and back them up when they do it."[18] Lindsay, by contrast, wanted to add four civilian members to the review board, all of whom would be appointed by the mayor. He also wanted one of the three police members of the board to be a patrolman. As many police officers saw it, Buckley would support the police while Lindsay would side with their accusers.

There was another aspect to the political affinities of the police. As Lindsay campaigned around the city, he was greeted by hecklers carrying signs proclaiming DOWN WITH CIVILIAN REVIEW BOARDS and the Bircher slogan SUPPORT YOUR LOCAL POLICE. Some of the hecklers were menacing. They yelled "traitor," "communist," and other epithets at Lindsay and sometimes jostled the candidate and his supporters. Lindsay's aides observed that some police seemed more eager to side with the hecklers than to protect their candidate. Some police had BUCKLEY FOR MAYOR buttons pinned on their uniforms or joined in booing Lindsay. There were a few scraps. In Queens, a teenager attacked Sid Davidoff, a Lindsay aide who was physically protecting the candidate. On Coney Island, someone wielded a Buckley sign as something of a weapon, using the edge to rip Lindsay's shirt and scratch his chest. Lindsay's wife, Mary, slapped the attacker across the face.

Throughout the summer, Lindsay ignored Buckley. The conventional wisdom is that it is counterproductive to attack minor party candidates, and thereby make them more visible. But in early fall—when some polls showed Buckley closing in on 20 percent—Lindsay's campaign strategists changed course. They first attacked Buckley indirectly by leaking a story to the *New York World-Telegram* that the Buckley campaign was encouraging supporters to smash the windows of Lindsay storefront headquarters and engage in other "vicious right-wing hate tactics."[19] This backfired. Although the *New York World-Telegram* ran a story under the headline HATE TACTICS HIT LINDSAY, the *New York Times* reported the next day that the hooliganlike tactics were so isolated that Lindsay was not personally aware of them, and that Lindsay did not blame Buckley for whatever had occurred. This setback caused the Lindsay campaign to defer—but not abandon—their intention to vigorously go after Buckley.

On October 14, Buckley and Lindsay appeared, one after the other, before a group called the Parents and Taxpayers Association at a high school in Queens. The audience of roughly eight hundred clearly favored Buckley. It listened in stony silence to the first fifteen minutes of John Lindsay's speech, but when he got to his proposal for the civilian police review board, he was assailed with boos and jeers. As Lindsay was leaving the auditorium, one heckler screamed, "Down with Lindsay—Shoot him in the back!" The *Herald Tribune* ran a story about the event the next morning. This gave Lindsay the hook he needed. He called a press conference to say that what happened the night before was stimulated by "a doctrine of hate" that "reminded him of some of the worst moments in history," such as Nazism. He called Buckley "a candidate of the ultra-Right" whose campaign was "beset" with extremism. "In the streets, the Buckley campaign becomes a racist campaign," he added. A reporter asked if he was calling Buckley a racist. Lindsay said he did not believe that Buckley was himself a racist but that he was exploiting racism. "The city is a powder keg and Buckley is doing his best to light the fuse," said Lindsay. Buckley thought this was political theatrics on Lindsay's part. As he saw it, hecklers are common on the campaign trail, and candidates cannot be held responsible for them.

Buckley's policy of not appealing to voters as members of ethnic groups created a different kind of hubbub in October.[20] All three candidates were to sit in the reviewing stand during the Pulaski Day Parade, an annual event of pride for the Polish community. Buckley was not personally informed of the invitation. When it arrived, Buckley's assistant campaign manager, Neal B. Freeman, took it upon himself to decline on Buckley's behalf. "I am sorry to report that Mr. Buckley will be unable to attend the annual Pulaski Day Parade primarily because he has pledged himself to make no specifically ethnic or nationalist appeals," wrote Freeman. Buckley's policy, Freeman explained, was "to treat the voters of New York as responsible adult-individuals and not as members of monolithic voting blocks." Buckley learned about the invitation when the *Herald Tribune* published an article reporting that Buckley had been the favorite of most of the three hundred members of the Pulaski Day organizing committee—until the letter spurning their invitation was read to them. Buckley's press secretary declared the story would cost the campaign a hundred thousand votes. That was probably more than he'd get in the first place, Buckley snorted. Freeman offered to fall on his sword: He volunteered to resign or have Buckley publicly reprimand him. Buckley chose a different approach. He wrote the parade organizers a second letter, advising them that he had not previously been aware of their invitation. "I endorse the main point Mr. Freeman has made, which is that too many politicians believe they can manipulate nationality groups by attending their parades," Buckley said. He had also declined to attend the Steuben Day and Columbus Day parades. He continued, "If I had written the letter myself, I'd have added . . . that if you invite me next year to attend, when my presence would not be construed as politically motivated, I shall accept with pride and pleasure. And I might have added, as a longstanding supporter of the American Friends of the Captive Nations, that my sympathy for the ordeal of your people is more than ritualistic."

Lindsay had a different kind of problem during the campaign. On the very first day of his candidacy, a reporter asked Lindsay if he was running with Rockefeller money.[21] Lindsay was always considered a man of rectitude, but he denied outright that Rockefeller was contributing to his campaign—ungraciously adding that he found the very suggestion that he would accept the governor's money offensive. Lindsay followed this up by having a spokesman tell the city that the congressman didn't want Rockefeller campaigning for him or contributing to his campaign. Rockefeller was so furious that he called *Newsweek* columnist Emmet John Hughes and told him his version of events. Hughes published a two-page story in the July 12 issue of *Newsweek*, in which he reported the details of the meeting between Rockefeller and Lindsay and Rockefeller's promise to guarantee half a million dollars of campaign costs. Hughes (who was close to Rockefeller and would become an adviser and speechwriter for his 1968 presidential campaign) adeptly wrote the piece in a way that portrayed both men as entirely honorable—Rockefeller eager as leader of the party to encourage the strongest possible candidate to run for mayor, and Lindsay eager to insure his political independence.

After Hughes's story appeared, Lindsay was asked to comment on the now-specific report that Rockefeller pledged half a million dollars to his campaign. Lindsay's initial response was, "Hogwash, hogwash." Lindsay changed his tune the next day on *Meet the Press* however. While insisting that no specific sum had been pledged, Lindsay admitted that the Rockefeller family had "promised to raise a substantial amount" for his campaign and that he gathered from press reports their goal was half a million dollars. "I have said that . . . the campaign would cost a minimum of half a million dollars," he added. Lindsay also said he would support Rockefeller if he ran for reelection the following year. That was significant: The governor's approval level was then so low that prominent Republicans were publicly saying the party needed to run someone else for governor, and it was being reported that Senator Jacob Javits, who was Lindsay's campaign chairman, wanted to be the candidate. Lindsay also said he would support Rockefeller if he decided to run again for president in 1968. Later Lindsay reversed course yet again, announcing that he would accept no aid of any type from Governor Rockefeller, neither contributions nor loans, and would return $100,000 that Rockefeller had advanced to the campaign. Lindsay said he was rejecting Rockefeller's help because the governor was not a New York City resident—an explanation that considering the normal customs and practices of American politics was unusual, even bizarre. There was nothing untoward in Rockefeller supporting Lindsay's campaign and nothing improper with Lindsay accepting his help. Moreover, Lindsay was so clearly a forceful, independent-minded personality that few worried about Lindsay becoming the governor's vassal. But Lindsay's strange repudiations of Rockefeller got remarkably little attention during the campaign. There were, however, long-term consequences to what happened between Lindsay and Rockefeller during the campaign; the two would remain on bad terms forever, with serious ramifications for city-state relationships.

Nearly 81 percent of eligible voters went to the polls on Tuesday, November 2, 1965—the third-largest turnout in city history and a reflection of how much the race had seized the public's attention. Lindsay won with 43.3 percent of the vote. Beame had 39.5 percent. Buckley captured 341,226 votes, 12.9 percent of the total, a surprisingly strong finish for a third-party candidate who had conceded he had no prospect of winning.

Obviously, Buckley did not succeed in his objective of costing Lindsay the election; indeed, Buckley's plaintive arguments to the contrary, there is good reason to suspect Buckley's efforts were responsible for Lindsay's victory. Only 102,407 votes separated Lindsay and Beame. If Buckley had not entered the race, and the votes he garnered had instead divided one third to Lindsay and two thirds to Beame, Beame would have won. That may well have been the case. Buckley drew strong support from Irish, Polish, and Italian neighborhoods—Catholic areas that normally voted heavily Democratic.[22] One telling fact is that Lindsay emerged the victor in every one of the twelve assembly districts in which Buckley compiled his highest vote percentages. Nevertheless, Buckley's race turned out to be an enormous success for both him and the conservative movement. Buckley and his conservative message had been communicated to a much wider audience. Previously, his precincts had been conservative intellectual circles and his audience people who read books and political journals of opinion. Now he had preached his gospel to a much wider audience. Over a period of four and a half months, he had appeared numerous times on radio and television, both in extended debates and short newscasts, in the nation's largest media market. His name and comments had been spread across the pages of New York City's great newspapers. The race, and Buckley, had received considerable national coverage as well. People—and especially young people—who had not previously considered themselves conservative or even been especially interested by politics were smitten. Many scurried to their school and community libraries to find *National Review* and Buckley's earlier books. When the following year Buckley published what turned out to be his finest book, a campaign memoir titled *The Unmaking of a Mayor*, readers eagerly snapped it up. *National Review's* paid circulation swelled from about sixty thousand the year before the election to nearly one hundred thousand the year after the election.[23] It had become clear the camera and microphone loved Buckley. Five months after the election, Buckley had his own weekly television show, *Firing Line*, in which he interviewed— or, as the case may be, skewered—distinguished guests. The show, originally produced and syndicated by WOR-TV in New York, was taken over by PBS in 1971. It would continue for thirty-three years.

The Conservative Party had also gained respectability. It was, to be sure, an unusual political party. Buckley had made it clear throughout the race that he was, and intended to remain, a Republican. He was running under the Conservative Party banner because the Republican nomination was unavailable to conservatives. Everyone understood that the objective of the Conservative Party was not to supplant the Republican Party but to force it into a more conservative direction by providing a vehicle for conservative candidates—including spoiler conservative candidates—only as long as liberals controlled the Republican apparatus. In 1968, however, James Buckley, Bill's older brother and the manager of Bill's mayoral campaign, would run for the United States Senate as the Conservative Party candidate—against Democratic and Republican candidates—and win. Later Jim would himself acknowledge that would not have been possible but for Bill's 1965 campaign.

One of Buckley's objectives in running was to extinguish the political career of John V. Lindsay. Lindsay, however, had won. Moreover, not only had he failed to stop Lindsay's election but Buckley may have helped elect him. Though no one could foresee it while Buckley and his supporters were licking their wounds, Lindsay's election would turn out to be a gift to the conservative movement. The nation's eyes were on John Lindsay. The week after his election, *Time* and *Newsweek* both put Lindsay on their covers. Now everyone was going to see how Lindsay would do.

The Lindsay administration was not merely a test for Lindsay. It was a test for liberalism. What liberalism stood for, more than anything else, was that social problems could be solved, and that it was government's role to solve them. This was at the heart of the debate between liberalism and conservatism fifty years ago (and it remains at the heart of the debate between them today). In significant part, the debate sprang from the competing visions of liberty. Conservatives tended to hold to the negative view of liberty—being free from coercion, especially government coercion. Liberals tended to favor the positive vision of liberty—having a reasonable opportunity to do with one's life what one desires, which in a modern society requires providing children, especially, with good schools, safe neighborhoods, and adequate nutrition and health care.

Liberals, moreover, believed that government could solve (or significantly ameliorate) social problems that destroyed genuine liberty. What it took to do so was enlightened leadership—that is, leadership that did not follow rote ideology, was not in the pocket of special interest groups, and would not permit its policies to be muddled by political comprise. Enlightened leadership would assemble the best minds— sociologists, criminologists, epidemiologists, economists, educational experts, political scientists, and historians—and with their help devise programs based on the best learning. In 1961, President Kennedy called upon the nation to make a commitment to put a man on the moon and return him safely "before this decade is out." The nation was half of the way toward meeting that goal when John Lindsay was elected, and it would achieve the goal during Lindsay's administration. Liberals believed it possible to undertake similar efforts with respect to social problems. It was a constant liberal refrain that if it were possible to put a man on the moon, then it was possible to end poverty or solve other social issues. Conservatives had a different view about what was possible. They were, at best, skeptical about government's capacity to solve social problems. In 1964, for example, James Burnham argued that the liberal's desire to solve the problem of the most extreme form of poverty— homelessness, or "skid row" as he and others then called it—was doomed to failure. It was wrongheaded to think about skid row as a social problem at all. Skid row was "a natural, and indeed inevitable, condition of every articulated community of any size."[24] Skid rows existed in every city and always would. It was the "end of the line," the place where those "individuals who by destiny or choice drop out of normal society" wind up. In Burnham's mind, if people did not wind up on skid row as a result of their own choices, they would up there as a result of *destiny*, that is, forces that were not susceptible to societal intervention. Burnham felt the same way about people who did not have enough to eat, whether in the United States or in third world countries. The problem, he said, is that those people placed a higher priority on other things than on food. They chose to "sacrifice food for the sake of power, glory, piety, laziness, resentments and large families."[25] The reality of the world, said Burnham, was that men were not angels and the earth could not be made into heaven.[26] Attempts to solve the problem of poverty would be futile. The natural order could not be changed. Although Burnham's statements may be tinged with enough cynicism to make some readers wonder whether he was simply indifferent about the plight of the homeless, conservatives could be compassionate but genuinely believe that social programs were likely to do more harm than good.

The Lindsay administration put the liberal argument to the test. Whether or not it was a fair or meaningful test, that is how many perceived it. It many ways, the stars were well aligned for this liberal experiment. New York City, of course, was affected by national and regional circumstances. But when Lindsay was elected, Lyndon Johnson was in the White House. In June 1965, while Buckley and Lindsay were preparing their campaigns, Johnson made a major speech endorsing the positive vision of liberty and declaring war on poverty. "Freedom is not enough," Johnson declared at Howard University's commencement. "It is not enough just to open the gates of opportunity. All our citizens must have the ability to walk through those gates."[27] During the Lindsay administration, Johnson was implementing a panoply of social programs, including the Job Corps, Head Start, VISTA, and Community Action Programs.[28] Nelson Rockefeller—an energetic and powerful liberal—was governor of New York State throughout the Lindsay administration.[29] During the Lindsay administration, therefore, there were concerted efforts to implement liberal programs at the national, state, and local level.

It was a great blow to liberalism that Lindsay failed.

The biggest test was whether poverty could be reduced. Poverty and welfare were linked; that is, in the large cities, poor people were on welfare. When Lindsay took office in 1965, over half a million New York City residents—8 percent of the city population—were on the welfare rolls.[30] By the end of his two terms, in 1972, the welfare rolls had swelled to 1.25 million residents—16 percent of the city's population.[31] This was not necessarily Lindsay's fault. New York City's experience closely paralleled national trends.[32] However, regardless of whether the performance of the Lindsay administration was a fair test of liberalism, the fact remains that it was considered a test. Lindsay was elected on the bright promise that the liberal approach would make a positive difference, but despite concerted federal, state, and city efforts, the problems of poverty and welfare became significantly worse.

Similar failures—or perceived failures—occurred across the board. With respect to crime, for example, the violent crime rate in New York City more than doubled between 1965 and 1973.[33] Here too, while New York City paralleled national trends, the Lindsay administration failed

to make a positive difference. There were similar disappointments with
respect to the public schools and drug treatment programs. Meanwhile,
at great cost, Lindsay expanded city services across a wide spectrum of
areas. For example, one of Lindsay's initiatives was to open the City
University of New York—a system that included four-year colleges,
community colleges, professional colleges, and a graduate school—to
any graduate of a city high school who wanted to attend. This was a
great liberal initiative; students previously turned away—many of them
minorities—would be able to pursue one of the great American dreams
of a college education. The cost of the CUNY open admissions policy
was staggering, however. When Lindsay became mayor, the city spent
$35 million per year on higher education. When he left office, it was
spending $200 million per year.[34] Lindsay borrowed money to fund
those services. When he left office the city was paying about $100 mil-
lion in interest expense and headed for financial collapse. Three years
after Lindsay left office, New York become insolvent, and the state created the Municipal Assistance Corporation to control and restructure
the city's finances.[35]

John Lindsay was courageously effective in one important respect.
He wanted the city's minorities to know that he cared—and he did this
by personally walking through their neighborhoods, including the city's
most dangerous areas. Moreover, he typically did so without police en-
tourages or preannouncement to the press. During the summer of 1966,
there were riots in forty-three American cities. New Yorkers could look
across the Hudson River and see fires burning in Newark, but there
were no major disturbances in New York City. When, during the evening of April 4, 1968, Lindsay learned that Martin Luther King Jr. had
been assassinated, he immediately went to Harlem—despite pleas from
the police commissioner that he not go. When the mayor's car arrived
in Harlem, the situation looked so menacing that an aide accompanying
him thought, *My life is over.*[36] Lindsay talked extemporaneously to the
crowd about how sad he was about King's death. A scuffle broke out
between two groups near the mayor. In the confusion, Percy Sutton, a
black civil rights lawyer and Manhattan borough president, thought
one group was trying to harm the mayor, and Sutton quickly whisked
Lindsay away in his own car. In fact, the two groups—one Muslim, the
other from a Harlem labor union—were vying for position to protect

the mayor. Although there was rioting in New York that dreadful night, things were not as bad in New York as they were in many of the other 168 cities that experienced rioting in the wake of King's assassination. Lindsay kept up his practice of walking through the city's ghettos. It became his trademark. Nearly everyone credits Lindsay's walks with keeping the city relatively "cool" during desperate years. Even a critic of his administration calls this Lindsay's "finest hour."[37]

But failures dwarfed successes. Lindsay was lucky to be reelected in 1969. After losing the Republican nomination, which sent him into the general election as the candidate of the Liberal Party only, Lindsay won reelection against weak Democratic and Republican candidates by capturing 41 percent of the vote. But later campaigns are more revealing. When, in 1972, Lindsay switched parties and ran for the Democratic presidential nomination, he won no primaries and received 7 percent of the vote in Florida, the state in which he invested the most resources. When, in 1980, he ran for election to the United States Senate, he placed third in a three-candidate contest and captured only 16 percent of the vote.

Liberal analyst Charles R. Morris and conservative scholar Vincent J. Cannato have published superb analyses about the Lindsay years. They both agree that the Lindsay administration represents a failure of American liberalism.[38] The title of Morris's book—*The Cost of Good Intentions: New York City and the Liberal Experiment, 1960–1975*—captures in a nutshell how liberals perceived the Lindsay years.

It was not just Lindsay who failed, of course. Liberal leaders failed in other cities, and the war on poverty failed nationally. Lindsay, however, is a prominent symbol of all of these failures. His administration dashed liberal hopes. It left liberals disheartened and adrift, and gave conservatives increased confidence. It was a significant turning point in America's ideological debate.

CHAPTER 7

Vietnam

During the second half of the twentieth century, nothing had a greater impact on political and ideological debate than did the Vietnam War. It could hardly be otherwise. Nothing affected Americans as tangibly as Vietnam. More than 58,000 Americans lost their lives in the war, and 300,000 more were wounded, half of them seriously. In April 1969, at the height of the war, there were 543,400 American troops in Vietnam. The number of Americans directly affected by the war was much larger. During the course of the war, about two million Americans served in Vietnam or on military vessels offshore. Nearly nine million Americans performed military service during the Vietnam era. America's direct expenditures for the war totaled $106.8 billion (the equivalent of about $425 billion today).[1] No debate during this time was more passionate than whether the war was worth that expenditure of blood and treasure.

History has revealed that the war in Vietnam was a terrible mistake. America lost the war and Vietnam fell to the communists—with no dire no consequences for America's national interest. According to the U.S. State Department, "U.S. relations with Vietnam have become increasingly cooperative and broad-based in the years since political normalization [in 1995]. A series of bilateral summits have helped drive the improvement of ties, including President George W. Bush's visit to Hanoi in November 2006."[2] Even before formal normalization of relations, the United States and Vietnam entered into a bilateral trade agreement, and by 2009 trade between the two countries totaled $15.4 billion. Vietnam no longer has troops in Cambodia or elsewhere beyond its borders. The United States continues to express concern about suppression of political dissent in Vietnam, but it has also praised Vietnam for expanding religious freedom.[3]

Classic Cold War thinking—domino theory, in particular—got America into Vietnam. The war must be considered principally a liberal failure. It was President Lyndon Johnson who embroiled America in a major war in Vietnam, although the genesis of American involvement was President John F. Kennedy's sending 16,300 "advisers" to support the South Vietnam government. But the war was a conservative failure as well.

If competing ideologies are to benefit America, one school of thought must be able to ring alarm bells when the other school is about to misstep. That did not happen in Vietnam. On the contrary, conservatives—led by Buckley, Burnham, and *National Review*—repeatedly urged presidents Kennedy and Johnson to make larger missteps. Both the liberal administrations and the conservatives made the same fundamental mistake: They failed to study the history of Vietnam. They failed to understand the Vietnamese people. They assumed that the Vietnamese were fighting the war for the same reasons we were fighting it, that is, that they also saw the war as a struggle between the communist bloc and the Western democracies. They assumed that the Vietnamese communists were trying to topple a domino for the same reasons we were trying to prop up the domino.

To put the debate over Vietnam in a truly meaningful context, it is necessary to spend some time understanding the relevant history.

The story begins in the colonialist era when European powers believed they bore the "white man's burden" of bringing civilization to primitive peoples and were entitled to appropriate their lands and natural resources. Britain, Spain, Portugal, and France all sought to bring portions of Southeast Asia under their control during this period, among other reasons to position themselves for projecting their influence still further to China.[4] Competing with its European rivals, France began seizing significant areas of what was then called Indochina beginning in 1858. An emperor had long ruled—loosely, through mandarins—over Vietnam, and over a period of nearly a thousand years preceding France's

arrival the Vietnamese had repelled repeated Chinese invasions. Although the Vietnamese people had a sense of national identity, they
identified more strongly with their villages than with the country as a
whole.

French forces met little resistance as they took control of areas
throughout Vietnam. French technology was so superior that the Vietnamese people tended to think, rather like the French themselves, that
French domination must be the will of heaven. In the mountainous
north, the French dug coal, tin, and zinc mines. In the fertile south, the
French created large plantations—sold to whoever had enough money
to purchase them, French or Vietnamese—which produced rubber, sugar,
rice, and other commodities for export. The French built roads and
canals, even railroads, connecting their enterprises. On the site of what
had been a small fishing village in the Mekong Delta in the south, they
built Saigon, the city they called "the Paris of the Orient." The French
financed their enterprises by taxing Vietnamese peasants on rice and
other crops they produced and by creating government-owned monopolies
that sold alcohol, opium, and salt to the Vietnamese people at prices six
times higher than what the people paid for these products prior to the
French occupation. Even before their colonial occupation of Vietnam,
French missionaries worked at converting Vietnamese—who traditionally had adhered to ancestor-worship philosophies, including Confu-
cianism, Buddhism, and Taoism—to Catholicism. They had considerable
success among Vietnamese elites who worked with the French and
considered it advantageous to be Catholic and educate their children in
French schools. As Neil Sheehan writes, however, "Roman Catholics
were a tainted minority in Vietnam."[5] That is, many Vietnamese considered their Catholic countrymen to be collaborators with the French
occupiers.

In 1890, Ho Chi Minh was born to a family in the northern central
region of Vietnam, an area that was especially resistant to French rule.
His father was a Confucian scholar and aristocrat who served as a district magistrate. Ho was well educated in Confucian philosophy, which
included becoming proficient in Chinese, and he was then sent to a
French lycée in Hue, the coastal city in central Vietnam that was then
the nation's capital. At some point, Ho's father was dismissed from his
position as district magistrate for espousing nationalistic views and the

family was thrown into poverty—an event that may have had as profound an influence on Ho as her father's expulsion from his chemistry
shop had on Ayn Rand. Ho completed his studies, taught in a private
school for a while, and then took a job as a cook's helper on a ship
bound for America. He lived for periods of time in Harlem, Boston,
Brooklyn, and London, working as a baker and in other odd jobs, before moving to Paris in 1919, the year the Treaty of Versailles was
signed. In France, Ho joined the Socialist Party. Its principal attraction
for him was that the party's more radical elements advocated independence for the French colonies.

Shortly thereafter a passionate debate erupted in the Socialist Party:
whether to remain allied with socialist parties following the Second
International, organized in Paris three decades earlier, or to switch over
to the Third International that Vladimir Lenin had just organized in
Moscow. Ho asked which International had greater sympathy for colonial peoples. A friend told him that was the Third, and gave him a copy
of Lenin's "Thesis on the National and Colonial Questions." Many
years later, Ho recalled that when he read that document, he was "over-
joyed to tears." This, he thought, was his people's path to liberation. Ho
voted with the group that wanted to join the Third International and
found the French Communist Party.

In 1923, the party sent Ho to Moscow as a delegate to the Congress of
the Peasant International. A year later, it sent him to Canton, China, to
serve as an interpreter with its mission to the Chinese Nationalist Party,
which was founded by Sun Yat-sen and then included communists and
nationalists such as Chiang Kai-shek. While in Canton, Ho founded the
Revolutionary Youth League, dedicated to the liberation of Vietnam.
Ho traveled to other Chinese cities to recruit Vietnamese who were
living in exile after having been forced out of Vietnam for nationalist
activities. Most of his recruits were, like him, "Marxist mandarins"—
children of Vietnamese scholar-aristocrats who rejected French rule of
their country.[6] For twenty years, Ho labored among scattered groups,
slowly building a movement.

It was not until February 8, 1941, that Ho Chi Minh crossed the border
into his homeland. It was an opportune time to begin an armed revolt
against French occupation; the Nazis had overrun France, and the French
colonial authorities in Vietnam were part of the Vichy government and

principally working to serve the Japanese war effort. Vietnamese exports were now being shipped not to France but to Japan, and Japanese forces controlled the ports. Ho founded the Vietnam Independence League—the Viet Minh—to organize a guerilla movement and expel the French and Japanese. Twenty years earlier there had been several indigenous groups working to expel the French from Vietnam and for revolutionary change in Vietnam society, but they were divided in their goals and never coalesced into a unified movement. But under Ho's leadership, the Viet Minh was extraordinarily successful. By the end of 1944, it numbered half a million members in a nation of about twenty-six million. Its affairs were directed by the Xa Hoi Dang, a socialist party composed of roughly five thousand members, but the main message of the Viet Minh was nationalistic. The Viet Minh was, Sheehan writes, "the nearest thing Vietnam had to a national movement."[7]

Changes on the international stage profoundly affected what was happening in Vietnam. On June 6, 1944, the Allies landed in Normandy, and two months later the Vichy government came to an end. This led the Japanese to replace the French administrators running the Vietnam government with their own Vietnamese lackeys under the titular authority of Emperor Bao Dai. Meanwhile, because the Japanese were diverting rice to their own war effort and homeland, a terrible famine gripped North Vietnam—so terrible, in fact, that as many as two million Vietnamese starved to death during 1944 and 1945. The famine intensified hatred of both the French and the Japanese. The Viet Minh, rapidly growing, seized granaries from French and Japanese landlords and distributed the rice to starving Vietnamese. The U.S. Office of Strategic Services (OSS) was supplying Viet Minh forces with arms to help them fight the Japanese.

In August 1945, Ho led a thousand Viet Minh out of the mountains and jungles and into the city of Hanoi. They encountered no resistance. Later that month, in a ceremony in the imperial city of Hue three hundred miles to the south, Emperor Bao Dai abdicated his title and turned his dynastic seal and sword over to representatives of the Viet Minh. The following month, Ho proclaimed the establishment of the Democratic Republic of Vietnam. He read the Vietnamese declaration of independence to a crowd of half a million people in Hanoi. It began: "All men are created equal. They are endowed by their Creator with certain inalienable rights; among these are Life, Liberty, and the pursuit of Happiness." Ho catalogued the abuses of the French and Japanese against the people of Vietnam in the same manner that Thomas Jefferson and the American founders catalogued the abuses of King George against the American colonies. Ho concluded, "For these reasons, we, members of the Provisional Government of the Democratic Republic of Vietnam, solemnly declare to the world that Vietnam has the right to be a free and independent country—and in fact is so already."[8]

The Allies had different plans. At the Potsdam Conference a month earlier, France demanded a return of all its colonial possessions in Indochina. Indochina was a backwater issue for the big three at the conference—Truman, Stalin, and Clement Attlee, who replaced Winston Churchill as British prime minister in the middle of the conference—and the Allies acceded to France's demand. They agreed, moreover, that British and Free French forces would land in southern Vietnam and disarm the Japanese south of the sixteenth parallel, and that Chinese Nationalist forces, marching south into Vietnam, would do the same north of that line.[9] The Viet Minh were temporarily replaced as Chinese Nationalists marched—looting and pillaging as they went—into Hanoi. After seven months, the Chinese Nationalists withdrew from Vietnam, but the French forces stayed. Ho Chi Minh sent eleven telegrams to President Harry Truman appealing for help in negotiating his nation's independence with France. Truman ignored the telegrams. Ho sent similar telegrams to Chiang Kai-shek, Stalin, and Clement Attlee, but none of the Allies wanted to offend France, and all of Ho's telegrams went unanswered. In September 1946, Ho traveled to Paris and signed a working agreement with France, but the very next month France violated the agreement over customs and revenue issues. Following a skirmish that left twenty French soldiers dead, French general Jean-Etienne Valluy ordered a naval, air, and artillery bombardment of Hanoi that killed six thousand Vietnamese civilians. "We apparently stand quite alone; we shall have to depend on ourselves," Ho concluded. On December 19, 1946, Viet Minh forces attacked French garrisons in Hanoi and other cities in northern and central Vietnam. The Vietnamese war of independence against France now began.

France sought help from the United States. America had little sympathy for French colonialism, but France had a simple and compelling argument: Ho Chi Minh was a communist. France argued that either it or a communist-led movement would control Indochina just at about the time George Kennan was persuading the American government to adopt a policy of containment. Kennan had formulated that policy to contain the Soviet Union, not communist countries everywhere, but American policy makers were not making distinctions about communists.[10] They viewed communism as a monolith. In the eyes of American policy makers, Ho's nationalism was not as salient as his communism. By the end of Truman's term, the United States was subsidizing about 40 percent of France's military costs in Indochina.[11] During the early phase of the war, the Viet Minh received no help from either the Chinese communists, who were preoccupied with their struggle against the Chinese nationalists, or from the Soviets.[12]

During the roughly nine years of what is known to history as the First Indochina War, the Viet Minh were both outmanned and outgunned. The French Expeditionary Corps in Vietnam totaled around 150,000 while Viet Minh forces totaled approximately 100,000.[13] French forces had modern weaponry—much of it supplied by the United States— while the Viet Minh fought with a hodgepodge of weapons. But the Viet Minh were fighting for independence on their own soil and among their own people, and that proved decisive.

Befuddled by losing to what it considered a ragtag army of peasant guerrillas, France replaced one commander with another, to no avail. France continually requested more American assistance. Eisenhower succeeded Truman as president. After Mao Zedong and the Chinese communists drove Chiang Kai-shek and the nationalists from the mainland to Formosa, Eisenhower told his cabinet that he could not afford to let his political opponents—who were fond of asking "Who lost China?"—start asking "Who lost Vietnam?" A communist government in Vietnam was not acceptable. On the other hand, Eisenhower was determined to keep American troops out of Indochina. "The jungles of Indochina . . . would have swallowed up division after division of United States troops . . . Furthermore, the presence of ever more numbers of white men in uniform probably would have aggravated rather than assuaged Asiatic resentments," Eisenhower later wrote. Eisenhower substantially increased American contributions to France's war effort. Best estimates are that in the later years of the war, America subsidized about 75 percent of France's war costs. Not everyone was sanguine about America dipping its toes into the Indochina quagmire. When, in February 1954, Eisenhower sent ten American bombers and two hundred air force technicians to service them, senators from both sides of the aisle questioned that judgment. Eisenhower privately promised that he would remove the two hundred Americans by midyear.[14]

In March 1954, the war culminated in the battle of Dien Bien Phu, a remote forested valley in northern Vietnam, where the French sought to lure the Viet Minh into a trap. To bait the trap, the French commander positioned his forces to yield the highest ground to the enemy, thereby encouraging the Viet Minh to attack. An American adviser who visited the site before the battle was confused when he observed this. If the Minh placed artillery on high ground, would they not destroy the French positions? A French officer informed him that the Viet Minh had no artillery, and even if they somehow came into possession of artillery they would not know how to use it. That turned out to be wrong on both counts. The French force of thirteen thousand found themselves under devastating bombardment from more than two hundred Viet Minh artillery pieces, many on high ground and able to fire along direct lines of sight to their targets. Fifty thousand Viet Minh cut off all possibilities of resupply or reinforcement.

French army chief of staff Paul Ely flew to Washington to plead for help. Ely met Admiral Arthur Radford, chairman of the joint chiefs of staff, who Ely believed committed to sending B-29s from the Philippines and navy fighter-bombers from U.S. aircraft to pound the surrounding Viet Minh forces with a devastating attack of conventional bombs—plus three atom bombs thrown in for good measure. When word of this reached Eisenhower, the president said any bombing without congressional approval would be unconstitutional. Seeking such approval, Radford and Secretary of State John Foster Dulles met with congressional leaders, but were rebuffed. That result pleased Eisenhower. Still, Eisenhower was uncomfortable about a communist government in Vietnam, and it was during his explanation about why that was unacceptable—at a press conference on April 7, 1954, while the battle of Dien Bien Phu still raged—that he first used the domino metaphor. Radford made one more attempt to get Eisenhower to agree to use atom bombs against the Viet Minh, sending him a draft of a National Security Council recommendation suggesting that option. "You boys must be crazy," Eisenhower exclaimed. "We can't use those awful things against Asians for the second time in less than ten years. My God!"

On May 7, 1954, the French troops at Dien Bien Phu surrendered. The Viet Minh took 11,721 French soldiers prisoner. It allowed about nine hundred of the most severely wounded prisoners to be evacuated by the Red Cross, and marched the rest to prison camps hundreds of miles away. Many died from disease, starvation, and abuse. Some members of the French Foreign Legion at Dien Bien Phu were of Indochinese ancestry, and some of these may have joined the Viet Minh or been permitted to return to their homes. When the war ended four months later, the Viet Minh returned 3,290 prisoners to France. Viet Minh losses were far greater: about eight thousand killed and twice as many wounded. Eisenhower tried to persuade the French that they lost a battle but not the war—after all, only 10 percent of the French Expeditionary Corps had been involved in the battle—but he was unsuccessful. The battle was decisive for political reasons. Dien Bien Phu punctured the illusion that the sophisticated French military would ultimately prevail over a peasant rebellion, and the French public no longer supported holding on to its colonial possession in Indochina.

Shortly thereafter, the warring parties—meeting in Geneva together with representatives of the United Kingdom, the United States, the Soviet Union, the People's Republic of China, Laos, and Cambodia—agreed to peace terms, set forth in two documents. The first was an armistice agreement. It provided for a cease-fire and an exchange of prisoners. It also provided that French forces would regroup south of the seventeenth parallel, that Viet Minh forces would regroup north of that line, and that for a period of three hundred days civilians would be permitted to cross to whatever side of the line they desired. It also prohibited all foreign military intervention in Vietnam, including the introduction of troops and munitions. The second agreement, termed the final declaration of the conference, had two major provisions. First, it stated that the seventeenth parallel constituted a "military demarcation line [that] should not in any way be interpreted as constituting a political or territorial boundary." Second, it declared that "the settlement of political problems, effected on the basis of respect for the principles of independence, unity, and territorial integrity, shall permit the Vietnamese people to enjoy the fundamental freedoms, guaranteed by democratic institutions established as a result of free general elections by secret ballot," which were to be held two years hence—in July 1956—under international supervision.[15] The armistice was signed by the commanders in chief of the French Union Forces in Indochina and Democratic Republic of Vietnam. No one signed the final declaration however. It was not to be a legally binding treaty but an informal agreement. The United States, moreover, did not even informally agree to the final declaration. Instead, the United States issued a statement acknowledging the agreement and stating that it intended to "continue to seek unity through free elections" supervised by the United Nations, though it said nothing about the timing of such elections. That carefully worded language was camouflage. Eisenhower privately said that the Vietnamese considered Ho Chi Minh the father of their country and that if elections were held Ho would likely receive 80 percent of the vote. The United States, therefore, did not want an election to take place unless that situation changed.

There was another party that did not even attend the conference: a pseudoentity known as the State of Vietnam. The French created this fictitious creature in 1950 to give its administration of Vietnam cosmetic legitimacy. Since abdicating his authority to the Democratic Republic in Vietnam at the ceremony in Hue four years earlier, Emperor Bao Dai had lived in France. When the war ended, France brought him to Saigon and proclaimed him the head of the so-called State of Vietnam. Bao Dai had little credibility with the Vietnamese people. Not only had he abdicated his authority years earlier in Hue and left the country, but even before that he had been little more than a figurehead for French rule. Indeed, he was fluent only in French. For the next four years, Bao Dai had little or nothing to do with administrative affairs. He did not even live in Saigon, where the administrative offices were headquartered, and spent most of his time game hunting. As France withdrew, the United States turned its attention to trying to transform this empty shell into a genuine government—and, of course, an anticommunist government that would be a dependable ally of the United States.

The man entrusted with that responsibility was Edward G. Lansdale, a colonel in the United States Air Force, who was head of the U.S. military mission and later CIA station chief in Saigon. Lansdale worked along two tracks simultaneously. On one track, he tried to destabilize the Democratic Republic of Vietnam through sabotage and "black propaganda," that is, fake reports that ostensibly came from Viet Minh and were designed to discredit them. He generated false reports that the Viet Minh were going to persecute dissidents, thereby causing 860,000 people—most of them Catholics—to migrate across the seventeenth parallel to the south, an enterprise Lansdale called Operation Exodus.

On the second track, Lansdale tried to get a government up and running in the south. His first task was to find a suitable person to prop up as prime minister of this government. The man he selected was Ngo Dinh Diem. Diem, fifty-three, came from a family closely allied with the French. His father had served as minister for the emperor Thanh Thai, who, like other emperors during the period of French colonization, was considered a pawn of the French. Diem had been educated at lycée in Hue and a French school of law and public administration in Hanoi. He had risen through the civil service ranks in the colonial administration, ultimately serving as interior minister for Emperor Bao Dai. But Diem then got into trouble with the French by advocating the establishment of a Vietnamese legislature. He lost his position, and for the next two decades had no formal job at all, devoting himself mostly to study and religious devotion. Lansdale liked four things about Diem. First, Diem was staunchly anticommunist. Ho Chi Minh had, in fact, offered Diem a position in his cabinet but Diem had refused, telling Ho that the Viet Minh had murdered his older brother. Second, Diem was pro-Vietnamese independence, but in a low-key sort of way. His attitude toward the United States was not that the United States should leave Vietnam but that the United States should provide Vietnam with as much aid as possible. Third, Americans could relate to Diem. He was a Catholic, indeed passionately and devoutly Catholic. Fourth, Diem enjoyed political support in the United States. He had spent the past four years there. One of his principal benefactors was Francis Cardinal Spellman, the politically connected and staunchly anticommunist archbishop of New York. During his time in the United States, Spellman introduced Diem to prominent American politicians, including the senators Mike Mansfield and John F. Kennedy, both of whom joined a pro–South Vietnam lobby called the American Friends of Vietnam when it was formed in 1955.

Lansdale's first step in making Diem head of a new state—now called the Republic of Vietnam, and known principally to Americans as South Vietnam—was to have Bao Dai appoint Diem prime minister. The second step was to hold a referendum on whether the new state should be a monarchy under Bao Dai or a republic under Diem. The referendum was held in October 1955, and Diem received nearly 99 percent of the six million ballots cast.

Diem's leadership strategy was to lead an exemplary life. He was religiously devout and celibate. He worked hard; indeed, he was such a micromanager that government administration slowed to a turtle's pace as nearly everything, whether important or trivial, required his approval. He trusted no one beyond his family. Relatives composed half of his original cabinet. His younger brother Ngo Dinh Nhu controlled the intelligence services and police agencies. Nhu had been educated in Paris. He was an admirer of totalitarian leaders, especially Adolph Hitler. Nhu's beautiful and flamboyant wife, known to the West as Madame Nhu or the Dragon Lady, was the unofficial first lady of South Vietnam. She lectured the people about morality. She also supported legislation that imposed conservative Catholic doctrine on the population—banning contraceptives, making divorce next to impossible, prohibiting spiritualism and occultism. Madam Nhu traveled frequently to the United States, where she was a popular lobbyist for her brother-in-law's government. Her father became South Vietnam's ambassador to the United States.

The most important issue to the Vietnamese was land reform. Eighty-five percent of the population made its living in agriculture. The Viet Minh had won many hearts by taking land from French plantation owners and Vietnamese landlords who collaborated with the French and redistributing it to the people, who had previously been tenant farmers. Diem appropriated all of the land that the Viet Minh had redistributed and gave it to Catholics who were streaming south from North Vietnam or back to the original plantation owners and landlords. Some farmers were permitted to keep their land, if they purchased it from the government in annual installments. The army and police enforced this program. Neil Sheehan writes, "Through unstinting resort to the armed forces and the police, he reversed the pattern of land ownership in the Mekong Delta back toward one resembling the prewar pattern, when 2 percent of the owners had held about 45 percent of the land and approximately half of the farmers had been landless."[16]

Diem's government was basically a continuation of the French administration. The civil servants and retainers of the French now served Diem. The fuel on which the engine ran was American aid, much of which went to helping Diem build an army. Diem was as pure as the driven snow, but his government was riddled with less virtuous people, and much of the money and supplies that poured into the country was diverted toward corrupt ends. Rather than making the South Vietnamese more independent, American aid made them more dependent. But by 1959, the United States was sending $20 million worth of food to South Vietnam per year (the equivalent of $145 million today), even though agriculture was the country's principal activity.

Diem had been suspect from the start in the eyes of the majority of the population. As they saw it, the United States had supplanted France, and Diem was the handmaiden of another colonial power. As time went on, suspicion turned to antipathy—and that caused Diem and his family to become increasingly repressive. In 1956, he created a law authorizing the arrest and imprisonment of people deemed dangerous to the state, and he established political prison camps. He ended the practice of villages electing their own councils, and instead appointed outsiders, many of whom were Catholics.

In July 1955, Diem announced that he would not hold general elections to reunify the nation. He sealed the border and stopped trade and postal services between North and South Vietnam. Ho Chi Minh protested those actions, but he was too preoccupied with problems in North Vietnam to do more. In the postwar environment, he needed to concentrate on rebuilding. Moreover, famine was always at the door. South Vietnam had long been the breadbasket of the nation, and when trade with the South terminated, Ho faced grave challenges in feeding the North's fourteen million people. In 1956, the North implemented its own land reform program. The Communist Party urged peasants to arrest landlords and try them for treason. This precipitated an orgy of violence in which fifty thousand people lost their lives. Unlike the conventional dictator, however, Ho Chi Minh declared that he and the party had been wrong to instigate this program, and he launched a so-called Rectification of Errors to correct his own mistakes.

In compliance with the Geneva accords, ninety thousand Viet Minh soldiers—most of them originally from the south—had regrouped north of the seventeenth parallel. However, much larger numbers of Viet Minh returned to their villages in the south, stashed away their arms, and waited for the election that would unify the nation. Were they civilians or members of a military organization controlled by Ho? The reality was between the two extremes. The Viet Minh were comprised of people with an assortment of ideologies. Many had only a passionate desire to rid Vietnam of foreign powers and vassal governments. That was especially true of Viet Minh who remained in the south. Although Ho and the Communist Party exerted considerable influence over the Viet Minh, it is too simplistic to say that they directed the affairs of the Viet Minh. After visiting an area in southern Vietnam that was still under Viet Minh control in 1955, American journalist Joseph Alsop (who favored American involvement in Vietnam) wrote, "I could hardly imagine a Communist government that was also a popular government and almost a democratic government."[17]

Starting in 1957 and 1958, as the Diem regime grew increasingly repressive, guerrilla operations began to resume, probably more or less spontaneously. Early in 1960, a group of former resistance fighters in a southeastern area issued a proclamation that declared the existing situation "intolerable" and called upon patriots to regroup in preparation for collective action. On December 20, 1960, a group of one hundred unnamed persons issued a statement from "somewhere in Nam Bo" announcing that they had established the National Liberation Front of South Vietnam (NLF).[18] A little over a year later, the NLF held a congress, which selected a central committee representing a diversity of constituencies and included communists, intellectuals, and religious leaders. No one doubts that NLF leaders considered themselves allied with North Vietnam. Nevertheless, as Frances FitzGerald writes, "The personnel of the NLF was, with few exceptions, southern. Northern troops did not enter the south until the American troops had already arrived."[19] Diem started calling NLF guerrillas "Vietcong"—Vietnamese communists—a term that NLF members themselves never used because they did not consider themselves an exclusively communist movement.

The response of Diem and his American advisers was to institute a "strategic hamlet program." Vietnamese villages were not small, concentrated affairs; they were composed of farmers who lived in houses scattered among paddies. They were now moved into central fortified positions in which they could be protected from the Vietcong. Ngo Dinh Nhu set a goal of converting two thirds of South Vietnam's villages into strategic hamlets within a fourteen-month period.[20] Moving these farmers into the strategic hamlets effectively deprived them of use of their lands, which might be five miles away. The hamlets were surrounded by barbed wire. Houses outside the perimeter were demolished, sometimes by sorties from American fighter-bombers. Areas outside the strategic hamlets were considered free-fire zones at night, and anything that moved could be fired on. The program was supported by large amounts of American aid that was intended to enable the villages to build their own defenses and improve their communities. But the material was sent to province chiefs, who often forced the farmers to purchase it. Thus, Vietnamese were deprived of the use of their farmlands, watched their relatively nice farmhouses destroyed, and were then forced to build inferior dwellings with galvanized sheet metal roofs in congested surroundings, and often were required to pay for the privilege of doing so. They were confined within these unpleasant hamlets from sundown to sunrise on risk of being shot.[21]

In October 1961, President Kennedy dispatched Walt Rostow and General Maxwell Taylor, his advisers on national security and military affairs, to Vietnam. Diem was asking Kennedy to send combat troops, and the president was trying to determine what to do. When they returned, Rostow and Taylor told the president that the Diem government was unlikely to last more than three months without the help of American troops. Secretary of State Dean Rusk and Secretary of Defense Robert McNamara gave the president a memorandum that stated, "The chances are against, probably sharply against, preventing the fall of South Viet-Nam by any measures short of the introduction of U.S. forces on a substantial scale." Two advisers disagreed. Undersecretary of State George Ball told the president that "within five years, we'll have three hundred thousand men in the paddies and jungles and never find them again. That was the French experience." John Kenneth Galbraith, Kennedy's ambassador to India who visited Vietnam at the president's request, thought the problems were political, not military. Galbraith told Kennedy that Diem had "a comparatively well-equipped army" numbering a quarter of a million men and opposed by "a maximum of fifteen to eighteen thousand lightly armed men." Galbraith recommended dumping Diem and finding a more effective leader. Kennedy decided to send 2,067 "military advisers" to Vietnam. Many were helicopter pilots and technicians.[22]

In May 1963, Buddhists in Hue demonstrated in protest to an order forbidding them to carry Buddhist flags. Catholic province officials tried to disperse the large crowd—including both Buddhist monks and laity—with fire hoses and tear gas. When that did not work, they fired live ammunition into the crowd, killing nine. Diem's government claimed the deaths were caused by Vietcong plastic explosives. On June 15, 1963, Buddhist monks told several Western journalists that an event of importance would occur the next day at one of the main intersections in downtown Saigon. When the journalists arrived at the appointed place and time, they watched a large procession of Buddhist monks walk to the intersection. A monk named Thich Quang Duc seated himself in the lotus position at a main intersection of downtown Saigon and set himself on fire. Bystanders fell to their knees weeping. Images of the event were broadcast by media throughout the world. Even today on YouTube one can watch Saigon police holding back a large crowd as a monk slowly pours gasoline over Duc, while other monks bow their heads in prayer. Why the police did not stop the striking of the match is a mystery to the Western mind. Indeed, the unprecedented event was something of a mystery to the Vietnamese themselves. But in a culture where the sacred and the political are intertwined, it had a profound effect. During the summer and fall, six more Buddhist monks and nuns burned themselves to death. Madame Nhu derisively dismissed the spectacles as "barbecues," and at her husband's orders troops invaded a pagoda near the presidential palace and killed more than thirty monks. These responses intensified the monks' message: Something was terribly wrong.[23]

Realizing that South Vietnam would fail under Diem, Kennedy had the CIA deliver a message to certain South Vietnamese generals that the United States would look favorably upon a military coup. The coup occurred on November 1, 1963, and a military junta took power. Kennedy believed that the generals had promised Diem safe passage out of the country, and Ambassador Henry Cabot Lodge was relaying that message to Diem by telephone when Diem found himself surrounded in the presidential palace. The junta troops killed Diem. Two days later, Kennedy was assassinated in Dallas.

Little purpose would be served by recounting the next twelve years because, by this stage, the Vietnam War was already lost. North Vietnamese prime minister Pham Van Dong correctly assessed the situation in 1962, before Diem's assassination, when he was interviewed in Hanoi by the American historian and journalist Bernard Fall. Fall wanted to know whether North Vietnam was upset by a recent announcement of increased American aid to Diem. Poor Diem, Dong replied. He is unpopular. Because he is unpopular, the Americans must give him aid. And because the Americans give him aid, he is less popular. It sounds like a vicious cycle, Fall remarked. "Not a vicious circle," Dong replied, "but a downward spiral."[24] That dynamic remained unchanged notwithstanding subsequent changes in South Vietnamese leadership. All of Diem's successors remained in power only through American support.

In 1995, Robert S. McNamara—Kennedy and Johnson's secretary of state and one of the main architects of the war—traveled to Vietnam and met with men who were high North Vietnamese officials during the war. One of the people he talked to was Nguyen Co Thach, who had been the foreign minister of Vietnam. Thach told McNamara:

> Mr. McNamara, You must never have read a history book. If you had, you'd know we weren't pawns of the Chinese or the Russians. McNamara, didn't you know that? Don't you understand that we have been fighting the Chinese for 1000 years? We were fighting for our independence. And we would fight to the last man. And we were determined to do so. And no amount of bombing, no amount of U.S. pressure would ever have stopped us.[25]

This seems to have been a revelation to McNamara. He and his colleagues had thought of Vietnam as a war of communist aggression.

They believed America was helping South Vietnam defend itself from infiltration and invasion from North Vietnam, which in turn was sponsored by Red China and the Soviet Union. American policy makers had been so locked into Cold War mentality that they never even considered another possibility. Now, looking back more than two decades later, McNamara saw Vietnam as a civil war. But that was not really correct either, at least not in terms of a civil war between North and South Vietnam. Most members of the NLF were from South Vietnam; even many North Vietnamese regulars had been from South Vietnam until Viet Minh forces regrouped to the North following the Geneva accords.

The Vietnamese, in turn, were locked into their own false mind-set. For nearly a century, they had been in the grip of a colonial power, and they saw the United States as merely a successor to France. During their conversation in 1995, Thach told McNamara, "You were fighting to enslave us." McNamara knew that was not true. The United States did not intend to enslave or even to control South Vietnam—as long as South Vietnam did not become a communist country, whether through foreign aggression or democratic choice.

We are now ready to turn to the conservative movement's reaction to the war.

"Mr. Ngo Dinh Diem, visiting these days in Washington, can, along with South Vietnam, be chalked up as a triumph of American foreign policy—one of the triumphs of recent years," *National Review* declared in a May 1957 editorial.[26] Naysayers who griped that Diem—a shy, ascetic Roman Catholic—was not the man for the job had been proved wrong, the magazine argued. Diem had won a popular referendum. Moreover, despite complaints by Britain, France, and the Soviet Union that he was violating the Geneva accords, Diem "refused even to discuss all-Vietnam elections for the summer of 1956—when they would have resulted in Communist domination of the country." South Vietnam "is well on the way to stability, if not democracy," the magazine announced, and if he requested an increase in American aid during his visit, "he should be given a favorable hearing."

It had become clear by 1962 that the Diem government was in trouble, but as *National Review* saw it, that was because the United States was not taking sufficiently aggressive military measures. In his The Third World War column in March, James Burnham wrote that South Vietnam and Laos were both under attack "from Communist North Vietnam, proximately, and also from the Soviet Union and Communist China."[27] If America "were serious" about South Vietnam it would attack enemy bases throughout Indochina and "very decidedly" in North Vietnam. In an article in the spring of 1963, Anthony Harrigan complained that the United States was playing to the enemy's strength by itself engaging in guerrilla-style operations. Harrigan argued that America ought to use its "real strength"—superior weaponry. He recommended that the United States "sanitize" areas with chemical weapons that "destroy vegetation, animal life and crops" but happily "do not destroy property." He informed readers that a "single helicopter equipped with a gas dispenser, could flush out an entire band of guerrillas in a few minutes work." The United States, in fact, was already taking Harrigan's advice. A year and a half earlier, Kennedy had authorized the spraying of herbicide defoliants both to deprive the Vietcong of cover and to destroy rice, sweet potatoes, corn, and other crops in areas controlled by the Vietcong. This program became more robust as the war continued. In 1966 alone, chemical spraying from specially fitted aircraft destroyed 850,000 acres of forest and crops. By the end of war, the United States sprayed eighteen million gallons of herbicides over 20 percent of the total forest area in South Vietnam.[28]

National Review backed Diem to the bitter end. Liberals were vilifying Diem for persecuting Buddhists, for being a despot and an incompetent, and for running a corrupt, nepotistic government, but all of that was wrong. Diem "has maintained as much stability and freedom in South Vietnam as George Washington was able to maintain in the Colonies, while engaged in a revolutionary war," the magazine declared in the early fall of 1963.[29] James Burnham reiterated the point in his column a few weeks later. "Diem is the best that has been available in South Vietnam, and a damn sight better than we had any right to expect," he wrote.[30] The good news, said Burnham, was that the strategic hamlet program was moving along and that two communists were being killed for every noncommunist. The bad news was that the Kennedy administration was abiding by the axiom that the war must be kept from escalating and thus unduly restricting the military. "To keep the conflict from escalating, we must forbear using the advanced weapons—including chemical, biological, and nuclear—that constitute our distinctive strength and advantage," declared Burnham.

In September 1963, William F. Buckley Jr. received a phone call from Clare Boothe Luce. Luce was a formidable personality. She was the author of magazine articles, books, and Broadway plays; a former member of Congress; and a former ambassador to Italy for President Eisenhower. It is said that while in the latter position Luce—quite characteristically, for she was more than outspoken—lectured Pope Pius XII about why it was important to the church to be tough on communism. "You know, Mrs. Ambassador, I am a Catholic too," the pontiff allegedly responded. As a young woman, Luce was strikingly beautiful, and newspapers and magazines had been fond of running photos of her. Now, at sixty, she was still elegantly attractive. To top things off, she was married to Henry R. Luce, the immensely powerful publisher of *Time*, *Life*, and *Fortune* magazines. Buckley had long admired Clare Boothe Luce but never met her. She invited him over to her and her husband's Fifth Avenue apartment to discuss the worsening crises in South Vietnam, and of course he accepted. The Luces were both close to Francis Cardinal Spellman and active in American Friends for Vietnam. *Time* magazine had long sung the praises of Ngo Dinh Diem, and had twice put him on its cover.[31] Buckley later wrote about how charming Clare Boothe Luce had been at their first meeting—she was painting when he arrived, and gave him a painting lesson before discussing Vietnam—and about how they became friends.[32] Although Buckley did not reveal the substantive content of their conversation on their first meeting, it can be deduced from its result. Two months later, *National Review* published three pieces about the Diem government. The first, titled "The Lady *Is* for Burning: The Seven Deadly Sins of Madame Nhu," was by Clare Boothe Luce herself. It was a five-page full-throated defense of the Diem regime as a whole and of Madame Nhu in particular. Luce, however, implicitly conceded that Diem lacked the political strength to survive without the United States propping him up. She wrote:

> If the United States gives firm support to Diem now, the crisis [precipitated by the self-immolation of Buddhist monks] will pass and the war may still be won. If the United States support

is withdrawn on the grounds that the U.S. can no longer support the Diem government because six men—or sixteen—insist
on making human torches of themselves, South Vietnam will
fall and the political vacuum left by the Ngo Dinh family
will soon be filled by the "Yu-No-Hu" family: the Chinese
Communists.[33]

The same issue included a second article titled "What's Really Going
On in Vietnam" by Ngo Dinh Thuc—the archbishop of Hue and Diem's
brother—who was then being widely accused of persecuting Buddhists.[34]
Thuc's piece was all about denigrating Buddhist monks (or bonzes, as
they were also called). With only a few exceptions, Thuc claimed, the
amount of education Buddhist monks received was "almost nil." Thuc
said people scoffed at them, saying "that only the lazy and incompetent
became bonzes because their upkeep was and is assured by the income
of the pagodas." Thuc also purported to give readers the lowdown on
how Thich Quang Duc's internationally reported self-immolation was
arranged. "They chose three good old bonzes, and drew lots to see which
should be burned." And they drugged Duc so he could go through with
the act.

As it happened, both Clare Boothe Luce and Ngo Dinh Thuc's articles appeared in the issue of *National Review* that was on the stands
when Diem was assassinated. In its next issue, *National Review* ran a
third piece: excerpts from an interview with Diem that the magazine
had conducted earlier but withheld pending final approval of the transcript. One of the most interesting exchanges was the following:

NATIONAL REVIEW: Mr. President, your critics say the Communists
    have been able to organize a large guerrilla army here in Vietnam,
    because the people have stopped supporting you.
DIEM: This is not true. The Communists took over much of the
    country when the Japanese left in 1945, and built their strength for
    the next nine years while the French only controlled the main
    centers and some roads. The people had to cooperate with the
    Communists, and they recruited from the local population both
    north and south . . . The people came to support the Republic
    [Diem's government] because of its advances and respect for the

individual. The Communists lost—not gained—strength, and it was because of our successes that full-scale war was begun by them in February 1960.[35]

Diem's claim that the communists forced the people to cooperate with them fit perfectly with the then-common American frame, namely, that the people really hated communists and cooperated with them only under pain of death. There was some truth to this claim, to be sure. Neither the Vietcong nor the North Vietnamese were above using terror. However, South Vietnamese and American propaganda widely exaggerated the enemy's use of terror. Sir Robert Thompson, a British adviser to Diem, wrote, "Normally communist behavior towards the mass of the population is irreproachable and the use of terror is highly selective." Vietcong doctrine, in fact, required extensive bureaucratic consideration and approval of assassinations.[36] Although the frame of sweeping communist terror was widely accepted in the United States, by both liberals and conservatives alike, critical analysis should have produced greater skepticism. Each use of terror alienates the terrorized. Terror is more effective when its perpetrators have complete control over the population than when two sides are vying for people's loyalty.

After Diem's assassination, *National Review* was in a quandary. It had argued that Diem was essential to success in South Vietnam. If that was true, then was the game up? And if America could not succeed, should it not withdraw? That conclusion seemed both demanded by logic and un- acceptable because it would mean a communist victory. The magazine flailed over this conundrum. James Burnham predicted disaster. Diem had "represented the only serious and cohesive anti-Communist forma- tion in South Vietnam" and the officers who succeeded him had no "so- cial base." The new regime—or inevitable succession of regimes—would "begin disintegrating at once" and wind up in some accommodation with the NLF.[37] Similarly, in an editorial the magazine wrung its hands and offered no solution. "It was Ngo Dinh Diem and his family and friends who made South Vietnam into a functioning political entity," the magazine lamented. What made this so, the magazine suggested, was that the Diems were Catholic. Although they constituted 20 percent of the population, Catholics were not only "the most literate and skilled" but also "by far the most pro-Western and anti-Communist" elements of the population.[38]

Burnham was right about the generals who overthrew Diem lacking any political or social base beyond the troops they commanded, and his prediction that there would be a succession of regimes turned out to be painfully accurate. There would be so many coups that the South Vietnam government came to resemble a perpetual game of King of the Mountain. General Duong Van Minh (Big Minh as he was known to the Americans), the leader of the twelve-general coup against Diem, remained on top for only three months before being displaced by a second coup led by General Nguyen Khanh, who was replaced shortly thereafter in what was known as the coup of the Young Turks. Among the kaleidoscope of generals who flashed before the eyes, none is more memorable than Air Vice-Marshal Nguyen Cao Ky, a handsome thirty-four-year-old who carried pearl-handled pistols, and jetted about the country with his wife, an attractive former airline stewardess, dressed in matching black flight suits. Ky found special ways to get under American skins: He scheduled free elections and then canceled them, he denounced Americans as "colonialists," and he liked to refer to the American ambassador as the "Governor General" of South Vietnam, the term used by the French colonial authority.[39] The man who lasted the longest at the top of the mountain was General Nguyen Van Thieu, who at America's insistence did hold elections, eked out a small plurality of 35 percent of the vote, and responded to charges that he had stolen the election through fraud by imprisoning defeated candidates and their supporters. He learned from this incident however. When he again held elections years later, Thieu amassed a literally incredible 94 percent of the vote.[40] Although all of this lay in the future, James Burnham's crystal ball was working well enough for him to discern the dim outline of this future should the United States remain in Vietnam. But he thought the alternative would also lead to grief.

National Review still seemed lost seven months later when it published a cover story by V. L. Borin, a journalist and former member of the Czechoslovakian Communist Party.[41] Titled "Who Killed Diem and Why?" the confused six-page article never got around to directly answering the question posed by its title. Borin informed readers that Communist China was subsidizing North Vietnam's attempt to conquer South Vietnam, and it was doing so because "the Vietcong army is the vanguard of the Chinese Communist Army." China and North Vietnam had realized that they were no match for the Diem government, supported by America, and therefore they had to discredit Diem in the United States. A collection of liberals and the liberal press were hoodwinked into taking on this chore "unaware that they are Communist dupes." Readers were left with the vague impression that American liberals killed Diem, but the only such assassins that Borin identified were a group of sixteen individuals who took out an advertisement in the *New York Times* to publish an open letter asking President Kennedy to allow the South Vietnamese people "to achieve independence from dictator Diem and the United States, which has maintained him in power." Six of the signatories of the letter were professors of history, political science, and law at Yale University and one was chemist Linus Pauling, a recipient of two Nobel Prizes. Why the Kennedy administration was persuaded by statements such as these rather than its own reports from intelligence, military, and diplomatic officials Borin did not explain.

Eventually *National Review* clarified its post-Diem thinking. The essence of its position was that the United States had to militarily defeat the communists in Vietnam—not to defend the South Vietnam government, for which the magazine would never again muster much enthusiasm, or even to help the Vietnamese—but because that was important to the United States's own national interest. "If we have an excuse for being in Vietnam, it can only be for our *own* security," James Burnham explained.[42] That did not mean that American involvement was at the expense of the Vietnamese people. Burnham believed that U.S. involvement, if successful, would "incidentally" benefit the Vietnamese. He stressed, however, that America's actions should not be dependent on the desires of the Vietnamese people but on its own interests.

Other *National Review* contributors followed Burnham's lead. Ernest van den Haag, for example, took stock of the situation as follows: Maybe the South Vietnamese government was as bad as, or worse, than the North Vietnamese government. Maybe we should not have gotten involved in Vietnam in the first place. Maybe we had no right "to intervene in a far-away civil war." Maybe our allies disapproved of our involvement in Vietnam. Nevertheless, we had to "deny any semblance or

hope of military or political victory to North Vietnam and its supporters, including the Vietcong, without spreading the conflict. As long as
we can do so we are winning," he wrote.[43] This kind of analysis hardly
makes the blood run quickly about America's mission in Vietnam. We
are trapped in a very bad situation, Van den Haag is saying, and the best
it can hope for is not achieving a positive result—such as building a free
and independent South Vietnam that will be a blessing to its people as
well as a responsible ally of the United States—but avoiding the negative result of a communist victory.

In the fall of 1971, however, Van den Haag wrote a thoughtful twelve-
page article about United States war crimes that *National Review* published in two installments.[44] American soldiers had been charged with
massacring all of the inhabitants in the villages of My Lai and Son
My—504 defenseless men, women, and children. The description of
events that emerged at their court-martial shocked and disgusted many
Americans. The soldiers had beaten, raped, and sodomized victims before murdering them; laughed when one soldier twice missed a baby
who was lying on the ground before killing the baby with his third shot;
burnt the villages to the ground; and had even slaughtered all of the
water buffaloes and pigs in the villages. But some Americans were upset
at prosecuting American soldiers who had been forced to fight a terrible
war in which they had trouble differentiating friend from foe. In their
eyes, prosecuting American soldiers was somehow equivalent to attacking America or siding with critics of the war. The only soldier convicted
was Lieutenant William Calley, who not only commanded many of the
soldiers but personally shot to death at least twenty-two victims. He was
sentenced to life imprisonment at hard labor. President Nixon reduced
Calley's sentence to three years and allowed him to serve his sentence in
his own apartment with visitation privileges for his girlfriend.

It was in the wake of these emotionally charged events that Van den
Haag traveled to Vietnam, interviewed American soldiers to determine
how they viewed these events and how common these kinds of crimes
were, and wrote his articles. He described his interview techniques,
which seemed well considered, and reported and evaluated the data.
Van den Haag said atrocities occurred and those that were reported
were probably "only the tip of the iceberg." He explained why he believed the rate of war crimes was almost always high, and said that he

believed that the frequency of war crimes in Vietnam was roughly the same as it had been in Korea. He was, however, by no means an apologist for war crimes or commanders who did too little to avoid them. He found that the number of prosecutions of such crimes was disturbingly low and the punishments meted out "far too lenient." Most surprising of all to find in the pages of a conservative journal, Van den Haag criticized the United States for "cling[ing] to our belief in technological superiority as a panacea long after it was proven wrong in Vietnam," which was not only "at the root of our military failure" but may have resulted in avoidable death and destruction. One curious aspect of Van den Haag's thinking was that he blamed war critics for creating an environment that made it too difficult to prosecute the perpetrators of atrocities. His point was that war critics blamed the system rather than individuals. "They plead for indulgence, and insist that none but 'society' is ever guilty," he wrote. But here Van den Haag was confusing how some liberals viewed domestic crime with how they viewed war crimes. It was the hard-right "my country right or wrong" crowd that favored leniency for the likes of William Calley.

Once *National Review* and its editors had lost hope for a political victory—that is, building a South Vietnam that could win the hearts and minds of its people—they were left with the only remaining option of advocating a military solution. In a major piece in the fall of 1967, Burnham sounded two themes that would continue to be the motif of *National Review*'s position throughout the rest of the war. First, America could not win the war exclusively within South Vietnam. The only way to win was to cause North Vietnam so much pain and devastation that it would sue for peace. As the pain and devastation that America inflicted upon North Vietnam increased—to no avail—*National Review* consistently urged the infliction of more pain and devastation. Escalation, moreover, was not to be feared but welcomed. Second, the magazine was constantly fretting that American leaders were plotting to leave Vietnam before forcing North Vietnam to surrender.

James Burnham set the tone in a long article in the fall of 1967.[45] The article was prompted by a statement that Secretary of Defense Robert S. McNamara provided to the Senate Armed Services Committee about the effectiveness of the United States's bombing campaign against North Vietnam. Burnham had considerable respect for McNamara. "He invariably presents his case with logical rigor, confidently uttered statistics, and a notable absence of sentiment," Burnham said of Mc-Namara. Nevertheless, Burnham took issue with the central conclusion of McNamara's statement. McNamara said that the bombing campaign was intended to reduce the flow of infiltration of men and supplies into South Vietnam and to make North Vietnam pay a heavy price for any continued infiltration. The campaign, said McNamara, had been successful. Other than food, the amount of material reaching South Vietnam was "very, very small." Increased bombing could not reduce this flow any further because there were so many different ways—not only via rails, roads, and barges, but also via sampans, foot, and bicycles—of getting material from the North to the South. Therefore, short of targeting the North Vietnam population, increased bombing would have little utility. McNamara might be correct that increased bombing could not further restrict the flow of enemy supplies to South Vietnam, conceded Burnham, but the flow of supplies could be stopped entirely if Ho Chi Minh's regime decided to stop it. That should be the goal of American bombing. Burnham was unimpressed by the argument that the Vietnamese were fighting for their independence and would persevere despite any amount of pain. "There is some point at which any nation or people will yield," he said.

What did this mean? Did it mean that the United States should target the Vietnam population? Burnham seemed to equivocate on that question. "A full-scale air campaign (restricted only from area bombing directly targeted against population—though even that restriction is not inevitable) would permit what we have so far failed to achieve," he wrote. Meanwhile, Burnham wanted to smash the roads, rail lines, ports, and airfields that were being used to transport material from China to North Vietnam. In other words, if the flow of material into South Vietnam could not be further reduced by increased bombing of the lines of communication from North Vietnam to South Vietnam, then we should start vigorously bombing the lines of communication from China to North Vietnam. But there were two flaws in Burnham's analysis. McNamara said the amount of material reaching South Vietnam was "very, very small . . . significantly under a hundred tons per day." McNamara had at least implied that the amount of material was not militarily significant. If that were the case, and Burnham did not challenge McNamara's suggestion that it was the case, then there might be little military advantage in reducing the flow further. The second flaw in Burnham's analysis was that if it were not possible to eliminate this small flow of men and material by bombing the lines of communication between North Vietnam and South Vietnam, then there was no reason to believe it would be possible to do so by bombing the lines of communication between China and North Vietnam. Indeed, it would be far more difficult. The border between China and North Vietnam is more than seven times as long as the border between North Vietnam and South Vietnam, even if one includes in the latter adjacent areas in Laos through which the Ho Chi Minh trail (i.e., the pathways used by the North Vietnamese) ran.

A great deal turned on two military questions: First, how many men and how much material did North Vietnam have to move south in order to sustain its war effort in South Vietnam? Second, could the flow of men and material be reduced below those levels? In fact, the central strategy of American military planners was to achieve what they called the "crossover point," that is, the point where the attrition of enemy forces and material exceeded the enemy's ability to replenish them.[46] To that end, American forces focused on killing as many of the enemy as possible, destroying as much enemy material as possible, and reducing enemy reinforcements as much as possible. Burnham understood this. At the time Burnham wrote his article, General Westmoreland, the top American commander in Vietnam, was publicly stating that he believed America was reaching the crossover point. Burnham was alarmed because McNamara suggested that this was not the case—and might never be the case. Did this mean that McNamara "was in reality preparing himself psychologically, and perhaps the rest of us" for pulling out of Vietnam, a prospect that Burnham considered "catastrophic"? Burnham was, in fact, reading McNamara correctly. The secretary of defense was coming to the conclusion that "short of genocidal destruction" it was not possible for America to win in Vietnam. In time, he would settle firmly and permanently on that conclusion. In his memoirs, McNamara states that the central assumption of American war strategy—that it was possible to reach the crossover point—was "deeply flawed" because it "grossly underestimated the Communists' capacity to recruit in the South amid war and to reinforce from the North in the face of our air attacks."[47] (Burnham was not the only one who was alarmed over McNamara's state of mind. Within two months, President Johnson appointed Robert McNamara head of the World Bank.*)

Would the policy Burnham recommended—bombing the line of communication from China to North Vietnam—bring China into the war? China might be unnerved by bombing along its border. After all, that was what had brought China into the Korean War. Moreover, Chinese trucks, railcars, and ships might well be destroyed. Burnham thought that it was unlikely but possible that such bombing would bring China directly into the war. He conceded that getting into a war with China was perilous but argued that "for the West, Chinese intervention would be an opportunity as well as a danger" because it would provide "adequate motivation for destroying Chinese nuclear installations." What Burnham meant by the phrase "the West" is not clear. America's only allies in Vietnam were South Korea, Australia, New Zealand, and Thailand, and if the United States provoked China into entering the war it would likely face China pretty much alone. Moreover, Burnham's off-hand comment that this would give the United States an opportunity to destroy China's nuclear arsenal was curious coming from someone who prided himself on rigorous analysis; this was too big a deal to address in an almost blasé manner. China probably had its nuclear arsenal dispersed and placed in hidden and hardened facilities. Would America have to use nuclear weapons to try to destroy those weapons? What would the consequences be if the United States failed to destroy all of China's nuclear weapons? Would China strike back with its remaining nuclear weapons? Would China invade South Vietnam, South Korea, or Formosa? Burnham addressed none of these questions.

What was clear, however, is that Burnham thought considerable risks were justified because he placed so great a weight on prevailing in Vietnam. If Vietnam fell, he said, communism would expand into "Southeast Asia, the Indian subcontinent, the South Seas and the Pacific and Indian oceans . . . shift[ing] the global strategic balance decisively and

---

*So deftly did Johnson maneuver McNamara out the door of the Pentagon that many years later McNamara said, "I do not know to this day whether I quit or was fired."

perhaps finally against the West." As Burnham saw it, Vietnam was a domino at the intersection of multiple lines of dominoes running throughout much of the world. Burnham was hardly alone in accepting the domino metaphor as a truism without examining it. Yet despite his practiced style of ratiocination, Burnham did little heavy lifting on Vietnam. His writings reflected little study about the history of the country and the conflict and displayed less than rigorous analysis. He made sweeping but unsupported statements about geopolitical ramifications, perhaps too accustomed to his colleagues and readers accepting his pronouncements ex cathedra.

William F. Buckley Jr. also addressed American bombing of Vietnam.[48] Over the past couple of years, America expanded the classification of targets it was willing to bomb, and the bombings had accomplished a great deal, Buckley said. However, because of "the enemy's genius for extravasation," bombings were yielding diminishing returns. The Vietnamese were becoming ever more skillful at rebuilding bridges overnight, employing elaborate detours, and adapting to terrain—exploiting the lees of mountainsides, tunnels, and the like—to render their routes "all but unbombable." This, said Buckley, presented "a good case for zeroing in on the sources of the infection." Buckley did not specify what this meant, but the implication of what he and Burnham were both saying seemed to be: Bomb the population centers in North Vietnam, wreaking enough death and destruction to force North Vietnam to capitulate. However, Buckley never claimed special expertise about the conflict. Although when he rolled his sleeves up and thought through key questions his pieces were often more thoughtful than Burnham's, Buckley generally accepted Burnham's position and followed his lead on overarching strategic and geopolitical questions. More often than not, Buckley addressed narrow questions about the war. He was zealous in attacking liberals for opposing the war. Why was it, he asked for example, that liberals never protested Vietcong barbarities?

Too often, Buckley concentrated on flippantly deriding the war's opponents rather than analyzing the merits of their arguments. When Senator J. William Fulbright, the cerebral chairman of the Senate Foreign Relations Committee, delivered a series of lectures at Johns Hopkins University questioning American involvement in Vietnam, Buckley wrote, "Senator Fulbright appears not to be able to think about anything besides Vietnam, and his statements concerning it are like a fanatic's, growing stronger and stronger, more and more disorderly." Rather than challenging Fulbright's substantive arguments, Buckley fastened upon Fulbright's stating that "both literally and figuratively, Saigon has become an American brothel." Buckley took issue with the word *figuratively*. Ignoring Fulbright's obvious point—the Saigon government served at the pleasure of the United States in the sense that it was an American puppet—Buckley suggested Fulbright had gone off the rails by asserting that America was deriving pleasure from the war, enjoying expending lives and money. Surely Buckley did not really think that was what Fulbright was saying, but he used that suggestion to set up the following witticism: "We must hope, reaching for charitable alternatives that Senator Fulbright lost his hold on the language and used the term 'figuratively' more or less because he was scratching around for a verb to waltz about with 'literally.'" Truly silly targets were easier. Buckley wrote a column accusing David Ifshin—the president of the National Student Association, who had traveled to North Vietnam and broadcast anti-American comments over Radio Hanoi—of being ignorant. Outraged at this insult, Ifshin, a newly minted Syracuse University graduate, asked Syracuse to withdraw the honorary degree it bestowed on Buckley when he delivered the commencement address two years earlier. Ifshin argued that because he received high grades at Syracuse, Buckley defamed the university by calling him ignorant. For Buckley, this was shooting fish in a barrel. Buckley quoted Ifshin as saying, "The Thieu-Ky regime is one of the most oppressive regimes in history." Ifshin had majored in political science. How, Buckley asked, was it possible to have read a single book on political science and made that remark? "I demand," continued Buckley, that Syracuse "either call back Little Lord Haw Haw and explain a few things to him, or else beg him not to bring up, while exhibiting his ignorance, the matter of his having graduated from Syracuse University. It is too embarrassing for us Syracuse degree-holders."[49]

Regrettably, Buckley's problems with race leeched into his writings about Vietnam. On April 15, 1967, four hundred thousand Vietnam War protestors marched from Central Park to the United Nations, and another hundred thousand marched in San Francisco on the same day. A number of black leaders—including Martin Luther King Jr., Stokely

Carmichael of Student Nonviolent Coordinating Committee, and Floyd B. McKissick of Congress of Racial Equality—had spoken at the rally, along with white leaders such as Dr. Benjamin Spock and Jan Barry Crumb, cofounder of Vietnam Veterans Against the War. Buckley wrote a column about the event, which began with the following sentence: "The most depressing aspect of the Vietnam protest in New York City was the heavy involvement in it of Negro leaders."[50] Buckley was upset because he thought the communists were manipulating America's blacks by turning them against the war and against America itself. "The obvious goal of the present movement is to stir the Negro people, whom the Communists continue to consider the most ductile, and (quite justifiably) the most generally discontent, into violent protests of whatever kind," he wrote. This was awfully late in the day to still be looking behind the curtain for communists. It made about as much sense in 1967 to suggest that antiwar leaders were brainwashed by the American Communist Party as it would have been to suggest that war supporters were brainwashed by the American Nazi Party. Buckley threw in some insults against American Indians for good measure. He ridiculed an Indian chief who also spoke at the rally by calling him Big Chief Hatum War and reporting that when he was speaking someone had whispered, "Say ugh and sit down." When he introduced the chief, Dr. Spock had said that Americans were doing to the Vietnamese what their forefathers had done to the Indians, which prompted Buckley to make the dubious observation that there were more American Indians alive in 1967 than there had been when Columbus discovered America.[51]

By the end of the war, America pretty much resorted to everything except what McNamara called a strategy of "genocidal destruction." It bombed military and industrial targets in Hanoi and Haiphong extensively. The Johnson administration bombed tank farms in Haiphong and in other areas in North Vietnam, destroying 80 percent of North Vietnam's known petroleum reserves. While the Johnson administration worried about hitting Soviet or Chinese ships or railcars, the Nixon administration—freed somewhat by these concerns by the Sino-Soviet split and the desire of both China and the Soviet Union to not allow the other to have a more favorable relationship with the United States— bombarded the port of Haiphong so aggressively from B-52s and large guns on U.S. Navy warships that it accidently hit four Soviet ships, killing Soviet seamen in the process. Later Nixon mined Haiphong harbor, closing the port entirely. America bombed lines of communication between China and North Vietnam, including roads, rails, and ports. It attacked the communists via air and ground in Laos and Cambodia. American bombing of communist lines of communications throughout Indochina was so vigorous that the mortality rate of enemy truck drivers was as high as 30 percent and working on a road-repair crew was as hazardous as being a foot soldier. At the outset of his administration, Nixon's bombing of Hanoi was sufficiently savage for Buckley. "When Richard Nixon decided to bomb, he decided to bomb definitively," Buckley wrote.[52] And in a paroxysm of devastation known as the Christmas bombing just before reaching a settlement with North Vietnam, Nixon conducted fierce B-52 bombing throughout North Vietnam.[53] None of this had strategic value. Nixon and Kissinger ultimately settled with North Vietnam for little more than an agreement that American troops would be allowed to withdraw without being fired upon, and Nixon's ability to make what were at this point entirely unbelievable statements that American objectives had been achieved because the South Vietnamese government was now viable on its own. Saigon, of course, fell and Vietnam was united under communist rule—a final result that had no adverse consequences on the United States.

Most of the war occurred—and the majority of American lives were lost—after American policy makers had reached the conclusion that victory was not possible. Time and again they thought if they ratcheted up American involvement one more notch they would convince North Vietnam that America was committed to persevere until North Vietnam offered a settlement that allowed America to leave on at least a face-saving basis. "Peace with honor," they called it. But the problem was not that North Vietnam thought America was on the verge of cutting and running. Quite the contrary; it believed that the rhetoric of American politicians was subterfuge, and that America—like any true imperialistic or colonialist power—truly intended to remain in Vietnam permanently.

Buckley, Burnham, and *National Review* did read American politicians accurately however. They were constantly worried that American leaders were about to give up before defeating the communists and guaranteeing a noncommunist South Vietnam. Their worries were often warranted; there were continually debates within the high councils of American government about whether the United States should leave. In 1966, Senator George Aiken suggested that America simply declare that it had won the war and leave, and some variations on that theme were always being considered. In the beginning, only a few American politicians argued against America's involvement in Vietnam. When, in the summer of 1964, President Johnson claimed that North Vietnam boats had fired torpedoes at the American destroyers USS *Maddox* and USS *Turner Joy*—a claim that was exaggerated[54]—and requested the congressional resolution that served as the legal basis for the war, only two members of Congress, Senator Ernest Gruening and Senator Wayne Morse, voted against it. Governor Mark O. Hatfield of Oregon was then the only other major American politician opposing the war. Senators J. William Fulbright and George McGovern and John V. Lindsay became early converts against the war.* As time progressed, the ranks of opponents grew. But American policy makers were generally more worried about the political right than the political left. In his memoirs, McNamara says he worried that if the administration was not tough enough, right-wing pressure to escalate the war to dangerous levels might become irresistible. He was especially worried about "right-wing pressure to attack targets near the China border, as had been done shortly before Beijing intervened in the Korea War." President Johnson told George Ball: "Don't worry about the hippies and the students and the Commies; they'll raise a lot of hell but can't do real damage. The terrible beast we have to fear is the right wing; if they ever get the idea I am selling out Vietnam, they'll do horrible things."[55]

In 1970, Garry Wills wrote an article for *National Review* in which he argued against the war on conservative grounds (or so Wills thought).[56] "In the case of Vietnam," asked Wills, "did we ever have a legitimate national interest there, on a scale that justifies mass killing?"[57] Wills

---

*A still-popular conservative narrative is that Eastern elites drove opposition to the war. Gruening, Morse, Fulbright, and McGovern were, respectively, from Alaska, Oregon, Arkansas, and South Dakota. Senator Eugene McCarthy, who challenged Lyndon Johnson for the 1968 Democratic presidential nomination over the war, was from Minnesota.

argued that the only kind of national interest that justifies war is self-defense. Some argued that America's involvement in Vietnam was an act of self-defense. "By the domino theory, Vietnam was just one step along a course that would lead to our destruction. But if that argument is to be made," Wills continued, "it must be based on solid evidence." Wills examined what America's leaders were saying about why the nation was fighting in Vietnam and did not find solid evidence. What he found instead was "muddled idealistic talk" about saving Asia for Asians or defending the right of self-determination of the Vietnamese people. The political realists were then saying it no longer mattered why we first entered the war; staying in Vietnam had become a matter of "living up to our commitment." "That sounds very noble," wrote Wills, "as if we were serving simple truth and honor—until we push the analysis: then it becomes evident that a failure to our commitment would be evil because it would hurt American prestige."

Wills went on to talk about George Washington's testamentary address and Dwight D. Eisenhower's farewell address. Both presidents had given the nation similar warnings. Washington had spoken of "overgrown military establishments which, under any form of government, are inauspicious to liberty," and Eisenhower spoke about "the military-industrial complex." Wills argued that Washington and Eisenhower had been warning about exactly the kinds of traps that had gotten America into Vietnam. It is not genuinely patriotic, Wills continued, "to prefer muddled abstractions of 'confrontation with Communism' in Vietnam to the lives of our young men." If we were going to fight for our country "right or wrong," then we had to be truly fighting for our country—"and Vietnam is not our country."

Wills may have published more articles in the magazine than anyone except Buckley himself—more than 150, not counting other articles published under a pseudonym so that his byline would not appear too often.[58] Buckley rejected this piece, however. Arguments against the war were beyond the permitted parameters of debate within the pages of *National Review*.

Buckley would never believe the Vietnam War was a mistake. We lost, he believed, not because the war was inherently unwinnable but because we lacked the political will to continue. After our ignominious departure, "the Communist victors killed hundreds of thousands and forced more than 1.5 million into reeducation camps, causing more than 2 million others to flee Vietnam."⁵⁹ "Southeast Asia," he wrote, "learned what it can mean to rely on the United States."⁶⁰

The intellectual left argued against American involvement in the war from the earliest days of the Johnson administration. The *Nation* and the *New Republic* both published articles explaining the history and relevance of French colonialism in Vietnam and why the war was wrongheaded and unwinnable.⁶¹ It is entirely possible that history would have been different if—instead of continually urging increased military action— the intellectual right, led by Buckley and *National Review*, had also advocated against American involvement. But would that have been feasible from an ideological point of view? Would that have been a coherent conservative position?

Under a Burkean form of conservatism, the answer is a resounding yes. Burke warned England against pursuing its disastrous tax policy against the American colonies—and more importantly, against trying to subdue the colonies through military force. He had carefully studied the colonies and their histories, cultures, and the writings of their leaders. And he rigorously considered what military force could and could not accomplish.⁶² Burke believed it was important to appreciate differences in culture. He thought it was a mistake to expect that people with different histories and circumstances would see the world the same way. He made strong efforts to understand the American colonists. "I think I know America—if I do not, my ignorance is incurable, for I have spared no pains to understand it," he said. This allowed him to predict far better than the king's ministers and other members of Parliament how the colonists would react to attempts to bring them to heel. Burke explained that the Americans believed they were fighting for "everything that was valuable in the world." He cautioned his colleagues to "reflect how you are to govern a people who think they ought to be free, and think they are not." Could the vastly superior English army and navy subdue the colonies? Burke thought they could but asked his colleague to carefully consider what that would mean. "To send [the army] to one town would not be sufficient; every province of America must be traversed, and must be subdued. I do not entertain the least doubt this

could be done. We might, I think, without much difficulty, have destroyed our colonies," Burke said. And, to preserve its victory, how long
would England have to maintain large army and naval forces in America? "Permit me to observe," said Burke, "that the use of force alone is
but *temporary*. It may subdue for a moment; but it does not remove the
necessity of subduing again; and a nation is not governed which is perpetually to be conquered."

It is important not to be seduced into drawing parallels between the
American colonies and twentieth-century Vietnam. The Vietcong were
not the Continental Army, Ho Chi Minh was not Thomas Jefferson,
and Vo Nguyen Giap was not George Washington. It is also important
to bear in mind that at bottom Burke's sympathies were with England,
not America. He wanted to preserve as much of the British Empire as
possible. The question was what was possible. A second question in-
volves values. Burke wanted to preserve as much of the British Empire
as possible not merely for the benefit of England but for the benefit of
all the inhabitants of the empire. He believed all people should be ac-
corded equal respect and dignity. He also did not believe it possible over
the long run for one nation to exploit another; relationships had to be
built on mutual advantage. These two aspects of Burke's approach are
related because—both as a means of analysis, and as a means of promoting values—they involve putting oneself in the other's shoes. This is
what we Americans as a whole failed to do in Vietnam. Rather than
trying to understand the Vietnamese people and seeing the world through
their eyes, we saw them as pawns in the global Cold War struggle. As a
result, we treated them as pawns. We did not think of it that way, of
course. Imprisoned by our own worldview, we believed that the South
Vietnamese people and we were fighting together, with the same interests
and desires, for freedom and against communist aggression. It is the same
kind of mistake that Burke tried in vain to warn his fellow countrymen
against in dealing with the American colonies.

Buckley, however, had followed a different path. He was not a Burkean,
and under his leadership conservatism was decidedly not Burke's philosophy. Neither he nor Burnham, on whom he relied so heavily on issues
of foreign affairs, tried to understand the war from the Vietnamese perspective. They did not make a strong effort to study Vietnamese history
and culture. They assumed that the Vietnamese saw things pretty much

the same way as did Americans, and that if the Vietnamese were free to choose, they would make the same choices as would Americans. They assumed that the best Vietnamese leader was someone with whom they could relate—someone staunchly anticommunist, Western educated, and Catholic. In all of these things, liberal American policy makers made similar mistakes, but the nation failed to benefit from a check on those errors.

Conclusion

Nineteen sixty-eight was a traumatic year for America. First came the Tet Offensive. For much of the preceding year, the nation's leaders—particularly President Johnson and General William C. Westmoreland, America's top military commander in Vietnam—had been telling the American people that the war in Vietnam was going well. They claimed that fully two thirds of the country was considered "pacified" and the "light at the end of the tunnel" was in view. In the not too distant future, they said, the South Vietnamese would take over and prevail on their own. That illusion was shattered in the early morning hours of January 31, 1968, when Vietcong and North Vietnamese launched coordinated attacks throughout the country, including what were considered the most secure areas. They attacked five of South Vietnam's six largest cities and one hundred provincial and district capitals. They seized most of the city of Hue, including the provincial headquarters, the university, and the central marketplace, and they ran the banner of the National Liberation Front (the formal organization of communist and noncommunist South Vietnamese who were fighting for national reunification) up the flagpole in the imperial citadel. It took a month for American and South Vietnamese forces to retake the city. Six thousand Vietcong soldiers attacked targets throughout the city and suburbs of Saigon. They blasted a hole in the eight-foot wall surrounding the American embassy. They failed to breach the armored doors of the embassy building, but held the outer courtyard for six hours against counterassaults by U.S. Marines. In due course, American and South

Vietnamese troops retook the cities, inflicting punishing casualties on the Vietcong. From a strictly military point of view, the Tet Offensive was considered a defeat for the National Liberation Front and North Vietnam. But that was beside the point. The Tet Offensive told the American people that what they had been led to believe was wrong. The light at the end of the tunnel was not in sight; maybe it never would be. People who had been willing to stand behind their leaders in time of war no longer had confidence in those leaders.

On March 12, Senator Eugene McCarthy—running against the incumbent president of his own party on the issue of the war—captured 42 percent of the vote in the New Hampshire Democratic presidential primary. No one had expected McCarthy's strong showing. One of his more improbable supporters happened to be Russell Kirk. Kirk liked that McCarthy considered Edmund Burke his mentor and believed that McCarthy was, at least in theory, a conservative. James Burnham also admired McCarthy. He considered him unusually intelligent, learned, and decent for a politician, even if McCarthy was, in Burnham's view, wrong on the most important issue of the day.[1]

Four days after McCarthy demonstrated that Johnson was vulnerable, a more formidable challenger entered the race: Senator Robert F. Kennedy of New York, the presumptive heir to his brother's legacy. Two weeks later, Lyndon Johnson announced he would not seek reelection.

On April 4, 1968, Martin Luther King Jr. was assassinated in Memphis, Tennessee. America was convulsed by riots. A struggle for the heart and soul of the civil rights movement was already under way between moderate black leaders and more extreme black leaders who wanted to jettison King's commitment to nonviolence. What would happen with King gone and rage unleashed?

Two months after King's death—on the night he defeated Eugene McCarthy in the critical California presidential primary—Robert F. Kennedy was assassinated in Los Angeles. America felt lost. It was in the midst of a war it no longer believed it could win, but had long been told it could not afford to lose. Race relations were more troubled than ever before—perhaps doomed—and the nation, quite literally, was burning. Just when America needed leaders more than ever, madmen were snuffing them out. There was a sense of spiraling into chaos.

The sixties touched Buckley personally, causing a painful rupture to one of his most valued friendships. This relationship began eleven years earlier, when *National Review* had received an unsolicited submission from someone in Cincinnati. James Burnham read the piece first, then sent it to Buckley with a note that the author "writes in places as only a true writer can."[2] Buckley was so impressed with the piece that he immediately called the author and invited him to come to New York. The author demurred. Sensing the obstacle, Buckley said *National Review* would, of course, pay for the trip. That brought Garry Wills—then a twenty-three-year-old graduate student at Xavier University—to Buckley's office at *National Review*. As previously mentioned, Garry Wills became one of the magazine's most published writers. Buckley and Wills also became personally close. Buckley appreciated Wills's great talent as a writer and thinker, as well as Wills's devout and learned Catholicism (Wills spent six years in a Jesuit seminary before deciding that the celibate life was not for him). The two men developed a social as well as a professional relationship; Wills was a frequent guest on Buckley's sailboat, for example. Buckley even selected Wills as his official biographer.[3]

Wills, however, had never been a Buckley-style conservative. Neither Wills nor Buckley realized that at first. Wills had been largely apolitical, and when Buckley asked him whether he was a conservative, Wills did not know. It was Frank Meyer who first diagnosed Wills's ideological leanings. Wills wrote book reviews for Meyer, who was *National Review*'s literary editor. When Wills handed in a review of a book about Russia that Meyer had assigned, Meyer informed Wills that he was surely no conservative—but not to worry, Meyer would protect him by having him review nonpolitical books. Although articles bearing Gary Wills's byline were spectacularly numerous and diverse, an astute reader may have noticed they were nearly all about culture and religion—not politics.

Politics became impossible to avoid in the sixties, however. In 1968, Wills wrote two articles that contributed to the painful rupture between him and Buckley. The first was a long article that Wills wrote for *Esquire* (later expanded into a book), titled "The Second Civil War."[4] It was about how both black and white America were arming for riots, with potentially dire consequences. Calamity would only be avoided if black Americans felt respected. Policy makers were talking about removing the causes of rioting, by which they meant ending poverty. "But money is not the solution it itself," wrote Wills. "More important is the way the money is gained by the Negro; it must not be given, but surrendered, on his terms, or he will think it is another bribe to 'keep him in his place.'" This piece did not sit well with *National Review* editors. Wills's second piece, for *National Review*, was about the 1968 Democratic National Convention in Chicago, at which there were violent confrontations between police and antiwar demonstrators. Frank Meyer unsuccessfully tried to persuade Buckley not to allow Wills to cover the convention in the first place, and when Wills handed in his piece heavily criticizing Chicago mayor Richard J. Daley, Meyer urged Buckley not to run it. Buckley did publish it—to the displeasure not only of the magazine's editors, but its readers as well.[5] Buckley defended his decision to publish the piece, but no one thought he would have done so if someone else had written it.

The divergence on politics was bad enough, but things started to become personal as well. Wills let it be known that he had decided not to write a biography of Buckley. Buckley wasn't important enough, Wills told one person. Maybe he would write an analysis of the American right instead. This prompted a letter to Wills by Neil McCaffrey, the head of Arlington House, which was to publish Wills's biography of Buckley. "Since a contract may not be altered unilaterally," McCaffrey wrote, "I offer you two alternatives: either return to the plan for a biography of Bill, or return the advance and let us cancel the contract."[6] In the latter event, Wills was to return the $8,000 advance for the Buckley biography (the equivalent of $48,000 today), as well as another advance Wills had received for a book about John Henry Newman. Wills returned the money. By late 1969 or early 1970, when Wills submitted his piece against the Vietnam War to Buckley, there was little chance Buckley would run it. There followed some reciprocal sniping, and then Buckley and Wills stopped speaking.

By this time, Wills knew much more about political ideology than he had as a callow twenty-three-year-old, and Meyer's opinion notwithstanding, Wills considered himself a conservative. In 1979, Wills wrote a book titled *Confessions of a Conservative*, in which he defended his ideological self-identification. "*Conservatism*," he wrote, "looks to the cohesion and continuity of society—what makes people band together and remain together with some satisfaction."[7] Libertarianism was just the opposite. "It is easy to see at the outset that libertarians lived in a dream world of hypothetical atoms interacting with each other dynamically. No society can ever be formed on the basis of individualism, togetherness deriving from apartness," Wills wrote.[8] He argued that conservatives value continuity and tradition. An ideology that placed the free market at the center of its philosophy was not genuinely conservative because capitalism was all about risk taking and seeking new markets, and therefore not a force for continuity and stability.

How did conservatism take this wrong turn? In the Old World, Wills observed the king and the church were the institutions of stability and continuity, which is why conservatives valued them. But, of course, king and church were also the institutions of power. The source of power in modern America was business. "We rather simple-mindedly kept the nexus *power = conservative*, even when the power involved was a revolutionary and unstable one."[9] Wills did not mention Will Buckley—and there is no reason to believe Wills was thinking of his former friend's father—but Wills's observation helps explain how an entrepreneur like Will Buckley, who happened to be a devout Catholic, would confuse power with conservatism. Will arrived in Mexico during a time of superficial stability. The autocrat Porfirio Díaz had been in power for thirty-four years. The Catholic Church was the wealthiest institution in the nation, and Díaz and the church supported each other. Díaz, moreover, was good for business, and welcomed foreign investors like Buckley and the oil companies with which he did business. It is easy to see how, for Will, stability, continuity, traditional authority, religion, business, and power would conflate.

"The right wing in America," Wills wrote, "is stuck with the paradox of holding a philosophy of 'conserving' and an actual order it does not want to conserve. It keeps trying to create something new it might think worthy, someday, of conserving."[10] That sounded very much like Clinton Rossiter and Peter Viereck. And although Wills may not have realized it, much of what he said sounded like Edmund Burke.

The year after Wills published *Confessions of a Conservative*, Kirk left *National Review* and, after a twenty-five-year hiatus, resumed his slashing attacks on libertarianism and his insistence that true conservatism followed in the footsteps of Edmund Burke. But it no longer mattered what Wills or Kirk thought conservatism should stand for—or that they could persuasively claim to be the rightful heirs of a genuine conservative heritage. Over the past thirteen years, Buckley and *National Review* had changed nearly everyone's understanding of the term. "Conservatism" was no longer the conservatism of Robert A. Taft. It was not about conserving the best in American traditions and institutions while seeking slow and moderate improvements. It was not a philosophy of caution and prudence. It did not share Edmund Burke's concern about the dangers of unintended consequences. Boldness had supplanted caution and zealousness had replaced prudence. Conservatism was no longer a philosophy about community—a hallmark of Burkeanism; it had become a philosophy of individualism. Conservatism was no longer wary of military adventurism. It worried less about what could be achieved with force than it did about what would transpire if America were too hesitant to use force. It was not pragmatic. It did not set and revise policy directions based on changing circumstances and analyses of history and data. Those approaches led to being blown hither and yon as circumstances, facts, and analyses changed. Conservatism was now based on immutable truths of human nature and Christian values.

Buckley's conservatism had been shaped by turmoil, but not turmoil he personally experienced or even turmoil that America experienced. Bill inherited his father's philosophy, and that philosophy had been formed from Will Buckley's experiences during the Mexican Revolution. According to family legends (and there are no reasons to doubt them) Will Buckley had survived—and prospered—during a time of extreme chaos and personal danger on the basis of courage, ingenuity, and righteousness. He had pursued personal ambition while remaining faithful to his religious convictions. Will valued wealth, but did not worship mammon. He believed in business but even more in the entrepreneurial skill of the individual. He came to see sharp divisions between people, between the worthy and the unworthy. He considered the revolutionaries who purported to act for the benefit of the people nothing more than barbarians—unlettered, undisciplined, hypocritical, greedy, corrupt, sacrilegious, and brutal. He believed that the revolution was ignited by government concessions. Compromise had not satiated desires; it had inflamed them. He came to doubt the efficacy of democracy. The people were liable to elect charlatans who promised to redistribute wealth. The most powerful civilizing force was the church. As Will saw it, it was far from incidental that the revolutionaries attacked the church and sought to destroy its authority in the eyes of the people. In many ways, the essence of what was to become Bill Buckley's conservatism—its combination of libertarianism, neoconservatism, and religiosity—was established by the time Will Buckley left Mexico.

William F. Buckley Jr. made his father's brand of conservatism into a political movement. The talents he brought to this endeavor—both numerous and extraordinary—need not be recounted again. One asset, however, is worth mentioning. Buckley was leading a movement fueled by fear: fear of international communist expansion; fear of domestic communist infiltration; fear that American leaders were naïve or perhaps worse; fear that the civil rights movement would destroy civilization; fear that American capitalism would be devoured by socialism; fear that Americans would lose their self-sufficiency and become soft, self-indulgent, and dependent on government largesse; fear that America would embrace secularism and cease to become a nation under God. Buckley, however, did not appear afraid. He was a cheerful, confident, and attractive personality with a rare and wonderful sense of humor. As *Time* magazine had pointed out in its cover story, Buckley showed that conservatism could be fun. An ideology so weighted with worries would have been misery if it were led by someone whose personality reflected its fear, pessimism, or even paranoia. Buckley gave voice to his followers' fears and yet was himself a powerful antidote to those fears.

By 1968, Buckley had given the conservative movement both robust life and sharp definition. *National Review* had achieved a paid circulation of one hundred thousand, a considerable number for a political journal of opinion.[11] Buckley was then at the apogee of his personal fame and influence. In 1967, *Time* magazine put him on its cover, and that same year he won the Best Columnist of the Year Award for On the Right, which was then carried by 350 newspapers. He received an Emmy for *Firing Line* in 1969. He continued editing *National Review* until 1990, when he handed over those duties to John O'Sullivan. He continued to give public speeches until 1998; for decades he averaged seventy speeches per year. He continued filming *Firing Line* until 1999. He continued to hold legal control of *National Review* until 2004, when he transferred his voting stock to a board he had selected. He continued to write On the Right for newspapers and *National Review* to the end.

In some ways, his views changed markedly. In 1990, at age sixty-five, Buckley published a small book titled *Gratitude*. "The points I raise," he warned in the introduction, "will disturb some 'conservative' presumptions."[12] The book is a proposal for a massive new federal program—a national service program that Buckley hoped would enroll more than 80 percent of young Americans.[13] Enrollees would spend a year working full time and without pay for organizations that provided services to those in need or to the community at large, such as hospitals, nursing homes, day care centers, orphanages, programs for the mentally or physically disabled, literacy programs, and the like. In accordance with conservative principles, the program would be voluntary. No one would be drafted. But government would wield large carrots and sticks to herd young people into the program. Those who served would receive immunity for the first $10,000 they owed to the Internal Revenue Service, and only they would be eligible for federally insured college loans. A uniform federal program would be administered by a new agency—the National Service Franchise Administration ("every conceivable Grand New National Idea ought not to be discarded out of hand," Buckley argued).[14] The states, however, would decide what types of work and organizations qualified for service. Buckley would also encourage states to impose auxiliary sanctions on those who failed to serve—perhaps even denying high school diplomas to them (which, as a practical matter, would come close to making the program mandatory).[15]

Buckley argued for the program on Burkean grounds, even citing Robert Nisbet about claims the community can rightfully make on the individual.[16] The program, for Buckley, had two objectives. The first was to provide manpower for worthy community services that could not afford to purchase it in the marketplace. The program, he acknowledged, "would be injecting into the marketplace an artificial enhancement of supply, intending to meet a demand, which, in orthodox economic terms [cannot] generate its own supply by reaching out and paying for it."[17] In other words, the free market does not operate perfectly. One of its deficiencies is that it does not sufficiently value some services needed by the community, and it was appropriate that government make adjustments. The second objective—which Buckley considered the more important—was to foster a sense of satisfaction in those who provide national service.[18] Buckley recognized that those who give are often more profoundly affected than those who receive. By providing service to others, participants would develop a greater appreciation for and sense of connection to the community at large. Both those who gave and those who received would experience gratitude—especially the givers.

This is hardly a proposal that the younger Buckley is likely to have made. He included an entire chapter defending national service from anticipated libertarian arguments—arguments he himself may have made decades earlier. This migration (some might say growth) of Buckley's personal ideological views is interesting, but by this time it was not of great importance to the conservative movement. Buckley was like a man who built a ship, recruited a crew, charted a course, and set sail for a particular destination. He persuaded others not to follow him per se but to join him in sailing for the same destination. That was the right destination; hence, the course was the correct course. Over time, Buckley's ship became one among a great flotilla. In the early years, Buckley's was the lead ship. Others recognized his special skills with sextant and map. If he thought a course correction was necessary, they paid attention. But other captains and navigators developed confidence in their own skills. Over time Buckley's voice became merely one among many.

At times, Buckley may have been wistful about his diminished influence. But at bottom, that is what he wanted. As Buckley understood—and this cannot be overemphasized—a genuine political movement transcends any single leader. Buckley's career was not about his own glorification. As Garry Wills put it, even while he and Buckley were estranged, Buckley was "a man truly serving something outside himself."[19] Buckley's great accomplishment was building something that had a life beyond his own remarkable presence. Although, by 1968, Buckley was only forty-three years old and less than halfway through his career, his goal had largely been accomplished. Fellow conservatives had come to consider what he had to say important but not inviolable. If in 1968 William F. Buckley

Jr. had been struck down by a bolt of lightning, the conservative movement would have continued unabated and on the same trajectory.

Although by 1968, conservatism had been redefined, it had not yet come to political power on the national level. In that year of turmoil, the leading candidates for the two major party presidential nominations were former vice president Richard M. Nixon and sitting vice president Hubert H. Humphrey. Despite rage against the war, Humphrey was not going to have much difficulty defeating Eugene McCarthy for the nomination. Nixon's situation was dicier. He faced challenges from both the left and right of the party—from Nelson A. Rockefeller and Ronald Reagan, governors of the nation's two largest states.

Ronald Reagan, of course, was a movement conservative. Indeed, his political conversion from New Deal Democrat had in large part been brought about by reading *National Review* on long train rides while he was working for General Electric. Although Nixon had come to the national stage by pursuing Alger Hiss, Nixon was a centrist and a pragmatist. With the notable exception of Whittaker Chambers, movement conservatives had little love for Nixon, and Nixon had little love for them. In the 1960 general election, *National Review* declined to endorse Nixon over Kennedy, with the explanation that "*National Review* was not founded to make practical politics. Our job is to think and write."[20] When Buckley ran for mayor of New York City, Nixon twice told reporters that Buckleyites were a greater threat to the Republican Party than Birchers.[21] Nevertheless, as soon as Reagan started to be mentioned as a possible presidential rival, Nixon invited Buckley, Bill Rusher, and several other movement conservatives to his Fifth Avenue apartment, where he offered them South African brandy (a sly touch, Bill Rusher believed, to suggest his affinity for the apartheid nation), served them lunch, and treated them to a three-hour analysis about the state of the world and the nation. Buckley and Rusher were impressed by the performance but had reservations about Nixon's ideology. Buckley, however, believed that conservatives had no choice but to support Nixon. He told Nixon that nominating a former actor who had just been elected governor of California was "preposterous" and "loony." In his column, Buckley publicly discounted Reagan as a serious challenger and suggested that because Nelson Rockefeller could conceivably win the nomination, conservatives should support Nixon.[22] It took 667 delegate votes to secure the nomination. Nixon narrowly won the first ballot with 692 votes; Rockefeller received 277 and Reagan 182. In the closing days of the general campaign—despite the strong antipathy that Rusher and other members of the *National Review* family felt toward Nixon—the magazine endorsed Nixon at Buckley and Burnham's urgings.

The year 1968 was also a time of party realignment. The Southern wing of the Democratic Party, furious at Johnson for the civil rights acts, was ready to bolt. Alabama governor George C. Wallace seized the opportunity to launch a third-party campaign. He was not a credible national candidate. He was patently racist, and he selected as his running mate General Curtis LeMay, the man who firebombed Tokyo during World War II and wanted to use nuclear weapons against Cuba and Vietnam. Taking advantage of a backlash against school desegregation efforts, Wallace captured 13.5 percent of the national popular vote. He won five states, all in the Deep South, and by his candidacy delayed the South's complete defection to the Republican Party. Nixon beat Humphrey by a whisker in the popular vote; less than 1 percent separated them. Nixon's electoral victory was more decisive, however. He carried nearly all of the Midwest, the plains states, and the West, though Humphrey carried Texas.

The magazine's fears that Nixon was more liberal than conservative were fully realized in the Nixon presidency. Bill Rusher titles the chapter of his memoirs about *National Review*'s decision not to support Reagan for the Republican nomination "The Blunder of 1968." Nixon ultimately withdrew from Vietnam, promoted détente, entered into arms control agreements with the Soviet Union, recognized Red China, expelled Nationalist China from the UN, endorsed a more liberal welfare system, established the Environmental Protection Agency and the Occupational Safety and Health Administration, jettisoned the gold standard, and instituted wage and price controls—a policy James Burnham called "fascistic." Throughout his presidency, Nixon sought to soften conservative criticism of his ideological apostasies by deploying Henry Kissinger, originally his national security adviser and later his secretary of state, and Patrick Buchanan, then an aide and speechwriter, as his ambassadors to Buckley and Burnham, with some limited success.[23]

The modern conservative movement finally reached the political mountaintop with Ronald Reagan's election as president in 1980. As John O'Sullivan put it, "Reagan's victory was the triumph of Bill Buckley's philosophy and a catastrophic defeat for the suffocating liberalism that had dominated America in 1951. The rest was details."[24]

Without Buckley and *National Review*, Reagan's election would not have been possible. Without the role that Buckley and *National Review* played in his ideological conversion, Reagan may not have become a conservative. Buckley and *National Review* also provided much of the material for Reagan's basic message. (Years later, at *National Review*'s twenty-fifth annual dinner, Buckley tried to joke about this. With Reagan in the White House, said Buckley, he [Buckley] would henceforth list his occupation as ventriloquist.[25] Not everyone thought this funny.) Buckley and *National Review*'s greatest contribution to Reagan's election may have been making conservatism respectable. That allowed voters who were not themselves conservative to feel comfortable considering a conservative candidate. After all, while some Americans voted for Reagan because he was a conservative, others voted for him because he was Ronald Reagan. They liked him, they trusted him, and at least they did not consider his political philosophy disqualifying. Reagan alluded to this important change in conservatism's respectability at *National Review*'s thirtieth anniversary dinner, when he said, "The man standing before you was a Democrat when he picked up his first issue [of *National Review*] in a plain brown wrapper; and even now, as an occupant of public housing, he awaits as anxiously as ever for his biweekly edition—without the wrapper."[26]

Indeed, Reagan's ascendancy helped turn on ideological respectability. The word *liberal* acquired a pejorative tinge. Politicians on the left avoided "the L word." For reasons not entirely clear, they often preferred the term *progressive*.

This brings us to the final question. William F. Buckley Jr. and *National Review* were good for the conservative movement, but was the conservatism they fashioned good for America? Buckley and his colleagues fashioned an ideology that was brilliantly suited for political growth, but was it well suited for governance?

These are, of course, complicated questions, and a full exegesis of how conservative ideology has been translated into matters of policy, and with what consequences, is beyond the scope of this book. Nevertheless, some observations are in order.

Ronald Reagan is credited with three main achievements. First, he restored national pride and good feeling. The liberal tendency is to focus on problems, and that can become wearing. Moreover, as the example of the Lindsay administration showed, liberals often raised hopes only to dash them. During the three administrations prior to Reagan's, the nation lost a war, had a president leave office in disgrace, and was humiliated by a long hostage crisis. Reagan made the nation feel good about itself. Although Reagan's sunny disposition and acting skills may have been the biggest reasons he was able to achieve this, his message of conservative patriotism was also an important ingredient.

Second, Reagan changed the debate about government and public policy. Reagan's most famous phrase—repeated time and again with variations—was: "Government is not the solution to our problems. Government is the problem." This message was classic Buckley-styled conservatism. As president, Reagan did not, in fact, reduce either the size or expenditures of the federal government.[27] Nevertheless, he succeeded in bringing about a sea change in how Americans thought about their government. He persuaded much of the nation that government was too often looked to as the solution to problems, and that government was often asked to do too much. Even Democrat president Bill Clinton felt compelled to declare that the nation should not expect to solve its problems "through big government." "The era of big government is over," he declared.[28] After Reagan, Americans were not only more skeptical about government programs; they were skeptical about government itself. Although Reagan said nothing of the kind expressly, he persuaded many Americans that government was not only often inefficient or unduly burdensome—especially in the regulation of business—but that government was somehow untrustworthy. And of course, many of the people Reagan brought into his administration shared that view. We shall return to this issue shortly.

Third, Reagan is often credited with helping bring about the collapse of the Soviet Union and the end of the Cold War. Everyone remembers Reagan calling the Soviet Union "the evil empire." And everyone remembers Reagan's stirring speech of June 12, 1987, when he stood before Brandenburg Gate in Berlin and called out, "General Secretary Gorbachev, if you seek peace, if you seek prosperity for the Soviet Union and Eastern Europe, if you seek liberalization: Come here to this gate! Mr. Gorbachev, open this gate! Mr. Gorbachev, Mr. Gorbachev, tear down this wall!" Reagan's speechwriters—Tony Dolan and Peter Robinson—were, in fact, protégés of William F. Buckley Jr. and Jeffrey Hart, a Dartmouth College professor who also served as an editor of *National Review*.[29] They had both been hired on Buckley's recommendation, and they produced a speech that made their mentors proud.

Nevertheless, it must be said that Reagan's contributions to bringing about the demise of the Soviet Union and the end of the Cold War were made just as much in spite of modern conservatism as because of it. Movement conservatives like to argue that Reagan caused the collapse of the Soviet Union by stimulating an expensive arms race that drove the Soviet Union into bankruptcy. But, ironically, conservatives tend to overlook the inherent weaknesses of the communist system that over a period of decades produced a fatally weak economy. As former neoconservative Francis Fukuyama puts it, "Conservatives of all stripes tend to put too much emphasis on the American military buildup as the cause of the USSR's collapse, when political and economic factors were at least as important."[30] Reagan understood the critical weaknesses of the Soviet economy, and while it gave him an optimistic long-term view, it also made him worry that as its system began to convulse, the Soviet Union might become dangerously aggressive.[31] During his second term, this concern spurred him to work even more ardently to reduce tensions. Conservatives were not cheering on Reagan during these efforts; they were booing him. When, at the Moscow summit in May 1988, Reagan said that he thought the Soviet Union was no longer an evil empire, conservatives were outraged. Buckley denounced Reagan's statement as Orwellian. "Big Brother," Buckley wrote, "decides to change a historical or present fact, and evidence inconvenient to the new thesis is simply made to disappear."[32]

The Cold War ended not merely because of the economic collapse of the Soviet Union, but also because of the reforms instituted by Soviet premier Mikhail Gorbachev. Historians have convincingly demonstrated that Reagan's personal relationship with Gorbachev—accompanied by reduced tensions between the superpowers—gave the Soviet premier the room he needed to institute those reforms. However, movement conservatives opposed Reagan's four summit meetings with Gorbachev, opposed the accord Reagan reached with Gorbachev providing for UN-sponsored peace talks between Afghanistan and Pakistan that made it possible for the Soviets to pull out of Afghanistan, and opposed Reagan's arms control negotiations with Gorbachev. And they disputed Reagan when he claimed that Gorbachev was different from other Soviet leaders and was negotiating in good faith and not as part of a plot to acquire strategic advantage and achieve world domination. At the time, conservatives accused Reagan of betraying the cause of anticommunism.

Conservatives had a pitched battle with Reagan over the Intermediate-Range Nuclear Forces Treaty, for example. On September 18, 1986, Reagan's secretary of state, George Shultz, and Soviet foreign minister Eduard Shevardnadze announced that they had agreed in principle to an INF treaty. The treaty called for the elimination of shorter-range and intermediate-range Soviet nuclear missiles based in East Germany and Czechoslovakia and similar American nuclear missiles in West Germany. Over three years, 859 U.S. nuclear missiles and 1,836 Soviet missiles were to be destroyed. It was a historic agreement. Although it eliminated only a tiny fraction of each side's total nuclear arsenals, the INF treaty was the first superpower agreement to destroy nuclear weapons, and the first agreement requiring on-site monitoring of compliance.[33] Hard-line conservatives were outraged. They believed the Soviets could never be trusted; Soviets cheated or found loopholes in treaties, they argued. As Buckley rather euphemistically put it years later, "President Reagan seemed to me and to many conservatives to come perilously close to trusting the Soviet Union."[34] Buckley and *National Review* campaigned passionately against Senate ratification. Buckley wrote a number of personal letters to Reagan, arguing against the treaty. In one letter, Buckley apologized for the harsh tone of a recent *National Review* article about INF, and assured Reagan that he would not publish anything questioning the president's motives.[35] Reagan asked Buckley to come to the White House for a chat, but failed to sway him. In an Oval Office interview with television network news anchors on December 3, Reagan struck back. Some conservatives, said the president, "were ignorant of the advances that had been made in verification," and others refused to accede to the possibility of the superpowers ever reaching any understanding and "in their deepest thoughts have accepted that war is inevitable and that there must come to be a war between the superpowers."[36]

The right-wing coalition continued its battle against ratification. They mailed three hundred thousand letters opposing the treaty to grassroots supporters; they distributed five thousand cassette tapes of NATO supreme commander general Bernard Rogers denouncing the treaty; they ran full-page ads in conservative newspapers that compared Reagan to Neville Chamberlain, the British prime minister who infamously declared he had guaranteed "peace in our time" by signing an accord with Hitler.[37] *National Review* devoted much of its May 22 issue—published just before the Senate debate—to the treaty. The cover read REAGAN'S SUICIDE PACT. Archconservative senator Jesse Helms (R-NC) led a filibuster against the treaty. In the end, the president won decisively. On May 27, the Senate ratified the treaty by a vote of 93–5.

In other ways, Reagan did not govern as a pure movement conservative. In eight years, for example, he never once submitted a balanced budget proposal to Congress. His influential aide, Richard Darman, said that was because "the hard-core Reagan revolutionaries turned out to be little match for the dominant forces of moderation in the American political system."[38] But Reagan's premier biographer, Lou Cannon, observes, "If so, this is partly because Reagan's penchant for compromise often led him to side with the moderating forces."[39] Reagan himself thought he was not as hard right as others thought. In a private diary entry, he noted that the press was trying to portray him as someone intent on reversing the New Deal. "I remind them," he wrote, "I voted for FDR 4 times. I'm trying to undo the 'Great Society.'"[40] (Burkean conservative columnist George F. Will saw things much the same way. "Americans are conservative," Will wrote. "What they want to conserve is the New Deal.") Reagan also had a pragmatic streak, which was on display, for example, when—after a suicide bomber killed 241 marines and wounded more than a hundred more in Beirut—he decided to withdraw all U.S. Marines from Lebanon. Movement conservatives also urged Reagan to send American troops into Nicaragua and Panama, but Reagan resisted doing so.[41]

Modern conservatism came more fully to power with the administration of George W. Bush. Commentators have argued that politically Bush was Reagan's disciple.[42] That is, as president he tried to emulate not his father, but Reagan, whom he considered the quintessential conservative president. But, in fact, Bush was more faithful to the modern conservatism—that is, the philosophy fashioned by William F. Buckley Jr. and *National Review* during the seminal period—than he was to Reagan. Where Bush departed from Reagan, Reagan had departed from conservative orthodoxy.

In the eyes of many Americans, Bush left office in disgrace. According to the final CBS News-*New York Times* poll of his presidency, 73 percent of Americans disapproved of the job George W. Bush did as president. Twenty-two percent approved of the job he had done, the lowest rating in history. Some other polls had him slightly higher—just ahead of Richard M. Nixon, who left under threat of impeachment. The judgment of presidential historians is even worse. According to a 2009 survey, they rank George W. Bush the seventh-worst president in history, far below any other modern president, even Nixon.[43] (They rank Ronald Reagan the tenth-best president in history.) *National Review* disagreed. In an editorial at the end of his presidency, the magazine placed Bush "in the middle ranks of American presidents."[44] It conceded that history's verdict about Iraq depended on whether it became a stable country. If that came to pass, then Bush would "deserve major credit for a major strategic advance."

It is, of course, possible that the judgments of the public and historians will change. Historians considered Truman a disaster when he left office but now rank him the fifth-best president in history, a fact that George W. Bush and his admirers like to cite.[45] Nevertheless, the first draft of history has condemned Bush as a failure.

In nearly all circumstances, moreover, George W. Bush's failures stem from his administration's purist devotion to conservative ideology. His most consequential decision was to invade Iraq. Whether or not he did so because he genuinely believed Saddam Hussein possessed weapons of mass destruction we need not address here. What is important for our purposes is that his administration did so without adequately analyzing the ramifications of the invasion. Before the invasion, conservatives argued that Iraq was well suited for democracy because it had an educated population and a substantial middle class, and that it would serve an important geopolitical purpose to create a democratic Arab country in the heart of the Middle East. This goal was one of the reasons, if not the principal reason, that the Bush administration wanted to invade Iraq. It was, moreover, a neoconservative goal. In 2000, William Kristol and Robert Kagan, two pillars of neoconservatism, wrote that they believed "the idea of America using power to promote changes in nations ruled by dictators [was] entirely realistic."[46]

Yet there had never been democracy in Iraq or anywhere else in the Arab world. It's a neoconservative assumption that people the world over are like us and despite their different histories and cultures want to live the way we do. "I think democracy is a universal idea. And I think letting people rule themselves happens to be something that serves Americans and America's interests," declared Paul Wolfowitz, Bush's neoconservative deputy secretary of defense.[47] Similar beliefs undergirded both Burnham's rollback strategy and our assumptions in Vietnam.

William F. Buckley Jr. originally supported Bush's 2003 invasion of Iraq, though not on the neoconservative grounds of bringing democracy to that nation. The issue, for Buckley, was whether the invasion was necessary for self-defense. Vice President Cheney had said that there was "no doubt that Saddam Hussein now has weapons of mass destruction [and] that he is amassing them to use them against our friends, against our allies, and against us." Buckley noted that Cheney had been vague about a nuclear program. The vice president had said that Iraq was continuing "to pursue" a nuclear program, but he did not say how long it would be before Iraq had nuclear weapons. Buckley thought it reasonable to take Cheney at his word that a preemptive strike was essential. "[I]t is inconceivable that he should be speaking in the high pitch of resolution unless he has evidence on which he frames his analysis," Buckley wrote in his syndicated column.[48] When, after the invasion, no WMDs were found, some called Bush and Cheney liars. Buckley called those charges "hysterical."[49] "Those who reasonably doubt that George Bush and Dick Cheney would consciously lie to Congress and the American people and [British prime minister] Tony Blair and, for that matter, the entire world are, again, reasonably, asked to look for other explanations." More than two years later, Buckley continued to believe that Bush and Cheney's WMD claims must have resulted "from ignoble failures of the intelligence community."[50] As more information emerged, Buckley decided the culprit was George Tenet, who had been director of central intelligence during the invasion. Tenet's own statements in a television interview revealed that the CIA had been "run by a man who cannot think straight, advising the national security advisor, who went on to make false allegations, and the vice president, who made more false allegations, and the president, who took ill-considered actions."[51]

By March 2006, Buckley had concluded there was "no doubt the American objective in Iraq has failed."[52] But should America withdraw? On this question, Buckley was torn. His thinking was haunted by Vietnam, especially by the slaughter of Vietnamese who had cooperated with the United States after it left Saigon.[53] He also equated withdrawal with "capitulation," an act of humiliation that would weaken America in the eyes of other nations.[54] On the other hand, he wrote, "A point is reached when tenacity conveys not steadfastness of purpose but misapplication of pride."[55] When Buckley died, the troop surge was under way with results then unknown.

It will be many years before we find out whether Iraq is able to build a viable democracy, but regardless of the final outcome, the fact remains that the Bush administration's expectation that American soldiers would be warmly welcomed and that democracy would spring up relatively easily was a pipe dream. So patently flawed was this neoconservative adventure that one of the most prominent neoconservative thinkers, Francis Fukuyama, declared that he no longer supported that ideology.[56] Burkeans—who are acutely aware that people are the products of their different histories and cultures, who understand the importance of traditions and institutions, and who worry about unintended consequences— would not have made these choices.

A series of calamities occurred in the governmental bureaucracies. The best known is the failure of the Federal Emergency Management Administration to deal capably with the devastation caused by Hurricane Katrina in 2005. FEMA's ineptitude was caused, in part, by President Bush's choice of director for the agency—a man named Michael D. Brown, whose last job before joining FEMA was commissioner of the International Arabian Horse Association and who had no meaningful relevant experience. An ideology that has disdain for government cares little who heads a federal agency such as FEMA. Meanwhile, abuses were ongoing at the Department of Justice, where then-thirty-two-year-old Monica M. Goodling held the influential position of liaison to the White House. Goodling graduated from Regent University

School of Law—an institution founded by evangelist Pat Robertson that boasts that it recognizes "the critical role the Christian faith should play in our legal system"—in a class in which only 40 percent passed the bar exam.[57] Her principal and perhaps only credential for the important position she held was her ideology. The Department of Justice had a long tradition of hiring the most talented law school graduates, but Goodling used her position to substitute ideology for professional competence. She considered a commitment to religious conservatism especially important and quizzed job applicants about their views about abortion and same-sex marriage. When investigations about these practices were undertaken, Goodling refused to cooperate and invoked her Fifth Amendment rights before Congress. She was ultimately disbarred. There will from time to time be scandals about the improper politicization of governmental positions, but what was different in the Bush administration was both how sweeping those problems were and, in Goodling's case, how what mattered was not political loyalty as much as ideological loyalty. She was not doing what was politically expedient. She was, in her view, doing God's work.

One may dismiss the likes of Michael Brown and Monica Goodling to poor management, that is, to poor choices by the people who selected them. But to put these choices down solely to poor decision making, unconnected to ideological beliefs, would miss a central point. When it comes to governance, there is an inherent weakness in an ideology that has little regard for government, and even being disdainful of government. People steeped in such ideology can hardly care who heads FEMA or what lawyers work in the Department of Justice. The nation is best served by a government staffed by individuals who consider their positions important to the nation, and therefore a sacred public trust. Of course, Ronald Reagan and George W. Bush thought of the presidency in those terms, and presumably their cabinet secretaries had the same regard for their positions. But that is hardly enough. It is not reasonable to expect government to work well when it is staffed at lower levels by people with contempt for government. Why should they be expected to fill positions on the basis of competence and dedication to the mission of the department or agency that they serve? Why should we not expect them to instead only take into account considerations of politics and ideology?

And, of course, the Bush administration ended with a calamity in the domestic economy. As Bush left office, America was plunging into the worst recession in its history and was on the verge of a full-scale economic depression. This was caused, in significant part, by the deregulation of investment banks and other financial institutions, which permitted subprime lending in the housing mortgage market. The nation's largest financial institutions held enormous quantities of bad debt, or toxic assets as they were called. As shocks cascaded throughout the financial system, the federal government had to take unprecedented actions—including bailing out some of the nation's largest corporations and financial institutions—to prevent a collapse of the entire financial system. Not all of the deregulation occurred on George W. Bush's watch. The repeal of the Glass-Steagall Act, which was enacted in 1933 to prevent risky speculation by savings banks insured by the federal government, occurred during the closing days of the Clinton administration. Nevertheless, the deregulation was driven by libertarian philosophy, especially the ideas that regulation causes more problems than it solves and that the free market works best unimpeded by government rules and oversight.

It was enough to worry a thoughtful and deeply committed libertarian. On October 23, 2008, Alan Greenspan—chairman of the Federal Reserve from 1987 to 2006, and the man his mentor, Ayn Rand, called the Undertaker—testified about the financial crisis before Congress. During those hearings, he had the following exchange with Congressman Henry Waxman, chair of the House Committee on Oversight and Government Reform:

WAXMAN: Do you feel that your ideology pushed you to make decisions that you wish you had not made?

GREENSPAN: Well, remember that what an ideology is, is a conceptual framework with the way people deal with reality. Everyone has one. You have to—to exist, you need an ideology. The question is whether it is accurate or not. And what I'm saying to you is, yes, I've found a flaw. I don't know how significant or permanent it is. But I've been very distressed by that fact.

. . .

WAXMAN: You found a flaw?

GREENSPAN: I found a flaw in the model that I perceived is the critical functioning structure that defines how the world works, so to speak.

WAXMAN: In other words, you found that your view of the world, your ideology, was not right, it was not working.

GREENSPAN: Precisely. That's precisely the reason I was shocked, because I was going for more than 40 years with very considerable evidence that it was working exceptionally well.[58]

William F. Buckley Jr. never heard this exchange. He had died on February 27, 2008, at age eighty-two, in his garage study at Wallack's Point in Stamford, Connecticut. He was alone at the time. His wife, Patricia, had passed away ten months earlier. Buckley's son, Christopher, thought his father might have been working on his syndicated column when he died.[59] That seemed fitting. Buckley had written fifty-six hundred columns during his lifetime. They alone total about 3.75 million words, enough to fill twenty-eight volumes of the size of this book. In addition, Buckley had written countless other articles and fifty-six books (six of which were collections of columns and magazine articles).[60] For a while, it looked like even death would not slow him down: Two of his books, reminiscences of his relationships with Barry Goldwater and Ronald Reagan, were published posthumously.

Buckley lived a satisfying life. He had a long and happy marriage. He was the proud father of a man who became a fine writer in his own right, and whose satiric novels bumped his own books off bestseller lists. He had loving siblings. He sailed in his own boat twice across the Atlantic Ocean, once across the Pacific, and wrote books about all three adventures. He was beloved by countless people who knew him personally—and by millions who did not.[61] A couple of years before his death, Buckley's sister Priscilla had made arrangements for Buckley and Garry Wills to dine together at Buckley's favorite restaurant in New York City, making it possible for the two friends to reconcile.[62]

Several years earlier, Buckley had talked with Christopher about his wishes for his memorial service. "If I'm still famous, try to convince the Cardinal to do the service at St. Patrick's. If I'm not, just tuck me away in Stamford," Buckley told his son. Christopher told this story in his remarks to the twenty-two hundred mourners packing St. Patrick's Cathedral in New York City. "Well, Pup," he remarked, "I guess you're still famous."[63] Buckley, in fact, will not only long be famous but will also remain a hero to millions of Americans who read his writings, watched his television shows, and listened to his speeches. He made an indelible imprint on the nation.

Acknowledgments

I am enormously grateful to Peter Ginna and Pete Beatty, two great editors at Bloomsbury Press, who read the manuscript with great care and made copious suggestions—large and small—that greatly improved the final product. Many thanks as well to Paula Cooper for meticulous copyediting.

I am appreciative to Priscilla and James Buckley, as well as to Jeffrey Hart, for granting me lengthy interviews and allowing me to pester them with follow-up e-mails. They did this knowing that I am a liberal, and that on many matters I was likely be critical of their brother, or in Jeff Hart's case, dear colleague and friend. They understood, of course, that the events in which they participated are too historically important to be left exclusively to analyses by the like-minded, but I was deeply moved by their generosity and good will. There is sure to be much in this book with which they disagree. I hope that I have not disappointed them too much. In the same vein, I am grateful to William F. Buckley Jr. for granting me access to papers at Yale University.

I am grateful to Dean David A. Logan and the Roger Williams University School of Law for supporting their law professor in this lawless project, with both encouragement and a semester sabbatical. I could not have accomplished this project without able research assistance from Michelle Fleming, Daniel Morton-Bentley, and Amy Goins, all of whom are now, or soon will be, alumni of the Roger Williams law school. Among other things, they toiled for many hours at the Roger Williams main library over reels of microfilm containing the early years of *National Review*. They became so proficient at spinning through the reels to find particular articles, and aligning everything just so before hitting the photocopy button, that university librarians pressed them into service to teach those skills to others—something they had not signed on for when they had agreed to be my research assistants. I hope they found our discussions, in which they served as sounding boards for my impressions and ideas as we worked through material together, a little less tedious.

Last but not least, many thanks to my agent, John W. Wright, for his wise counsel and advice. Without him, this book would not exist.

Notes

"WFB" refers to William F. Buckley Jr. "WFBP, Yale" refers to the William F. Buckley Jr. papers at Sterling Memorial Library of Yale University.

Preface

1. Clinton Rossiter, *Conservatism in America: The Thankless Persuasion* 259 (2d ed. 1962) quoting Griswold.

Introduction

1. Letter from WFB to H. L. Hunt, April 21, 1955 (WFBP, Yale).
2. Rick Perlstein, *Before the Storm: Barry Goldwater and the Unmaking of the American Consensus* 49–53, 61–63 (2001); William A. Rusher, *The Rise of the Right*, chpts. 4–5 (1984).
3. Lou Cannon, *President Reagan: The Role of a Lifetime* 67–68 (1991). See also Perlstein, supra note 2, at 499–504.
4. Thomas W. Evans, *The Education of Ronald Reagan: The General Electric Years and the Untold Story of His Conversion to Conservatism* (2006); Linda Bridges and John R. Coyne Jr., *Strictly Right: William F. Buckley Jr. and the American Conservative Movement* 233–34 (2007).
5. George H. Nash, *The Conservative Intellectual Moment in America Since 1945* 140 (1998 ed.). First published in 1996. Page references are to the 1998 edition.
6. Lionel Trilling, *The Liberal Imagination* ix (1950).
7. Herbert McClosky, "Conservatism and Personality," 52 *American Political Science Review* 27 (1952).
8. Letter from WFB to William Loeb, March 5, 1962 (WFBP, Yale).
9. Letter from WFB to Dr. A. G. Blasey, June 5, 1959 (WFBP, Yale).
10. Letter from William Loeb to William F. Buckley Sr., March 20, 1958 (WFBP, Yale).

11. Letter from WFB to William Loeb, March 24, 1958 (WFBP, Yale).
12. Letter from James J. Kilpatrick to WFB, April 17, 1962 (WFBP, Yale).
13. Letter from WFB to William Loeb, March 8, 1961 (WFBP, Yale).
14. Interview with Priscilla Buckley, Sept. 10, 2008; letter from WFB to William Schulz, Nov. 17, 1959 (stating "I ought to tell you frankly that I am carrying a terrible load for *National Review* where I work without compensation, and can't afford to go out of town to speak without exacting a fee") (WFBP, Yale).
15. Bridges and Coyne, supra note 4, at 173.
16. Letter from WFB to Russell Kirk, Sept. 14, 1955 (assuring Kirk that "if Chodorov and Meyer are unreasonable in their dealings with NR, they will simply be banished") (WFBP, Yale).
17. Scott McLemee, "A Conservative of the Old School," *Chronicle of Higher Education*, May 7, 2004, A18. For the publisher's story behind the publication of *The Conservative Mind*, see Henry Regnery, "The Making of The Conservative Mind," in Russell Kirk, *The Conservative Mind from Burke to Eliot* (7th rev. ed. 2001).
18. Frank S. Meyer, "Why Freedom," *National Review*, Sept. 25, 1962, at 223, reprinted in Frank S. Meyer, *In Defense of Freedom and Related Essays* 155 (1996). Meyer conceded that it is essential to man's being to seek virtue, and that a "double allegiance to virtue and to freedom is the overall consensus of contemporary American conservatism." Meyer, *In Defense of Freedom and Related Essays*, at 156. But that is about as far as he went in accommodating traditional conservatism—or at least what he took to be the principles of traditional conservatism, for it is unlikely that Burke and traditional conservatives would accept Meyer's description of their beliefs.

Meyer maintained that "virtue is only virtue when freely chosen." Ibid. at 157. He believed that traditional conservatism sought to impress individuals into conforming to visions of virtue mandated by the state, by institutions, or by traditions. He thought traditional conservatism confused "the temporal with the transcendent," that is, that it confused the authority of God or the authority of truth with the authoritarianism of men and institutions who considered it their province to proclaim what the transcendent truths are—and thereby suppressed freedom. Ibid. at 200. See also Frank S. Meyer, "The Roots of Libertarian Conservatism," *National Review*, April 6, 1957, at 331. Meyer rejected Edmund Burke root and branch. He argued that it was "impossible to derive a firm political position" from Burke and that it was blindness to take Burke as a mentor. Meyer, *In Defense of Freedom and Related Essays*, at 10. He said that Burkeanism favored a social order that was "constrained and controlled by the tyranny of habit, custom, and prescription; a philosophy so held to precedent that it is deprived of the freedom to deepen and develop human understanding; an ethos tightly swaddled in the multitudinous wrappings of code and custom." Ibid. at 131. He inveighed "against the concept of community as a decisive concept in political and social thought." Ibid. at 133.

Many histories suggest that Meyer fashioned an elaborate system combining traditional conservatism with libertarianism. See, e.g, Kevin J. Smart, *Principles and Heresies: Frank S. Meyer and the Shaping of the American Conservative Movement* xx–xxi, 49–55 (2002). Yet Meyer spent more time excoriating traditional conservatives—especially Russell Kirk, but also Robert Nisbet and other Burkeans—than he did attempting to blend their views with libertarianism. It may be more accurate to say that Meyer attempted to blend libertarianism with what we today call religious conservatism. Meyer wrote, for example: "Conservatism assumes the existence of an objective moral order based upon ontological foundations. Whether or not individual conservatives hold theistic views—and a large majority of them do—this outlook is derived from a theistic tradition." Meyer, *In Defense of Freedom and Related Essays*, supra note 18, at 10. It might appear that here Meyer was borrowing from traditional conservatism. Yet Meyer quickly went on to warn that believing in objective standards for human conduct should not lead conservatives toward collectivist politics—and Meyer had repeatedly accused traditional conservatives of succumbing to collectivism. See, e.g., Meyer, *In Defense of Freedom and Related* Essays, at 122. And so at every turn, Meyer appeared more intent upon rejecting traditional conservatism than fusing it with other principles. An accurate description of fusionism appears in George H. Nash, *The Conservative Intellectual Movement in America Since 1945*, supra note 5, at 161–67 (1996).

19. David Boaz, *Libertarianism: A Primer* 59 (1997).
20. Edmund Burke, "Speech on Conciliation with the Colonies," in Isaac Kramnick, *The Portable Edmund Burke* 262 (Isaac Kramnick ed. 1999).
21. Meyer, *In Defense of Freedom*, supra note 18, at 99.
22. Meyer was drawing on Adam Smith, whom libertarians often praise yet only selectively follow. In his great work, *The Wealth of Nations*, Smith also said that government had three natural functions. The first two he listed—to protect its citizens from "violence and invasion" and to provide for "an administration of justice"—are the same listed by Meyer and other libertarians. However, Smith's third governmental function is anything but libertarian. Government, said Smith, has the responsibility of "erecting and maintaining those public institutions and those public works

which may be in the highest degree advantageous to a great society" but that "are of such a nature that profit could never repay the expense to any individual or small number of individuals," Robert L. Heilbroner, *The Worldly Philosophers* 68–69 (7th ed. 1999)(quoting Adam Smith).

22. Meyer, *In Defense of Freedom*, supra note 18, at 100.

23. Russell Kirk's quotations in this paragraph are drawn from W. Wesley McDonald, *Russell Kirk and the Age of Ideology* 140, 162, 178 (2004).

24. Interview with Priscilla Buckley at Great Elm, Sharon, CT, Sept. 10, 2008.

25. McDonald, supra note 23, at 153.

26. Daniel Kelly, *James Burnham and the Struggle for the World* 149–70, 212 (2002).

27. Ibid. at 153.

28. Interview with Jeffrey Hart in Hanover, NH, June 20, 2008.

29. Nash, supra note 5, at 330.

30. E.g., Kelly, *James Burnham*, supra note 26, at 370 (quoting Richard Brookhiser); H. W. Brands, *The Devil We Knew: Americans and the Cold War* 141 (1993).

31. Garry Wills, *Confessions of a Conservative* 78–79 (1979).

32. My information regarding the *Freeman* is drawn from the following sources: Nash, supra note 18, at 11, 21, 79, 133–34, 378 n. 105; John B. Judis, *William F. Buckley, Jr.: Patron Saint of Conservatives*, supra note 16, at 89, 102–04; (1988); Rusher, *The Rise of the Right* 33–35.

33. Regarding Robert A. Taft, as well as his father and grandfather, I have relied principally on James T. Patterson, *Mr. Republican: A Biography of Robert A. Taft* (1972). Other sources are used when specifically noted.

34. John Fischer, "The Editor's Easy Chair: Why Is the Conservative Voice So Hoarse?" *Harper's*, March 1956, at 16 ("dominant conservative of his time"); Clinton Rossiter, *Conservatism in America: The Thankless Persuasion* 173 (2d rev. ed. 1962) ("very model of the American conservative"). First published in 1955. Page references are to the 1962 edition.

35. James Chase, *1912: Wilson, Roosevelt, Taft & Debs—the Election That Changed the Country* 17, 33 (2004).

36. Ibid. at 221.

37. Patterson, supra note 33, at 191.

38. William Manchester, *The Glory and the Dream: A Narrative History of America 1932–1972*, at 680–81 (1973); James MacGregor Burns, *Roosevelt: The Soldier of Freedom 1940–1945*, at 216 (1970).

39. Manchester, *The Glory and the Dream*, supra note 38, at 493.

40. The description of the secret meeting at the Pentagon comes mainly from Eisenhower. Sources disagree about when the meeting occurred; some

believe it took place during a trip home after Eisenhower assumed the NATO position. Patterson, *Mr. Republican*, supra note 33, at 483–84; Stephen E. Ambrose, *Eisenhower: Soldier and President* 251–52 (1990); Tom Wicker, *Dwight D. Eisenhower* 11 (2002). Regarding Eisenhower's views about Taft's isolationism, see Fred I. Greenstein, *The Hidden-Hand Presidency: Eisenhower as Leader* 48–49 (1982); Steven Wagner, *Eisenhower Republicanism: Pursuing the Middle Way* 3–4, 116, 145 (2006).

41. Patterson, *Mr. Republican*, supra note 33, at 590; Greenstein, *The Hidden-Hand Presidency*, supra note 40, at 49.

42. Greenstein, *The Hidden-Hand Presidency*, supra note 40, at 167.

43. "Taft's conservatism contained a strong strain of pragmatism, which caused him to support intensive Federal activity in those areas that he believed not adequately served by the private enterprise system. Taft did not believe that this was inconsistent with the conservative doctrine; conservatism in his opinion was not irresponsibility," John F. Kennedy, *Profiles in Courage* 194–95 (fiftieth-anniversary ed. 2006).

CHAPTER 1: THE MAKING OF THE
MAN WHO REMADE CONSERVATISM

1. An eleventh child, Mary Ann, born in 1929, died when she was two days old.

2. John B. Judis writes, "What education did not take place in the classroom took place at the dining table, which Will presided over . . . He used the dinner hour not only to quiz his children about their work at school, but to acquaint them with his political views on the European payment of war debts or the Spanish Civil War." Judis quotes a family friend as saying, "'At table, their father made them defend their intellectual and political positions. He would catechize them, so to speak, on the various things they had learned.'" John B. Judis, *William F. Buckley, Jr.: Patron Saint of the Conservatives* 31 (1988).

3. Interviews with Priscilla Buckley and James L. Buckley at Great Elm, Sharon, CT, Sept. 10, 2008. Priscilla and James agree that there was not especially a lot of talk about politics in the household when they were children. Priscilla told me about her father's storytelling about his Mexican years, and her comments are confirmed in a chapter she wrote in a privately published book about her father, *W. F. B.—An Appreciation* (Priscilla L. Buckley and William F. Buckley Jr. eds. privately published, 1959), and by Reid Buckley, the eighth of the ten siblings, in his book, *An American Family: The Buckleys* (2008). The conclusion about the influence of these stories is mine.

4. Buckley, *An American Family*, supra note 3, at 171 (2008).

5. Claude H. Buckley, "My Brother's Early Years," in *W. F. B.—An Appreciation*, in supra note 3, at 10.

6. Because a more complete description of the Mexican Revolution would be too long a discursion from the central thesis of this book, my account is enormously simplified. I rely heavily on Frank McLynn, *Villa and Zapata: A History of the Mexican Revolution* (2000). Other sources consulted include Earl Shorris, *The Life and Times of Mexico* (2004); and Robert M. Buffington and William E. French, "The Culture of Modernity," and John Mason Hart, "The Mexican Revolution, 1910–20," both in *The Oxford History of Mexico* (Michael C. Meyer and William H. Beezley eds. 2000).

7. Hart, "The Mexican Revolution," supra note 6, at 436.

8. Buffington and French, "The Culture of Modernity," supra note 6, at 400.

9. Ibid.

10. Villa complied with Madero's wishes. The situation regarding Zapata is complicated. Although Zapata wanted to be governor of Morelos in order to push his land reform program, he nonetheless agreed to retire to private life. When a spontaneous "Zapata for governor" sprang up, however, a porfirista general invaded Morelos to arrest Zapata and destroy the Zapatistas. Zapata appealed to Madero to stop this assault, but Madero vacillated. When Madero finally ordered the suspension of offensive operations against Zapata, it did not matter: The generals, including Victoriano Huerta who was then leading the assault, misled Madero about what was happening in Morelos and continued the attack. The result was that Zapata turned against both Madero and the porfiristas. Zapata issued his Plan of Ayala, which called for expropriating land in Morelos that had been illegally acquired by haciendas and redistributing it to independent farmers.

11. Carranza's revolt against Huerta began about one year after Huerta seized power. When Huerta failed to respect his authority as governor of Coahuila, appointing military commanders as state governors instead, Carranza obtained approval for rebellion from the Coahuila legislature.

12. Nemesio Garcia Naranjo, "A Friend of Mexico," in *W. F. B.—An Appreciation*, supra note 3, at 36.

13. McLynn, supra note 6, at 290. For the prior statement about Villa supporting the American intervention at Veracruz and the comment about not being dragged into a war with a friend, see McLynn, supra note 6, at 228.

14. Hart, supra note 6, at 454.

15. Ibid. at 453; McLynn, supra note 6, at 317–19.

16. Carranza once famously said: "I never was a revolutionary, nor am I, nor will I ever be." McLynn, supra note 6, at 355.

17. The Senate Subcommittee on Mexican Affairs was chaired by Senator Albert B. Fall (R-NM), who later became secretary of the interior during the Harding administration and was convicted of corruption in the Teapot Dome scandal.

18. McLynn writes, "The Church had done well under Díaz and even under Madero, but received a rude awakening when Huerta came to power. In his anticlericalism Carranza was the continuation of Huerta by other means . . . [Carranza] wanted the Church firmly under his heel, so that it could not emerge as an ideological rival to his version of the Revolution or mobilize supporters to form a political party. However, he was no anticlerical zealot, for he knew that virulent anti-Catholicism was dangerous." McLynn, supra note 6, at 343.

19. Ibid. at 162–63, 290, and 343–44.

20. Arthur M. Schlesinger Jr., *The Politics of Hope* 117 (Princeton University Press 2008) (quoting Theodore Roosevelt). First published in 1963. Page references are to the 2008 edition.

21. Buckley, *An American Family*, supra note 3, at 162–69.

22. The dinner at Xochimilco concluded the first of two days of discussions. The second day, depicted in a famous photograph, took place two days later at the presidential palace in Mexico City. The two men never met again. This particular story was told to Reid Buckley by a family friend who claimed to have witnessed the event, but it apparently typifies several meetings between Villa and Will Buckley.

23. Priscilla L. Buckley, "The Other Mexico He Talked About," chap. 4 in *W. F. B.—An Appreciation*, supra note 3.

24. Buckley, *An American Family*, supra note 4, at 53n. †.

25. C. Wright Mills said there were only eight socially proper prep schools but sociologist E. Digby Baltzell, who is famous, among other things, for coining the term WASP, counted sixteen. C. Wright Mills, *The Power Elite* 64–65 (1959); Peter W. Cookson Jr. and Caroline Hodges Persell, *Preparing for Power: America's Elite Boarding Schools* 43 (1987)(setting forth Baltzell's list). About the upper-class view that only a small number of schools are truly acceptable, Nelson W. Aldrich Jr. famously teased, "There are fifteen prep schools in the country . . . It's a complete list, though mine. (In maintaining that there are no prep schools beyond these fifteen, I claim the right, as theater people do, to say that anything beyond Broadway is Bridgeport.) A Preppie from any other school springs like Gatsby 'from some Platonic conception of himself.'" See Cookson and Persell, *Preparing for Power*, supra, at 43 (quoting Aldrich). Every prep school mentioned in this chapter, with the exceptions of Millbrook and Portsmouth Abbey, is on both Baltzell's list of the sixteen "Most Socially Prestigious American

Boarding Schools," which he compiled in 1958, and Aldrich's list of fifteen, which he compiled in 1979.

26. Buckley, *An American Family*, supra note 3, at 143–46; Charles Lam Markmann, *The Buckleys: A Family Examined* 32–42 (1973); Douglas Reed, "Odyssey of an Oil Man" 158–59, and George S. Montgomery, Jr., "Post-Mexico: The Business History" 177, both in *W. F. B.—An Appreciation*, supra note 5.

27. Buckley, *An American Family*, supra note 4, at 88 (classifying his mother's family origins as petite bourgeoisie) and 258 (regarding her resentment from being looked down on by Sharon society).

28. E-mail from Priscilla Buckley to author, July 8, 2009.

29. See James McLachlan, *American Boarding Schools: A Historical Study* 287–98 (1970); and Cookson and Persell, *Preparing for Power*, supra note 25, at 125.

30. McLachlan, *American Boarding Schools*, supra note 29, at 32 (quoting Arthur Mann).

31. One of the more famous definitions of the so-called Eastern Establishment is Theodore H. White's seven-page description, which contains the following: "The Eastern Establishment seems to inhabit a belt that runs from Boston through Connecticut to Philadelphia and Washington. Its capital is New York, a city shrouded in a blur of symbolic words like 'Wall Street,' 'International Finance,' 'Madison Avenue,' 'Harvard,' '*The New York Times*,' 'The Bankers Club,' 'Ivy League Prep Schools,' all of which seem more sinister and suspect the farther one withdraws west or south . . . It is by no means a closed community; but raw money cannot buy entrance." Theodore H. White, *The Making of the President 1964* 62–69 (1965).

32. Buckley, *An American Family*, supra note 3, at 229.

33. Ibid. at 387.

34. See, e.g., Judis, *William F. Buckley, Jr.*, supra note 2, at 30; Linda Bridges and John R. Coyne Jr., *Strictly Right: William F. Buckley Jr. and the American Conservative Movement* 9–10 (2007); Charles Lam Markmann, *The Buckleys: A Family Examined* 23 (1973);

35. Interview with Priscilla Buckley, supra note 3.

36. Buckley, *An American Family*, supra note 4, at 83.

37. Ibid. at 8.

38. See, e.g., Judis, *William F. Buckley, Jr.*, supra note 2, at 27n.*

39. See Cookson and Persell, *Preparing for Power*, supra note 25, at 52 (describing Portsmouth Abbey as "prestigious") and 40 (classifying it as "within the elite tradition").

40. Judis, *William F. Buckley, Jr.*, supra note 2, at 44 (reporting that Nock's *Memoirs* became Buckley's favorite book).

41. Albert Jay Nock, *Memoirs of a Superfluous Man* 157 (1943). First published

in 1943. Page references are to the 2007 edition published by the Ludwig von Mises Institute. Nock also writes: "As far as the individual was concerned, all State systems seemed to tend about equally towards the same end of State-slavery." Ibid. at 129.

42. Ibid. at 175–76 (original emphasis).

43. Ibid. at 128 and 211.

44. Ibid. at 129–30.

45. Ibid. at 145. Regarding economism, see also ibid. at 111–13, 117–19, 147, and 175–76.

46. Ibid. at 102–04 (regarding the history of American imperialism).

47. Ibid. at 38–39, 48–49, and 250–51.

48. William F. Buckley Jr., *Miles Gone By: A Literary Autobiography* 403 (2004).

49. Judis, *William F. Buckley, Jr.*, supra note 2, at 50 (quoting Bill's letter).

50. Yale College—Scholarship Record for WFB (WFBP, Yale).

51. See, e.g., Bridges and Coyne, *Strictly Right*, supra note 34, at 17 (stating that WFB majored in economics).

52. Judis, *William F. Buckley, Jr.*, supra note 2, at 58 (quoting Coffin).

53. William F. Buckley Jr., God and Man at Yale 14–15 (2001 ed.). First published in 1951. Page references are to the fiftieth-anniversary edition.

54. Buckley was wrong on the facts. The ACLU never banned anyone from membership. Charles Lam Markmann suggests that Buckley may have been confusing this with an ACLU policy barring adherents of any totalitarian doctrine from holding office or being employed by the organization. Markmann, *The Buckleys*, supra note 34, at 81.

55. Bridges and Coyne, *Strictly Right*, supra note 34, at 23.

Chapter 2: Choosing the Path

1. For the Korean conflict and historical background of the times, I rely heavily on James T. Patterson, *Grand Expectations: The United States, 1945–1974* (1996).

2. David Caute, *The Great Fear: The Anti-Communist Purge Under Truman and Eisenhower* 38 (1978).

3. *W. F. B.—An Appreciation* 247 (Priscilla L. Buckley and William F. Buckley Jr. eds., privately published, 1959). Regarding Bill's decision about whether to pursue graduate study, see also John B. Judis, *William F. Buckley, Jr.: Patron Saint of the Conservatives* 79 and 103 (1988).

4. Judis, *William F. Buckley, Jr.*, supra note 3, at 79 (quoting John Kenneth Galbraith, who was present during the conversation).

5. Ibid. at 103; Linda Bridges and John R. Coyne, Jr., *Strictly Right: William F. Buckley Jr. and the American Conservative Movement* 24 (2007).

6. David H. Bennett, *The Party of Fear: From Nativist Movements to the New Right in American History* 293 et seq. (1988).

7. Eisenhower believed that he would have only given McCarthy more publicity and stature by taking him on. "I really believe that nothing will be so effective in combating this particular kind of trouble-making as to ignore him. This cannot stand," Eisenhower wrote in his diary on April 1, 1953. Fred I. Greenstein, *The Hidden-Hand Presidency: Eisenhower as Leader* 169 (1982). Greenstein reveals that Eisenhower worked behind the scenes to help weaken McCarthy, and concludes that "it is difficult to see how, at least for the purposes of defusing McCarthy, another technique would have worked faster and more decisively in the context of the time." Greenstein, 227. Others argue that Eisenhower's failure to publicly denounce McCarthy constituted a failure of leadership. E.g., Tom Wicker, *Dwight David Eisenhower* 139 (2002) (criticizing Eisenhower for not expressing "moral outrage at McCarthy's sins against decency)."

8. Patterson, *Grand Expectations*, supra note 1, at 203.

9. Caute, *The Great Fear*, supra note 2, at 36 and 305–06. See also Patterson, *Grand Expectations*, supra note 1, at 199 and 203.

10. Alan Brinkley, *The End of Reform: New Deal Liberalism in Recession and War* 141 (1995).

11. Whittaker Chambers, *Witness* 550 ("roots" quote), 476 (accosted by socialite), and 741 ("sling" quote)(1952). First published in 1952. Page references are to the fiftieth-anniversary edition.

12. Judis, *William F. Buckley, Jr.*, supra note 3, at 124 (quoting Chambers).

13. The poll was taken in March 1954. See Caute, *The Great Fear*, supra note 2, at 109. McCarthy reached the apex of his popularity in January 1954, when he had a 50 percent approval rating in the Gallup Poll.

14. Patrick Allitt, *Catholic Intellectuals and Conservative Politics in America 1950–1983* (1993) at 7.

15. Ibid. at 2.

16. Bennett, *The Party of Fear*, supra note 6, at 295.

17. Patterson, *Grand Expectations*, supra note 1, at 202.

18. Paul Johnson, *A History of the American People* 833 (1997)(quoting Kennan). First published in 1997. Page references are to the 1998 edition.

19. Ibid. at 834.

20. For Buckley's remark, see Bridges and Coyne, *Strictly Right*, supra note 5, at 30.

21. See William F. Buckley Jr. and L. Brent Bozell, *McCarthy and His Enemies: The Record and its Meaning* 277 (1954)(original emphasis).

22. Ibid. at 300.

23. Ibid. at 333.

24. George Gallup Jr., "Americans More Religious Now Than Ten Years ago, but Less So Than in 1950s and 1960s," *Gallup News Service*, March 2001.

25. Buckley and Bozell, *McCarthy and His Enemies*, supra note 21, at 334.

26. Ibid. at 333.

27. Ibid. at 331.

28. Ibid. at 281.

29. Allitt, *Catholic Intellectuals*, supra note 14, at 20–21.

30. This debate was more than academic. McCarthyism was then an issue with personal ramifications, not only nationally but at Yale. The immediate past president at Yale had famously declared, "There will be no witch hunt at Yale, because there will be no witches," thereby implying that Yale would not hire or grant tenure to professors with questionable loyalties. The two professors, Fowler Harper and Vern Countryman, were ardent critics of McCarthy—the latter without tenure. When, during the same year as the debate, Yale denied Countryman tenure, some attributed the denial to Countryman's fierce opposition to McCarthyism. One Yale faculty member, Addison Mueller, resigned his own position in protest. See Bridges and Coyne, *Strictly Right*, supra note 5, at 32 (regarding debate); Nick Ravo, "Vern Countryman, 81, Professor and Commercial Law Expert," *New York Times*, May 17, 1999 (regarding Countryman); Patterson, *Grand Expectations*, supra note 1, at 185 (regarding "no witches" quote).

31. Jeffrey Hart, "Buckley at the Beginning," *New Criterion*, Nov. 2005.

32. Judis, *William F. Buckley, Jr.*, supra note 3, at 114.

33. Interview with Priscilla Buckley at Great Elm, Sharon, CT, Sept. 10, 2008.

34. Letters from WFB to L. Brent Bozell, April 13 and August 18, 1955, (WFBP,Yale) (regarding attempts to have McCarthy solicit supporters).

35. Judis, *William F. Buckley, Jr.*, supra note 3, at 121, 129; Bridges and Coyne, *Strictly Right*, supra note 5, at 34; William A. Rusher, *The Rise of the Right* 46 (1984); Thomas W. Evans, *The Education of Ronald Reagan* 105–06 (2006).

36. Regarding Buckley's attempt to recruit Chambers, I rely on Sam Tanenhaus, *Whittaker Chambers: A Biography* 487–92 (1997); William F. Buckley Jr., *Miles Gone By* 299–317 (2004); and Judis, *William F. Buckley, Jr.*, supra note 3, at 127–29.

37. Tanenhaus, *Whittaker Chambers*, supra note 36, at 486.

38. Ibid. at 482 (demagogic, fascistic) and 492 ("raven of disaster.")

39. Tanenhaus, *Whittaker Chambers*, supra note 36, at 488; Judis, *William F. Buckley, Jr.*, supra note 3, at 126.

40. Russell Kirk, *The Conservative Mind: From Burke to Eliot* 5 (7th revised ed. 1985)(1953). First published in 1953. Page references are to seventh revised edition. Kirk expanded the book in subsequent editions and changed the subtitle to *From Burke to Eliot*.

41. WFB, "Essay in Confusion," *Freeman*, July 1955, at 576.

42. Letter from WFB to Henry Regnery, May 16, 1955 (WFBP, Yale).

43. Letter from Henry Regnery to WFB, May 19, 1955 (WFBP, Yale).

44. Meyer also included Walter Lippmann among the New Conservatives. Lippmann, however, was not a self-avowed Burkean and did not fit quite as clearly along with Kirk, Nisbet, Rossiter, and Viereck. Frank S. Meyer, "Collectivism Rebaptized," *Freeman*, July 1955, at 559, reprinted in Frank S. Meyer, *In Defense of Freedom and Related Essays* (1996). Arthur Schlesinger Jr. named Kirk, Rossiter, and Viereck as the New Conservatives in "The New Conservatism: Politics of Nostalgia," *Reporter*, June 16, 1955, at 9. Although Schlesinger credited the New Conservatives with reviving conservatism "as a respectable social philosophy," he criticized their philosophy as representing "the ethical afterglow of feudalism," a nostalgia for the concept of reciprocal duties among different classes. But as America never had a feudal system, how, he asked, could it have feudal traditions? Schlesinger also argued that when the New Conservatives left the realm of abstract philosophy and ventured into concrete social issues, they—and Kirk especially—simply adopted the views of the business community. "For better or worse," Schlesinger wrote, "our upper classes base their position not on land or tradition or a sense of social responsibility but on the folding stuff."

45. Kirk was, at this point in time, preparing to launch his own journal, which he then planned to call the *Conservative Review*, and two years later appeared under the name *Modern Age*. The *Freeman* issue containing Meyer and Buckley's articles was sent to members of the board of advisers of that putative journal. This effort to undermine Kirk's base of support by convincing his supporters that Kirk sought to take conservatism down the wrong path was, according to Kirk, unsuccessful. Kirk said his advisers "expressed their delight that we would not be saddled with the oppressive endorsement of the Supreme Soviet of Libertarianism, the kiss of death." Letter from Russell Kirk to WFB, Sept. 1, 1955 (WFBP, Yale).

46. Letter from Russell Kirk to WFB, Sept. 1, 1955 (WFBP, Yale).

47. Letter from WFB to Russell Kirk, May 20, 1955 (WFBP, Yale).

48. Letter from Russell Kirk to William F. Buckley Sr., July 13, 1955 (WFBP, Yale).

49. Letter from WFB to Russell Kirk, undated (WFBP, Yale).

50. Buckley would later label himself a libertarian in the subtitle of his book, *Happy Days Were Here Again: Reflections of a Libertarian Journalist* (1993).

51. Interview with Priscilla Buckley, supra note 33.

52. W. Wesley McDonald, *Russell Kirk and the Age of Ideology* 140 (2004) (quoting Kirk on "true community"); Kirk, *The Conservative Mind*, supra note 40, at 242 ("social atomism").

53. Burke's full statement, from which that maxim is drawn, reads "The individual is foolish; the multitude, for the moment is foolish, when they act without deliberation; but the species is wise, and, when time is given to it, as a species it always acts right." Kirk, *The Conservative Mind*, supra note 52, at 57 (quoting Burke).

54. Ibid. at 47.

55. Edmund Burke, "Sketch of a Negro Code," in *The Portable Edmund Burke* 183 (Isaac Kramnick ed. 1999).

56. Russell Kirk, *The Sword of Imagination: Memoirs of a Half-Century of Literary Conflict* 83 (1995).

57. William F. Buckley Jr., *Up from Liberalism* 207 ("economic freedom is the most precious temporal freedom") and 220 ("omnicompetence of the free marketplace") (1984). First published in 1959. Page references are to the 1984 edition.

58. Kirk, *The Conservative Mind*, supra note 40, at 489–90; McDonald, supra note 52, at 162 and 217 (stating that Kirk rejected capitalism as an absolute good).

59. See McDonald, *Russell Kirk*, supra note 52, at 217 (stating McDonald's assessment that Kirk was not an uncritical worshipper of the free market); and Russell Kirk and James McClellan, *The Political Principles of Robert A. Taft* 13, 67, 68, 70, 138 (1967) (repeatedly observing that Taft was not a laissez-faire absolutist; quotation about injustices produced by free market at 70).

60. Buckley, *Up from Liberalism*, supra note 57, at 200 and 202–06.

61. Kirk and McClellan, *The Political Principles of Robert A. Taft*, supra note 59, at 134–37.

62. Ibid. at 164.

63. Portions of the discussion about Edmund Burke are adapted from Carl T. Bogus, "Rescuing Burke," 72 *Missouri Law Review* 387 (2007). For citations to further sources, see especially 422–34 (regarding Burke and America), 452–54 (regarding *Reflections on the Revolution in* France), 472–73 (regarding Burke and religion).

64. Kirk, *The Conservative Mind*, supra note 40, at 426 and 454.

65. Ibid. at 426 ("expansive conceit") and 454 (new imperialism).

66. Kirk, *The Sword of Imagination*, supra note 56, at 214.

67. McDonald, *Russell Kirk*, supra note 52, at 178 (quoting Kirk).

68. Clinton Rossiter, *Conservatism in America: The Thankless Persuasion* 220–21 (1962). First published in 1955. Except where indicated, page references are to the second revised edition.

69. Edmund Burke, "Speech on the Act of Uniformity," in *The Portable Edmund Burke* (Isaac Kramnick ed. 1999), at 107–08.

70. Kirk, *Sword of Imagination*, supra note 56, 66–69, 229–47.

71. Kirk, *The Conservative Mind*, supra note 40, at 8.

72. Kirk, *The Sword of Imagination*, supra note 56, at 232.

73. See McDonald, *Russell Kirk*, supra note 52, at 43.

74. William F. Buckley Jr., *Let Us Talk of Many Things* 13 (2000).

75. Letter from Max Eastman to WFB, Jan. 28, 1958 (WFBP, Yale).

76. Letter from Max Eastman to WFB, Nov. 28, 1958 (WFBP, Yale).

77. Buckley added "but that is a semantic problem to a certain extent, I agree." Letter from WFB to Max Eastman, Aug. 21, 1962 (WFBP, Yale).

78. Kirk, *The Sword of Imagination*, supra note 56, at 250.

79. Finances became a little easier for Kirk after 1961 when, largely for fun, he wrote a gothic romance novel titled *Old House of Fear* that was to outsell all of the other books he would write combined. Nevertheless, his association with *National Review* remained important to his reputation as a prominent conservative for twenty-five years.

80. Buckley Jr., *Miles Gone By*, supra note 36, at 288.

81. Kirk, *The Sword of Imagination*, supra note 56, at 188.

82. Garry Wills, *Confessions of a Conservative* 46 (1979).

83. For biographical information on Peter Viereck, see Margalit Fox, "Peter Viereck, Poet and Conservative Theorist, Dies at 89," *New York Times*, May 19, 2006; and Tom Reiss, "The First Conservative: How Peter Viereck Inspired-and-Lost-a-Movement," *New Yorker*, Oct. 24, 2005, at 38.

84. Peter Viereck, *Conservatism Revisited* 33 (rev. and enlarged ed. with the addition of *The New Conservatism—What Went Wrong* (1962).

85. Ibid. at 84–85.

86. See George H. Nash, *The Conservative Intellectual Movement in America Since 1945* 137 (1996), arguing that Whittaker Chambers, among others, taught Buckley and *National Review* that "the Left was, in basic philosophy, united."

87. *See* Viereck, *Conservatism Revisited*, supra note 84, at 45–46 and 158.

88. Rossiter, *Conservatism in America*, supra note 68, at 40–41 (economic individualism, 42 (religious feeling), 44 (history), 111 (education), 247 (civil rights), 247 (taking traditionalism to an extreme), 252 and 255 (businessmen), 268 (Judeo-Christian tradition).

89. Russell Kirk, "American Conservative Action," *Chicago Review*, Fall 1955, at 65.

90. Rossiter, *Conservatism in America*, supra note 68, at 222.

91. Kirk, *The Sword of Imagination*, supra note 56, at 68.

92. Nash, *The Conservative Intellectual Movement*, supra note 86, at 182–84.

93. James Burnham, review of *Conservatism in America* by Clinton Rossiter and *The Liberal Tradition in America* by Louis Hartz, 301 *Annals of American Academy of Political and Social Science* 234 (1955).

94. Rossiter, *Conservatism in America*, supra note 68, at 96.

95. Ibid. at 208.

96. Burnham, *Review of Conservatism in America*, supra note 93. Russell Kirk would not have recoiled at Rossiter's suggestion that liberalism and conservatism had commonalities, or even that both could coexist within a single individual. Kirk repeatedly observed that Edmund Burke was both a liberal and a conservative, and he later called Taft a "liberal conservative." Kirk, *The Conservative Mind*, supra note 40, at 13; and Russell Kirk, *Edmund Burke: A Genius Reconsidered* 161 (1997) (calling Burke a liberal and a conservative). First published in 1967. Page references are to the 1997 revised and updated edition. Kirk and McClellan, *Robert A. Taft*, supra note 59, at 51 (calling Taft a "liberal conservative").

97. Rossiter, *Conservatism in America*, supra note 68, at 269.

98. Letter from Frank Chodorov to Dr. Robert Johnson Needless, July 21, 1955 (WFBP, Yale). Dr. Johnson was a physician who wrote both scientific journals and political magazines. Chodorov appears to have failed to turn Needless against Kirk as Needless later published a number of articles in early issues of *Modern Age*.

99. Letter from Clinton Rossiter to WFB, Feb. 29, 1956; letter from WFB to Clinton Rossiter, March 6, 1956; letter from Clinton Rossiter to WFB, March 8, 1956 (WFBP, Yale).

100. Rossiter, *Conservatism in America*, supra note 68, at 251.

101. Viereck, *Conservatism Revisited*, supra note 84, at 125 (unhistorical appeal to history), 140 (humanistic conservatism of the past), 141 (desegregation), 145–56 (attacking Welch but not McCarthy), 150 (morally bankrupt).

102. "Death of a Teacher," *Cornell Alumni News*, Sept. 1970, at 18.

103. Caleb Rossiter, "Cornell's Student Revolt of 1969: A Rare Case of Democracy on Campus," *Progressive* (Ithaca, NY), May 5, 1999.

104. For information about Nisbet's life, I rely on Brad Lowell Stone, *Robert Nisbet: Communitarian Traditionalist* (2000), and Robert G. Perrin, "Robert Alexander Nisbet," 143 *Proceedings of the American Philosophical Society* 695 (1999). I also consulted Nash, supra note 86.

105. Robert Nisbet, *The Quest for Community: A Study in the Ethics of Order & Reform* 42, 89, 220 (ICS Press 1990). First published by Oxford University Press in 1953. All citations herein are to the ICS 1990 edition.

106. Ibid. at 38–39.

107. Ibid. at 53–54.

108. Ibid. at xxiii.

109. Ibid. at 207 (regarding Dewey).

110. It is worth adding here some notes about Hayek's relationship to conservatism, and Hayek's relationship with William F. Buckley Jr. The

conservative movement embraced Hayek as one of its idols. Yet Hayek was less than comfortable in conservative circles. He explained why in a piece titled "Why I Am Not a Conservative," included in his book, *The Constitution of Liberty* (1960). Hayek accused the modern American conservative movement of having "a propensity to reject well-substantiated new knowledge" when it disliked consequences that followed from that knowledge. Evolution, he said, was such an example. He decried the "strident nationalism" of the conservative movement, which he said led to imperialism. "The more a person dislikes the strange and thinks his own ways superior, the more he tends to regard it as his mission to 'civilize' the other," he wrote. Moreover, sounding somewhat like Robert Nisbet, Hayek argued that conservatism's nationalistic bias might wind up serving as a bridge to collectivism because it could easily lead to demands that national assets be devoted to the national interest. Hayek associated his political views with those of Thomas Babington Macaulay, Alexis de Tocqueville, and Edmund Burke. His connection to Burke would grow stronger. "I am becoming a Burkean Whig," Hayek declared later in life. E. H. H. Green, *Ideologies of Conservatism* 259 (2004)(quoting Hayek).

In November 1961, William F. Buckley Jr. was surprised to receive a short letter from Hayek, complaining about a *National Review* editorial that, said Hayek, accused Dag Hammarskjöld—the secretary-general of the United Nations who had recently been killed in an airplane crash—of cheating at cards. This overstepped "the boundaries of decency," said Hayek, and he did not want any further issues of the magazine. Letter from F. A. Hayek to WFB, Nov. 2, 1961 (WFBP, Yale). Buckley sent an uncharacteristically aggressive reply, suggesting that Hayek must have had an ulterior motive. "As I think back on your coolness towards our enterprise (I have not, in the six years that the magazine has been published, had from you a single letter commending a single article, editorial, or book review), it occurs to me that you must be harboring some grudge against me or the magazine which you now, for your own reasons, seek occasion for externalizing." The editorial was an attempt at "logical fantasy," "mock solemnity," "intended playfulness," and no one else had complained. Letter from WFB to F. A. Hayek, Dec. 6, 1961 (WFBP, Yale).

Hayek was not moved. "I fear our standards about what is admissible in attacks on public figures seem to differ considerably," he wrote, adding that after receiving Buckley's letter he reread the editorial but found nothing playful in it. Hayek had been receiving *National Review* through someone's generosity—he always assumed it had been Buckley's—and he "no longer wished to be indebted to such a courtesy." Letter from F. A. Hayek to WFB, Dec. 8, 1961 (WFBP, Yale).

Apparently Hayek was sharing his opinion with others; Buckley had already heard from one individual to that effect. Buckley may have been worried that Hayek's letter was a precursor to a public attack on *National Review*. Why else, Buckley may have wondered, would a prominent public intellectual take the time to cancel a complimentary subscription to a magazine? Writing back again, Buckley signaled he would fight fire with fire. Pride, he said, caused Hayek to overlook the possibility that he misunderstood the editorial because it "was not written in your native tongue." Whether or not Hayek chose to read *National Review* was a matter of private concern. "But it is a matter of public concern that you are capable of making such unstable judgments," Buckley warned menacingly. Letter from WFB to F. A. Hayek, Dec. 13, 1961 (WFBP, Yale). No public attack on *National Review* materialized. Hayek, we must assume, wrote to Buckley simply because the editorial—and *National Review*'s practice of snidely and personally disparaging liberals, often under the guise of parody—offended him. Thirty years later, fate drew the two men together. On November 18, 1991, President George H. W. Bush awarded the Presidential Medal of Freedom to ten men and women, including both Buckley ("for a lifetime of achievement in American political and social thought") and Hayek (mentioning *The Road to Serfdom*, along with Hayek's economic achievements).

111. F. A. Hayek, *The Road to Serfdom* 66 (University of Chicago Press 1994) (1944). First published in 1944. Page references are to the 1994 edition. Hayek at 75 (economic dictator), 98–99 (money), 120–21 (distributive justice, equality), 127–31 (resentment of middle class), 133–34 (safety net and social insurance).

112. Ibid. at 247 (original emphasis).

113. Ibid. at 214 and 180.

114. Stone, *Robert Nisbet*, supra note 104, at 84. See also Nisbet, *The Quest for Community*, supra note 105, at 240.

115. Stone, *Robert Nisbet*, supra note 104, at 33.

116. Rossiter, *Conservatism in America*, supra note 68, at 224 (praise for Nisbet's book), 226 (Kirk and Nisbet united by Burkeanism).

117. David Brooks, "Robert Nisbet's Quest," On the Issues: American Enterprise Institute Online, Sept. 30, 1996 (quoting Nisbet).

118. William F. Buckley Jr., *The Jeweler's Eye* 13–14 (1969)(republishing 1963 article). As did Frank Meyer, see supra note 44, Buckley counted Walter Lippmann among the new conservatives.

119. Kirk, *The Sword of Imagination*, supra note 56, at 164.

120. Russell Kirk, "Libertarians: The Chirping Sectaries," *Modern Age*, Fall 1981, at 345; republished in *The Essential Kirk: Selected Essays* 373 (George A. Panichas ed. 2007).

CHAPTER 3: CIVIL RIGHTS

1. John B. Judis, *William F. Buckley, Jr.: Patron Saint of the Conservatives* 128 (1988).
2. Letter from WFB to Roger Milliken, April 6, 1956, with accompanying invoice for 1,221 gift subscriptions (WFBP, Yale); Thomas W. Evans, *The Education of Ronald Reagan* 105–06 (2006)(regarding Boulware). I infer that ten thousand copies were destined for newsstands because *Newsweek* reported that the initial press run was fifty thousand.
3. Letter from WFB to Frank Meyer, Nov. 4, 1955 (WFBP, Yale).
4. John Fischer, "Why Is the Conservative Voice So Hoarse?" *Harper's*, March 1956, at 16; Dwight Macdonald, "Scrambled Eggheads on the Right," *Commentary*, April 1956, at 367; Murray Kempton, "Buckley's National Bore," *Progressive*, July 1956, at 13.
5. William F. Buckley Jr., "A Report from the Publisher: Reflections on the Failure of 'National Review' to Live Up to Liberal Expectations," *National Review*, Aug. 1, 1956, at 7.
6. Priscilla L. Buckley, *Living It Up at National Review: A Memoir* 6 (2005).
7. Ibid. at 13–14.
8. Ibid. at 19.
9. William A. Rusher, *The Rise of the Right* 15–19 (1984).
10. For the history of the civil rights movement, I particularly rely on Taylor Branch, *Parting the Waters: America in the King Years 1954–63* (1988), as well as on James T. Patterson, *Grand Expectations: The United States, 1945–1974* (1996); and Steven E. Ambrose, *Eisenhower: Soldier and President* (1990).
11. Folsom ran again in 1962. He sat out the 1958 election because Alabama governors cannot serve consecutive terms.
12. Edmund Burke, *Reflections on the Revolution in France* 19 (Yale University Press 2003). First published in 1790. Page references are to the 2003 edition published by Yale University Press.
13. Carl T. Bogus, "Rescuing Burke," 72 *Missouri Law Review* 387, 415–16 (2007).
14. Patterson, *Grand Expectations*, supra note 10, at 387.
15. "Segregation and Democracy," *National Review*, Jan. 25, 1956, at 5. Unsigned editorials set forth *National Review*'s corporate position, while signed articles expressed only the personal opinion of the writer. Unless otherwise stated, I shall use the word editorial to mean only unsigned editorials.
16. A previous *National Review* article had also portrayed the Gray Plan as moderate, middle ground. The author had written: "As she has done so often in her historic past, Virginia is providing the leadership in seeking a way out of this embittered socio-legal crisis." Sam M. Jones, "Tidewater

State Leads South in Seeking Way Out of Desegregation Crisis," *National Review*, Dec. 28, 1955, at 23.

17. Forrest Davis, "The Right to Nullify," *National Review*, April 25, 1956, at 9.

18. Branch, *Parting the Waters*, supra note at 10, at 413–14; *Griffin v. County School Bd. of Prince Edward County*, 377 U.S. 1226 (1964).

19. Sam M. Jones, "South Carolina: State Will Offer Formidable Opposition to Liberals at the Democratic National Convention," *National Review*, Feb. 22, 1956, at 18.

20. "The South Girds Its Loins," *National Review*, Feb. 29, 1956.

21. The Week, *National Review*, March 4, 1956, at 6.

22. "Foul," *National Review*, April 18, 1956, at 6; "How Much Is It Worth?" *National Review*, Jan. 19, 1957, at 55.

23. "Less Sound and Fury," *National Review*, March 28, 1956, at 5.

24. "Behind the Filibuster Vote," *National Review*, Jan. 19, 1957, at 53.

25. William F. Buckley Jr., "Reflections on Election Eve," *National Review*, Nov. 3, 1956, at 6.

26. Rick Perlstein, *Before the Storm: Barry Goldwater and the Unmaking of the American Consensus* 227, 565 n.227 (2001)(citing *Newsweek* poll).

27. Sam M. Jones, "Voice of the South," *National Review*, July 27, 1957, at 105.

28. "Why the South Must Prevail," *National Review*, Aug. 24, 1957.

29. Judis, *William F. Buckley, Jr.*, supra note 1, at 138–39.

30. Though he was not a racist, Goldwater nevertheless, in the words of Theodore H. White, "pinpointed himself as the outright anti-Negro candidate in the campaign." Theodore H. White, *The Making of the President 1964*, 304 (1965). See also Perlstein, *Before the Storm*, supra note 26, at 333–335, 460–65, 469–70 (2001). There is voluminous literature about Nixon's "Southern strategy" in 1972. For a brief description, see Patterson, *Grand Expectations*, supra note 10, at 730–35.

31. L. Brent Bozell, "Open Letter: Mr. Bozell Dissents from Views Expressed in the Editorial, 'Why the South Must Prevail,'" *National Review*, Sept. 7, 1957, at 209.

32. William F. Buckley Jr., *Up from Liberalism* 156 (1959).

33. Branch, supra note 10, at 410.

34. E.g., Judis, *William F. Buckley*, supra note 1, at 139.

35. George H. Nash, *The Conservative Intellectual Movement in America Since 1945* 260 (1996). One notable exception is Ramesh Ponnuru, who concedes that William F. Buckley Jr. and *National Review* took racist positions. "Most contemporary conservatives who know this history regret it and find it embarrassing," he writes. Moreover, Ponnuru argues that this legacy of racism has not been fully purged from the right, and that it lives on in conservative skepticism about congressional power to enforce the equal

protection provisions of the Fourteenth Amendment. See Ramesh Ponnuru, "The Right's Civil Wrongs," *National Review*, June 21, 2010, at 16.

36. Jeffrey Hart, *The Making of the American Conservative Mind: National Review and Its Times* 103–04 (2005).

37. "Intelligence or Prejudice?" *National Review*, Dec. 1, 1964, at 1059.

38. For example, Van den Haag said, "I do not think that in this matter we have conclusive evidence one way or the other, though the indications are the two groups have different aptitudes (or different distributions of aptitudes). Please note that I am not saying that I have proved genetic inferiority of Negroes." In another artifice, Van den Haag offers this hypothetical: "Suppose four-fifths of Negroes fall into the lower half of intelligence distribution. Chances are that, say, one-third of whites will too." He does not say that is what data show. It's just a hypothetical, ostensibly offered to illustrate that different distributions on intelligence tests do not mean that all blacks are less intelligent than all whites, or as Van den Haag puts it, under his example "if intelligence is the criterion, four-fifths of the Negro group would be no more 'inferior' than one-third of the white group." The hypothetical is transparently designed to give the reader the impression that most blacks are, in fact, less intelligent than most whites, while allowing Van den Haag to deny that he said any such thing.

39. William F. Buckley Jr. "Obituary: Ernest van den Haag, R.I.P.," *National Review*, April 22, 2002; Richard Brookhiser, *Right Time, Right Place: Coming of Age with William F. Buckley Jr. and the Conservative Movement* 237 (2009).

40. Buckley, *Up from Liberalism*, supra note 32, at 155–60.

41. Peter Duignan and Lewis Henry Gann, "White and Black in Africa," *National Review*, Jan. 28, 1961, at 47.

42. J. D. Futch, "It's All Quite Simple," *National Review*, July 1, 1961, at 417.

43. William F. Buckley Jr., *Rumbles Left and Right* 122–27 (1963).

44. Joseph J. Thorndike, " 'The Sometimes Sordid Level of Race and Segregation': James J. Kilpatrick and the Virginia Campaign Against Brown," at 51 in *The Moderates' Dilemma*, (Matthew D. Lassiter and Andrew B. Lewis eds. 1998).

45. James Jackson Kilpatrick, "Right and Power in Arkansas," *National Review*, Sept. 28, 1957, at 273.

46. The magazine once observed that "However paradoxical it may sound, it is so that Northern ideologues are responsible for the outbreak of violence in the South and that, nevertheless, no one is responsible for that violence save those who commit it." The Week, *National Review*, Jan. 12, 1957, at 27.

47. James Jackson Kilpatrick, "The South Sees Through New Glasses," *National Review*, March 11, 1961, at 141.

48. James Jackson Kilpatrick, "Civil Rights and Legal Wrongs," *National Review*, Sept. 24, 1963, at 231.

49. Branch, *Parting the Waters*, supra note 10, at 408–09.

50. L. Brent Bozell, "To Mend the Tragic Flaw," *National Review*, March 12, 1963, at 199.

51. James Jackson Kilpatrick, "Must We Repeal the Constitution to Give the Negro the Vote?" *National Review*, April 20, 1965, at 319.

52. "*Still* Federal," *National Review*, Aug. 16, 1958, at 125 (original emphasis, praising Forbus); "The Lie to Mr. Eisenhower," *National Review*, Oct. 5, 1957, at 292 (denouncing Eisenhower); The Week, *National Review*, Oct. 19, 1957, at 340 (reporting that one of the students publicly thanked a woman who was procommunist, active in communist front organizations, and married to a man who asserted his Fifth Amendment rights before the House Un-American Affairs Committee). For other editorials along the same line, see "Surrender to Decency?" *National Review*, March 22, 1958, at 271; "Back to Reality," *National Review*, July 5, 1958, at 53; "Verdict for Ideologues," *National Review*, Aug. 30, 1958, at 149; "No Trips to Newport," *National Review*, Sept. 28, 1957, at 270; "Bayonets and the Law," *National Review*, Oct. 12, 1957, at 316.

53. Two former editors of *National Review* have recently written, "The concept of states' rights could be and often was used by racists for their purposes, but it is also a fundamental principle of the American Republic, which at its founding was a union of states and not a unitary entity." Linda Bridges and John R. Coyne Jr., *Strictly Right: William F. Buckley Jr. and the American Conservative Movement* 81 (2007). They are right about the republic being a union of states only if they are speaking about the Articles of Confederation. The founders assembled in Philadelphia because they believed that the confederation model had produced a national government that was too weak to be effective. They also believed that the nearly-all-powerful states were becoming threats to liberty. The founders scrapped the confederation model in favor of a system with a much stronger federal government that derives its authority not from the states but directly from the people. The Constitution begins, "We, the people of the United States . . . do ordain and establish this Constitution for the United States." An individual is a citizen of the United States as well as his or her state. By contrast, the Articles of Confederation declared, "The said States hereby severally enter into a firm league of friendship with each other." For more on this topic, see Garry Wills, *A Necessary Evil: A History of American Distrust of Government* (1999).

54. Two Cambridge undergraduates also participated in the debate. The debate can be viewed at http://rivendell.lib.uic.edu/news/2008/03/04/william-f-buckley-1965-debate-available-online (visited June 21, 2010). The slightly

condensed transcript of the debate was published under the title "The American Dream and the American Negro," *New York Times Magazine*, March 7, 1965, at 87.

55. Garry Wills, "Buckley, Buckley, Bow Wow Wow," *Esquire*, Jan. 1968, at 72.
56. William F. Buckley, Jr., "The Negro and the American Dream," *National Review*, April 6, 1965, at 273.
57. James Baldwin, *The Fire Next Time* 8; 9–10 (Vintage 1993)(original emphasis). First published in 1963. Page references are to the 1993 edition.
58. James Carney, "10 Questions for William F. Buckley," *Time*, April 12, 2004.
59. William F. Buckley Jr., *Gratitude: Reflections on What We Owe to Our Country* 24 (1990).

CHAPTER 4: "THE LOONIES"

1. Letter from WFB to Robert Welch, Nov. 2, 1958 (WFBP, Yale).
2. "Who Was John Birch?" *Time*, April 12, 1961.
3. For biographical information about Welch, see the G. Vance Smith's foreword to Robert Welch, *The Politician* (Robert Welch University Press 2002.) First circulated as an unpublished manuscript in 1958. First formally published in 1963. Page references are to the 2002 edition; William A. Rusher, *The Rise of the Right* 59 (1984).
4. Welch contributed $1,000 when the magazine was established in 1955, and another $1,000 in response to an appeal for help two years later. John B. Judis, *William F. Buckley, Jr.: Patron Saint of the Conservatives* 193 (1988); Letter from Robert Welch to WFB, June 6, 1957 (WFBP, Yale).
5. Letter from Robert Welch to WFB, Nov. 24, 1958 (WFBP, Yale).
6. Letter from WFB to Robert Welch, Nov. 26, 1958 (WFBP, Yale).
7. Welch, *The Politician*, supra note 3, at 224.
8. Ibid. at 254, 255.
9. Ibid. at 15, 202, 204, 214.
10. Ibid. at 212.
11. Ibid. at 205.
12. Ibid. at 71 (Javits), 90–91 (Stout), 186 (Einstein), 194 (Case), 195 (Harriman, then governor of New York), 196 (Smith), and 199–222 (others mentioned).
13. Ibid. at 475 n569.
14. Ibid. at xxxiii.
15. *The Blue Book of the John Birch Society* 9 (four separate provinces), 10–11 (Lenin quote), 5 (virtual control of many slices of national life), 6 (army), 25 (mass media), 53–53 (the cancer of collectivism), (10th printing 1961).

First printing in 1959. Page references are to the tenth printing, except as otherwise indicated.

16. This letter from Buckley appears to have gone missing, along with Welch's reply; but excerpts from both letters appear in Judis, *William F. Buckley, Jr.*, supra note 4, at 194. See also William F. Buckley Jr., *The Jeweler's Eye* 19 (1969)(describing his principal disagreement with Welch).

17. "So Long, Ike," *National Review*, Jan. 14, 1961, at 6.

18. Letter from Robert Welch to WFB, Jan. 12, 1958 (WFBP, Yale).

19. Letter from WFB to Robert Welch, March 3, 1959 (WFBP, Yale).

20. Eugene Lyons, "Folklore of the Right," *National Review*, April 11, 1959, at 645.

21. Letter from Robert Welch to WFB, March 18, 1959 (WFBP, Yale).

22. Rusher, supra note 2, at 61.

23. *Blue Book*, supra note 15, at ix n14 (page ix follows page 112).

24. People listed on the original masthead of the Committee Against Summit Entanglements (CASE) included Spruille Braden, Clarence Manion, and lawyer Robert B. Dresser of Providence, Rhode Island, all of whom were financial backers of *National Review*, as well as Revilo P. Oliver. Later the masthead grew to include Roger Milliken and Morrie Ryskind, also financial backers of *National Review*. All became members of the John Birch Society; Manion and Oliver were on the JBS council. J. B. Matthews, Medford Evans, and E. Merrill Root—all of whom were associates and contributors to *National Review*—also became members of the John Birch Society; Matthews was on the JBS council. Jeffrey Hart, *The Making of the Conservative Mind:* National Review *and Its Times* 156 (2005); Judis, *William F. Buckley, Jr.*, supra note 4, at 194; Rick Perlstein, *Before the Storm: Barry Goldwater and the Unmaking of the American Consensus* 154 (2001). For the original CASE masthead, see form letter dated May 28, 1959, attached to letter from WFB to Revilo P. Oliver, June 23, 1959 (WFBP, Yale). For the enlarged, later CASE masthead, see center insert in the tenth printing of *The Blue Book of the John Birch Society*. For a list of members of the Council of the John Birch Society, see letter from Robert Welch to WFB, April 25, 1961 (WFBP, Yale).

25. Letter from WFB to Revilo Oliver, June 25, 1959 (WFBP, Yale).

26. *National Review* announced that Oliver had joined as an associate and contributor in its April 4, 1956 issue (at 7). Correspondence reflecting that Buckley knew about Oliver's bigotry include: letter from Ralph de Toledano to WFB, Dec. 16, 1958 (stating, "It was good to see you and Pat in New York . . . even though I found certain aspects of Oliver's rhetoric distressing"); letter from WFB to L. Brent Bozell, Dec. 15, 1959 (asking whether

National Review should publish an article by Oliver with Bozell's reply: "A persuasive case of anti-Semitism could be made out against N.R. by showing we assigned a Jewish story to a demonstrable anti-Semite"); letter from Oliver to WFB, Dec. 22, 1959 (referring to "the heathen Chinee"); letter from Oliver to WFB, March 12, 1960 (stating, "We all know that, in addition to the large [but diminishing] number of rabbits who are panic-stricken when they hear 'anti-Semitic,' there is a very large, well organized, extremely powerful and utterly ruthless body of Jews whose only standard of judgment is . . . 'Is it Good for the Jews?'") For more about Oliver, see Benjamin R. Epstein and Arnold Forster, *Report on the John Birch Society 1966* 16, 20–22, 33 (1966). Jeffrey Hart writes that Oliver was expelled from *National Review* because Buckley found out he was a member of the John Birch Society. Hart, *The Making of the Conservative Mind*, supra note 24, at 55–57. However, correspondence reflects that Buckley terminated Oliver for publicly associating with anti-Semites and crackpots. Letter from Oliver to WFB, Dec. 24, 1960; letter from WFB to Oliver, April 5, 1961. Among other things, Oliver's speeches were being published by the anti-Semitic periodical *Common Sense*. Even as he terminated Oliver from *National Review*, Buckley wrote, "I know that you know that this action has no bearing whatever on our personal relationship, which will not, I pray, be in the least affected by it. All the editors and members of the board who know you esteem you as I do." Letter from WFB to Oliver, May 16, 1960. All correspondence cited from WFBP, Yale.

27. William F. Buckley Jr., *Rumbles Left and Right* 42 (1963). For background on the Carnegie Hall rally, see Linda Bridges and John R. Coyne Jr., *Strictly Right: William F. Buckley Jr. and the American Conservative Movement* 67 (2007); Rusher, *Rise of the Right*, supra note 3, at 75–78; Judis, *William F. Buckley, Jr.*, supra note 4, at 175–77 (also describing Chambers's reaction).

28. Judis, *William F. Buckley, Jr.*, supra note 4, at 184.

29. Alan F. Westin, "The John Birch Society: Fundamentalism on the Right," *Commentary* (Aug. 1961): at 93. Others estimate that at its height, the JBS had about eighty thousand members. E.g., Eckard V. Toy Jr., "The Right Side of the 1960s: The Origins of the John Birch Society in the Pacific Northwest," 105 *Oregon Historical Quarterly* 260 (2004).

30. "Organizations: The Americanists," *Time*, March 10, 1961 (first article about JBS); "The Nation: Storm over Birchers," *Time*, April 7, 1961 (Kuchel's speech; Goldwater's comment); "Organizations: Beware the Comsymps," *Time*, April 21, 1961 (Welch's speech in L.A.); Kenneth Reich, "O.C. Politician and Ex-Senator Kuchel, 84, Dies," reprinted in extension of re-

marks by Representative Stephen Horn, *Congressional Record* E1858 (Oct. 11, 2002)(background to Kuchel's speech).

31. Rusher, *Rise of the Right*, supra note 3, at 62 (Welch as poetry).

32. William F. Buckley Jr. "The Uproar," *National Review*, April 22, 1961, at 241.

33. Rusher, *Rise of the Right*, supra note 3, at 115–16; Judis, supra note 4, at 197–98; Perlstein, *Before the Storm*, supra note 24, at 155. Regarding the YAF's formation, see also M. Stanton Evans, *Revolt on the Campus* 108–12 (1961).

34. For a brief description of the history and effectiveness of the liberal and conservative parties in New York State, see James Underwood and William J. Daniels, *Governor Rockefeller in New York: The Apex of Pragmatic Liberalism in the United States* 64–68 (1982).

35. William A. Rusher, *The Rise of the Right*, supra note 3, at 96–98.

36. William F. Buckley Jr., *Flying High: Remembering Barry Goldwater* 65–70 (2008). For brief biographical information about Frank Cullen Brophy, including his membership on the JBS council, see *Blue Book*, supra note 15, at 169 (8th printing).

37. Perlstein, supra note 24, at 43–46, 51–53, 61–63.

38. Brent and Trish Bozell spent awhile in Spain, where they fell in with Carlists and became radicalized. After separating from *National Review* and writing *Conscience of a Conservative*, Brent founded a Catholic journal of opinion named *Triumph*. In time, he renounced conservatism in favor of what he called Christian politics. He and Trish founded a militant anti-abortion group. In 1970, Brent was arrested for using a large wooden cross to smash the glass door of the George Washington University Health Service, which Brent claimed was performing abortions. In 1971, Trish was arrested for rushing a stage at Catholic University and assaulting feminist speaker Ti-Grace Atkinson. That same year Brent told a newspaper that being Bill Buckley's brother-in-law was "a hindrance" because Buckley was "the right-wing establishment" while he considered himself "outside the establishment." Judis, *William F. Buckley, Jr.*, supra note 4 at 317–22.

39. *Blue Book*, supra note 15, at 119.

40. Barry Goldwater, *The Conscience of a Conservative* 13 (CC Goldwater ed.) (swindled); 61–64 and 67 (collectivist plot); 84 (treason) (Princeton University Press 2007). First published in 1960. Page references are to the 2007 edition.

41. "The Question of Robert Welch," *National Review*, Feb. 13, 1963, at 83.

42. Epstein and Foster, *Report on the John Birch Society*, supra note 26, at 88–97.

43. Perlstein, *Before the Storm*, supra note 24, at 392.

44. Theodore H. White, *The Making of the President 1964* 217–18 (1969).

45. Two prominent Republicans questioning American involvement in Vietnam

were Senator Mark O. Hatfield of Oregon and Congressman John Lindsay of New York.

46. Bill Hirschman, "Wichitans Found Welch Extreme," *Wichita Eagle*, Jan. 8, 1985.

47. I rely on two excellent biographies of Rand: Jennifer Burns, *Goddess of the Market: Ayn Rand and the American Right* (2009), and Anne C. Heller, *Ayn Rand and the World She Made* (2009).

48. Burns, *Goddess of the Market*, supra note 47, at 36 (quoting the *Nation*).

49. Ayn Rand, *The Fountainhead* 217 (Signet 1993). First published in 1943. Page references are to the centennial edition.

50. Burns, *Goddess of the Market*, supra note 47, at 86 (quoting Rand).

51. William F. Buckley Jr., *Let Us Talk of Many Things* 231–32 (2000).

52. See Rand's notes in afterword by Leonard Peikoff, in *The Fountainhead*, supra note 49, at 696.

53. Ibid. at 697.

54. Burns, *Goddess of the Market*, supra note 47, at 90 (quoting reviews in *Providence Journal* and *New York Times*). Burns reports that the *New York Times* review was the best of Rand's career.

55. For sales data, see Burns, supra note 47, at 90 and 106–07, and Heller, supra note 47, at 219 (2009).

56. William F. Buckley Jr., "Ayn Rand, RIP," *National Review*, April 2, 1982, at 380. See also Heller, supra note 47, at 245–46; and Burns, supra note 47, at 139–40.

57. See Burns, *Goddess of the Market*, supra note 47, at 74–78 (regarding the formation of Rand and Paterson's friendship), 125–32 (regarding the falling out between Rand and Paterson), and 140 (regarding Buckley asking Paterson about Rand).

58. William F. Buckley Jr., *God and Man at Yale* lxvi (fiftieth-anniversary ed. 2002). First published in 1951. Page references are to the fiftieth-anniversary edition.

59. Ayn Rand, *The Virtue of Selfishness* 38 (1964).

60. Burns, supra note 47, at 146.

61. Ayn Rand, *Atlas Shrugged* (Signet 1996). First published in 1957. Page references are to the fiftieth-anniversary edition.

62. William F. Buckley, Jr., "Ayn Rand, RIP," supra note 56.

63. See generally Rand, "Objectivist Ethics," chap. 1 in *The Virtue of Selfishness*, supra note 59.

64. See generally Rand, "Government Financing in a Free Society," chap. 15 in *The Virtue of Selfishness*, supra note 59.

65. Whittaker Chambers, "Big Sister Is Watching You," *National Review*, Dec. 28, 1957.

66. Burns, *Goddess of the Market*, supra note 47, at 176.

67. Heller, *Ayn Rand and the World She Made*, supra note 47, at 286 (selecting Chambers); William F. Buckley Jr., *The Jeweler's Eye* 14 (1969)(reading Rand out of the movement).

68. Letter from T. Coleman Andrews to WFB, Jan. 3, 1958 (WFBP, Yale).

69. Jennifer Burns observes that *"Atlas Shrugged* was a throwback to Socialist realism, with cardboard characters in service of an overarching ideology." Burns, *Goddess of the Market*, supra note 47, at 179.

70. Heller, supra note 47, at 287.

71. Ibid. at 287; Esther B. Fein, "Book Notes," *New York Times*, Nov. 20, 1991.

72. Burns, supra note 47, at 203.

73. Ibid. at 205.

74. Ibid. at 212.

75. George H. Nash, *The Conservative Intellectual Movement in America Since 1945* 1530 (1996)(quoting Herberg's two-part article, "Conservatives, Liberals, and Natural Law").

76. Burns, *Goddess of the Market*, supra note 47, at 144–45, 151–54, 182–84. See also David Gordon, "Biography of Murray N. Rothbard (1926–1995)," available at http://mises.org/about/3249 (last visited June 21, 2010).

77. Burns, supra note 47, at 258.

78. Ibid. at 153.

79. The description of this event is drawn principally from Murray N. Rothbard, "Listen YAF," *Libertarian Forum*, Aug. 15, 1969, at 1; and Jerome Tuccille, "Report from St. Louis: The Revolution Comes to YAF," *Libertarian Forum*, Sept. 15, 1969, at 1. See also Burns, *Goddess of the Market*, supra note 47, at 254–57.

80. Ibid. at 144–45, 151–54, and 182–84.

81. Buckley, "Ayn Rand, RIP," supra note 56.

82. Burns, *Goddess of the Market*, supra note 47, at 4.

83. The most recent attack on Rand, which was given cover story status, is also the most perceptive: Jason Lee Steorts, "The Greatly Ghastly Rand," *National Review*, Aug. 30, 2010, at 43.

Chapter 5: The Cold War

1. Regarding Burnham's life and much of his thinking, I rely heavily on Daniel Kelly's biography, *James Burnham and the Struggle for the World: A Life* (2002).

2. Ibid. at 68 and 128–29.

3. James T. Patterson, *Mr. Republican: A Biography of Robert A. Taft* 436–37 (1972).

4. Stephen E. Ambrose, *Eisenhower: Soldier and President* 275–77 (1990);

5. Tim Weiner, *Legacy of Ashes: The History of the CIA* 33–36 (2007).

6. Ibid. at 22–23, 29, 32–33 (Kennan) and 36 (OPC and rollback).

7. Regarding Burnham's involvement with the CIA, CCF, and ACCF, see Kelly, supra note 1, 149–93. See also ibid. at 212 (regarding Burnham interviewing Buckley). See also Michael Kimmage, *The Conservative Turn: Lionel Trilling, Whittaker Chambers, and the Lessons of Anti-Communism* 180–81 (2009).

8. James Burnham, *Suicide of the West: An Essay on the Meaning and Destiny of Liberalism* 265 (Gateway 1985). First published in 1964. Page references are to the 1985 edition.

9. James Mann, *The Rebellion of Ronald Reagan: A History of the End of the Cold War* 23 (2009)(quoting a statement Reagan wrote in 1975).

10. Kelly, *James Burnham*, supra note 1, at 178–79 (quoting Kennan). Through some inference on my part, I expand slightly on what Kennan wrote.

11. See, e.g., John B. Judis, *William F. Buckley, Jr.: Patron Saint of the Conservatives* 122 (1988); Linda Bridges and John R. Coyne, Jr., *Strictly Right: William F. Buckley Jr. and the American Conservative Movement* 35–37 (2007).

12. Richard Parker, *John Kenneth Galbraith: His Life, His Politics, His Economics* 260–61 (2005).

13. See, e.g., David Caute, *The Great Fear: The Anti-Communist Purge Under Truman and Eisenhower* 31 and 51–52 (1978).

14. In addition to Kelly, *James Burnham*, supra note 1, I have consulted George H. Nash, *The Conservative Intellectual Movement in America Since 1945* 105–07; Judis, supra note 11, at 122–23; Bridges and Coyne, supra note 11, at 36.

15. Diana Trilling related encountering James and Marcia Burnham while she and her husband were in a shoe store in Manhattan during this period. The two couples had been good friends and chatted briefly. Then, according to Diana, Marcia asked in a "wistful voice" whether Diana and Lionel would be would be "willing" to visit James and her in their home in Connecticut. "Her tone and her use of the word 'willing' made me very unhappy for her. They were being ostracized by Burnham's old friends and university associates," explained Diana. Kelly, *James Burnham*, supra note, at 204.

16. William F. Buckley Jr., *Miles Gone By: A Literary Autobiography* 289 (2004).

17. Jeffrey Hart, *The Making of the American Conservative Mind: National Review and Its Times* 15 (2005).

18. Burnham also tells the fictional liberal that tests "have been *alleged* to rate intellectual abilities independently of environment and education" (emphasis

added). Burnham adds the following footnote to this section: "My interest in this section is solely in the *method of reasoning*, and has nothing to do with the merits of the positions defended or questioned in these hypothetical instances [such as] the belief in the innate equality of races" (original emphasis). Burnham, *Suicide of the West*, supra note 8, at 101–03.

19. Elsewhere in the very same book, Burnham talks about two men who he says worked a few blocks away from *National Review*'s offices. His purpose is to provide an example of how a minimum wage would throw people with low skills out of work. Here is how he describes these two men: "The two Negroes were cheerful, pleasant fellows. They worked amicably together. I got to know them a little that day and thereafter, and it was plain that they had IQ's down almost out of sight; but they could handle the work they were doing [collecting discarded cardboard], and they took pride in doing it well." Ibid. 108–09. This story is meaningful only to someone with an "Amos 'n' Andy" image of black people, for the race of the men gives the vignette verisimilitude. In a speech about the United Nations, Burnham asked, "Why in the world should any sensible person give a damn what some spokesperson for cannibalistic tribes or slave-holding nomads thinks about nuclear tests?" Kelly, *James Burnham*, supra note 1, at 264. Burnham did not think of himself as a racist. When he addressed racial issues directly, he thought he was being objective and evenhanded. He said he wanted the United States to integrate—but "more piecemeal, involving at any given stage less sharp a break with existing conditions." Ibid. at 60. However, because of what shone through about Burnham's deeply held views, he—like Buckley and *National Review* as a whole—lacked credibility on racial issues.

20. Weiner, *Legacy of Ashes*, supra note 5, at 149–56 (2007). Weiner reports that Frank G. Wisner, head of the OPC, ordered the radio broadcasts, and that Allen Dulles told Eisenhower no such broadcasts were taking place, but Weiner does not take a position on whether Dulles lied or was misinformed.

21. Historians would later learn that Mao Zedong had vigorously pressed Khrushchev to extinguish the Hungarian uprising. Mao thought the Soviets were losing their revolutionary zeal. "If they don't want the sword, we do," Mao told his advisers. John Lewis Gaddis, *The Cold War: A New History* 107–11 (2005).

22. I draw upon Ambrose, *Eisenhower*, supra note 4, at 412–35 (1990); Gaddis, *The Cold War*, supra note 21, at 107–11, 124–28 (2005); James T. Patterson, *Grand Expectations: The United States, 1945–1974* 304–09 (1996); Tom Wicker, *Dwight D. Eisenhower* 87–93 (2002).

23. Ambrose, *Eisenhower*, supra note 4, at 427. Tom Wicker says that Eisenhower's decision to oppose the British-French-Israeli initiative was "one of

his finest hours as president." Wicker, *Dwight D. Eisenhower*, supra note 22, at 89.

24. Gaddis, *The Cold War*, supra note 21, at 66.

25. Ambrose, *Eisenhower*, supra note 4, at 430.

26. Ibid. at 423.

27. "The Kremlin and the Poles," *National Review*, Nov. 3, 1956, at 4.

28. "Action at Two Levels," *National Review*, Dec. 8, 1956, at 4.

29. "The Reoccupation of Suez," *National Review*, Nov. 17, 1956, at 4.

30. "The Dulles Plan," *National Review*, Jan. 12, 1957, at 29.

31. See, e.g., Burnham, *Suicide of the West*, supra note 8, at 268–70.

32. Ernest van den Haag, "Communism, Democracy and Religion," *National Review*, March 22, 1958, at 275.

33. "More Light!" *National Review*, Nov. 16, 1957, at 437.

34. Richard Reeves, *President Kennedy: Profile of Power* 31 (1993).

35. Weiner, *Legacy of Ashes*, supra note 5, at 180. For background about the Bay of Pigs and the Cuban missile crisis, I rely on Weiner; Patterson, *Grand Expectations*, supra note 22, at 427–28, 486–509; Reeves, *President Kennedy*, supra note 34, at 86–106 and 338–427; Seymour M. Hersh, *The Dark Side of Camelot* 202–221 (1997).

36. "Intervention: Eventually—Why Not Now?" *National Review*, April 23, 1960, at 253.

37. Gaddis, *The Cold War*, supra note 21, at 168.

38. "Cuba, RIP," *National Review*, May 6, 1961, at 269.

39. Hersh, supra note 35, at 268–93; Weiner, *Legacy of Ashes*, supra note 5, at 214–16 and 239–41.

40. Anthony Harrigan, *National Review*, July 16, 1960, at 13.

41. Barry Goldwater, "A Foreign Policy for America," *National Review*, March 25, 1961, at 177.

42. Gaddis, *The Cold War*, supra note 21, at 75–78.

43. The letter is available at http://www.jfklibrary.org/jfkl/cmc/cmc_corre spondence.html (visited July 30, 2010).

44. "Action Stations?" *National Review*, Nov. 6, 1962, at 340.

45. Frank S. Meyer, "Principles and Heresies," Nov. 6, 1962, at 352. Though this piece was published after Kennedy's speech, Meyer's column reads as if it might have been written beforehand. That is entirely possible as Meyer lived in Woodstock, New York, and generally mailed his pieces to the magazine.

46. E.g., "Surrender to Castro," *National Review*, Oct. 23, 1962, at 299; James Burnham, "Intelligence on Cuba," Nov. 20, 1962, at 386; "Fire the Softs on Cuba!" *National Review*, Nov. 27, 1962, at 2; "Who Won in Cuba?" *National*

Review Bulletin, Nov. 13, 1962, at 2; James Burnham, "The Gentle Khrushchev," *National Review*, Dec. 31, 1962, at 505.

47. "At Home," *National Review Bulletin*, Nov. 27, 1962, at 4.

48. See, e.g., Donald G. Brennan, "When the SALT Hit the Fan," *National Review*, June 23, 1972 (criticizing arms control talks by Nixon), and Mann, *The Rebellion of Ronald Reagan*, supra note 9, at 49 and 55 (quoting *National Review* articles criticizing arms control talks by Reagan).

49. "The Great Fallout Hoax," *National Review*, Sept. 23, 1961, at 183.

50. See Kelly, *James Burnham*, supra note 1, at 319–20 (regarding Burnham on environmentalism).

51. Garry Wills, *Confessions of a Conservative* 58 (1979).

CHAPTER 6: LIBERALISM FALTERS

1. Vincent J. Cannato, *The Ungovernable City: John Lindsay and His Struggle to Save New York* 60 (crime increase), 155 (NYPD demographics), 156–59 (Weiss's proposal and data about police brutality)(2001).

2. I draw most of the facts about Bloody Sunday and the murder of Viola Gregg Liuzzo from "Nation: The Central Points," *Time*, March 19, 1965, and "Civil Rights: Protest on Route 80," *Time*, April 2, 1965. See also James T. Patterson, *Grand Expectations: The United States, 1945–1974*, at 579–84 (1996).

3. I draw Buckley's version of events from his book, *The Unmaking of a Mayor* 9–15 (1966). The full transcript of Buckley's speech to the Holy Name Society was published in *National Review*, April 20, 1965, at 324. For other information about the campaign, I rely on Cannato, *The Ungovernable City*, supra note 1, at 19–74, and John B. Judis, *William F. Buckley, Jr.: Patron Saint of the Conservatives* 235–56 (1988).

4. Buckley, *The Unmaking of a Mayor*, supra note 3, at 103 (vendetta).

5. E-mail from James L. Buckley to author, Dec. 14, 2009.

6. "New York: Incitement to Excellence," *Time*, Nov. 12, 1965, cover story.

7. For the story about how Price maneuvered Lindsay into the race, I rely on Cannato, *The Ungovernable City*, supra note 1, at 27–29 and 41–42; Emmet John Hughes, "An Untold Tale," *Newsweek*, July 12, 1965, at 18.

8. William A. Rusher, *The Rise of the Right* 185–87 (1984). See also John B. Judis, *William F. Buckley, Jr.*, supra note 3, at 237–38 (1988).

9. Priscilla Buckley's memory is that the streamer was a lark. E-mail from Priscilla Buckley to author, Dec. 13, 2009.

10. Judis, *William F. Buckley, Jr.*, supra note 3, at 191.

11. E-mail from James L. Buckley to author, April 30, 2011.

12. "Statement by Wm. F. Buckley Jr. Announcing His Candidacy for Mayor

of New York, June 24, 1965," *National Review*, July 13, 1965, at 586. The statement is also reproduced in Buckley, *The Unmaking of a Mayor*, supra note 3, at 115–24.

13. E-mail from James L. Buckley to author, April 30, 2011 (stating that WFB wrote the position papers himself).

14. Buckley, *The Unmaking of a Mayor*, supra note 3, at 196.

15. David Soll, "Watershed Moments: An Environmental History of the New York City Water Supply," available at www.rockarch.org/publications/resrep/soll.pdf (visited Dec. 15, 2009).

16. In addition to references to Glazer and Moynihan in Buckley, *The Unmaking of a Mayor*, supra note 3, see William F. Buckley Jr., "Harlem is in New York City," *National Review*, Nov. 2, 1965, at 978.

17. Buckley, *The Unmaking of a Mayor*, supra note 3, at 202 (welfare), 247 (addicts), 182–88 (hullaballoo).

18. Ibid. at 118 ("lust") and 222 ("duty").

19. Cannato, *The Ungovernable City*, supra note 1, at 54. For this aspect of the campaign generally, see ibid. at 54–56; Buckley, *The Unmaking of a Mayor*, supra note 3, Ibid. at 259–71.

20. Buckley, *The Unmaking of a Mayor*, supra note 3, at 285–88.

21. Regarding Rockefeller's contributions and Lindsay's comments about them, see Cannato, *The Ungovernable City*, supra note 1, at 41–42 and 591n60; Joseph E. Persico, *The Imperial Rockefeller* 216 (1982); Richard Witkin, "Lindsay to Support Rockefeller in 1966; Welcomes His Aid," *New York Times*, July 12, 1965, at 1; Hughes, "An Untold Tale" supra note 7; and "Lindsay Bars Rockefeller Aid," *New York Times*, Sept. 17, 1965.

22. "New York: Incitement to Excellence," supra note 6. Professor Vincent J. Cannato observed that "Buckley did well among conservative, white ethnic Democrats who would normally vote for Beame." Cannato, *The Ungovernable City*, supra note 1, at 70.

23. See "Statements of Ownership Management and Circulation," *National Review*, Oct. 6, 1964, at 882, and Oct. 18, 1966, at 1022.

24. James Burnham, *Suicide of the West: An Essay on the Meaning of Liberalism* 106 (Gateway 1985). First published in 1964. Page references are to the 1985 edition. See Daniel Kelly, *James Burnham and the Struggle for the World: A Life* 284 (2002).

25. Burnham, *Suicide of the West*, supra note 24, at 117.

26. Ibid. at 118.

27. Patterson, *Grand Expectations*, supra note 2, at ix.

28. See generally James T. Patterson, *Freedom Is Not Enough: The Moynihan Report and America's Struggle over Black Family Life from LBJ to Obama* (2010).

29. William Rusher captured Rockefeller's reputation well when he wrote that although Rockefeller was "hard-line" on foreign affairs, "his attitude on the general subject of welfare was 'compassionate' enough to satisfy the most demanding liberal." William A. Rusher, *The Rise of the Right*, supra note 8, at 96 (1984).

30. Charles R. Morris, *The Cost of Good Intentions: New York City and the Liberal Experiment, 1960–1975* 68 (1980).

31. Cannato, *The Ungovernable City*, supra note 1, at 539.

32. See Morris, *The Cost of Good Intentions*, supra note 30, at 196.

33. In 1965 and 1973, there were, respectively, 58,802 and 135,468 violent crimes recorded in New York City. The violent crime rates per 100,000 residents were 325.4 in 1965 and 741.7 in 1973. See New York Crime Rates 1960–2009, available at www.disastercenter.com/crime/nycrime.htm (visited March 13, 2011).

34. Morris, *The Cost of Good Intentions*, supra note 30, at 192; Cannato; *The Ungovernable City*, supra note 1, at 457–59.

35. Morris, *The Cost of Good Intentions*, supra note 30, at 170–214 (city finances analyzed in detail); Cannato, *The Ungovernable City*, supra note 1, at 564–66 (insolvency and creation of MAC).

36. Cannato, *The Ungovernable City*, supra note 1, at 211 (quoting David Garth, who accompanied Lindsay to Harlem).

37. Morris, *The Cost of Good Intentions*, supra note 30, at 74.

38. Morris, *The Cost of Good Intentions*, supra note 30; Cannato, *The Ungovernable City*, supra note 1.

Chapter 7: Vietnam

1. Robert S. McNamara, *In Retrospect: The Tragedy and Lessons of Vietnam* 321 (1995) (U.S. troop and casualty figures); Paul Johnson, *A History of the American People* 877 (HarperPerrenial 1968). First published in 1967. Page references are to the 1968 edition.

2. U.S. State Department, "Background Note: Vietnam," Nov. 30, 2010, available at www.state.gov/r/pa/ei/bgn/4130.htm (visited March 14, 2011).

3. Ibid.

4. For background about Vietnamese history and the American war in Vietnam, I rely on Frances FitzGerald, *Fire in the Lake: The Vietnamese and Americans in Vietnam* (Back Bay 2002.) First published in 1972. Page references are to the 2002 edition; Jean Lacouture, *Vietnam Between Two Truces* (1966); Robert S. McNamara, *In Retrospect*, supra note 1; Neil Sheehan, *John Paul Vann and America in Vietnam* (1988).

5. Sheehan, *John Paul Vann*, supra note 4, at 143.

6. FitzGerald, *Fire in the Lake*, supra note 4, at 158 (quoting the term originated by historian Alexander Woodside).

7. Sheehan refers to the political party within the Viet Minh as the Communist Party, but FitzGerald observes that Ho Chi Minh deliberately created a distinctively Vietnamese form of socialism "linking the future distribution of wealth with the sacred communal traditions of the old village," and that was what the party's name signified. Sheehan, *John Paul Vann*, supra note 1, at 163. FitzGerald, *Fire in the Lake*, supra note 4, at 60–63, 220 (quotation), and 467n9.

8. The text of the Vietnamese Declaration of Independence is available at www.fordham.edu/halsall/mod/1945vietnam.html (visited Aug. 8, 2010).

9. I have found the following timeline, from Philip Gavin's "History Place" Web site, helpful: www.historyplace.com/unitedstates/vietnam/index-1945 .html (visited July 8, 2010).

10. Robert S. McNamara has written that "George [Kennan] would, I am sure, be pained to think that any senior U.S. government official viewed our intervention in Vietnam as a logical extension of 'containment.' It is unlikely he ever visualized extending the strategy globally to this extent." McNamara, *In Retrospect*, supra note 1, at 215n*.

11. Alonzo L. Hamby, *Man of the People: A Life of Harry S. Truman* 570 (1995).

12. Sheehan, *John Paul Vann*, supra note 14, at 165–66.

13. Harry D. Bloomer, "An Analysis of the French Defeat at Dien Bien Phu," available at www.globalsecurity.org/military/library/report/1991/BHD.htm (visited Aug. 8, 2010).

14. Regarding Eisenhower and Vietnam, I rely on Stephen E. Ambrose, *Eisenhower: Soldier and President* 357–59 1990); David Halberstam, *The Best and the Brightest* 136–51 (1972); Tom Wicker, *Dwight D. Eisenhower* 30–35 (2002). Regarding the battle of Dien Bien Phu, I also consulted Bernard Fall, "Battle of Dien Bien Phu," *Vietnam*, April 2004, available at www.historynet.com/battle-of-dien-bien-phu.htm (visited Aug. 9, 2010), and Bloomer, "An Analysis of the French Defeat at Dien Bien Phu," www.globalsecurity .org/military/library/report/1991/BHD.htm.

15. The text of the armistice agreement is available at www.mtholyoke.edu/ acad/intrel/genevacc.htm, and the text of the final declaration is available at http://avalon.law.yale.edu/20th_century/inch005.asp (both visited on Aug. 10, 2010).

16. Sheehan, *John Paul Vann*, supra note 4, at 183.

17. Lacouture, *Vietnam: Between Two Truces*, supra note 4, at 52 (quoting Alsop).

18. Ibid. at 54.

19. FitzGerald, *Fire in the Lake*, supra note 4, at 147. According to Neil Sheehan,

the NLF was nothing more than a front organization for North Vietnam. See Sheehan, *John Paul Vann*, supra 4, at 195–96. FitzGerald implies that the NLF congress and central committee were something more than mere toadies and that the makeup of the central committee "opened the way to a coalition in the event that the United States should withdraw its support from the Saigon government." FitzGerald, *Fire in the Lake*, supra note 4, at 149 (also stating the NLF had presence in 80 percent of rural communities in South Vietnam).

20. FitzGerald, *Fire in the Lake*, supra note 4, at 123.

21. Ibid. at 123–26; Sheehan, supra note 4, at 309–11.

22. Richard Reeves, *President Kennedy: Profile of Power* 253–62 (1993); McNamara, *In Retrospect*, supra note 1, at 321.

23. Fitzgerald, *Fire in the Lake*, supra note 4, at 129–34. The event may be witnessed at www.youtube.com/watch?v=fBj6ac_uVD4 (visited Aug. 11, 2010).

24. Halberstam, *The Best and the Brightest*, supra note 14, at 183.

25. As recounted by McNamara in the documentary film *The Fog of War: Eleven Lessons from the Life of Robert S. McNamara* (Sony Pictures Classics 2003).

26. "Mr. Diem Goes to Washington," *National Review*, May 18, 1957, at 465.

27. James Burnham, "Southeast Asian Contradiction," *National Review*, March 13, 1962, at 163.

28. Reeves, *President Kennedy*, supra note 22, at 259 (Kennedy authorizing program); Sheehan, *John Paul Vann*, supra note 4, at 618–19 (gallons sprayed and acreage affected).

29. Editorial, *National Review Bulletin*, Sept. 17, 1963, at 1.

30. James Burnham, "What Chance in Vietnam?" *National Review*, Oct. 8, 1963.

31. *Time*, April 4, 1955, and Aug. 4, 1961.

32. William F. Buckley Jr., *Happy Days Were Here Again: Reflections of a Libertarian Journalist* 416–20 (1993); William F. Buckley Jr., *Miles Gone By: A Literary Autobiography* 262–65 (2004). Buckley's two accounts differ as to whether he met Luce before or after she mailed her manuscript to him; I adopt the version in *Happy Days Were Here Again*, which was written closer in time to the events and is more detailed.

33. Clare Boothe Luce, "The Lady *Is* for Burning: The Seven Deadly Sins of Madame Nhu," *National Review*, Nov. 5, 1963, at 395, 399.

34. Archbishop Ngo Dinh Thue, "What's Really Going On in Vietnam," *National Review*, Nov. 5, 1963, at 388.

35. "Diem from the Grave," *National Review*, Nov. 19, 1963, at 426.

36. FitzGerald, *Fire in the Lake*, supra note 4, at 173 (quoting Thompson) and 174 (bureaucratic control of assassinations).

37. James Burnham, "The Revolution in the Mekong," *National Review*, Nov. 19, 1963, at 436.

38. "Once Again: No-Win, *National Review*, Dec. 3, 1963, at 467.

39. FitzGerald, supra note 4, at 273–75 (personal style), 287–88 (election), 319–21 and 419 (denouncing U.S.).

40. Ibid. at 330–38.

41. V. L. Borin, "Who Killed Diem and Why?" *National Review*, June 2, 1964, at 441. For biographical information about the author, see Stephen Holt, "Nothing If Not a Survivor: Vladimir Lezak Borin," *National Library of Austrian News*, July 2001, at 10, available at www.nla.gov.au/pub/nlanews/2001/jul01/story-3.pdf (visited Aug. 13, 2010).

42. James Burnham, "What Are We Doing in Vietnam?" *National Review*, March 23, 1965, at 232 (original emphasis).

43. Ernest van den Haag, "Vietnam: After All Is Said and Done," *National Review*, Nov. 29, 1966.

44. Ernest van den Haag, "U.S. Crimes in Vietnam," *National Review*, Oct. 22, 1971, 1171; Ernest van den Haag, "When Is a Crime a War Crime?" *National Review*, Nov. 5, 1971, at 1227.

45. James Burnham, "McNamara's Non-War," *National Review*, Sept. 19, 1967, at 1012.

46. Sheehan, supra note 4, at 694.

47. Ibid. at 210.

48. William F. Buckley Jr., "The Bombing of Innocents," *National Review*, March 21, 1967, at 293.

49. For examples of thoughtful pieces, see Buckley, "The Bombing of Innocents," ibid., "Terrorism—Weapon of Warfare," *National Review*, March 7, 1967, at 237. The former does a good job of analyzing the limited effectiveness of bombing even if it leads Buckley to the vague and possibly ominous recommendation of "zeroing in on the sources of the infection." The latter deals with what an army psychological warfare expert said about how Vietnamese react to terrorism. For Buckley's attack on Fulbright, see William F. Buckley Jr., *The Jeweler's Eye* 48 (1969)(republishing a 1966 column). For Buckley's attack on Ifshin, see William F. Buckley Jr., "Young Ifshin Objects," *National Review*, May 4, 1971. All of these pieces were On the Right columns.

50. William F. Buckley Jr., "The Protest," *National Review*, May 2, 1967, at 470. See also William F. Buckley Jr., "The Search For a Nexus—Vietnam and the Negroes," *National Review*, Aug. 22, 1967, at 894.

51. While estimates of the number of American Indians in 1492 range from one to twelve million, it is generally accepted that "the native population shrank by millions" following Columbus's landing in America. John D. Daniels, "The Indian Population in North America in 1492," 49 *William and Mary Quarterly* (1992). Even by 2000, there were only 4.3 American

Indians and Alaskan natives in the United States. Stella W. Ogunwole, "We the People: American Indians and Alaskan Natives in the United States," U.S. Census Bureau (2006), available at www.census.gov/popula tion/www/socdemo/race/censr-28.pdf (visited Aug. 17, 2010).

52. John B. Judis, *William F. Buckley, Jr.: Patron Saint of the Conservatives* 343–44 (1988) (quoting Buckley).

53. Sheehan, supra note 4, at 675–81 (air war generally, destruction of petroleum reserves, mortality rate of truck drivers and road crews) and 745–47 (Cambodian incursions); FitzGerald, *Fire in the Lake*, supra note 4, at 414–18 (incursions into Laos and Cambodia, air war generally); Henry Kissinger, *White House Years* 1122 (hitting Soviet ships), 1178 (bombing road and rail links to China), mining Haiphong 1171–96 and 1446–57 (Christmas bombing) (1979).

54. Two days after South Vietnamese patrol boats attacked North Vietnamese positions on two islands in the Gulf of Tonkin, North Vietnamese patrol boats attacked the *Maddox* with torpedoes and automatic weapons, but did no damage. President Johnson decided not to take any action in response to this incident. Several days later, during a dark night of thunderstorms and high seas, both the *Maddox* and *Turner Joy* reported that more than twenty torpedoes had been fired at them. No physical evidence confirmed such attacks, and senior navy officials believed it was possible that young, jittery radar crews overreacted to weather effects. It was the second attacks that caused President Johnson to ask Congress for the Tonkin Resolution. See McNamara, *In Retrospect*, supra note 1, at 127–43. McNamara's final opinion was that it was "indisputable" that the first attack occurred and "probably but not certain" the second attacks occurred. Ibid. at 128.

55. McNamara, *In Retrospect*, supra note 1, at 229 (quote) and 252–53.

56. Garry Wills, *Confessions of a Conservative* 78–79 (1979).

57. See Garry Wills, *Nixon Agonistes: The Crisis of the Self-Made Man* 485 (1970) (including the article Buckley rejected as the chapter titled "Our Country!").

58. Wills, *Confessions of a Conservative*, supra note 56, at 39.

59. William F. Buckley Jr., "What If We Left?" *National Review*, Sept. 45, 2006, at 58.

60. Buckley, *Happy Days Were Here Again*, supra note 32, at 194.

61. E.g., editorial, "The Serpent in the Garden," *Nation*, May 11, 1965, at 969; editorial, "Mr. Johnson's War" *Nation*, May 25, 1965, at 518; Jonathan Kapstein, "In the French Footsteps," *Nation*, Dec. 21, 1964, at 479; Isaac Deutscher, "Another Dienbienphu?" *Nation*, March 1, 1965, at 212; editorial, "Vietnam—What Now?" *New Republic*, Dec. 5, 1964, at 3; editorial, "The Sooner, the Better," *New Republic*, June 19, 1965, at 5.

62. For a summary of Burke's position about the American colonies and cita-
    tions to sources for all of Burke's quotations, see Carl T. Bogus, "Rescuing
    Burke," 72 *Missouri Law Review* 387, 422–434 (2007), from which portions
    of the main body have been adapted.

Conclusion

1. Russell Kirk, *The Sword of Imagination* 324–28 (1995); Daniel Kelly, *James
   Burnham and the Struggle for the World* 318 (2002).
2. John B. Judis, *William F. Buckley, Jr.: Patron Saint of the Conservatives* 157
   (1988). See also Garry Wills, *Confessions of a Conservative* 3–16 (1979).
3. Garry Wills, "Daredevil," Atlantic, July/August 2009, at 102.
4. Garry Wills, "The Second Civil War," *Esquire*, March 1968, at 71.
5. Regarding the split between Buckley and Wills, see Judis, *William F.
   Buckley, Jr.*, supra note 2, at 272–73 and 322–26; Wills, "Daredevil," supra
   note 3; Wills, *Confessions of a Conservative*, supra note 2, at 75–79.
6. Letter from Neil McCaffrey to Garry Wills, Aug. 14, 1968 (WFBP, Yale).
7. Wills, *Confessions of a Conservative*, supra note 2, at 213.
8. Ibid. at 210.
9. Ibid. at 213.
10. Ibid. at 211.
11. Linda Bridges and John R. Coyne Jr., *Strictly Right: William F. Buckley Jr.
    and the American Conservative Movement* 162 (*National Review* circulation)
    and 139 (columnist award and Emmy)(2007). For number of newspapers
    carrying On the Right, see, *Encyclopedia of American Journalism* 111(Stephen
    L. Vaughn ed. 2008).
12. William F. Buckley Jr., *Gratitude* xv (1990).
13. Ibid. at 139.
14. Ibid. at xix.
15. Ibid. at 148.
16. He cited Nisbet for acknowledging the claims of community. Ibid. at 66.
17. Ibid. at 55.
18. Ibid. at 26.
19. Wills, *Confessions of a Conservative*, supra note 2, at 36.
20. Judis, *William F. Buckley, Jr.*, supra note 2, at 179 (quoting *National Review*).
21. William A. Rusher, *The Rise of the Right* 198–200 (1984).
22. Judis, *William F. Buckley, Jr.*, supra note 2, at 280.
23. See, e.g., Kelly, *James Burnham*, supra note 1, at 325–26 (regarding Kiss-
    inger); Rusher, *The Rise of the Right*, supra note 21, at 197–202, and Judis,
    William F. Buckley, Jr., supra note 2, at 333–36 (both regarding Buchanan
    and Congressman John M. Ashbrook's primary 1972 primary challenge).

24. John O'Sullivan, "William F. Buckley, Jr.: Man of Thought, Man of Action," *National Review*, March 24, 2008, at 18, 26.

25. William F. Buckley Jr., *The Reagan I Knew* 129 (2008).

26. Speech delivered by President Ronald Reagan at *National Review*'s thirtieth anniversary dinner, available at http://old.nationalreview.com/document/reagan200406100924.asp (visited March 14, 2011).

27. Lou Cannon, *President Reagan: The Role of a Lifetime* 744–45 and 756–57 (2000).

28. Radio address by President Clinton, Jan. 27, 1996, available at www.cnn.com/US/9061/budget/01-27/clinton_radio (visited March 14, 2011).

29. James Mann, *The Rebellion of Ronald Reagan: A History of the End of the Cold War* 157–58 (backgrounds of Dolan and Robinson), 150–96 (writing the speech and battles about what it should contain), 199–206 (text of speech) (2009).

30. Francis Fukuyama, *America at the Crossroads: Democracy, Power, and the Neoconservative Legacy* 59 (2006).

31. Lou Cannon and Carl M. Cannon, *Reagan's Disciple: George W. Bush's Troubled Quest for a Presidential Legacy* 40–41 (2008); Mann, supra note 29, at 28–29.

32. William F. Buckley Jr., "So Long, Evil Empire," *National Review*, July 8, 1988, at 56.

33. Cannon, *President Reagan*, supra note 27, at 696.

34. Buckley, *The Reagan I Knew*, supra note 25, at 118.

35. Ibid. at 204–05 (letter of Oct. 18, 1987). Other letters appear at 198 and 202.

36. Cannon, *President Reagan*, supra note 27, at 700.

37. Hedrick Smith, "The Right Against Reagan," *New York Times Magazine*, Jan. 17, 1988.

38. Cannon, *President Reagan*, supra note 27, at 756. Regarding the battle between movement conservatives who referred to themselves as "Regan revolutionaries" and moderates in the Reagan administration, see ibid. at 263–64; Cannon and Cannon, *Reagan's Disciple*, supra note 31, at 25 and 52; and Mann, *The Rebellion of Ronald Reagan*, supra note 29, at 50–51, 98–99, 167, 232, 254–55, 256, 263–64, 276, 287–88, 291–92, and 344 (2009).

39. Cannon, *President Reagan*, supra note 27, at 756.

40. Cannon and Cannon, *Reagan's Disciple*, supra note 31, at 32n (Reagan's diary entry), 38 (Will's quote), 135–57 (Lebanon) (2008).

41. Ibid. at 165–66.

42. Cannon and Cannon, *Reagan's Disciple*, supra note 31; Bill Keller, "The Radical Presidency of George W. Bush, Reagan's Son," *New York Times Magazine*, Jan. 26, 2003; Bruce Bartlett, *Imposter: How George W. Bush Bankrupted America and Betrayed the Reagan Legacy* (2006).

43. This 2009 survey of sixty-four historians and professional presidential observers by C-SPAN is available at http://legacy.c-span.org/Presiden tialSurvey/Overall-Ranking.aspx (visited May 3, 2011).

44. Editorial, "Looking Back," *National Review*, Dec. 29, 2008, at 14.

45. See Cannon and Cannon, supra note 31, at 295–319 (giving views of the authors and others). Lou Cannon was one of the participants in the C-SPAN 2009 Historians Presidential Leadership Survey.

46. Fukuyama, supra note 30, at 56 (quoting Kristol and Kagan).

47. Thomas E. Ricks, *Fiasco: The American Military Adventure in Iraq* 17 (2006) (quoting Wolfowitz).

48. William F. Buckley Jr., "Iraq: Question Closed?" *National Review*, Sept. 30, 2002, at 54.

49. William F. Buckley Jr., "Who Screwed Up?" *National Review*, June 30, 2003, at 59.

50. William F. Buckley Jr., "Iraq: The Last Word" *National Review*, Dec. 31, 2005, at 54.

51. William F. Buckley Jr., "Torture on 60 Minutes," *National Review*, May 28, 2007, at 55.

52. William F. Buckley Jr., "It Didn't Work," *National Review*, March 27, 2006, at 58.

53. See, e.g., William F. Buckley Jr., "Exiting Iraq," *National Review*, June 6, 2005, at 58; William F. Buckley Jr., "What If We Left?" *National Review*, Sept. 25, 2006, at 58.

54. William F. Buckley Jr., "High Decision Time," *National Review*, March 19, 2007, at 58.

55. William F. Buckley Jr., "The Mounting Protests," *National Review*, July 18, 2005, at 54. See also Buckley, "Exiting Iraq," supra note 53 (stating, "We are entitled to say to our ourselves: If the bloodletting is to go on, it can do so without our involvement in it").

56. Fukuyama, supra note 30, at xi.

57. For Regent law school's statement about the role the Christian faith should play in the law, see "A Message from Dean Brauch," available at www.re gent.edu/acad/schlaw/dean/home.cfm (visited Sept. 1, 2010). See also Carrie Johnson, "Internal Justice Dept. Report Cites Illegal Hiring Practices," *Washington Post*, July 29, 2008; Alan Cooperman, "Bush Loyalist Rose Quickly at Justice," *Washington Post*, March 30, 2007; Dan Eggen, "Aide to Gonzales Won't Testify," *Washington Post*, March 27, 2007.

58. Hearings of the House Oversight and Government Reform Committee, Oct. 23, 2008, available at http://oversight.house.gov/index.php?option= com_content&task=view&id=3470&Itemid=2 (visited Sept. 1, 2010).

59. Douglas Martin, "William F. Buckley Jr., 82, Dies; Sesquipedalian Spark

of the Right," *New York Times*, Feb. 28, 2008, at A1 (quoting Christopher Buckley). See also Christopher Buckley, *Losing Mum and Pup: A Memoir* 189 (2009).

60. Christopher Buckley, *Losing Mum and Pup*, supra note 59, at 144n.
61. The joy and exuberance with which Buckley lived his life may even have been infectious. Social scientists are now reporting that conservatives are much happier than liberals. Jamie L. Napier and John T. Jost, "Why Are Conservatives Happier Than Liberals?" 19 *Psychological Science* 565 (2008) (reporting three studies that found that conservatives are happier than liberals, as well as a Pew Research Center survey that found that 47 percent of Republicans describe themselves as "very happy" compared to 28 percent of liberals). Moreover, conservatives are happier even though some social scientists are still claiming that conservatives have lower IQs and less education than liberals. E.g., Lazar Stankov, "Conservatism and Cognitive Ability," 37 *Intelligence* 294 (2009). (Compare with research conducted in 1952, described at note 6 in the introduction.) Why are conservatives happier? Researchers Napier and Jost claim it is because conservatives are more successful at rationalizing social inequality. George Will says it is because liberalism is a "complicated," "grim," and "scolding" creed." See Napier and Jost, supra. But perhaps, as much as anything else, it is because William F. Buckley Jr. showed that conservatism can be fun.
62. Wills, "Daredevil," supra note 3.
63. "A Eulogy for My Father," *National Review*, April 11, 2008.

Index

A Note on the Author

Carl T. Bogus is a professor of law at Roger Williams University and a nationally recognized expert in the fields of tort law and gun control legislation. His previous books include *Why Lawsuits Are Good for America*, and he has written for the *Nation*, the *American Prospect*, and *Tikkun* magazines, as well as *USA Today*, the *Boston Globe*, and the *Providence Journal*. He lives with his family in Washington, D.C.